Justice in the Balkans

CHICAGO SERIES IN LAW AND SOCIETY
A series edited by William O'Barr and John M. Conley

JOHN HAGAN

Justice in the Balkans
PROSECUTING WAR CRIMES
IN THE HAGUE TRIBUNAL

THE UNIVERSITY OF CHICAGO PRESS
CHICAGO AND LONDON

John Hagan is the John D. MacArthur Professor of Sociology and Law at North-western University (on leave from the University of Toronto) and a senior research fellow at the American Bar Foundation. He is the past president of the American Society of Criminology and the author or coauthor of ten books, including two award-winning studies, *Structural Criminology* (1988–89) and *Mean Streets: Youth Crime and Homelessness* (1997, with Bill McCarthy). His most recent book is *Northern Passage: American Vietnam War Resisters in Canada* (2001).

The University of Chicago Press, Chicago 60637
The University of Chicago Press, Ltd., London
© 2003 by The University of Chicago
All rights reserved. Published 2003
Printed in the United States of America
12 11 10 09 08 07 06 05 04 03   1 2 3 4 5

ISBN: 0-226-31228-3 (cloth)

Library of Congress Cataloging-in-Publication Data

Hagan, John, 1946–
    Justice in the Balkans : prosecuting war crimes in the Hague Tribunal/John
Hagan.
        p.   cm.—(Chicago series in law and society)
    Includes bibliographical references and index.
    ISBN 0-226-31228-3 (cloth : alk. paper)
    1. International Tribunal for the Prosecution of Persons Responsible for Seri-ous Violations of International Humanitarian Law Committed in the Territory of the Former Yugoslavia since 1991.   2. War crime trials—Netherlands—The Hague.   3. Yugoslav War, 1991–1995—Atrocities.   I. Title.   II. Series.

KZ1203.A12H34 2003
341.6'9—dc21

                                                        2003008546

To Linda

CONTENTS

ACKNOWLEDGMENTS

This research was supported by generous grants from the American Bar Foundation, the Social Sciences and Humanities Research Council of Canada, and the National Science Foundation. The Russell Sage Foundation and its president, Eric Wanner, gave me the remarkable opportunity to write the largest part of this book as a visiting scholar, providing me with thoughtful and stimulating colleagues, including Peter Katzentein, Bob Hauser, Jim Gibson, and Peter Evans, as well as the unique assistance of Becky Verreau. Bryant Garth supported this work not only as director of the American Bar Foundation but even more significantly as a superb scholar and colleague with a unique understanding of international law. The International Criminal Tribunal for the Former Yugoslavia met my insistent requests for cooperation with respect and equanimity, and Mary McCall of the Office of the Prosecutor was unfailingly gracious in assisting with my visits. Ron Levi is an invaluable collaborator in parallel papers that flow from this research and was my able assistant throughout this study. Deans Ron Daniels and Dan Linzer were remarkably supportive and understanding about my travels and resulting absences during the several years of fieldwork. I am especially grateful to my colleagues—Carol Heimer, Ron Gillis, John Simpson, Ronit Dinovitzer, Holly Foster, and Blair Wheaton—for reading and commenting on this work. I am indebted beyond the possibility of repayment with these few words for the remarkable assistance of Patricia Parker in helping with every detail of this research. My greatest debt is to Linda, Jeremy, and Joshua, whose love, support, and patience made this research possible.

KEY CHARACTERS

Madeleine Albright   U.S. ambassador to the UN and secretary of state during the Clinton administration

Christiane Amanpour   CNN newsperson known for international reporting and for "being there first"

Kofi Annan   Secretary-general of the UN who oversaw creation of the international tribunals for the former Yugoslavia and Rwanda

Louise Arbour   Canadian jurist and chief prosecutor at The Hague who served from 1996 to 1999 and signed the criminal indictment for Slobodan Milosevic

Paddy Ashdown   Former member of the British Parliament who visited Kosovo several times, including June 1998, when he warned Milosevic of his responsibility for war crimes

Lloyd Axworthy   Canadian foreign affairs minister who advanced the Human Security Agenda, pledging the protection of the human rights of world citizens in the 1990s

Milan Babic   The former dentist who held leadership positions in the former Republika Srpska government that was carved out by the Serbs in Croatia

James Baker   U.S. secretary of state during the administration of George H. W. Bush who famously declared that the United States had "no dog in this fight" involving atrocities in the Balkans

Julia Baly   Legal officer who worked on the Prejidor prison trial team with Dirk Ryneveld and Daryl Mundis

Gary Bass   Author of the political history of war crimes tribunals, *Stay the Hand of Vengeance*

Cherif Bassiouni	Chairman of the commission of experts established by UN Security Council Resolution 780 in October 1992
Morten Bergsmo	Lawyer in the Legal Advisory Section of the ICTY and former member of the commission of experts who with Hanna Sophie Greve wrote the Prijedor Report, which concerned ethnic cleansing as genocide
Tony Blair	Prime minister who reversed British policy regarding the Balkan conflict and provided timely support to the ICTY
Tihomir Blaskic	Croatian general whose controversial trial was among the first to pursue important issues of command responsibility
Mike Blaxill	British lawyer who was among the first hired by the tribunal
Graham Blewitt	Deputy chief prosecutor for the tribunal who has served in this role from its beginning, with background in the prosecution of organized crime and Nazi war criminals in Australia
John Bolton	Undersecretary in the U.S. State Department during the administration of George W. Bush who advocated a legal exclusionist policy for Americans at the new ICC
Boutros Boutros-Ghali	Secretary-general of the UN who established the commission of experts and appointed Richard Goldstone as the first chief prosecutor of the ICTY
Terree Bowers	Assistant U.S. Attorney in Los Angeles who worked as a senior trial attorney and chief of prosecutions under Richard Goldstone and Louise Arbour at the ICTY
Rick Butler	Military analyst seconded from the U.S. Army for the ICTY who gave detailed testimony in the Srebrenica case based in large part on his analysis of thirty thousand documents seized from the Zvornik and Bratuanc brigades
Antonio Cassese	Italian chief judge and first president of the tribunal who was also the guiding hand behind Goldstone's appointment as its first chief prosecutor

Andrew Cayley

Prosecution lawyer who served as co-counsel in the Blaskic and the Krstic cases

Jacques Chirac

French president who was a central figure in the Dayton Accords

Jean Chrétien

Canadian prime minister who appointed Louise Arbour to the Supreme Court of Canada

Wesley Clark

U.S. general who was in command of NATO during the war in Kosovo and negotiated with Milosevic during Louise Arbour's efforts to enter Kosovo after the Racak massacre

Christine Cleiren

Dutch law professor appointed to the commission of experts in 1993 who prepared a report on legal aspects of rape and sexual assault and also helped with the Prijedor project and work on rape in Bosnia

Robin Cook

British foreign secretary under Tony Blair who released highly publicized intelligence to assist in the preparation of the Milosevic indictment

Carla Del Ponte

the former Swiss attorney general who became the third chief prosecutor of the ICT in 1999 and oversaw the transfer of Milosevic for trial in The Hague for genocide as well as crimes against humanity

John Deutch

CIA director during the Clinton administration who worked with Richard Goldstone to increase the transfer of intelligence to the ICTY

Zoran Djindjic

the Serbian prime minister who cooperated in the transfer of Slobodan Milosevic to The Hague

Djordje Djukic

Senior Bosnian Serb officer who was transferred to the ICTY after making a wrong turn into a Bosnian-controlled area of Sarajevo and later released weeks before dying of cancer

Slavko Dokmanovic

Serb mayor of Vukovar whom Louise Arbour secretly indicted and arrested in connection with the Ovcara farm massacre and who took his life while on trial in The Hague

William J. "Wild Bill" Donovan

Headed the Washington office of strategic services during the planning for Nuremberg and served as a prosecutor at Nuremberg until unresolvable conflicts emerged with Robert Jackson concerning prosecution strategy

Simo Drljaca

Secretly indicted Prijedor police chief shot dead after pulling a gun when a British-led NATO SWAT team arrested his brother-in-law, Milan Kovacevic

Lawrence Eagleburger

Secretary of state for George H. W. Bush who in late 1992 made but did not follow up on a "naming names speech" calling for a "second Nuremberg tribunal"

Drazen Erdemovic

Croatian member of the Serb military who confessed to and testified about his participation in an execution squad that killed twelve hundred Muslims at a farm outside Srebrenica

Ramon Escovar-Salom

Attorney general of Venezuela who agreed to become the tribunal's first chief prosecutor but ultimately withdrew

Bill Fenrick

Canadian lawyer on the commission of experts and subsequent head of the tribunal's legal advisory section who developed early legal strategy for establishing command responsibility in connection with the siege of Sarajevo

Ben Ferencz

Lifelong activist for international criminal law who conducted early war crimes trials during the liberation of German concentration camps and later led the Nuremberg prosecution of the *Einsatzgruppen* case, then known as "the biggest murder trial in history"

Robert Franken

Dutch deputy commander during the massacre at Srebrenica

Stefanie Frease

Young crime analyst who worked with Jean-René Ruez on "the ghost team" to develop the radio and telephone intercepts used in the Srebrenica genocide trial

Stanislav Galic

Indicted Serbian major general who commanded eighteen thousand military personnel in ten brigades during most of the forty-four-month siege of Sarajevo

Sheldon Glueck

Harvard law professor who advocated an international tribunal before the end of World War II and helped Robert Jackson plan for the Nuremberg trials

Richard Goldstone

South African judge named as the ICT's first chief prosecutor after serving as the very visible chair of a South African commission that exposed high-level right-wing government involvement in police violence by the apartheid regime

Hanne Sophie Greve   Norwegian jurist and member of the commission of experts who developed with Morten Bergsmo the report on ethnic cleansing in the Prijedor region that became a basis for subsequent prosecutions

Roy Gutman   Journalist who broke the news of the death camps of Bosnia with the chilling headline "Like Auschwitz: Serbs Pack Muslims into Freight Cars"

Mark Harmon   U.S. Department of Justice lawyer on the *Exxon Valdez* case who became the lead prosecutor in a succession of major ICTY trials, including the conviction of General Radislav Krstic in the Srebrenica genocide case

Richard Holbrooke   U.S. assistant secretary of state and ambassador to the UN who led the peace initiative that produced the Dayton Accords and was involved in the Kosovo negotiations

Brenda Hollis   U.S. Air Force lawyer who was one of the original American military secondees to the ICTY and played a leading role in prosecuting the case against Dusko Tadic

David Hunt   Australian judge who confirmed the initial Milosevic indictment by Louise Arbour charging crimes against humanity in Kosovo

Robert Jackson   Charismatic U.S. Supreme Court justice appointed to prosecute the Nazi leadership at the Nuremberg International Military Tribunal

Michael Johnson   U.S. prosecutor on loan to the OTP who had periodically worked on procedural issues and fundraising efforts until becoming chief of prosecutions in 2001

Fritz Kalshoven   Retired Dutch law professor who was the first designated chair of the commission of experts before Bassiouni's appointment

Radovan Karadzic   President of the Bosnian Rupublika Srpska and head of the Serbian Democratic Party who was indicted for genocide by the ICTY and removed from office by the Dayton Accords and at the insistence of Richard Goldstone

Michael Keegan   U.S. Marine Corps lawyer who assisted in the
                                    prosecution of the ICTY trial of Dusko Tadic

Joseph Kingori   Kenyan colonel assigned as by the UN to monitor
                                    violations of the Srebrenica ceasefire agreement
                                    who testified in the Radislav Krstic genocide trial

Mirko Klarin   Former Yugoslav reporter who called for a
                                    "Yugoslav mini-Nuremberg" tribunal to head off
                                    the larger-scale crimes against humanity and
                                    genocide and subsequently became the senior
                                    editor of the Institute for War and Peace
                                    Reporting, the key Internet cite for ICTY news

Jacques Klein   Retired U.S. Army general and UN administrator
                                    in Eastern Slavonia for UNTAES who facilitated
                                    the first use of a secret indictment to arrest Slavko
                                    Dokmanovic in Vukovar for the Ovcara massacre

Radomir Kovac   Indicted along with Zoran Vukovic as
                                    subcommander under Dragoljub Kunarac in the
                                    Foca rape case

Mico Kovacevic   Serbian deputy mayor of Prijedor who was
                                    arrested under secret indictment by the
                                    British-led NATO SWAT team in a raid that led to
                                    the death of Simo Drljaca

Momcilo Krajisnik   Secretly indicted Bosnian Serb politician who
                                    worked closely with Radovan Karadzic and was
                                    one of the most important figures taken into
                                    custody prior to the arrest of Milosevic

Milorad Krnojelac   Secretly indicted and subsequently arrested
                                    former warden of a Foca prison that was turned
                                    into a detention camp where many Muslim men
                                    were tortured and killed

Aleksa Krsmanovic   Senior Bosnian Serb officer apprehended with
                                    Djordje Djukic and transferred to the ICTY after
                                    making a wrong turn into a Bosnian-controlled
                                    area of Sarajevo, only to be released within
                                    months without being charged

Radislav Krstic   Bosnian Serb commander of the Drina Corps who
                                    was arrested on a secret indictment by U.S.-led
                                    SFOR troops and convicted for his role in the
                                    Srebrenica genocide

Dragoljub Kunarac   Charged with command responsibility for
                                    activities carried out in association with Radomir

Kovac and Zoran Vukovic in Foca rape houses and detention centers

Peggy Kuo

Lawyer from the civil rights division of the U.S. Department of Justice who was a key addition to the trial team for the Foca rape case

Hersch Lauterpacht

Pioneer contributor to the conceptualization of crimes against humanity

Raphael Lemkin

Jewish human rights activist who introduced the concept of genocide and worked tirelessly for the inclusion of this term in the Geneva conventions and elsewhere

Patrick Lopez-Terres

French senior trial lawyer at the ICTY who was named the new chief of investigations in a reorganization of the OTP by Carla Del Ponte

Catherine MacKinnon

Internationally known legal scholar who accompanied Cherif Bassiouni into the field to conduct victim and witness interviews for the commission of experts

John Major

British prime minister who paralleled George H. W. Bush in his reticence to seriously engage the Balkan conflict

Mickey Marcus

U.S. general who offered Ben Ferencz a position in which to continue his work on war crimes in Germany after World War II

Richard May

Stern British judge who presided over the three-member judicial panel that tried the Milosevic case and sparred frequently with Milosevic in courtroom exchanges

Peter McCloskey

ICTY legal advisor and senior trial attorney from the U.S. Department of Justice's civil rights division who worked as part of the Srebrenica ghost team and as co-counsel in the Radislav Krstic genocide trial

Gabrielle Kirk McDonald

American successor to Antonio Cassese as chief judge of the tribunal who presided in the sentencing of Dusko Tadic

Theodor Meron

Respected New York University law professor who nurtured the linkage of groups such as Human Rights Watch to international humanitarian law and became an ICTY judge

Slobodan Milosevic — Leader of the former Yugoslavia, participant in the Dayton peace talks, and the first sitting head of state indicted by an international tribunal, for crimes against humanity in Kosovo and Croatia and genocide in Bosnia

Ratko Mladic — Bosnian Serb general twice indicted for crimes against humanity and genocide who served as Radovan Karadzic's military chief and eluded transfer to the ICTY

Sam Muller — German lawyer who played a leading organizational role for the ICTY registrar's office and in the five-person advance team for the ICC

Florence Mumba — Zambian judge at the ICTY who presided in the Foca rape trial

Daryl Mundis — Young Navy lawyer who joined the Foca team shortly before it went to trial

William Nash — U.S. general who worked with the Srebrenica investigation team to arrange IFOR security for exhumations

Aryeh Neier — Head of Helsinki Watch, Human Rights Watch, and George Soros's Open Society Fund who led early calls for an international war crimes tribunal for the former Yugoslavia and stepped in with a Soros grant for the first year of ICTY operations

Geoffrey Nice — British prosecutor at the ICTY who was sought as lead counsel for the Kordic and Milosevic trials

Grant Niemann — Australian lead prosecutor on the Tadic prosecution team

Jack Nowitz — Army private who at the end of World War II worked with Ben Ferencz in investigating and trying early war crimes cases in liberated German concentration camps

Dragan Obrenovic — Chief of staff for the Zvornik brigade who served during the Srebrenica genocide under Radislav Krstic

Otto Ohlendorf — German SS general who headed part of the *Einsatzgruppen*, the extermination squads that followed the German troops as they invaded Poland and the Soviet Union

Eric Ostberg

Swedish prosecutor who worked with Mark Harmon and Terree Bowers in the Rule 61 hearing of the Karadzic and the Mladic cases one year after the Srebrenica genocide

David Owen

British politician-diplomat who resisted the work of Cherif Bassiouni and the commission of experts as a perceived threat to peace negotiations undertaken with his U.S. counterpart, Cyrus Vance

Nancy Paterson

Senior ICTY legal advisor from the sex crimes unit of the district attorney's office in Manhattan who played a prominent role in many important investigations and prosecutions, including co-writing the Milosevic indictment with Clint Williamson

Biljana Plavsic

Bosnian Serb politician who played a leading role alongside Radovan Karadzic, eventually replacing him as president of Republika Srpska and as head of the Serbian Democratic Party

Colin Powell

U.S. secretary of state for George W. Bush who worked with Carla Del Ponte and the IMF and the World Bank to get Slobodan Milosevic transferred to the ICTY for trial

Samantha Power

Human rights lawyer and director of the Carr Center for Human Rights Policy, Kennedy School of Government, Harvard University, who is the author of a comprehensive political history of genocide

Pierre-Richard Prosper

U.S. ambassador for war crimes during Bush administration who previously prosecuted a major rape case at the ICTR

Radovan Radinovic

Former Yugoslav army general and later professor who testified for the defense in the Foca and Srebrenica trials

John Ralston

Australian chief of investigations at the ICTY who initiated search and seizure operations and oversaw the use of sealed indictments to accomplish early arrests

Zeljko Raznatovic

Paramilitary commander known as "Arkan" with ties to Milosevic and Serbian secret police who was indicted by Louise Arbour and later assassinated in Belgrade

Paul Risley

ICT prosecutor's spokesman and press secretary under Louise Arbour who was prominent in planning the announcement of the Milosevic indictment

Almiro Rodrigues

Presiding judge in the genocide trial of Radislav Krstic

Jean-René Ruez

French investigator who for five years led the Srebrenica "ghost team," whose extensive exhumation program and development of military and intercept evidence led to the prosecution and conviction of Radislav Krstic

Gavin Ruxton

Scottish legal advisor who played a role from the beginning of the ICTY in developing and implementing prosecutorial programs

Dirk Ryneveld

Canadian prosecutor who was placed in charge of the Foca rape case almost immediately on his arrival at the ICTY and has played a lead role in the Milosevic case and numerous other important cases

Michael Scharf

U.S. State Department legal advisor for UN affairs and prominent legal scholar and historian of the early years of the ICTY

David Scheffer

The first U.S. ambassador for war crimes; worked extensively with Madeline Albright and provided early and crucial support in the development of the ICTY during the Clinton administration

Pippa Scott

Co-owner of Lorimar Television Productions who became involved in human rights work and helped create a video archive for the commission of experts

Patricia Sellers

American prosecutor of sex crimes appointed by Richard Goldstone as special advisor on gender who planned strategy for Tadic, Foca, and other ground-breaking rape and sexual assault and enslavement trials at the ICTY and ICTR

John Shattuck

U.S. assistant secretary of state who traveled extensively in the Balkans to provide background assistance in establishing and advancing the work of the ICTY during the Clinton administration

Clifford Smith

ICTY criminal investigator formerly with London police who was extensively involved in

	exhumations and helped standardize exhumation site procedures
Clyde Snow	Forensic expert who participated in the exhumation at Ovcara during Louise Arbour's tenure
James Stewart	Canadian lawyer and chief of prosecutions for the ICTY
Asif Syed	Legally trained investigator from Pakistan with experience as a human rights police officer in Africa who became an essential part of the Srebrenica ghost team
Dusko Tadic	The first defendant indicted, during the Goldstone period; despite evidentiary problems he was convicted of persecution as a crime against humanity
Telford Taylor	Prosecuted the High Command case at Nuremberg and became chief prosecutor after Robert Jackson departed
Tejshree Thapa	A legally trained crime analyst from Nepal who worked with Hildegard Uertz-Retlaff and Peggy Kuo on the Foca case
Alan Tieger	Lawyer involved in the Rodney King case and a member of the prosecution team in the tribunal's first trial, which led to the conviction of Dusko Tadic
Hildegard Uertz-Retzlaff	German ICTY legal advisor and later senior trial attorney who headed the Foca investigation and was co-counsel in the resulting trial of Kunarac, Kovac, and Vukovic
Zoran Vukovic	Indicted with Radomir Kovac as subcommander under Dragoljub Kunarac in the Foca rape case
Clint Williamson	Legal advisor from the U.S. Department of Justice who with Louise Arbour played a major role in the formation of early ICTY arrest strategy and at the Racak border confrontation

ABBREVIATIONS

FRY	Federal Republic of Yugoslavia
ICC	International Criminal Court
ICT	International Criminal Tribunal
ICTR	International Criminal Tribunal for Rwanda
ICTY	International Criminal Tribunal for the Former Yugoslavia
IFOR	Implementation Force
IMF	International Monetary Fund
IMT	International Military Tribunal
IWPR	Institute for War and Peace Reporting
JNA	Yugoslav Peoples' Army
KLA	Kosovo Liberation Army
KVM	Kosovo Verification Mission
MUP	Ministry of Interior Police
NATO	North Atlantic Treaty Organization
NGO	Nongovernmental Organization
OTP	Office of the Prosecutor
PHR	Physicians for Human Rights
SDS	Serbian Democratic Party
SFOR	Stabilization Force
UN	United Nations
UNPROFOR	United Nations Protection Force
UNTAES	UN Authority in Eastern Slavonia
VRS	Bosnian Serb Army

Contempt of Court

There was no mistaking the image or the message Slobodan Milosevic intended to convey during his first appearance at the war crimes tribunal at The Hague in July 2001. With head tipped upward and jaw jutting forward, he was all defiance and disdain. Equally purposeful was the glare of Carla Del Ponte, the Swiss chief prosecutor nicknamed the Bulldog for her tenacious pursuit of organized crime figures across Europe. Seated next to Del Ponte was Dirk Ryneveld, the calm Canadian chosen to lead the Kosovo phase of the Milosevic prosecution. Judge Richard May, a poised British jurist perched on an elevated dais, preempted Milosevic's preliminary condemnations of this "false tribunal," warning that "this is not the time for speeches" and then asking if he wished to hear a formal reading of the indictment—the first filed against a head of state. Milosevic shrugged his response, "That's your problem," and with this summation the hearing was all but over, less than a quarter-hour after it began. As he was ushered away by armed guards and a security curtain was drawn across the bulletproof glass that separated the court from a gallery of sixty selected reporters, the still-running television monitors revealed Milosevic checking his watch and mouthing in mock disbelief, "Less than ten minutes."

Milosevic was scarcely out of his seat when Christiane Amanpour launched herself down the circular staircase into the tribunal lobby and out through the glass and steel security station appended like a high-tech cage to the front of the building. Amanpour sprinted across the grass and rounded a fountain decorated with dancing statuary to land first among a flurry of racing reporters, dead on her mark of the CNN live set. With a brush of her jet-black hair, Amanpour was ready to deliver her capsule summation of legal and human rights history in the making. Her support team, with producer Phil Turner in charge, was set for the news-breaking satellite report of Milosevic's arraignment to a waiting international audience.

When I reminded her between live feeds that she was the first to report the surprise Milosevic indictment two years earlier from nearly the same spot, Amanpour seemed to respond instinctively: "I was here first this time as well." She had arrived twenty-four hours earlier and spent all day outside the Scheveningen detention center before breaking the story that Milosevic would speak for himself before the tribunal, without the legal counsel that he reasoned would signal more legitimacy than he conceded to an international court he regarded as a pawn of NATO and the Anglo-Americans.

Milosevic's contempt made little or no difference to Jim Landale, a tribunal spokesperson and the subject of Amanpour's first interview following her report. He explained that Milosevic would be back before the court for a case status hearing at the end of the summer, and Landale already knew that today's display of defiance assured a follow-up audience for that procedural hearing, one that reporters would otherwise typically ignore. Landale had worked for weeks to organize this event, renting space in the convention center across from the tribunal for the chief prosecutor's earlier press briefing and to house an overflow crowd of reporters who watched Milosevic's appearance on remote monitors. He explained with relief afterwards that this would have been a much more complicated event to stage if it had come a week later, during the Northern Lights Jazz Festival, already scheduled for the convention center. The tribunal had a full-dress preview of this day during the May 1999 announcement of the Milosevic indictment by former chief prosecutor Louise Arbour. They were well prepared for the day's events.

A caravan of more than a thousand press representatives from more than a hundred news organizations surrounded the fountain in front of the tribunal. They brought satellite trucks and canopied live interview sets with tons of communications gear. Among the first to arrive was CNN, which staked out a prime spot for a background view of the fountain and the façade of the tribunal behind. Clusters of tribunal employees watched the media circus from the second-floor terrace overlooking the fountain and the press corps below. They celebrated more boisterously with a gathering on this same terrace at the end of the week, after the press had vanished. The press had never before appeared at the tribunal in such numbers, but they were gone almost as quickly by day's end, leaving this international criminal court to more peacefully pursue its work. The Milosevic trial was months away and would last for years after that.

Amanpour seems in some ways an extension of the tribunal community. She says she shares a similar feeling about why she does human rights journalism, as do many who work here: "because it matters." She doesn't like to dwell on her own sense of shock and fear of the atrocities she too often witnesses. Instead she emphasizes that "often our words and pictures are these people's only opening to the world." She enthusiastically describes the production team of camera people, editor, sound technician and field producer that helps make her reports happen. Producer Turner says that Amanpour "doesn't know how to cover news from the lobbies of hotels, like other correspondents," and she insists that her "you are there" approach is the only way she knows "to commit" journalism.

I ask how she got here first today. She answers, "I have my sources." Jim Landale says that this time it was Television B-92 in Belgrade that tipped her off to the story. Sometimes a "source" is also a "leak." The press is often little more than the repeated sounds of its sources. Few question Amanpour's gritty independence. Still, it is clear that the tribunal wants to put its own versions of its stories across, and in such a secretive and security-conscious institution, it is a challenge to get beneath the surface sounds to better explain these stories. I think that, with tape recorder in hand, I have succeeded in doing so. I am surprised, since I at first had difficulty even finding the building, much less gaining admission or authority to survey and then tape record more than a hundred interviews over a period of more than two years with the individuals who pursue the hunted targets of the tribunal's Office of the Prosecutor.

Previous treatments of the tribunal at The Hague, such as Gary Bass's remarkable *Stay the Hand of Vengeance,* which compares this tribunal to four others, have not sought to get inside the inner workings of this particular court but rather have focused on the central ideas, such as liberal legalism, that underwrite such tribunals and their place in international politics. My goal instead is to understand how this court works. To do so, I had to first find, gain access to, and then penetrate this institution.

The number 17 and number 8 trams in The Hague first take their riders past the World Court, or International Court of Justice, on the edge of the city center. This gorgeous Georgian castle of a building, complete with clock tower and fenced formal gardens, is often mistaken for the tribunal. This is the post–World War II court of civil law to which nations bring their collective disputes about treaties and conventions. It is a court of great diplomatic fanfare and intrigue that, many have argued, settles little or nothing, gaining greatest respect for its architectural grandeur, political protocol, and studied civility. Several stops beyond the World Court, past a heavily wooded park, the tram comes to a halt in front of the apex of the triangularly shaped International Criminal Tribunal (ICT)—the former site of a Dutch insurance company that when approached from the city seems almost to be hiding from its past claimants. This is the tribunal where individuals, and now a former head of state, are held criminally responsible for war crimes, genocide, and other crimes against humanity.

Not until you circle the building and encounter its formal face can you spot a United Nations flag. There is no sign to guide you to this court of international criminal law. You must circle the decorative fountain to find the security station where armed guards with puffed-up shirts covering bulletproof vests ask for a passport and ask your purpose before passing your belongings through a metal detector. A limited but growing number of visitors are allowed to observe the court from glassed-off galleries. A complicated security system with computer-coded personal passes restricts access to all other parts of the building. A massive vault in the center of the building, once used to secure files and insurance policies, now holds the tribunal's database, the closely guarded evidence of horrific atrocities in secret preparation for prosecution.

My goal was to penetrate and learn the ways of this novel institution. I planned to study the ways individuals work in the investigation and trial teams of the Office of the Prosecutor. I wanted to understand why and how these individuals do their work. After months of persistent inquiries and requests, using all the personal contacts and privileges I could muster from my university and foundation appointments, I finally was granted access in the spring of 2000.

My research began with a survey in 2000–2001 of 109 employees who form a representative one-third sample of the employees of the tribunal's Office of the Prosecutor. I followed the survey with more than one hundred in-depth tape-recorded and transcribed interviews conducted from 2000 to 2003. I also observed trials and analyzed trial transcripts for this same period. My stays at the tribunal were for periods of one week to a month, every second or third month, with courtroom observations filling periods between interviews. I interviewed the chairman of the commission of experts that preceded the tribunal, all three chief prosecutors (several repeatedly), the deputy prosecutor (repeatedly), four chiefs of investigations and prosecutions, and employees at all levels. My subjects included the office's lawyers and investigators most frequently but also data and case managers, crime and military analysts, clerical assistants, and several demographers and historians. The interviews from this research are quoted without citation, whereas excerpts from interviews done by others are cited in the notes. Public figures at the tribunal who did not request anonymity are quoted by name. I am the first social scientist to have such extensive access to the tribunal.

The three individuals who have served in sequence as chief prosecutors of the tribunal—Richard Goldstone, Louise Arbour, and Carla Del Ponte—are key protagonists in the history of this court, which is still a work in progress. My most detailed focus is on Louise Arbour and developments during her tenure, which climaxed with the indictment of Slobodan Milosevic. My thesis is that Arbour became a charismatic leader and that her experiences in this role provide important answers to fundamental questions about how—sometimes when it matters most—a single person can make a difference in an important institution such as the tribunal. Yet Arbour hardly stands alone in this account. The sociological lesson of this research is that charisma is a collective creation.

Louise Arbour is a diminutive yet powerful woman whom Milosevic's fellow indictee and henchman, known as Arkan, called "that bitch." Arkan was peeved and perhaps ultimately assassinated because Arbour not only indicted him but, more significantly, helped focus the attention of the world and a fledgling institution of international criminal justice on several menacing political tyrants, above all Milosevic, and also his paramilitary as well as military chiefs, while they were still in the midst of ongoing atrocities. The Milosevic indictment was the most visible in a chain of events that brought to preliminary account tens of thousands of criminal deaths, uncountable numbers of tortures, sexual assaults, and rapes, and more than a million deportations. Starting with a tribunal whose credibility was in grave doubt, Arbour became the leader of a prosecutorial team that brought meaningful international criminal law enforcement to the Balkans, nearly tripling the size of the tribunal in the process.

Yet the point of this research is more social than individual, and this is the larger significance of the Louise Arbour story. Arbour arrived at a crucial moment in the social history of the ICT, a moment when this institution gained the momentum it needed to become a successful instrument of international criminal justice, an active means of prosecuting and punishing crimes against humanity. The story of Louise Arbour illustrates that personal charisma is as much a social creation of the setting from which it emanates as it is a feature of the person it envelops, and that the significance of charisma lies as much in its social creation and consequences as in its personal origins.

The implication of the perspective adopted in this research is that a cast of characters must inevitably fill out the creative and consequential spaces around a charismatic figure, in this case beginning with and including the following:

Robert Jackson, Sheldon Glueck, and Ben Ferencz—Jackson was the charismatic U.S. Supreme Court justice who served as the first American prosecutor at Nuremberg with crucial assistance from less well-known figures such as Harvard Law professor Glueck and his student Ferencz. The little-known roles of Glueck and Ferencz illustrate the contingent nature of charisma and what it takes to create and keep its unique contributions unfolding.

Cherif Bassiouni—The determined Arab American head of the U.N. commission of experts who energetically laid the evidentiary ground-work for the establishment of the ICTY and then felt himself shunted aside when he unsuccessfully sought to serve as the ICTY prosecutor in The Hague.

Richard Goldstone—The distinguished South African judge who headed that country's inquiry into high-level abuses of police powers and became the first ICTY prosecutor in 1994. Goldstone oversaw the joint *in absentia* indictment hearing of Radovan Karadzic and Ratko Mladic, a low as well as high point in the early life of the tribunal.

Louise Arbour—The previously introduced Canadian judge who emerged as the media-savvy, charismatic second prosecutor, who from 1996 to 1999 built the scale and momentum of the ICTY prosecutions and ultimately masterminded the Milosevic indictment.

Carla Del Ponte—The above noted Swiss attorney general and third ICTY prosecutor beginning in 1999, whose hard-nosed, professional and tenacious administrative style streamlined the tribunal's prosecutorial procedures and produced a succession of arrests that included Slobo-dan Milosevic and his prosecution for genocide, following other crucial convictions, including the Srebrenica and Foca cases.

Graham Blewitt—The genial Australian deputy prosecutor who began in 1994 before Goldstone even arrived and served the prosecutors who followed, providing continuity while implementing a range of impor-tant innovations that ultimately made the ICTY an international insti-tution to be reckoned with.

Mark Harmon, Hildegard Uertz-Retzlaff, and Dirk Ryneveld—The American, German, and Canadian lead prosecutors in crucial leader-ship and thematic cases, including Srebrenica and Foca, that built the foundation for the prosecution of political figures such as Milosevic that would establish the longer-term reputation of the tribunal.

Clint Williamson, Nancy Paterson, and Jean-René Ruez—The Ameri-can legal advisors and French investigator who played key roles in the development of investigations without which the crucial arrests and convictions that led up to the Milosevic indictment could not have been achieved.

As each of the above individuals comes into this account, we learn something about how they contributed to the social organization of court life and helped create the circumstances in which Arbour emerged as a charismatic agent, as well as the consequences of the leadership role she played.

Even at Nuremberg, Justice Jackson needed the opportunities presented by a unique postwar political context, the direction and assistance of talented colleagues, and the cultivation of an initially unengaged press corps to play his charismatic role in the prosecution of Herman Goering and his Nazi colleagues, and it fell to others to follow through on his auspicious beginning at the famous Nuremberg Trial. By the time of Ted Turner and CNN's globalization of the news, the creation and consequences of charisma were even more important parts of international criminal justice.

Christiane Amanpour began the morning of Milosevic's first appearance at the tribunal by reading the *International Herald Tribune* next to the fountain where she would do her reports and interviews. Nancy Paterson was quoted at the conclusion of the lead story as saying that it would be challenging to establish all the necessary links in the chain of command that stretched from the atrocities committed in Croatia, Bosnia, and Kosovo to the governing actions of Milosevic in Belgrade. Amanpour wove this point into her later report of the day's events.

This point had been made earlier in the press by, for example, Graham Blewitt speaking as deputy prosecutor of the tribunal and by Louise Arbour as chief prosecutor. On this day, however, this observation took on special salience. The story prompted U.S. secretary of state Colin Powell to call Carla Del Ponte to inquire about the strength of the case against Milosevic. The call underlined a notable sequence. At its start most believed that the tribunal would achieve few if any arrests or convictions. After the arrests and convictions of low-level offenders, new doubts were raised about the tribunal's ability to move up the chain of command. As it did so, from soldiers through officers to generals, the absence of responsible politicians became the source of concern. Gary Bass was among the skeptics when in *Stay the Hand of Vengeance* he predicted that "the overall story of The Hague will be largely a dispiriting one" and that "Arbour . . . undermined the tribunal by jumping ship" before the end of her full term. Yet if the final measure of the tribunal is its ability to bring Milosevic and lesser figures to the bar of justice and provide them with fair trials that include establishing their command responsibility for atrocities in the Balkans, then this court and its leadership may be far closer to achieving success than most at first expected. How the tribunal got to this point is the story of this book.

The Prosecution's Theory

This book begins and ends with the prosecution of Slobodan Milosevic, although its larger topics are the development of the Office of the Prosecutor of the International Criminal Tribunal for the Former Yugoslavia and the evolving field of international humanitarian and criminal law. In many respects the development of the tribunal was focused around cases that formed the foundation for the Milosevic trial. The opening statement by the prosecution at the mid-February 2002 trial provides a historical overview of the wars that generated these cases and the tribunal.

As expected, Milosevic was a scowling and defiant presence, sitting alone and acting in his own defense.[1] He dismissed the prosecution's charges while insisting that he was the victim of a media lynching.[2] The chief prosecutor, Louise Arbour, who indicted Milosevic, and her deputy, Graham Blewitt, knew they would need a compelling lead counsel to advance the prosecution's theory of command responsibility against Milosevic. Arbour and Blewitt also knew they needed to look beyond their small group of largely American trial attorneys. "We thought," Blewitt recalled, "that this is going to become an American judicial office if we're not careful."

They began by looking for a lead trial attorney to handle a precursor case involving a political leader of the Croatian Serb mini-state in Bosnia, Dario Kordic.[3] Following a meeting with leaders of the London bar and several interviews, Geoffrey Nice was chosen. After Nice secured a conviction of Kordic, he returned to London. Blewitt observed that "we decided he was the person who had to do Milosevic. We specifically head-hunted him to do Milosevic."

The middle-aged Nice has a studious appearance and addresses the court with an accented British reserve that mixes thoughtfulness with courtesy. The colorful shirts and suspenders he sometimes favors outside of court are invisible beneath his dark barrister's gown. The current chief prosecutor, Carla Del Ponte, speaking first for the prosecution, stressed that Milosevic was on trial and not the Serbian people. She emphasized that Milosevic pursued power by making war by means of a "joint criminal enterprise" that combined "medieval savagery" with "calculated cruelty" and that "the search for power is what motivated Slobodan Milosevic."[4] Geoffrey Nice added that "the prosecution's case . . . from first to last has the accused being concerned by forcible removal of non-Serbs . . . to have and to control a centralized Serbian state."[5] Along with Del Ponte, Nice was joined at the prosecutor's table by two co-counsel, Dirk Ryneveld and Hildegard Uertz-Retzlaff, who feature prominently in the Foca rape case, discussed in chapter 6.

Nice conservatively estimated that there were at least several thousand deaths and 170,000 deportations in the early 1990s in Croatia, followed in the mid-1990s by more than 7,000 deaths and 200,000 to 300,000 deportations in Bosnia, leading in the late 1990s to more than 4,000 deaths and 750,000 deportations in Kosovo. He asked rhetorically with reference to Milosevic, "Did he know they were happening? Of course he did . . . he cannot *not* have known. And therefore the question is, 'Why did he not stop these things that were occurring?' "[6]

Nice argued that "Kosovo features from first to last in the sequence of tragedies with which we are concerned,"[7] or as participants in this conflict in Croatia and Bosnia also often predicted, "in the end it would end in Kosovo." Kosovo is the southernmost province in the Republic of Serbia and one of the constituent republics in the former Yugoslavia that was ruled after World War II by Marshal Tito until his death in 1980. By 1981 there were already student demonstrations for an autonomous "Kosovo Republika."

In response, the Serbian Academy of Sciences warned in a secret 1986 memorandum that there would be "the physical, political, legal, and cultural genocide against the Serb population of Kosovo." Real as well as imagined struggles have been a recurring feature of the Balkan region through the centuries, including a frequently remembered defeat of the Serbians by the Ottomans on the Field of Blackbirds in Kosovo in 1389.[8] Centuries later, during World War II, a half-million Serbian lives were lost to the Nazi-inspired Croatian "Ustasha," many at the infamous Jasenovac extermination camp. In retaliation, more than a hundred thousand Croatians were killed by Tito-led forces.[9] Still, a prominent contemporary historian of the Balkans is able to say that "for centuries, . . . life in the Balkans was no more violent than elsewhere" and that ethnic cleansing in the contemporary period has "represented the extreme force required by nationalists to break apart a society which was otherwise capable of ignoring the mundane fractures of class and ethnicity." It was Milosevic who most recently sparked these violent fires of nationalism.[10]

Milosevic was a protégé of the post-Tito leader, Ivan Stambolic, who sent him to quell the unrest in Kosovo in 1987. In a speech delivered that spring, Milosevic gave voice to an enduring sense of Serbian victimhood by reassuring his fellow countrymen that "you will not be beaten"—by implication, at the hands of the majority Albanian Muslims of Kosovo. Milosevic was learning the intoxicating power of nationalist rhetoric. He soon wrested the leadership of Serbia away from Stambolic and became a leading symbol in the Antibureaucratic Revolution of 1989. Serbia now instituted political and military measures to diminish the autonomy of Kosovo. Resistance to these moves in Kosovo was at this point largely nonviolent.

Milosevic simultaneously began to support Serb leaders in Croatia and Bosnia. So by the late 1980s, he was using political and military means to crush Muslim autonomy on several fronts. As the 1980s came to an end, Croatian Serbs in the city of Knin announced the creation of a Serbian autonomous district.

Meanwhile, the Montenegro-born psychiatrist and self-styled poet Radovan Karadzic was joining with Momcilo Krajisnik and Biljana Plavsic to form the leadership of a Serb party hostile to the majority Muslims in Bosnia. Plavsic complained that "they have introduced the term 'ethnic cleansing' to denote a perfectly natural phenomenon and qualified it as a war crime."[11] Milosevic soon established government ministries to form links with Serbs outside Serbia, including support for the SDS [Serbian Democratic] party—led by Karadzic, Krajisnik, and Plavsic—which would ultimately form Republika Srpska within Bosnia.

By 1991, Milosevic was actively laying the groundwork for wars in Croatia, Bosnia, and Kosovo. Geoffrey Nice provided an interim summary: "At the outset, he thought he could have . . . a new Yugoslavia; himself a second Tito. That impossible, the central Serbian state [was] to be carved out of Croatia and Bosnia, all the while keeping Kosovo in an iron grip." He explained that "this [was] all to be effected by the forcible removal of non-Serbs whenever and wherever they posed a challenge."[12]

The prosecution maintained that Milosevic made persistent use of state machinery, politicians, and military figures in a joint criminal enterprise. "He used his control and influence over elements of the army, first the JNA [Yugoslav Peoples' Army], later known as the VJ, over the MUP [Ministry of Interior Police] . . . , over individual politicians, over the political and military leadership of the Republika Srpska to be declared in due course in Bosnia, and in all cases using many resources at his disposal to ensure the efficient schemes designed to achieve the overall plan."[13] Croatia came first.

Croatia left the former Yugoslavia in 1991, following the election of its nationalist president, Franjo Tudjman. Within a year, several areas with concentrations of Serbs separated from Croatia. Local Serbian leaders were able to use military and paramilitary units from the former Yugoslavia to murder, detain, and deport Croats and non-Serbians, while the cities of Vukovar and Dubrovnik were largely destroyed.

The destruction of Vukovar was capped by the execution of several hundred individuals who were taken from a hospital, beaten, shot, and buried in a mass grave at the Ovcara farm. The exhumation of this mass grave five years later and the secret indictment and arrest of Slavko Dokmanovic in 1997 marked a major turning point in the success of the tribunal and its second prosecutor, Louise Arbour.

Serbia's Ministry of Defense financed much of the Croatian campaign. For example, the notorious paramilitary chief Zeljko Raznatovic, known as Arkan, led a group called the Tigers that was responsible for violence and terrorism in Croatia and later Bosnia, while receiving support from the Serbian State Security Service and direct command from the Yugoslav armed forces. Arkan proclaimed publicly that "these are paramilitary formations. They are people who voluntarily come to fight for the Serbian people. We surround a village. They enter it, kill those who refuse to surrender, and we go in."[14]

Bosnia was the second theater in the Balkan wars and the place where Milosevic was charged with genocide. Nice called genocide "the crime of crimes" and added that, at a minimum, as a superior authority, Milosevic knew or had reason to know that genocide was about to be committed and did not prevent or punish the perpetrators.

Three religious groups lived in Bosnia: the primarily Serbian Orthodox Serbs, the predominately Roman Catholic Croats, and the Bosnian Muslims.[15] Although the three groups coexisted relatively peacefully in Bosnia in the 1980s, the situation was sharply polarized by the early 1990s. In March 1991, Croatia's Tudjman met with Serbia's Milosevic to discuss the partition of Bosnia in a way that would allow each to expand and leave little for the Bosnian Muslims. However, Serbian JNA troops were increasingly deployed in Croatian territory and this soon allowed local Serbians to expand their control in Western Slavonia.

In early 1992, the Muslims and the Croatians in Bosnia voted to separate from the former Yugoslavia. Radovan Karadzic simultaneously declared the formation of an independent Republika Srpska, or Serbian Republic of Bosnia. Although Milosevic made efforts to conceal his support and direction of the Bosnian Serbs, the prosecution held that Karadzic "maintained regular and in certain crisis situations almost constant telephone communications with the accused and other officials in Belgrade. . . . He frequently but not always assumed the role of eager subordinate and willing collaborator in the ideas and designs originating in Belgrade."[16]

Among the efforts to disguise the links between Milosevic's Serbia and Karadzic's Republika Srpska was the placement of Bosnian-born Serbs into JNA units that then were located in Bosnia under the command of Ratko Mladic and demobilized. The officers and equipment of these JNA forces were immediately reconstituted into the new army, again led by General Mladic and now called the VRS, with continued assistance from Serbia.

The ethnic cleansing of Prijedor, the siege of Sarajevo, and the massacre at Srebrenica were three of the most devastating of the Bosnian Serbian aggressions against the Bosnian Muslims. Prijedor set a standard for barbarity. Men, women, and children were forced from their homes and into detention camps. The Keraterm and Omarska detention facilities in Prijedor became death camps. There were more than four hundred Serb-operated detention centers across Bosnia. Journalists and human rights groups such as Amnesty International and Helsinki Watch directed world attention to the atrocities in these camps.

A thorough investigation of the ethnic cleansing in Prijedor was undertaken by the UN commission of experts discussed in chapter 2. This commission presaged the establishment of the tribunal, as discussed in chapter 3. The authors of the Prijedor report concluded that the events there met the legal tests for genocide. A similar pattern of events led to establishment of rape houses and conditions of sexual enslavement in the area of Foca, in the southern part of Bosnia, as discussed in chapter 6. The first case prosecuted by the tribunal emerged from the commission's investigation in Prejidor and resulted in the conviction of Dusko Tadic, but weaknesses in this case also caused many problems that threatened the perceived legitimacy of the tribunal, as discussed in chapter 3.

The siege of Sarajevo was sustained by near-constant bombardment of this city's civilian population between 1992 and 1995. The aim was to divide the city and tie up the troops of the Bosnian Muslims. General Mladic publicly claimed that more than half of the military support for this bombardment came from Serbia. Nice illustrated the genocidal intent of the assault by noting that "the Bosnian Serb Minister of Health argued that their army . . . ought to destroy the Bosnian government civilian hospital in Sarajevo so that the enemy had nowhere to go for medical help."[17] The UN commission of experts applied early elements of the command responsibility thesis in an investigation of Sarajevo.

As the siege of Sarajevo was building, Lawrence Eagleburger, the American secretary of state in the first Bush administration, said publicly that crimes against humanity had been committed and that Milosevic, Karadzic, and Mladic would be held accountable. Nice suggested that "it will be for the Chamber to decide in due course whether he [Milosevic] took any notice of that warning and others like it at all."[18]

It was not until after the conspicuous failure of feeble Western arms embargos and no-fly zones that the tribunal was finally established by the UN in 1993. With Richard Goldstone as its first prosecutor, Karadzic and Mladic finally were indicted in 1995, two years after Eagleburger's empty warning. Goldstone staged a hearing of the case for their arrest in 1996, with Karadzic and Mladic conspicuously in absentia. Their absence gave the tribunal the image of being a "virtual" tribunal and revealed its inability to make actual arrests and try indicted war criminals. As noted above, it was not until 1997 that the tribunal's second prosecutor, Louise Arbour, was able to begin a string of turning-point arrests with the apprehension of Slavko Dokmanovic for the Ovcara farm killings.

The Srebrenica massacre occurred in the summer of 1995. Srebrenica was a UN "safe area" under the watch of a small number of Dutch troops before it was overrun. Under the direction of General Mladic and General Radislav Krstic, whose successful prosecution for genocide is the subject of chapter 5, approximately seven thousand Bosnian Muslim men and boys were massacred. This was the largest massacre in Europe since World War II. Without the persistence of the tribunal investigator Jean-René Ruez, the world might never have fully grasped the significance of this genocide. Shortly after the Srebrenica massacre, the Clinton administration gave support to NATO bombing of the Bosnian Serbs. This, combined with losses on the ground, forced the Serbs to finally go to the bargaining table at Dayton.

The Dayton Accords unintentionally entrenched Republika Srpska as a separate part of Bosnia, but at the insistence of Goldstone and the tribunal, Karadzic was subsequently prevented from holding onto power there, and Serbians in other parts of Bosnia were forced to leave. Karadzic was not allowed to attend the Dayton talks, but Milosevic participated and sought to present himself as a peacemaker.

Kosovo was next in line for Milosevic's warmaking.[19] Milosevic had already rolled back Kosovo's provincial autonomy and seen to it that Kosovo Albanians were dismissed from their institutions, jobs, and businesses. Geoffrey Nice characterized the earlier wars as battles Milosevic could afford to win and Kosovo as a battle he could not afford to lose.[20] Kosovo had since 1389 been a symbolic battleground for the Serbians, and Milosevic had staked his place in history on avenging perceived centuries of victimization. Meanwhile, the leaders of the Kosovo Liberation Army (KLA) were becoming increasingly persuasive advocates of violent resistance against the Serbian authorities.

In the summer of 1997 Milosevic delivered a speech in Kosovo, insisting that he would accept no international mediation and that Kosovo would be permanently a part of Serbia. Shortly thereafter, he was elected president and commander-in-chief of the newly named Federal Republic of Yugoslavia, making his control of the chain of command in Kosovo explicit, uncontestable, direct, and comprehensive. Louise Arbour explained that this legal authority was why she chose to indict Milosevic for crimes against humanity in Kosovo. The strategy that Arbour implemented to advance this indictment is the subject of chapter 4.

As early as 1997, Milosevic's representatives were warning the Kosovo Albanian leadership that demands for republic status would mean war and that a "scorched earth" plan would destroy Albanian villages within twenty-four hours. In 1998 the UN estimated that nearly three hundred thousand persons had been internally displaced within Kosovo or forced out of the province. In the summer of 1998 the Serbian military and paramilitary forces launched heavy strikes against the KLA by shelling towns and villages.

During the fall of that year a succession of foreign leaders, including the leader of Britain's Liberal Democrats, Paddy Ashdown, the American representative Richard Holbrooke, and NATO generals Naumann and Clark, all met with Milosevic to convince him of the seriousness of the Kosovo situation and his legal responsibility for it. Nice noted that one of these leaders would testify that "the accused spoke at one stage of knowing how to deal with the Albanians . . . in a way that they'd been dealt with in 1946," quoting Milosevic as saying, "we killed them all."[21] The threat of NATO intervention was looming.

Agreements came and went, but the assault on Kosovo continued. The tiny village of Racak finally caught the attention of the world in January 1999. "It was shelled and the fleeing villagers were shot. Twenty-five men found in a building were moved to a nearby hill and shot. Forty, in total, were killed."[22] Yet when Arbour attempted to cross the Kosovo border into Racak with her investigators, Milosevic had his crossing guards deny her admission for lack of a visa. A photograph of this scene landed on the front of the *New York Times,* and suddenly the world had a newly focused image of the self-serving nature of Milosevic's claim to sovereign immunity.

Similar insincerity characterized ensuing negotiations in Rambouillet, France. The record from Racak to Rambouillet was full of deceit. Milosevic seemed to be looking for an excuse to finish what the Croatians and the Bosnians earlier had warned would end in Kosovo. Nice observed that "the Serbian population in Kosovo had been mobilized . . . and the majority Albanians disarmed," and followed by asking rhetorically, "May it be that the NATO campaign he brought upon himself provided him with the opportunity to accomplish those goals while purporting to defend his country?"[23]

With the failure of the Rambouillet talks, the orange-colored trucks of the Kosovo Verification Mission exited Kosovo and the NATO bombs began to fall.[24] "As they did so and even before," Nice emphasized, "the forces of the FRY and Serbia began their systematic attacks against the Albanian population."[25] He went on to introduce time-specific data about the deportations and killings described in chapter 7 of this book. His point was that this was a crime against humanity that used the NATO bombing campaign as an excuse to explain the deportation of one-third of the Kosovo Albanian population.

As Geoffrey Nice concluded his opening statement, he introduced Dirk Ryneveld, his Canadian co-counsel, who would take the primary role in the presentation of the Kosovo part of the Milosevic case. Ryneveld had already gained international recognition as the co-counsel with Hildegard Uertz-Retzlaff and Peggy Kuo in the Foca rape case. Rape as a war crime would also be a feature of the Kosovo part of the case,[26] although because the rape witnesses would appear in closed session, this point would largely escape public attention. Ryneveld explained how sexual assault was a component of the deportation efforts: "Witnesses will describe how the soldiers taking part in the deportation roundup of civilians executed a group of about 17 men, and then selected a group of 50 to 100 women from among their captives and raped them in front of the rest of the group. You will hear of a 14-year-old girl being raped in front of her family." Ryneveld emphasized that cultural and religious customs created a situation in which "it takes great courage for these victims to come forward to tell the world the truth of what happened."[27]

Ryneveld also anticipated testimony about efforts to cover up war crimes in Kosovo by removing and reburying bodies, a tactic also used earlier in Srebrenica. In particular, he introduced a massacre in the Kosovo village of Izbica, where Serb authorities ultimately admitted that they removed and reburied bodies. Kosovo Albanian victims were exhumed from Kosovo burial sites and transported by refrigerator trucks to be reburied in sites throughout Serbia. Ryneveld presented a photograph and spoke of a truck that "was found in the Danube River and contained the bodies of about 80 Kosovo Albanians. You will see the feet sticking out of the back."[28]

These were among the final images in the prosecution team's opening statement. There were obvious parallels with the trials at Nuremberg that a half-century earlier had promised a new era of international humanitarian and criminal law to come. In the meantime, the world has swept aside the cruel evidence of many crimes against humanity and genocides. Ryneveld reminded the court of the thoughts of Justice Robert Jackson, who led the prosecution in the first Nuremberg trial. Jackson had offered fair warning for those to follow that "the wrongs which we seek to condemn and punish have been so calculated, so malignant and so devastating that civilization cannot tolerate their being repeated."[29] Yet repeated they were.

CHAPTER ONE

From Nuremberg

"**C**ollectively," Louise Arbour remarked as chief prosecutor at The Hague, "we're linked to Nuremberg. We mention its name every single day."[1] It was characteristic of the Canadian Arbour to begin a public statement about the tribunal with a reference to a shared experience. Robert Jackson was the charismatic U.S. Supreme Court justice who prosecuted the Nazi leadership at Nuremberg. His efforts to "stay the hand of vengeance" helped make Nuremberg the lasting influence Arbour described. Yet Jackson also shared prevailing prejudices of his day, and he notes in his oral history that "I had a great deal of argument and difficulty about the staff, particularly with Jewish people."[2] This bias coincided with an insular tendency in Jackson's leadership.

Jackson reasoned that having too many Jewish lawyers at the Nuremberg trial would undermine its objectivity. He acknowledged that "we had a good many Jewish persons on the staff" and that "some of them did excellent work." He rationalized, however, that "most of them felt . . . they ought to do their work in the background and not be put forward into places of great prominence in order to avoid the impression that it was a Jewish enterprise."[3] This kind of attitude made Jackson's leadership appear more singular than collective in character.

Jackson's views are the more striking today given that Louise Arbour *in part* was selected as prosecutor at The Hague because her gender was thought to be an *asset* in responding to rape as a war crime. In any case, a result of Jackson's attitude is an underappreciation of the roles played by others at Nuremberg who contributed to the collective creation of his charismatic image. Among the lesser-known Jewish contributors are the former Harvard University law professor Sheldon Glueck and his student Ben Ferencz. Glueck was the prescient author of *War Criminals: Their Prosecution and Punishment,*[4] and Ferencz assisted Glueck as a law student before going off to war and later becoming a Nuremberg prosecutor. Their experiences are instructive with regard to international legal activism and its early development at Nuremberg.

FROM WAR TO WAR CRIMES

Fresh out of law school, Ferencz arrived on the beaches of Normandy immediately after D-Day. The Germans had retreated and he at first was perched on a hill, manning a machine gun to guard against attack from the rear. This may have been the last time Ferencz looked back in a lifelong struggle for international criminal justice that has stretched from Nuremberg into the new millennium. I pulled Ferencz away from his computer late one evening. After updating me on his schedule, he lamented, "My wife says I have no time to live. I say I have no time to die."

Ferencz served under General Patton. "If the Germans had counter-attacked, we had relatively little way of repelling them, but they didn't, so off we went."[5] They chased the retreating Germans across France, Luxembourg, Belgium, and then Germany.

Back at Harvard, in the winter of 1944, Sheldon Glueck got a call from Washington asking him to suggest someone to work in a new war crimes program that preceded the Nuremberg trials. Promises were being made to do something about the execution of downed Allied flyers. Jewish victims of the Holocaust were still of less urgent concern. Glueck recommended Ferencz, and he was transferred to a new Judge Advocate section, where a colonel informed him, "We've been instructed to set up a war crimes branch and your name has been forwarded to us as a man who knows about this." The colonel knew nothing about war crimes, and Ferencz's first job was to brief him. "I swear to you," Ferencz recalls, "that's exactly how the war crimes program started in the United States Army."[6]

Ferencz knew the topic from his work on Glueck's book. "I had read everything that had been written about war crimes . . . and my job was to make summaries." Perhaps more significant, however, Ferencz also had read reports Glueck received about what had happened to the Jews in Poland beginning in 1939. "We knew that the Jews were being rounded up and sent to camps where they were being exterminated."[7] Now he would observe the results at first hand.

The new unit had five colonels, and Ferencz was the only enlisted man. None of the others were lawyers. Soon one Private Nowitz arrived, covered in mud from building a bridge but bringing the encouraging news that he was a Yale law graduate. Later a few other enlisted men with law degrees, never more than a half dozen in total, joined Ferencz and Nowitz. As Ferencz put it, "we were the war crimes team."[8] Ferencz and Nowitz were the nucleus of a nascent investigation and eventual trial team whose form is still today recognizable as the dominant organizational nexus of war crimes work at the Hague tribunal.

The work was grim enough at first when it involved finding bodies of downed Allied flyers. Then they began to encounter the concentration camps. Buchenwald was the first, but they soon were moving through a horrifying succession of camps. A report would come into headquarters that a tank division was approaching or had just overrun an area and had "come upon people who looked very strange, they were wearing pajamas, all looking like skeletons." Ferencz or Nowitz would jump into a jeep and join the unit going into the camp. They soon learned that to be most effective, two things are required before all others: the evidence and the perpetrators. The best chance of getting both was to be on the scene as quickly as possible. This was the importance of "real-time" war crimes investigation, a priority in Louise Arbour's later efforts at the Hague tribunal.

The scenes Ferencz encountered in the German concentration camps have been with him ever since. The memories come in a torrent: "Well, I'm sure that everybody by this time has seen the photographs of what the camp looked like and bodies lying in the dust, naked, a little item of clothing on, many of them not moving, some of them stirring, mostly bones; human beings, men weighing 50, 60 pounds. . . . And then, of course, the piles in front of the crematoria, stacked up like cordwood, and on the carts that were dragging them to the crematoria, these open carts just loaded with bodies, hands and arms hanging out on the sides."[9] Ferencz found that one defense against these horrendous images was to concentrate on the legal requirements of his job.

Conditions in the camps were chaotic. The American soldiers as well as the inmates would often vent their emotions by destroying everything, including those who ran the camps and their records. "It was bedlam, chaos everywhere, everything was destroyed, the inmates would go crazy, they would catch the guards and kill them, beat them up, burn them alive. I've seen all that, and so you have to move very fast . . . as soon as I got the evidence that I thought I needed I got out of the camp." From there it was on to the next camp. "We were moving fast . . . from one to the next, Abenzie and Muthausen and a whole string of camps." Ferencz noted that it usually took two to three days to get the material they needed.

In his movement through the camps, Ferencz also met up with Russian soldiers who wondered why he bothered with evidence. They asked incredulously, " 'What's the matter with you Americans—are you crazy? You know what they did, why do you ask them what they did? You're crazy! Kill 'em. Kill 'em.' And they did!"[10] As we will see later, this Russian attitude would prove crucial to what the Nuremberg trials eventually could and could not accomplish.

Ferencz and Nowitz kept on with their work, which was not only gruesome but seemingly endless. They kept finding more camps. "What we didn't know was all these sub-camps that were scattered all around. There were hundreds of them! Everywhere! . . . I have a list of over a thousand concentration camps run by the Germans and German industry. . . . We added three or four hundred later; I don't know how many thousand we have by now."

Throughout, Ben Ferencz felt a sense of the urgency; the fact that Ben and Jack were working together helped to hold off feelings of despair. Ferencz described putting himself "into a mental cocoon which was surrounded by an ice barrier which just enabled me to go on." He emphasized that working toward a shared goal with Jack Nowitz was important. "Interestingly enough," he added, "it was not somber in the sense that we never laughed . . . there were light moments as well."[11]

Ferencz explained that Nowitz was sometimes "exuberant" in his descriptions of crime scenes and that he would have to temper his prose. "He would come upon a typical concentration camp scene and had to write a report. He would say, 'These sadistic beasts, guards were murdering the people in cold blood, and it was outrageous and a violation of every act of human decency.' And I would have to calm him down and say, 'Look, Jack, we're just preparing legal documents to draw up an indictment. You refer to them as accused, you don't refer to them as dirty bastards. . . . Just describe the facts and the facts will speak for themselves.' We had a lot of fun actually together on that. We were good friends." The friendship and the humor helped both to deal with the horror and atrocity they were pursuing in ways that, as we will see, were important not only for them but also for others we will encounter throughout this book.

The first of the resulting war crimes trials were conducted in the Dachau concentration camp. Ferencz couldn't help but think there was ironic justice in hammering up a sign announcing their presence as "United States Army, War Crimes Unit, Dachau." The procedures were informal, but they had prisoners and something had to be done. The trials were conducted under rules developed for military court martials. There were three judges, the one with the highest rank presiding.

Ferencz freely acknowledges that their methods were flawed. They were in "hot pursuit," and "I wasn't going to take any crap from these SS officers. I had witnessed their deeds." Not proud that threats of coercion sometimes were used, he recalled, "When I got a confession I would take it and go out and find myself an officer and say to him, 'Here, I got a confession out of that son-of-a-bitch, you go in and be nice to him, give him a cigarette, have him write it and bring out the second edition. And if it's consistent with the first then we'll destroy the one that I got.'"

Although the trials may have been a rough form of victor's justice, they served an urgent need. Gary Bass, the political historian of international criminal tribunals, identifies this inclination as the beginning of a commitment to "liberal legalism."[12] Ferencz reasoned that "anytime you bring anybody to justice even if it is in an inadequate court, it's better than not bringing them to justice at all." His point of comparison was with the Russians, "who just shot them."[13] This was the comparison that Ferencz' former professor, Sheldon Glueck, was also pursuing in anticipation of the more important trials to come at Nuremberg. Glueck was the scholar behind Ferencz the activist, and his contribution was to better articulate liberal legal principles as a foundation for the work at Nuremberg.

LIBERAL LEGALISM AT HARVARD

Sheldon Glueck began teaching at Harvard University in the early 1940s and developed an understanding of at least three crucial factors: that the European Jews were nearly entirely powerless victims of the Nazis, that the Soviet Union was a powerful yet dubious partner at Nuremberg, and that these realities would make the use of international criminal law to punish German crimes against humanity a challenging undertaking.

Glueck was a pragmatist whose Jewish immigrant background gave him a direct interest in the war.[14] Glueck's involvement, however, unlike Ferencz's, lasted for less than a decade. His early contribution was to recognize the significance of the formal legal punishment of German war crimes. Writing before the war's end, Glueck urged as a fundamental principle of liberal legalism that "it is desirable that the United Nations set up an International Criminal Court . . . as a concrete token of the determination of civilized peoples to vindicate the rule of law in international affairs."[15]

In framing his position, Glueck did not reject out of hand the popular challenge to liberal legalism.[16] In fact, he accepted the early views of Churchill and Roosevelt that in disposing of the Nazi leaders "the United Nations have a perfect right to do as they please. . . . They can shoot them without any legal proceedings." But he also argued that "solemn arraignment followed by trial in an international court is to be preferred . . . in order to inform public opinion . . . and to fix the record of history."[17] Thus Glueck supported an international law of crimes against humanity. He joined the London Assembly in endorsing an early definition built on Hersh Lauterpacht's[18] conception of "crimes against humanity," which included "all crimes committed either within an Axis country or outside such country for the extermination of a race, nation or political party."[19]

The inclusion of "extermination" in this conception of crimes against humanity predated the Geneva Convention definition of genocide as "acts which were intended to destroy, in whole or part, a national ethnic or racial group."[20] Samantha Power notes that Raphael Lemkin first introduced this concept of genocide and then struggled to get it into the Nuremberg indictment.[21] Like those of Glueck and Ferencz, Lemkin's roots were European and Jewish. He placed an almost Talmudic faith in the power of law. Ferencz would later encounter Lemkin in the halls of the Nuremberg tribunal. He remembers that "this new idea of his was not something we had time to think about" and that "we wanted him to just leave us alone so we could convict these guys for mass murder."[22] Lemkin lost almost all of his family to the Holocaust and literally worked himself to death lobbying for the concept of genocide. The formal definition of genocide was ultimately provided in the 1948 Convention on the Prevention and Punishment of the Crime of Genocide, with Lemkin there to tirelessly assist.

The Hague tribunal's definition of crimes against humanity is summarized today as "inhumane acts of a very serious nature committed as part of a widespread or systematic attack against a civilian population on political, ethnic or religious grounds, whether committed in times of peace or war."[23] The distinction between "widespread or systematic attack against a civilian population," as a crime against humanity, and the "intentional destruction in whole or in part of a national ethnic or racial group," as the crime of genocide, is elaborated in the tribunal's Foca and Srebrenica trials, considered in the later chapters of this book.

First and probably foremost, Glueck did not want to see the results of World War I, when few and minor punishments were imposed on German war criminals at the Leipzig trials, repeated. Glueck served in France during World War I and knew that only twelve persons were tried and six convicted by the German Supreme Court, receiving sentences from two months to four years. Glueck set out his well-formulated arguments in influential and widely read articles, in his early book, and in a statement for congressional hearings.[24]

Glueck was unabashed in his pragmatism, insisting in his congressional statement that "the time for such clear-cut and level-headed policy-framing and program-implementing is getting short." He argued that politics must sometimes intrude on law, saying, "The issues to be faced cannot successfully be dealt with by regarding the absolute separation between the political and the legal as something sacrosanct for all times." Instead, he reasoned, "in the early stages of any system of law the executive and the judicial are not sharply differentiated."[25]

Glueck also rejected national sovereignty and claims of sovereign immunity as defenses, maintaining that national sovereignty was a privilege of power. Glueck argued that "to allow the fact that many atrocities were committed inside Germany . . . to prevent the trial of Germans for such atrocities, would be a triumph of bookish legalism and the death of both common sense and justice. There is nothing sacrosanct about the territorial theory of jurisdiction."[26] Subsequent decisions favorable to a broader, more universal conception of jurisdiction and hostile to the defense of national sovereignty have been distinguishing features of the Hague tribunal.

FROM WASHINGTON TO LONDON

Glueck contacted Jackson when he learned that he would be the American prosecutor.[27] Following the March 1945 congressional testimony and promulgation of the resulting resolution, events began to move rapidly. By spring, Glueck was in regular communication with the Office of Strategic Services (OSS) in Washington, headed by General William J. "Wild Bill" Donovan,[28] who was in charge of planning for Nuremberg.

With the end of the semester at Harvard, Glueck joined the OSS team in Washington. Jackson had just submitted a report to the president. Although this report noted "atrocities and offenses, including . . . persecutions on racial or religious grounds," it omitted specific mention of the Holocaust's primary victims, the Jews of Europe. Instead, for Jackson, the point of greater urgency was that "it is high time that we act on the juridical principle that aggressive war-making is illegal and criminal."[29] His report concluded with a lengthy review of the international law of war and its aggressive violation; Donovan was more focused on evidence of the Holocaust.

Glueck joined the group of seventeen lawyers, secretaries, and assorted staff that accompanied Jackson on a June 26 flight from Washington to London, where final planning began for the Nuremberg trial. Within two days of arriving at London's Claridge Hotel, Jackson issued work assignments. Glueck was appointed as the Consultant Supervising Installation of the Control System for the collection and classification of evidence. He saw the challenge before him with regard to evidence of the Holocaust. Many if not most of those involved in planning the Nuremberg trial were unconvinced about the Holocaust, and some were dismissive. Henry Stimson, the cabinet-level architect of Nuremberg, had earlier remarked to Roosevelt, "I have great difficulty in finding any means whereby military commissions may try and convict those responsible for excesses committed within Germany both before and during the war which have no relation to the conduct of war."[30]

Gary Bass observes that Stimson "was a rather mild and genteel anti-Semite, no worse but no better than the bulk of the American establishment in the 1930s and 1940s."[31] Jackson noted that most Americans simply didn't comprehend the enormity or significance of the Holocaust, saying, "The interest was greatest among people who had relations in Europe who had been persecuted, and the refugees. But the crimes of the Hitler regime were all a little remote to this country."[32] Americans were more focused on the Pacific theater and the defeat of Japan. Telford Taylor, who prosecuted the High Command case and who later became chief prosecutor after Jackson departed, readily acknowledged that "like so many others, I remained ignorant of the mass extermination camps in Poland, and the full scope of the Holocaust did not dawn on me until several months later at Nuremberg."[33] It was Taylor who in turn brought Ben Ferencz to Nuremberg to prosecute perhaps the most important Holocaust case after Jackson returned to the United States.

In an evidence planning meeting held the day after their arrival in London and attended by Glueck, the role of Jewish refugee groups was quickly discounted. The minutes of this meeting record that "the view was expressed that their materials are mostly gossip and that their evaluations are very emotional. It was considered that they are not a useful source for evidence."[34] There clearly was an evidentiary challenge to be met.

The control system devised by Glueck for collecting and managing evidence involved separately developed digest forms. These forms were numbered and began with the name of the defendant and the subject matter. Each numbered record of evidence was then cross-referenced in terms of other proof and data required, the point of law or possible defense at issue, connected OSS or other study material, and an indication of the subheading of the count and instrument of accusation to which the evidence was linked. Finally, each digest form ended with an open-ended prompt for "quotable material to be used by the prosecutor in summing up."[35] These forms were crucial in organizing the extraordinary volume of evidence left by the highly bureaucratized German war machine.

In the end, the overwhelming nature of the evidence of the Holocaust prevailed in shifting the focus of the trial from charges of waging aggressive war to crimes against humanity. Donovan, Glueck, and others foresaw this from the outset, but especially as the pictorial, witness, and interrogation accounts accumulated, Jackson as well was persuaded and turned the emphasis in court to the presentation of this evidence.

After the war, Jackson noted how essential Glueck's superbly organized efforts were to the trial's outcome: "When negotiations for a Four-Power agreement for the trial of Nazi war criminals began in London in June 1945, Professor Glueck's book was one of the few published studies of the problems involved in trial. . . . As captured documents began to pour in, he also devised a system for summarizing and indexing them, so that a large mass of material could be readily available on any particular point. His original plan is substantially the system pursued throughout the Nuremberg trial."[36] Glueck's evidence control system was a masterful organizational contribution and a reflection of his pragmatism and persistence. By these means, Glueck played a crucial role in translating the principles of liberal legalism into living law. He was not chosen to go on from London to Nuremberg for the trial. His legacy nonetheless continued through the lifelong work of his student, Ben Ferencz.

BETWEEN BERLIN AND NUREMBERG

Ferencz left the war crimes trials in Dachau in 1946, happy to be out of the army and looking forward to marrying Gertrude, the young woman he had pursued in the years before the war. Yet he wasn't home more than a matter of weeks before he received a telegram from General Mickey Marcus asking him to return to Dachau. Ben phoned Gertrude and asked, "How would you like to go to Europe for a honeymoon?" She was dismayed but agreeable, convinced they would be back in no more than six months.

Next Telford Taylor called from Washington with a more compelling offer. "I'm going back to Nuremberg, I've been over there, the International Military Tribunal is already in process, Justice Jackson is there, we're winding up that trial but I'm going to take over after him and we're going to set up a whole series of subsequent trials. I'm going to be in charge and I need staff and I've heard about you and I'd like you to come with me."[37] Taylor noted that the first trial was dealing with the highest-level Germans who presided over the war and the Holocaust. There remained the hierarchy below these leaders who were also responsible: the ministerial bureaucrats, industrialists, generals, SS members, doctors, and lawyers. This was a larger vision of the trial than Glueck had assumed possible.

Taylor picked Ferencz for his legal training and investigative experience. The team structure of this undertaking was especially attractive to Ferencz. They knew that much of the documentary evidence must be in Berlin, the core of the German war machine. Ferencz was assigned a team of fifty investigators, but he initially was given only a basement office. When he arrived he found a dusty picture of President Truman on the floor, which he promptly signed "To my friend Benny, from Harry." He framed and hung the picture and then placed a call to the colonel in command of the Berlin sector.

Ferencz asked the colonel to come by his office, explaining, "I'm here on assignment from the President of the United States to carry on a war crimes commission. . . . I want you to come over right away." When the colonel arrived, Ferencz asked, "You don't expect me to carry on this job in this office?"[38] Maybe it was the picture of the president. In any case, the colonel soon put half a building at his disposal.

The staff was a close-knit group. It included Ben's new bride, Gertrude, and a large number of German-speaking refugees, many of whom were Jewish, who knew the German scene and were uniquely motivated. An enormous stockpile of eight to ten million records was soon found in a bunker under a small chateau in Dahlem.

Ferencz next reencountered the influence of Glueck, specifically the digest forms he developed, which now were used to coordinate the investigative research. These forms became a crucial "way of funneling information from a document to the hands of a person who can see its merit and its relationship." Ferencz and Taylor were also flying between Berlin and Nuremberg during this time (and at one point wound up parachuting to safety).

A remarkable event in the first Nuremberg trial had involved the testimony of the SS general Otto Ohlendorf, who had headed a part of the *Einsatzgruppen* (EG), the extermination squads that followed the German troops as they invaded Poland and the Soviet Union. These squads included three thousand men whose assignment was to annihilate Jews, Gypsies, and others. At the first trial, Ohlendorf was a witness rather than a defendant. When he was asked how many people his soldiers had killed, he matter-of-factly responded, "In the year between June 1941 and June 1942 the *Einsatz* troops reported ninety thousand people liquidated."[39] Yet Ohlendorf was not among the targeted defendants for Taylor's subsequent Nuremberg trials. Ferencz could not believe that "we had trials against some SS officers, the *Reichssicherheitshauptamt,* but we hadn't planned an Einsatzgruppen trial."[40]

One nearly complete set of EG records was discovered in the burnt-out Gestapo basement headquarters. "One of my researchers came in with these Leitz folders, three or four of them, with all these daily reports from the front: how many Jews they'd killed in which towns, and the reports would read, you know, 'Today we entered the town of So-and-So. Within the first 24 hours we succeeded in eliminating'—they never—they always used euphemisms—'in eliminating 14,312 Jews, 127 Communist officials, 816 Gypsies' and they would list them. . . . I looked at it and said, 'My God, we have here a chronological listing of mass murder.' "[41] These records showed that the EG had slaughtered more than a million men, women, and children. Ferencz took the next plane to Nuremberg to inform Taylor.

Taylor was astonished but did not know where to fit this devastating information into the planned new trials. Ferencz protested, "It's enough for a separate trial by itself. Look, here we've got the names of all the commanding officers. There were 3000 men there, we have four big commands, Einsatzgruppen A, B, C, D, and each one with ten or twelve different units under them." Ferencz finally said that he would prosecute the case himself and Taylor responded, "Well, you've got your other job; you've got to do it in addition to your other job." Ferencz agreed and thus became the prosecutor in the case that a United Press article called "the biggest murder trial in history."[42] Ferencz was at this time still only twenty-seven years old.

The Einsatzgruppen case involved twenty-two defendants, including six SS generals, one of whom was Ohlendorf. The trial lasted nine months, although the prosecution presented its case in just three days. Thirteen of the accused were sentenced to death, but only four were actually executed. The maximum penalty at the Hague tribunal is life imprisonment.

BEYOND NUREMBERG

The victory of the Allied forces in World War II opened a window of political opportunity that lasted barely long enough for cooperation in prosecuting the captured Nazi leadership at Nuremberg. From the outset the American government had its doubts about how far the Nuremberg tribunal should go in imposing international criminal law on Germany, and this evolved into concerns about how this body of law could be institutionalized vis-à-vis the Soviet Union or, later, in relation to the use of American power in response to the cold war threat from the Soviets. The conflicting spheres of American and Soviet influence soon loomed large as the dominant postwar concern and added to problems that plagued the relationship between the Soviet Union and the other Allies from the beginning of the tribunal.[43] Not until this mentality subsided in the 1990s would there be sufficient global consensus to initiate another international tribunal.

This was the geopolitical context in which Justice Robert Jackson as prosecutor developed the Nuremberg tribunal. The responses of Glueck and Ferencz to their differing involvements with the tribunal offer hints about this kind of experience and its effect on individuals working in the area of international criminal justice and human rights. After writing his second book about war crimes and the Nuremberg tribunal following the war, [44] Glueck soon returned to his better-remembered longitudinal research on delinquency. [45] He did not have the experience of being a direct participant in Nuremberg, and he sensed that the geopolitical climate was not conducive to building a career in international law.

Ben Ferencz persisted in making international criminal law and human rights his life's work. After finishing at Nuremberg in 1948, Ferencz became director-general of the Jewish Restitution Successor Organization, which filed claims for more than one hundred sixty-three thousand properties in Germany. This effort led to further work with a German program of restitution and indemnification that eventually provided more than $60 billion and is still providing aid for victims of the Holocaust. Ferencz did not finally return to the United States until 1956, ten years later than he originally promised his wife.

Following a decade of legal practice with Telford Taylor in a prominent New York firm, and during the lead-up to the American involvement in Vietnam, Ferencz became heavily involved in work with the United Nations to more rigorously define international aggression and to make the case for an international criminal court. When his children left home and he had saved enough money, Ferencz turned back to his international work full-time. In the late 1970s he wrote a book titled *Less Than Slaves,* which established the liability of German industrialists who profited by working concentration camp inmates to their deaths.

In the early 1990s, nearly fifty years after Nuremberg, the geopolitics of international criminal law changed. The catalysts were the demise of the Soviet Union and the end of the cold war. A new public awareness also resulted from televised and eyewitness accounts of atrocities in the Balkans and later in Rwanda. The tacit acceptance of human rights violations on both sides of the cold war divide became simultaneously more visible and less tolerable. Human rights and women's organizations were able to work on their own and later through a UN commission of experts, discussed in the following chapter, to establish the International Criminal Tribunal for the Former Yugoslavia and later for Rwanda. This and the 1998 Rome Treaty to establish a permanent international criminal court were major steps toward the goals of liberal legalism to which Ferencz had devoted his adult life.

The trajectory of the cold war and the attention of the media to war crimes in the past decade tell us much about why international criminal law advanced so dramatically at Nuremberg and now has a renewed life at The Hague. This was the political opportunity structure in which the liberal legalism of international criminal justice first flourished, then failed, and recently has flourished anew.[46] It may be harder to explain why Ben Ferencz has persisted in his efforts throughout his life, while the pragmatic Sheldon Glueck and most others shifted their interests to other issues when the cold war made progress in this area so difficult. The firsthand exposure of Ferencz to the consequences of the Holocaust and the Nuremberg tribunal likely had much to do with his persistence.

The initial frenetic work of Ferencz with Jack Nowitz to enact some early form of justice in the concentration camps that they discovered during the German defeat and retreat may provide a further clue about the role of legal teamwork in fostering lifelong activism. We have seen that Ferencz then went to Berlin, where he became the leader of a larger team effort that linked Jewish refugee investigators with American lawyers to develop the evidence for the second set of postwar prosecutions. His early and later investigative work and the linkage of the latter to a historic trial anticipated the organization of investigation and trial teams at the Hague tribunal. The current study is able to more fully examine the organization of parallel efforts in the real-time unfolding of the Hague tribunal, with the goal of better appreciating and understanding how one person working with others can make an important difference of the kind made by Ferencz in World War II and beyond.

LEGAL ACTIVISM AS AGENCY

At little more than five feet in height, and now more than eighty years old, few today would call Ben Ferencz charismatic. Yet in his ninth decade he is clearly an example of human agency in action. Carol Heimer notes that social scientists use the term *agency* in two ways, both of which are relevant to legal and human rights activism.[47]

Sociologists use *agency* to analyze ways individuals autonomously enact meaningful choices that make a difference in their own and others' lives. Economists use the term to refer to effective methods for the selection and direction of others who act on the behalf of a principal. The latter usage is often referred to as the principal-agency problem—which can be a source of opportunity as well as a problem. Agency in the sociologists' sense can involve acting autonomously with respect to the wishes of a principal, and this may include developing these wishes in new and unexpected ways. Agency in this sense can be an ongoing process of negotiation and sponsorship with a principal or principals.

Robert Jackson was charismatic, and in many ways he was the salient figure at Nuremberg. His charisma mainly derived from his association with this tribunal and its accomplishments even after he left. Yet we have seen that the legacy of Nuremberg also benefited enormously, and perhaps ironically, from the agency of lesser-known figures such as the pragmatic Sheldon Glueck and his legal activist student, Ben Ferencz. Jackson's gate-keeping role at Nuremberg nicely illustrates the point that the principal-agent relation can be a source of both problems and opportunities. The way in which Jackson was a captive of the biases of his structural and cultural time and place and allowed these biases to limit Jewish participation at the tribunal illustrates the extent to which the principal-agent relation is as much socially shaped as it is individually determined. The contingency and dependence of charisma on agency and its structural and cultural dimensions is a persistent theme in this study of the Hague tribunal.

This chapter has featured several elements of the Nuremberg experience that illustrate the highly contingent influence of a charismatic figure such as Justice Jackson. These elements are all salient considerations in the sociological study of social movements,[48] and the identification of these elements makes the point that legal activism is in important ways a special form of social activism.

The first of these factors involves political opportunity. In this instance political opportunity presented itself in the form of the shaky alliance with the Soviet Union that allowed the Nuremberg tribunal to emerge. The beginning of the cold war subsequently closed off this opportunity and prevented the evolution of the IMT into a more permanent international criminal court. The Hague tribunal, the much-delayed next step toward such a court, had to await the new political opportunities presented by the end of the cold war.

The second factor involves investigation and trial teams as mobilization structures. Ben Ferencz started in the concentration camps with an investigation team that consisted of little more than himself and Jack Nowitz, but his work evolved in Berlin into a fifty-person investigation team, and then into a Nuremberg trial team that prosecuted the genocidal murders of more than a million people. We will see in following chapters how investigation and trial teams have emerged again as essential mobilization structures at the Hague tribunal. We will consider the crucial role that experiences in such teams have played in the advancement of the emerging field of international humanitarian and criminal law.

The third factor involves the emergence of liberal legalism as a cultural or interpretive framework featuring a normative commitment to the rule of law as the foundation of an institutional response to war crimes. Stalin, as well as Churchill and Roosevelt at early stages, endorsed more vengeful sentiments that form the background and sometimes the foreground challenges to the principles of liberal legalism. The Hague tribunal represents a renewed commitment to liberal legalism's rule of law.

The fourth factor is what social movement theorists have called an alternation experience,[49] in this instance involving the firsthand exposure of Ferencz and others to the conditions of the concentration camps. Although alternation includes "changes of life" that can be as common as movement from high school to college, the social movement theorist Doug McAdam notes that such experiences can also be "key turning points in life" that produce "powerful and enduring changes."[50] Whereas others were often simply shell-shocked by their exposure to the war and the concentration camps, Ferencz responded with a form of agency that was shaped by his exposure to liberal legalism while at Harvard University. Legalism became activism in the work of Ben Ferencz. The events in Croatia, Bosnia, and Kosovo have more recently created the circumstances of parallel alternation experiences for individuals and teams at the Hague tribunal.

When I closed my interview with Ben Ferencz at about ten o'clock in the evening, he offered a parting lecture on why I should press the case in this book for a permanent international court. "You have to do this," Ben implored. "The greater goal is for a permanent court where these principles apply equally to everyone and lead to a more humane and peaceful world." Then he concluded, "That's the story of my life. What I'm working on. What I was working on all day today. Probably doing all day tomorrow. People say, 'When are you going to take a vacation?' and I say, 'What's a vacation?' They say, 'When are you going to retire?' and I say, 'What's a retirement?' And my wife says, 'You have no time to live' and I say, 'I have no time to die.'"

CHAPTER TWO

Experts on Atrocity

Cherif Bassiouni was for all practical purposes the United Nations' first chief war crimes investigator for the former Yugoslavia, serving as chairman of the commission of experts established by UN Security Council Resolution 780 in October 1992. The commission came into being largely at the urging of U.S. ambassador Madeleine Albright as a political substitute for a meaningful military response to atrocities in the Balkans. It was purposefully called a commission of experts instead of a war crimes commission to dampen its symbolic and instrumental possibilities, and perhaps also to avoid embarrassing comparisons with the UN war crimes commission that met with such little success alongside Justice Jackson's London planning group for Nuremberg at the end of World War II.[1]

By the fall of 1992 women's and human rights groups had joined with the print and television media to provide a chilling picture from Bosnia of massacres, rapes, expulsions, and detentions that was reminiscent of the Nazi atrocities. Roy Gutman's *A Witness to Genocide* and Ed Vulliamy's *Seasons in Hell* are the best known of these accounts, but reporters for the *Washington Post,* the *Dallas Morning News,* the *Chicago Tribune,* and the *New York Times* joined Helsinki Watch and others in revealing the specter of a "Greater Serbia" pursuing "ethnic cleansing" in Bosnia, unlike anything since World War II.[2]

Aryeh Neier led Helsinki Watch and later Human Rights Watch in reporting that a genocide was in progress. Neier was an immigrant New York City high school student when he first heard Raphael Lemkin speak about genocide.[3] Neier led Helsinki Watch in calling for an international war crimes tribunal, which led the UN to establish the commission of experts.[4] A year earlier, Mirko Klarin, then a young Yugoslav reporter and now the senior editor of the Institute for War and Peace Reporting, had called for a "Yugoslav mini-Nuremberg" tribunal to head off the larger-scale crimes against humanity and genocide that were now occurring.[5]

Bassiouni characteristically battled his way to the chairmanship of the commission and left it in the same spirit—still fighting—after his candidacy to become the Hague tribunal's first chief prosecutor was rejected by the Security Council in the fall of 1993. Asked why Bassiouni generated so much conflict, the U.S. State Department legal advisor for UN affairs, Michael Scharf, answered that it was a result of his "being so committed and energetic and creative and stubborn that he wouldn't be worn down."[6]

Bassiouni recounted an incident that illustrates the challenge confronted by the commission of experts. The encounter featured the British politician-diplomat Lord David Owen and involved efforts of the commission to exhume the bodies of more than two hundred former patients taken in November 1991 from a hospital in the Croatian city of Vukovar. The patients were transported to a farm site in nearby Ovcara, where they were murdered and piled into mass graves. Vukovar was one of the first cities in the former Yugoslavia to fall victim to Serbian ethnic cleansing.[7] Bassiouni's encounter with Owen occurred during the lunch hour on the terrace outside the UN headquarters in Geneva.

Bassiouni spotted Owen during lunch but was hesitant to speak with him because Owen was known to oppose the commission's very existence.[8] When Bassiouni rose to leave he nodded and Owen rose to meet him, saying, "How are you, professor? Would you please sit down?" Owen had removed his jacket and with sleeves rolled up to his elbows was busily peeling an orange. Bassiouni recalled being "fixated at the sight of this elegant English Lord, the orange juice dripping through his fingers."

Owen began by saying, "I hear you're going to investigate a mass grave with some 200 Croat victims in it killed by the Serbs." Bassiouni nodded, and Owen responded by reporting that he had heard that two hundred Serb bodies were buried in the eastern Bosnian town of Bratunac. This was a town with a brutal history of revenge killings and horrible atrocities committed by Serbs against Muslims and vice versa. Bosnian Muslims were said to have massacred and mutilated sixty-three Serbs in December 1992.[9] Owen asked, "Why don't you investigate that?"

Bassiouni responded that he had multiple reports that varied in their attribution of the causes of death but were consistent in indicating that there were thirty-nine Serb bodies. He explained that they had developed a coding scheme to record the attributed causes of death— in combat, not in combat, after being taken prisoner—"I am proudly telling that to Owen to show him how good our work is." Owen impatiently replied, "You don't understand, it's 200." The puzzled Bassiouni repeated, "no, it's 39 bodies." Owen now pressed his point: "Professor, you have to investigate *three* mass graves of 200 each [Croats, Muslims, Serbians], do you understand?" This was a startling introduction to a policy sometimes known as moral equivalency that was associated with UN diplomacy and peacemaking efforts. Bassiouni was momentarily speechless. "My jaw dropped, I looked at him and I said, 'I can't do that.' And he looks at me as if I was the stupidest person in the world, stands up and contemptuously walks away."

Cherif Bassiouni is a middle-aged, distinguished-looking Arab American and Muslim, a member of an Egyptian family of lawyers and diplomats. He is president of the International Human Rights Law Institute at the DePaul University Law School in Chicago. When he was not in Bosnia during his chairmanship of the commission, he spent much of his time at the UN headquarters in Geneva, while also shuttling back and forth to Chicago, where he housed a large data archive for the commission.

Bassiouni's manner often provokes comment, and among the terms used to describe him are *charming, brilliant, aggressive, disruptive, dynamic, difficult, energetic, forceful, abrupt, arrogant,* and *aristocratic.* Put differently, he is a man of many missions. He insists that one of his main missions is "to remove from the political negotiator the ability to play the card of justice."[10] This mission was the core of his problem with Owen and is another variation of the principal-agent problem introduced in the previous chapter.

The "justice card" in this metaphor is the capacity of liberal legal institutions to collect evidence and establish responsibility for criminal violations of human rights. The commission of experts was the first UN institution officially charged with gathering evidence of war crimes in the Balkans. Bassiouni's encounter with Owen reflected the conflict between the commission's mandate and the role this politician-diplomat was playing with Cyrus Vance in brokering the Owen-Vance Peace Plan for the Balkans. Owen had worried from the first time he learned of the launching of the commission that it would expose new evidence of atrocities and upset the balance he was seeking in reaching a peace agreement. He attempted to block the commission's work from the start.

THE CHANGING POLITICS OF LIBERAL LEGALISM

The Bassiouni-Owen encounter can be understood in the context of broader conflicts that have emerged in recent years between elite politician-diplomats and advocates of international humanitarian law enforcement. In this instance, Vance and Owen were attempting to reach a brokered Balkans peace agreement, and Owen in particular believed that this was at odds with the joined goals of women's and human rights groups, the commission, and the subsequent tribunal to find evidence and convict war criminals in the Balkans. As the cold war came to an end, the political context of this conflict entered a new and crucial period of change.

George H. W. Bush was now moving into his 1992 presidential reelection campaign against Bill Clinton, who had endorsed a human rights agenda. With the cold war won and Iraq recently defeated in Kuwait, Bush did not want the United States bogged down in a Balkan war. His secretary of state, James Baker, famously observed in a visit to Belgrade that "we don't have a dog in that fight." The Bush administration sought to avoid involvement by discounting stories of Serbian atrocities and tending to equate them with Muslim and Croat infractions.[11] The British government under Prime Minister John Major was also dismissive of charges of atrocities against the Serbs. Major represented a generation that still remembered the Serbs as allies who heroically fought the Nazis in World War II and suffered as many as a half-million deaths at the hands of the Nazi-dominated Croatian Ustasha in an earlier wave of ethnic cleansing.

After World War II, Josip Broz Tito ruled Yugoslavia with a somewhat less repressive but still brutal iron fist until his death in 1980. Richard Holbrooke cogently characterized Tito's totalitarian regime as involving six republics, five nations, four languages, three religions, two alphabets, and one political party.[12] Perhaps only Tito's one-man rule, effectively mixing guile with ruthlessness, could hold this disparate assemblage together.

Soon after Tito's death, the Balkans began a downward spiral of violence, stimulated by Slobodan Milosevic's encouragement of "Greater Serbian" nationalist ambitions. The reluctance of the Bush and Major governments to confront the Milosevic-inspired regime of reawakened ethnic hatred left them both open to charges of "moral equivalency" from journalists and human rights groups. The latter groups claimed the higher ground of "moral universalism" with their relentless revelations of Serbian atrocities.

The sociolegal scholars Yves Dezalay and Bryant Garth argue that this kind of conflict between established political power brokers and advocates of legal humanitarian approaches has its roots in the emergence of a newly autonomous "transnational legal field" that joins what I have called the agency of human rights activism with international humanitarian law.[13] They note that this transnational field is steeped in a new kind of politics of the media, as well as anchored in professionalized advocacy groups, while drawing heavily on international human rights and criminal law. The individuals and groups within this field are characterized by increasing competition for media attention, funding, and political influence—especially in Washington, D.C.[14]

This competition evolved from the end of World War II, when government and philanthropic foundations were controlled by what has been called the foreign policy establishment and its focus on the cold war with the Soviet Union. The foreign policy establishment was an elitist group of cold warriors such as the Wall Street lawyer and high commissioner for Germany in World War II, John McCloy, who had little regard for succeeding cohorts of first-generation immigrant professors of international humanitarian law such as Sheldon Glueck, Ben Ferencz, and Cherif Bassiouni. The work of the latter group was regarded as having only marginal relevance to foreign policy. Instead, Dezalay and Garth observe that the strategy of the foreign policy establishment was made more or less exclusively in its own image. That is, its leadership was overtly elitist, allowing admission primarily to current and former government ministers, parliamentary deputies, and appeals court judges.

The first cracks in the dominance of the latter group emerged in the early 1960s with the founding of Amnesty International and its work in Chile. The cracks widened in the late 1960s with the Vietnam War and the challenges its failure posed to aggressive cold war militarism. The influence of international human rights law continued to grow, gaining a particular boost from the Carter administration. Human Rights Watch emerged in the 1980s and gained an influence that went beyond the successes of Amnesty International by cultivating the support of the Soros and MacArthur Foundations as well as opinion leaders in publishing and journalism.

The Ford Foundation gradually came on board, and Canadian, northern European, and Scandinavian countries lent important support. Respected legal scholars such as Theodor Meron of New York University nurtured the linkage of groups such as Human Rights Watch to international humanitarian law. Such efforts resulted in the consolidation of a transnational field that joined human rights activism and international humanitarian law in a more professional and penetrating form than had ever existed before. Dezalay and Garth emphasize that now "the leading human rights organizations began to recruit increasingly from the most elite law schools—which cemented their relationships through human rights programs and internships."[15] These individuals began to circulate and interpenetrate one another's worlds, giving the clearest evidence yet of the emergence of a new transnational legal field.

Vance and Owen were vestiges of the foreign policy establishment and were performing traditional elite roles as political peacemakers. However, by the middle of 1993 this mission was in pieces, and Owen was defending his initiatives against charges of appeasement that further underlined parallels to the Holocaust and World War II.[16] One observer noted that, "throughout, the two co-chairmen might have been more successful in promoting human rights if they had more vigorously championed the importance of pursuing war criminals—if not as part of the peace process, then through the separate mechanisms of the Commission of Experts and the Tribunal."[17] Cherif Bassiouni, on the other hand, represented the new transnational role to be played by human rights activists and the practitioners of international humanitarian law who were determined to use the media to expose Serbian atrocities in the Balkans. Owen used his influence within the UN bureaucracy to thwart the structural mobilization of this initiative through the commission of experts.

THE BATTLE FOR THE COMMISSION

The first attempt to block the commission's work came with the selection of its chair. The selection of such a person is often a turning point in determining for whom the principal-agent relation will be a problem and for whom it will be an opportunity. The UN was to be the principal, and the question was who would be its agent. Bassiouni reports that his longtime friend and secretary-general of the UN, Boutros Boutros-Ghali, initially called him to say, "I want you to be on the commission and I also want you to chair it." But when the commission appointments were announced, a retired Dutch law professor, Fritz Kalshoven, was the designated chair, with Bassiouni and three others as members.

Roy Gutman interviewed the commission's new chair and reported that Kalshoven "tells visitors he does not know why he got the job."[18] Bassiouni had an answer that led back to Owen. Bassiouni believed that Owen had interceded with Boutros-Ghali to sabotage his appointment, following the same kind of thinking Jackson used to limit Jewish participation in visible roles at Nuremberg, namely, that as a Muslim Bassiouni would be biased in favor of the Bosnians. This issue would arise again when Bassiouni was considered for the position of chief prosecutor of the tribunal. Meanwhile, a spokesperson from the UN's Office of the Legal Advisor put the best face he could on the commission appointment with the justification that "we felt we needed an anchor, someone calming."[19]

Bassiouni became more concerned when he found that the British were intent on limiting the work of the commission. When he learned at the first meeting of the commission in November 1992 that the UN was paying Kalshoven as a full-time chair and would provide no funds for investigation or operational expenses, he decided that he would solicit his own independent support to set up a document center in Chicago with a computerized database to collect and analyze the reports of atrocities the commission would receive.

Building on the kind of alliance between human rights activists, foundations, and legal scholars that Dezalay and Garth describe as characterizing the new transnational field of international humanitarian law, Bassiouni convinced the MacArthur and Soros Foundations to contribute a million dollars in funding and then persuaded his law school to donate space to create the document center. This led to questions about maintaining confidentiality, and Kalshoven raised this issue with Bassiouni at the commission's second meeting in Geneva in December 1992.

Bassiouni took elaborate security measures to ensure the confidentiality of the database with assistance from the FBI. "I went to the university's architects and I took half a floor, I sealed it off, had the university build a whole wall, put in secure doors, installed television cameras, got the FBI to come in and take a look at it, give us advice, I connected directly to the Chicago Police Department, and I submitted the whole security package to the U.N. 'That's what you want, here it is.' "

When Kalshoven raised issues of propriety and security at the December meeting in Geneva, Bassiouni reported, "I blew my stack." He insisted that Kalshoven withdraw his remarks and apologize, and when Kalshoven suspended the meeting Bassiouni pursued him out the door and down the hallway, demanding, "What the hell is going on?"[20] Kalshoven subsequently apologized, but Bassiouni persisted by writing Boutros-Ghali a letter questioning Kalshoven's suitability to chair the commission. The letter said, "I'm not advocating that you remove him. But whether you appoint me or somebody else as vice chairman to save face, somebody else has got to run it—because this guy isn't going anywhere." Bassiouni's most pressing concern was that he and another member of the commission, Bill Fenrick, were anxious to go into the field to begin investigations and collection of evidence.[21]

THE DEMANDING AND THE DETERMINED

Whereas Bassiouni was an unmistakably demanding presence in the life of the commission, Bill Fenrick was his less conspicuous but equally determined counterpart. Fenrick was a Canadian military lawyer. He brought four Canadian military lawyers and three military policemen with him, and for much of the time he worked with a small Dutch military engineering unit and volunteers from Physicians for Human Rights to form the core of the first UN war crimes investigation team in Bosnia. The work initially was to involve exhuming bodies and investigating crime scenes where the warring parties were often still shooting.

Bill Fenrick has a dry wit, and he recalls his early work in Bosnia with an irony that is part of a recurring theme of alternation in the experiences of many interviewed for this book. "Being in the former Yugoslavia was extremely exciting. It's a funny sort of thing. My wife described it as having the U.N. fund my mid-life crisis." He continued, "If you haven't spent time doing it, it's amazing how fast you can get an adrenaline rush from being around gunfire and things like that. It's terrifying, but if you're around it, it can be very exciting." It was this sense of excitement, linked to his firsthand experience in Bosnia, that made Fenrick insistent that the field work of the commission must begin. This is an intensity and commitment that I identify repeatedly in this book as emerging from the experience of work in the field. At the tribunal this work would later be referred to as going "on mission," and it was often the basis of a transitional alternation experience with a potentially transformative impact.

Meanwhile, at the same December meeting in Geneva at which Fenrick was assigned his on-site investigation role, down the hall in a larger UN meeting room the Bush administration's secretary of state, Lawrence Eagleburger, unexpectedly and belatedly seemed to be shifting the direction of U.S. policy in the Balkans by giving what came to be known as the "naming names speech." This speech named Slobodan Milosevic, Radovan Karadzic, Ratko Mladic, and others as suspected war criminals. Among the remarkable aspects of this call by Eagleburger for a "second Nuremberg tribunal" was that one of the named potential indictees, Karadzic, was sitting in the room.[22]

In any case, Eagleburger reported that after delivering his bombshell of a speech, Owen, who had been negotiating with Milosevic, Karadic, and Mladic for some time, "made it clear that he considered my remarks 'unhelpful.'"[23] Whether Owen considered the investigations of the commission helpful or not, Bassiouni and Fenrick were bound and determined to move ahead. They were not going to get much help from the Bush administration or even from Eagleburger, who later lamented that despite giving this speech he had not gone to Bush and said, "Mr. President, you've got to do something on this one."[24]

Bassiouni eventually took his difficulties with the UN and Owen to the media in an October 1994 interview with Mike Wallace on *60 Minutes*. Bassiouni regarded the press as his "equalizer," as a means of putting pressure on the UN and the governments that would determine the fate of the commission and the tribunal to follow. "The press really pushed the government into the corner where they couldn't say we're not going to establish a tribunal, we're not going to give it resources." Still, the process remained difficult: "having to shuttle between Geneva, Chicago and the field, having to fight the U.N. bureaucracy to get into the field, and being in the field in the midst of a war, and being shot at to try to get the evidence. Now, all of that does not make for a very efficient operation."

OVERLAP WITH THE TRIBUNAL

In advance of anyone on the commission actually setting foot in the Balkans, the Security Council passed a February 1993 resolution establishing the International Criminal Tribunal and requesting a report on this matter. This resolution made reference to the interim report of the commission, issued a month earlier, which described the Chicago-based data archive and outlined the legal foundation on which the rapes and other atrocities in the Balkans could be considered to be subject to international law.

In March Kalshoven finally became impatient and revealed to the press that "authoritative persons" in the Office of the Legal Advisor had instructed him not to pursue Serbian politicians such as Milosevic and Karadzic. Follow-up reports indicated that Owen was the likely source of the instructions.[25]

Bassiouni and Fenrick finally convinced Kalshoven to undertake the commission's first field mission to the former Yugoslavia in April 1993. The three went to Belgrade together and then Bassiouni and Fenrick went on to Zagreb and Sarajevo, where there was ongoing shelling and sniping at civilians. The significance of the delay in their work was brought home by a visit to Brcko, where they interviewed two teenage girls who had been held captive and raped by Serbian paramilitaries for a period of eight months. Bassiouni was shaken. "You're helpless because there's nothing you can do for them now, and there was nothing you could do for them at the time. Yet they look at you in one of two ways: one, they say, 'You're the U.N. Why weren't you there to help us?' Then they look at you and say, 'Are you going to bring these people to justice?'"

A May resolution instructed the commission to continue collecting information. Fenrick traveled to Vukovar, Belgrade, Zagreb, and Knin to obtain permission to exhume the mass grave at the Ovcara farm site near Vukovar. Prior to the war, Vukovar was a small, quiet city on the Danube, distinguished by its classic baroque architecture and peaceful mixture of ethnic groups.[26] Cyrus Vance had been conducting peace negotiations when he had heard about the ominous activities at the Vukovar Hospital and rushed to the scene in an armored car. Vance was refused entry at the front of the hospital while the Croatian patients were being taken out the back and transported to their deaths.[27]

Fenrick was stonewalled about the Ovcara grave site, and at one point his team was held at the Vukovar police station for taking pictures of the site without permission.[28] In December 1993 several forensic archaeologists traveled to Ovcara and conducted a preliminary survey. "Once the survey started, they found one body in the woods, and another protruding from the grave. They dug a meter-wide trench and took topsoil off several bodies. This was enough to determine that this was a mass grave."[29] Early in the new year, Madeleine Albright flew to the Ovcara site and forcefully warned local Serb leaders that they must allow an exhumation.[30] Fenrick's team was never able to actually begin its exhumation, although permission finally seemed to be in place when the commission was unexpectedly instructed by the UN to stop its work in April 1994.[31] In the meantime, Fenrick had moved his investigation team to Sarajevo.

BESIEGED IN SARAJEVO

Fenrick arrived in Sarajevo on June 20, 1993, for a three-week stay. The UN Security Council had designated Sarajevo as a "safe area" the previous month, but the siege continued unabated. Silber and Little report that the term *safe area* was a cruel misnomer and that "the military and strategic reality facing Bosnia in the spring and early summer of 1993 was that the country was gradually being wiped off the map of Europe."[32] More specifically, "a walk down any side street in Sarajevo provides visible evidence that nowhere was safe from the random mortar fire: the city's streets are pockmarked everywhere with the distinctive splatter of the mortar impact point. The local people called these imprints 'Sarajevo roses'—the color of blood . . . you could barely walk more than a few meters without passing one."[33]

This was the crime scene the team would investigate. "For Sarajevo, the mission lived luxuriously as most people simply did not have water, electricity, phones or adequate food." The recurring shelling made it necessary for the team to move around in armored personnel carriers. Fenrick observed with his typically droll humor that "strolling through the city to take pictures was not a recommended practice."[34]

The Sarajevo investigation was organized around three projects: a pilot study of systematic rape; a "law of war" study of a shelling incident; and an analytical survey of the siege of Sarajevo. Fenrick remarked that "nobody had ever done these things before, I mean, running around in the middle of all the shelling and that sort of stuff, trying to figure out whether or not you can develop a case." The question was one of "What can you do with X quantity of resources in Y period of time? How far along can you get to a proper investigation?" In spite of its problems, he felt that "as an experiment it was very useful."

Investigating rape is always difficult, but the heavy shelling and limited mobility presented further obstacles. They were able to acquire 105 files from the Bosnian War Crimes Commission that were identified as involving rapes. Preliminary investigation showed that 80 of the files actually contained allegations of rape, with the most complete files containing a single statement from a victim or a witness. The team clearly lacked the necessary resources to effectively investigate rape.[35]

The incident study focused on the mortar shelling of a soccer game in the Dobrinja suburb of Sarajevo on the first of June, 1993, just weeks before Fenrick arrived. The soccer field where the game was being played lies in the shadow of the showpiece Zetra sports stadium, built for the 1984 Winter Olympic games. The first day of June was clear and sunny, with good visibility, for the soccer tournament as well as for shelling.

No projectiles had landed in this area for several months, but Bosnian government radio had warned city residents that Serb forces might launch a heavy attack on Kurban Bayram, the name Bosnian Muslims give the day honoring Abraham's willingness to sacrifice his son to God. About 200 Sarajevans had gathered to ignore the war and watch the soccer game. "It wasn't a very good idea," an onlooker with a bandaged leg observed from his hospital bed afterwards.[36] The shells landed at 10:30 on the morning of the game, killing 13 persons and injuring 133. Although they could not identify probable offenders at the time, the team's incident study concluded that a prima facie case existed that "persons on the Serbian side deliberately attacked civilians and, therefore, committed a war crime."[37]

The team also completed a survey of the law of armed conflict as it related more generally to the siege. This report concluded that a compelling case could be made that civilians had been systematically targeted. Silber and Little estimated that "nearly 10,000 people had died in Sarajevo as the undisputed victims of Serb bombardment, most of them civilians, and many of them children."[38] Once an enumeration of those killed and injured in the siege was completed, Fenrick's team reasoned, it would be possible to specifically establish the relative percentages of military and civilian casualties incurred over time. They added that it probably also would be possible to establish where the projectiles causing the casualties came from, so that it would be feasible to determine the numbers of casualties caused by a unit located and commanded in a particular area. Meanwhile, UN military observers were operating on both sides of the battle lines and were sending back daily records of shelling, manpower, and military structures that subsequently could be used to establish command responsibility.[39]

The latter work on the law of armed conflict indicated for the first time that it should be possible "to develop a *prima facie* case against the commander of the Bosnian Serb forces surrounding Sarajevo for deliberately attacking the civilian population."[40] Prior thinking had assumed that because the perpetrators and documentary evidence were not in hand, as they had been at Nuremberg, that it would be necessary to develop legal cases from the bottom up, beginning with individual perpetrators and working up to the senior military and political figures. Fenrick's investigations instead led him to propose starting with the mid-level commanders and working up from there through the command structure.

This approach would become important not only in prosecuting the siege of Sarajevo, but also at Srebrenica and elsewhere. The general principle that Fenrick spelled out was that, "a commander does . . . , as a fundamental aspect of command, have a duty to control his troops and to take all practicable measures to ensure they comply with the law. The arguments that a commander has a weak personality or that the troops assigned to him are uncontrollable are simply unacceptable."[41] This focus on the responsibility of those in command roles anticipated the way in which the Hague tribunal would ultimately climb the ladder of leadership in targeting its prosecutions. It is useful to briefly "fast forward" in our story to get a glimpse of the later significance of this early work.

The work of Fenrick and his commission team in the summer of 1993 and of subsequent investigators and analysts at the tribunal finally paid off near the end of December 1999. It was a cold winter day and a desperate Stanislav Galic was taken into custody while driving his car down a road in southwestern Bosnia. Major General Galic had commanded eighteen thousand military personnel in ten brigades during most of the forty-four-month siege of Sarajevo. Fenrick noted that the Sarajevo investigation was one of "the first steps forming the intellectual underpinning of the Galic case." As 1999 came to an end, Galic realized that his time was running out—he was under sealed indictment from the ICT.[42] On the run, he was ambushed in his car by British commandos, who smashed through his driver's side window, dragged him out, pulled a black hood over his head, and flew him off to The Hague.

Fenrick's team, which had undertaken its three-week investigation in the early stages of the siege, left Sarajevo on July 9, 1993. In terms that Louise Arbour would later make central to her analysis of the work of the tribunal, this was a "real-time investigation" that was belatedly followed by a "historical time prosecution." It took seven and a half years to arrest the general who had been in charge of shelling the city on the day that Fenrick and his team departed through Snipers' Alley to Sarajevo's airport.

BASSIOUNI AND THE CHICAGO DATABASE

Kalshoven took a medical leave in August 1993, and in September, as the first year of the commission's existence came to a close, he announced that he was resigning. He singled out Britain and France as providing little support for the commission's work and specifically noted that Britain had refused to supply a combat engineering unit to undertake the exhumation at the Vukovar site where two hundred hospital patients were believed to have been massacred and buried.[43] After an interim replacement for Kalshoven died of a heart attack, Bassiouni finally was appointed chair.

In November 1993, Bassiouni made two new appointments to the commission: Hanne Sophie Greve, a Norwegian jurist who would later be appointed to the European Court of Justice, and Christine Cleiren, a Dutch law professor. Greve took responsibility for developing a project on ethnic cleansing in the Prijedor region, while Cleiren prepared a report on legal aspects of rape and sexual assault and also helped with the Prijedor project as described below.

Among the unusual components of the database Cherif Bassiouni developed was a video archive of violations of international humanitarian law in the Balkans. This initiative further reflects the kinds of new networks that were now being developed in the emerging transnational field that the commission represented. Bassiouni had formed a friendship with Pippa Scott, who with her husband, Ian Rich, owned Lorimar Television, which produced many of the most successful television sitcoms of the 1970s and 1980s. By the 1990s, Scott had become involved in human rights work and through Linden Productions in Los Angeles volunteered to create a video archive for the commission.

An archive was created with video materials shot in the Balkans and obtained from the major U.S. and European television networks. Individuals testified on videotape about detention centers, rape, torture, and ethnic cleansing more generally. Scott traveled with commission investigators and filmed some of what they were doing. Bassiouni reports that "each videotape was broken down, shot by shot, and every screen image was fully described in the video database and time-coded according to incidents, locations, dates, victims, witnesses, perpetrators, and other important characteristics that could be seen on the screen."[44] The result is a computerized data bank of more than three hundred videotapes.

The computerized database of textual materials developed and analyzed in Chicago contained nearly six thousand "cases" of alleged violations. These violations involved murder, torture, kidnapping or hostage-taking, forced eviction, and imprisonment, as well as a significant number of rapes and sexual assaults. Bassiouni was careful to emphasize that "while the reports adequately established the occurrence of large-scale victimization in the former Yugoslavia, they did not, for the most part, contain evidence in the legal sense, which is necessary to bring criminal charges under international criminal law."[45] Rather, Bassiouni conceived of the commission's task as an intelligence-gathering operation. "It was a dragnet. Everything that came in was thrown in there. And then it was divided in terms of locations and subjects. Prison camps, rapes, mass graves, ethnic cleansing, and you will see that reflected in the report." It could be quite convincingly concluded that "the data base contains substantially more allegations of violations committed by Serbian and Bosnian Serb forces against Bosnian Muslim civilians than by or against any other ethnic or religious group."[46]

THE ETHNIC CLEANSING OF PRIJEDOR

On the second day of August 1992, Roy Gutman of the New York tabloid *Newsday* broke the news of the death camps of Bosnia with the chilling headline, "Like Auschwitz: Serbs Pack Muslims into Freight Cars." The following story provided eyewitness accounts of the transportation of Muslims in crowded cattle cars to camps where killings were a daily event. Omarska, the first of the discovered camps, was one of three major concentration camps linked to an ethnic cleansing campaign in the Prijedor region of northwestern Bosnia. Ed Vulliamy broke the story in Europe in the *Guardian* and gave more than fifty radio interviews.[47] Satellite photos eventually revealed more than one hundred Serb concentration camps. A world that had promised "never again" after allowing the Holocaust to unfold in Nazi Germany now was confronted with a repetition of ethnic atrocities on the doorstep of southern Europe.

Within days foreign television crews gained access to the three major camps. Nearly fifty network television news stories appeared during the following weeks in the United States.[48] These eye-opening exposés revealed both the horrific atrocities taking place and the growing influence of the networks that were developing to deal with human rights issues.

A young mid-level official in the State Department's Policy Planning section reported, "There was a network of us, working for different agencies both in and out of government, sharing information."[49] Within a year of the ethnic cleansing and camp revelations, and in response to inaction by the Clinton administration, the state department was rocked by a wave of resignations by young policy officers who had been accumulating evidence.[50] The task remained, however, of providing the kind of specifically documented and fully detailed account that would establish the nature of this ethnic cleansing as a violation of international humanitarian law.

The commission provided such an account of Prijedor in a 131-page single-spaced report prepared by Hanne Sophie Greve and Morten Bergsmo. Greve had considerable experience working in Cambodian refugee camps. Bergsmo had completed several law degrees and was seconded to the commission by the Norwegian government. When the tribunal later filed its first indictments and launched its first trial with Dusko Tadic as the defendant, it was apparent that Greve and Bergsmo had produced a compelling case.

Their work joined extensive background materials gathered in Chicago with interviews involving nearly four hundred victims and witnesses of the events in Prijedor. Names were often redacted from the report for purposes of confidentiality, and full statements were separately collected into four large and confidential volumes transferred to the tribunal's database. The Prijedor team prepared their report to be like a legal case as much as possible, arguing that the facts of the case met the requirements for the charge of genocide.

The term *ethnic cleansing* per se was not actually the focus of the Prijedor report, because this concept is not a legal term and because, as noted, the team believed that the facts justified the charge of genocide. However, when Bassiouni prepared the final report of the commission, he included a series of introductory paragraphs which explained that in the context of the former Yugoslavia, *ethnic cleansing* refers to the use of force or intimidation to render an area ethnically homogeneous by removing persons of other groups.

These paragraphs further explain that the policy of ethnic cleansing is linked to political doctrines involving "Greater Serbia" and claims that date as far back as the 1389 battle in Kosovo. Ethnic cleansing can be seen as an integral, recurring part of an arc-like geography of aggression that began by linking Serbia proper with Serb-inhabited areas in Croatia and Bosnia[51] and then led to the semicircular sweep of Kosovo sometimes called Operation Horseshoe.[52] Rather than take on this larger story, which as yet had only partly taken place, the Prijedor team focused on issues of individual criminal responsibility within this more limited time and place. Nonetheless, Bassiouni emphasizes in the final report of the commission that the pattern documented in Prijedor matched closely similar information received in other regions, including Banja-Luka, Brcko, Zvornik, and Foca.[53]

The Prijedor analysis used Serbian-reported counts to establish that between 1991 and 1993 the Muslim population in the region decreased from nearly fifty thousand to slightly more than six thousand, while the Serbian population remained at about fifty thousand throughout. The Serb takeover of Prijedor officially began at the end of April 1992, when Simo Drljaca, who subsequently became chief of police in Prijedor, directed armed Serbians to assume all policing functions in the region.

The groundwork for this takeover had been laid during the previous six months as Serbians began establishing a parallel and exclusively Serbian administration of the region alongside the duly elected and appointed Bosnian authorities. In late March 1992, a Serbian paramilitary group also took over the television transmitter for the area and broke off reception from Sarajevo and Zagreb to broadcast disinformation about non-Serbian aggression against the Serbs. Noel Malcolm writes in his short history of Bosnia that "it was as if all the TV stations in the USA had been taken over by the Ku Klux Klan."[54]

Serbs now controlled the well-armed police, and the Serbian army distributed weapons to the Serbian citizenry. Serbian soldiers were returning from the war in Croatia, and the military commander of the area gave the local National Defense Council an ultimatum demanding that rather than being demobilized, these soldiers be redeployed to control the regional roads. Roadblocks were erected on all main roads to and from the region in mid-April.

As April came to a close, the Serbian army had established itself in all the strategic positions on the mountains surrounding the town of Prijedor, the major settlement in the region. When the townspeople awoke on the last day of April, "there were Serbian flags on all official buildings in Prijedor town. Sandbag shelters for soldiers with automatic weapons had been erected at all the main intersections, in front of the banks and other important buildings. There were snipers on the roofs of most tall buildings."[55] Radio Prijedor announced that the Serbian people and the SDS had taken control to "protect" the region from attack by forces in Sarajevo. Non-Serbs' financial assets were first frozen and then confiscated. Within days most non-Serbs were informed that they had been dismissed from their jobs.

The attacks on the town of Kozarac, just down the road from Prijedor, were especially savage. The first Serbian soldiers who entered Kozarac brought lists of leading figures in the town who were called forward and killed on the spot. Dusko Tadic, who lived in the town, allegedly provided the death lists. The final report of the commission indicates that "one informant was taken back to Kozarac from one of the concentration camps in the area together with 39 other men to collect dead bodies. He himself counted 610 dead people." Thousands are reported to have been killed in the town, and the rest were herded off to three prison camps.

The males were sent to the Omarska and Keraterm camps, while the women and the elderly were transported to the Trnopolje camp, which was monitored to some degree by the local Serbian Red Cross. The men were detained, tortured, and killed in their camps, which the report identifies as de facto death camps,[56] while the women in the Trnopolje camp were in some cases immediately deported by bus.

The Omarska camp was used first and most extensively for the prominent citizens of the Prijedor region who had survived the initial killings. These included political and administrative leaders, religious leaders, academics and intellectuals, business leaders, and others.[57] The exact number of these persons who were killed in Omarska could not be determined. When the deputy mayor in Prijedor, Mico Kovacevic, was confronted later with estimates of twelve hundred to two thousand deaths, he responded, "it's your choice."[58] Kovacevic was indicted by the Hague tribunal five years later, along with Simo Drljaca, the chief of police, and Milomir Stakic, the mayor of Prijedor.

Although Omarska was primarily a death camp for the male elite of Prijedor, thirty-six women in leading positions were also brought there.[59] Most of the women were badly tortured, raped, and repeatedly sexually humiliated. Men also were sexually assaulted. The report of the commission gave a detailed description of Dusko Tadic's presence during incidents involving the sexually sadistic torture and castration of men. The graphic nature of the allegations against Tadic, and the fact that he was arrested in Germany in February 1994 and thus available for extradition, later resulted in his becoming the first indictee placed on trial at The Hague.

The Keraterm camp was a smaller but probably equally deadly version of Omarska. Possibly the largest massacre at Keraterm occurred on the night of July 24, 1992, and is recorded in detail in the report of the commission.

At about midnight it could be heard that windows high up on the front wall to Hall No. 3 were broken. Someone cried out, "Do not shoot

unless the commander of shift A instructs that." . . . Then someone
else cried out, "They [detainees] are fleeing." Then heavy machine gun
fire started. The commander of Shift A yelled that the shooting should
stop. His instruction was ignored, and someone mocked him, saying,
"A Serbian mother has given birth to a Ustasha son." At first, prisoners
like himself detained outside Hall No. 3 thought that the long-lasting
shooting was merely to terrorize the prisoners. At dawn he was told
by fellow prisoners that it seemed that the prisoners in Hall No. 3 had
been killed. A little later he himself saw a huge pile of dead bodies
outside of Hall No. 3. At about 05.00 hours a large lorry—FAD 1620,
24 tons—driven by an identified man [whose name is not disclosed
for confidentiality or prosecutorial reasons] arrived at the camp. . . .
One prisoner participating in the loading of the dead—and with the
corpses also wounded prisoners—on the lorry afterwards told him he
had counted 98 dead and 62 or 63 wounded prisoners. Others claimed
the total of dead was 150, and that the wounded numbered between
30 and 40. Later in the day, two fire trucks came and hosed down Hall
No. 3 and the area outside it to remove all the blood there.

This account further indicated that the main road passing the camp was
closed to traffic the night and day following this massacre.

Children, women, and the elderly were detained in the third camp,
Trnopolje. The number of persons detained here varied from four
thousand to seven thousand. Killings were notably less frequent in
this camp, but rapes were widely reported. The conclusion was that
Trnopolje most accurately could be portrayed as a concentration camp,
whereas Omarksa and Keraterm were death camps.

When the Prijedor team completed their account of ethnic cleansing
in this region, they had no doubt about its legal meaning: "It is unques-
tionable that the events in Opstina Prijedor since 30 April 1992 qualify
as crimes against humanity. Furthermore, it is likely to be confirmed in
court under due process of law that these events constitute genocide."[60]
The principal authors of the Prijedor Report, Greve and Bergsmo, felt
strongly that all the different kinds and levels of criminal involvement
in Prijedor must be pursued, so that the highly placed and more responsible figures could be prosecuted to the fullest extent possible.

"We said," Bergsmo emphasizes in commenting on the report, "that
one must look at the full spectrum of crimes in order to identify those
most responsible, and build to higher levels of responsibility. You must
try to capture as much of the victimization as possible to build your
case against leaders. This is definitely necessary in order to contribute
to reconciliation in a way in which a trial should." These remarks iden-

tify a distinction often drawn by ICT prosecutors between "thematic" and "leadership" cases. Rape and sexual assault charges are regarded as thematic prosecutions among prosecutors at The Hague, whereas charges of crimes against humanity and genocide that move upwards through the military and political command structure are referred to as leadership cases. The charge of rape had not been well dealt with in international law enforcement until it was taken up by the commission and the tribunal as a thematic topic of prosecution, and the commission report was a part of this process.

RAPE AS A WAR CRIME

Cherif Bassiouni was well aware of the work of women's and human rights groups on rape in the Balkans, and he wanted to supplement the incident reports collected in the Chicago database with on-site investigations. Christine Cleiren joined Bassiouni in organizing the field work in Bosnia, and Nancy Paterson was the coordinator of the legal team. A team of about forty, most of them women, participated in the field work in the Balkans, and they completed 223 interviews.

The interviewing teams developed a close-knit camaraderie. Nancy Paterson described her field experience during this period as having a positive as well as a more disturbing side, echoing from one woman's perspective the kind of alternation experience recounted earlier in this chapter by Bill Fenrick. Paterson recalled, "When you're in the field, you're spending almost the whole day together. You may be off interviewing during the day, but . . . we usually stayed in flats, apartments, rather than hotels, so you'd be sharing the bathroom with your colleagues. You'd have breakfast, lunch and dinner with them. When we first started going to Bosnia the war was still going on. . . . It was quite intense but also often a lot of fun." Although the interviewing was halted by the premature termination of the commission's mandate, this investigation, in combination with the Chicago database, produced important results.

The rape study was probably the most contentious context in which the commission did its work. Fortunately, Christine Cleiren and Nancy Paterson were two unflappable members of this team who helped steady the work. Bill Fenrick recalled that "at times we squabbled like cats and dogs—I think the only one who never, who was always calm, was Christine Cleiren, and I always had the feeling that was because she had a number of small children and she was used to everybody rising up around her." He added, "Having said that, we did a hell of a lot of work."

One point of conflict involved sometimes tense relations between

legal scholars and the women's and human rights nongovernmental organizations (NGOs) working on rape and sexual assault and the women
investigators and interpreters doing the field interviews for the commission. Bassiouni noted that the internationally known legal scholar
Catherine MacKinnon accompanied him into the field and "gave generously of her time and help in contacting victims and witnesses whom
she had represented or otherwise knew."[61] He added that "we had almost 30 feminist organizations, mostly from outside the U.S., many German, French and other organizations that had been active in fighting
violence against women and rape. And they were much more sensitive
than the human rights organizations at the time were."

A major concern for the field interviewers was that the victims of
rape be treated with sensitivity both to their personal trauma and to
developing long-term relationships of trust that could be sustained
through the lengthy period leading up to and through prosecutions. Paterson and Bassiouni noted that this sensitivity was not present among
all those involved in interviews. Paterson described one prominent
participant who "claimed to be . . . very sympathetic to victims' rights,
and yet when you saw this person in action with these women it was
just outrageous. A couple of times this person insisted on sitting in on
some of the interviews, which, of course, we didn't need. We're dealing
with rape victims, we didn't need five people in the room. . . . Halfway
through the interview this person gets up and walks out, comes in again
20 minutes later, things like that, that were just shocking to me from
working with rape victims."

Interviewing in some cases proved nearly impossible, for example,
in trying to get male victims of sexual abuse to report their victimization. Paterson emphasizes that sexual assaults on men as well as women
played a key intimidating role in ethnic cleansing operations and concentration camps—"primarily for humiliation purposes, forcing them
to do it in public, in front of other people, often times forcing relatives
to do it with each other, fathers, sons, cousins, brothers." Paterson continues, "For half the men that you talk to it will be like 'you should
have seen what was going on in the cell next to us . . . . Now, it never
happened in our cell.' Of course later you talk to other witnesses: 'Of
course it happened in their cell; it happened in every cell.' But they
won't admit to it." Paterson argues that sexual assault on men is "the
most underinvestigated, unreported crime in all of Bosnia."

Bergsmo worried with Greve about how to situate the sexual assault
cases. Their concern was that the urgency of seeking justice in the
"thematic" rape cases could jeopardize the requirements of building the
larger "leadership" cases involving ethnic cleansing and genocide. We

will examine the efforts to join the thematic and leadership aspects of cases in the discussion of the Tadic prosecution in the following chapter and the Foca case in chapter 6.

The women's and human rights groups that did so much to attract world attention to the atrocities in the Balkans wanted to ensure that the commission and the tribunal did not let the rape and sexual assault investigations get swept aside because of difficulties associated with their prosecution. Women such as Nancy Paterson who had prosecuted sexual assault in their home countries and had come to the commission and the tribunal to extend this work were determined to see these cases advance as well. "Am I going to come here and suddenly not make 'rape' an issue?" she asked rhetorically. "Of course not. From day one, myself and other colleagues have been pushing the subject. I think every single woman here, investigator or prosecutor, has pushed the subject." This was the context in which rape was pursued as a war crime, with the special impetus that the commission provided from the outset. However, this beginning of work on rape cases in Bosnia by the commission was prematurely terminated in the process of selecting a first chief prosecutor and making the transition to the beginning of the tribunal in The Hague. Again Bassiouni was a focus of conflict.

BASSIOUNI DENIED

The politics of the commission became fully entangled with the politics of the tribunal in the summer of 1993, when the UN Security Council turned to the task of selecting the first chief prosecutor. Since Bassiouni was a longtime friend of Secretary-General Boutros-Ghali, was already engaged in building the foundation for prosecution cases, and was anxious to take on the position of chief prosecutor, he seemed a natural choice for the appointment. Bassiouni had sought and received strong support from Islamic nonaligned members of the Security Council and in addition had some support from the United States. However, he was blocked from the prosecutor position, as he had been earlier for the chairmanship of the commission, by the British.

Britain ostensibly opposed Bassiouni because he lacked prosecutorial experience and administrative skills.[62] One observer notes, however, that "Bassiouni's supporters are convinced that his candidacy was doomed by his religion (Muslim) and the very same personal qualities—impatience and ambition—that increased his appeal for the nonaligned governments."[63] The UN correspondent for the *Times* (London) reported that Britain blocked Bassiouni because it feared he would "quickly bring charges against the Serbs"[64] and further complicate Owen's efforts to negotiate a peace agreement. This assessment of

Britain's concern was bluntly supported by another representative to the Security Council who said, "He was seen as a fanatic who had too much information."[65]

The initial count of votes in the Security Council revealed that seven countries supported Bassiouni and seven opposed him, with one abstention. The United States was in favor, but France, Russia, and China joined Britain in opposition. Bassiouni further confirmed his capacity to complicate a situation by refusing to accept a compromise that would have made him second in command. Boutros-Ghali unsuccessfully attempted to intercede, and then Madeleine Albright tried to find a resolution that would make him the deputy prosecutor. "Madeleine Albright called and said, 'Do you want me to pull your name off the nomination, because you're going to be voted down. We can't turn the Brits off.' And I said, 'Absolutely not, let me be voted down.'"

Bassiouni explained that he did not want to become the second in command to a prosecutor with a less activist inclination than his own. The British in the meantime were able to convince council members that the choice of the prosecutor should be by consensus, a process that delayed the choice for several months. This delay likely suited both British and American preferences.

The Clinton administration was still feeling its way through its first year in office. Clinton as candidate had pushed for a more aggressive human rights approach in the Balkans, promising, "I will strongly support urgent and appropriate action to stop the killing."[66] But Clinton as president became more cautious. The administration's mantra, "it's the economy, stupid," trumped any foreign policy agenda. The selection of Madeleine Albright as U.S. ambassador to the UN, and her later elevation to secretary of state and the entry of Holbrooke into a negotiating role, would ultimately move the human rights agenda forward, but for the moment, caution was the American watchword.

Bassiouni had his own view of his fate, which he explained with an analogy to Patton and Eisenhower during and after World War II. "You have the George Patton who races through, does the impossible and distinguishes himself with his personal bravery and courage, is a maverick, is impossible but does what others can't. . . . In the modern era the commanding officer or person has to be the consummate bureaucrat, a self-effacing person, the ideal Eisenhower. I think I fit more in the Patton category than anything else, and at the time [at the commission] that is what was needed. We really needed to break through a lot and it was very difficult. When that period was past you needed another type of personality. . . . I started as a Patton and . . . they couldn't sell me as an Eisenhower afterwards." He was resigned to his fate.

FROM BASSIOUNI TO BLEWITT

Bassiouni continued his work as chair of the commission while the tribunal slowly began to take form in The Hague, albeit without a chief prosecutor. Finally, in the fall, Ramon Escovar-Salom, the attorney general of Venezuela, was chosen to become the tribunal's first chief prosecutor.

Bassiouni understood that work by the commission would continue for about a year, until the middle of 1994. He expected that the exhumation of bodies would be undertaken at the Ovcara farm site near Vukovar and that the rape study would be completed. This plan was derailed when the UN Office of Legal Affairs instructed completion of their work in April.

The timing of this decision was especially unfortunate in that it preceded by about a month the decision of Escovar-Salom *not* to assume his responsibilities as chief prosecutor of the tribunal. Ironically, Bassiouni was one of those who communicated this news to Boutros-Ghali after a meeting in Geneva. Bassiouni met with Escovar-Salom on January 14, 1994, to provide an update on the commission's work. "I gave Escovar-Salom an hour's briefing. I then realized he wasn't taking notes. Suddenly he interrupted me to say, 'Look, I'm not going to take the post.'"

Although Escovar-Salom had behaved irresponsibly, he did nonetheless make one important decision during his brief involvement. Graham Blewitt, an Australian prosecutor, had been in contact to indicate his interest in a senior position at the tribunal. Blewitt had earlier been asked to serve on the commission of experts but had had to decline because he was going to trial with several Nazi war crimes cases in Australia. When these cases were finished, Blewitt called the OLA and reported, "I'm about to go back to my former job. I read in the paper you're having all sorts of difficulties getting the prosecutor's office in this tribunal started. . . . If you're still interested in me, I believe I might have something to offer. I'm certainly not keen on the prosecutor's job, but maybe in some other senior capacity I could help." He was told to get himself on a plane and go to The Hague to be interviewed by Escovar-Salon.

Graham Blewitt's insistence that he was not interested in the *chief* prosecutor's position reflected his own clear sense about who he is and what he could best contribute. He is a far different person from Bassiouni. Blewitt is a skillful manager: a self-effacing middle-aged man with a keen sense of people. He is a team player, and perhaps even more important, a team builder—a behind-the-scenes partner in leadership. He is often the person seen at the edge of the television screen sitting by the chief prosecutor, measuring the moment, lending moral support, rarely misspeaking, the soul of discretion. Blewitt is the office morale builder who characteristically ends the week late each Friday afternoon by pulling his aides together for an after-hours drink, often with a bottle he delights in presenting as his own "Old Fat Bastard" wine.

Blewitt followed the instructions he received from the U.N. and met with Escovar-Salon. He was pronounced suitable for the job, for which there actually was no description in the Security Council mandate. Escovar-Salon told Blewitt that he should come to meet the judges, who at that time were sitting in a plenary planning session. Blewitt described the scene: "He came in and announced that he had interviewed me and was going to recommend to the Secretary-General my appointment as deputy prosecutor. He then proceeded to announce that he himself would not be taking up the post of chief prosecutor."

Blewitt was told by the judges that he should assume his position in The Hague as soon as possible, and he did so in February 1994. Boutros-Ghali insisted on making Blewitt's appointment an acting position, a sign of problems to come.[67] Nonetheless, Blewitt has served in the position of deputy prosecutor ever since, providing a continuity to this office that is all the more remarkable and ironic given its unusual beginning.

FINISHING THE COMMISSION'S WORK

Bassiouni made a provocative proposal in March 1994 to the U.S. State Department. The proposal involved his working with the tribunal to help prepare a case for the prosecution of the three generals, including Galic, who had commanded the Romanija Corps of the Bosnian Serb army for the shelling and sniping attacks on Sarajevo. Much of the legal conceptualization and field investigation for this case had already been done by Bassiouni in Chicago with the archival materials and by Fenrick in Sarajevo during their field mission at the beginning of the siege.

Bassiouni and Fenrick had invested much time and energy in developing this prospective case, although Fenrick thought the case was further from fruition than Bassiouni believed. Bassiouni described the possibilities as follows:

> I could tell you who the commanding general was over the three generals who were in command of the Sarajevo Romanija First Corps who surrounded Sarajevo. . . . I could document that in the three years of the siege, on a daily basis, how many rounds of artillery and mortar fell, how many sniper shots were fired, how many people were injured or wounded. If I can show you also the targeting of civilians, the recurrence of the targets, and even the timing of it, then I have made a case for command responsibility for that general. And it's

not a question of 'is it this cannon or that mortar that is targeting civilians.' If I can show you that the hospital was hit 289 times, you can't say it was a coincidence. If I can tell you that over 70 percent of those times were between the hours of twelve and two . . . and that happens to be visiting hours, . . . that's why 70 percent of the shelling occurred during that time. Now that suddenly gives a whole different dimension than the individual person who was targeting somebody. That puts the commanding general at risk, and if you see that the commanding general . . . was a member of what would be the equivalent to their Joint Chiefs of Staff, under Mladic, . . . and that the supplies and artillery shells came directly from Serbia, and so on and so forth, you've got a damned good case of command responsibility.

Bassiouni wonders whether the capability to make this case was again interpreted at high levels of the U.S. State Department as endangering the peace process. Or was it, as David Halberstam's analysis indicates, that the Clinton administration simply could not settle on a Balkan policy and in the meantime preferred a "go slow" approach?[68] In any event, Bassiouni never received a response to this proposal.

For his part, he is convinced that his nomination to be chief prosecutor and his proposals to extend the work of the commission by developing a major Sarajevo case were scuttled because he, in effect, aimed too high, and that this particularly disturbed the British.

From the beginning I said I was not interested in going after the little soldier who commits the individual crime. I was after building a case against the leaders who make the decisions. So I was going to establish that there was ethnic cleansing as a policy, that there was systematic rape as a policy, that there was destruction of cultural property as a policy, that the destruction of Sarajevo was a systematic process. What I didn't realize was that this was precisely what the British, and to some extent the French and the Russians, did not want. I can understand that the last thing in the world they wanted was someone who was going to screw up their negotiations. But I thought, they've got their work to do. Let them do it. I've got my work to do. But that was not the political reality, and that's why I did not get any support for what I was doing.[69]

The *Times* (London) agreed, noting that although the official reason given for rejecting Bassiouni was lack of administrative experience as a prosecutor, "diplomatic sources said the real reason is that the European countries are afraid Dr. Bassiouni will move too quickly to charge Serb and possibly Croat leaders with war crimes." The *Times* then quoted one official as saying, "He might try to indict high-level people imme-diately, and then we are in trouble."[70] Bassiouni was forced to settle for producing the most telling final report from the commission he could, a report that would leave a lasting record and provide a springboard for the tribunal.

The final report of the commission is summarized in an 84-page doc-ument that is a ringing indictment of Serbian crimes in the Balkans up to the spring of 1994. It is backed up by more than 65,000 pages of doc-uments and three hundred hours of videotaped testimony and news footage, as well as a 3,300 page, five-volume appendix supporting the conclusions in the final report. All of this material was accumulated in an enormous cargo container and sent by air freight from Chicago to the tribunal in The Hague.

FROM THE COMMISSION TO THE TRIBUNAL

Bassiouni visited the tribunal and assisted with the transition. Per-haps more significant, however, several of the leading individuals who worked with Bassiouni at the commission on each of its major projects soon joined the tribunal. Bill Fenrick, who developed the early legal conceptualization of command responsibility and linked this to the siege of Sarajevo, became the head of the tribunal's legal advisory sec-tion. Morten Bergsmo, who worked with Hanna Sophie Greve on the Prijedor Report and helped develop its detailed picture of ethnic cleans-ing as genocide, joined Fenrick in the legal advisory section. Nancy Paterson, who led the team of lawyers that conducted the rape victim interviews in Bosnia, became a senior tribunal legal advisor. Years later Paterson emphasized how great a role Cherif Bassiouni had played in getting them all to this juncture, noting that "our investigation never, ever would have happened if he hadn't pushed, pushed and pushed. He made a lot of enemies along the way. I have high respect for him. Now probably even more than I did then."

The Norwegian Bergsmo had just finished his legal education and was at the beginning stage of his legal career, the American Paterson was a criminal lawyer with extensive experience in sexual assault pros-ecutions, and the Canadian Fenrick was at the peak of his career as a military lawyer. These three lawyers were among the first recruited into the Office of the Prosecutor. They joined the new deputy prosecutor for the tribunal, Graham Blewitt, who was experienced in the prosecution of organized crime and Nazi war criminals in Australia.

It was of more than symbolic note that six months into his job, in June 1994, Blewitt still was designated as the acting deputy prosecu-tor and that there was as yet no chief prosecutor. Blewitt had little job security and could offer even less to others. Indeed, until he successfully appealed to be allowed to make appointments without going through the normal UN bureaucracy, it was uncertain that he could make binding offers of employment of any kind. He recalls this period as "one of the worst experiences of my life. I hope that I never have to go through it again."[71]

Blewitt even had trouble getting paid in the beginning. "I think it took several weeks to get my first pay check, a second pay check came, and then the pay checks just dried up. I wasn't getting paid at all." He flew to New York and found that his personnel file contained a directive saying that his pay should be withheld, without any explanation. "So having discovered that thing on my file, without embarrassment at all they said, 'Oh, that's why you're not getting paid. We'll fix that up.' And then the pay started to come. It's one of the mysteries of life that I'd like to clear up before I leave, to find out what prompted that."

Blewitt's capacity to ride out and resolve such problems, for others and himself, says much about how he and the tribunal have advanced and endured since its uncertain beginning. His co-workers from this period are quick to emphasize his centrality to the organization. One colleague notes that "to me the most important aspect of continuity has been the deputy prosecutor, Graham Blewitt. For good or bad, and I think mainly for good, and certainly never for evil, Graham to me has been the heart and soul of this organization." Another colleague observed that "he's incredibly diligent, very approachable and very kind and very understanding of people, and that's had a lot to do with it. He's a father figure in some ways to the whole place, and there have been changes, the president has changed, the registrar changes, the deputy registrar changes, the senior trial attorneys turned over, you need the rock of somebody that you can anchor the place on." Confronted with such a compliment, Blewitt is the kind of person who probably would deflect it as a comment about his battle with his waistline.

The lawyers Blewitt hired from the commission were now making their second adventuresome career moves. They were moving from their unique associations with the embattled commission to the uncertainty of the neophyte tribunal, launching careers in an emerging yet clearly struggling, unproved, and still quite tentative transnational institution of international criminal and humanitarian law. They were all there at the early stages to help Graham Blewitt "turn on the lights" in the summer of 1994. However, they soon discovered that they would have to generate a lot of the electricity themselves; the tribunal was still operating without a chief prosecutor. There was no source of agency at the top to lead an institution that remained largely undefined.

CHAPTER THREE

The Virtual Tribunal

More than a year after the UN Security Council established the tribunal, in July 1994, after a dozen nominees had been considered, Justice Richard Goldstone of South Africa was named as the ICT's first chief prosecutor. Goldstone is a short and sometimes stern man whose piercing gaze and determined demeanor might best be described as "owlish."[1] Alternately charming and combative, Goldstone is a match for the demands of the political moment. He is also legendary for his availability to human rights groups, the press, and academic and other audiences, and he maintains a punishing international travel schedule that frequently takes him far from his current seat on South Africa's Constitutional Court.

News coverage of Goldstone's work at the tribunal often pictured him in his judicial robes, and he notes in his memoir, "I was determined to use my title of Justice." He had his reasons for wanting to stand on ceremony: "The title would, in my opinion, attract more respect for the Office of the Prosecutor and result in a greater recognition of my independence." It is easy to understand why he was anxious to claim respect in his new role. Former British prime minister Edward Heath asked in mock amazement, "Why did you accept such a ridiculous job?"[2] when he was introduced to Goldstone soon after his appointment. The British press already was calling the UN tribunal a "fig leaf for inaction."

Goldstone was in some ways an unlikely choice for chief prosecutor. His training and early career were in commercial rather than criminal law. Yet he also had qualifications that made him politically unimpeachable. When he was tapped for the ICT job, he had just finished serving as the very visible chair of a South African commission that had exposed high-level right-wing government involvement in police violence by South Africa's apartheid regime.

In the course of this work Goldstone had interviewed hundreds and visited thousands of victims of apartheid who were being detained and often tortured without trial. He noted these were "innocent, uncharged, unconvicted people who were put away, indefinitely." His recurring experience was that although "I hated in the morning the thought of having to do this for another day, by the end of the day, I was exhilarated at the reaction and how important the work was." This sense of exhilaration repeats the theme of alternation highlighted in earlier chapters. Goldstone too was bitten by the bug of international humanitarian law.

The invisible hand behind his selection as prosecutor was the Italian chief judge of the tribunal, Antonio Cassese. Cassese telephoned Goldstone and asked about his availability. When Goldstone spoke with the South African minister of justice to explore this possibility, he learned that he also was about to be named by Nelson Mandela to his country's new Constitutional Court. Mandela ushered through a constitutional amendment that would grant Goldstone a leave to serve at the tribunal and then return to a spot on the Constitutional Court. Cassese was so pleased when he learned that Goldstone would accept the position that he faxed his fellow judges a message using the language of papal succession: "Habemus papum!" Some of the judges would later come to privately call their new chief prosecutor "Pope Goldstone," although not always with the enthusiasm of Cassese.

For entirely different reasons, both Nelson Mandela and Goldstone's persuasive wife, Noleen, wanted him to become the first ICT chief prosecutor. Noleen Goldstone and their two daughters had lived through the death threats and bodyguards that accompanied the chairmanship of the Goldstone Commission. Two years at The Hague, with its international reputation for diplomatic propriety, promised a respite.

For its part, the tribunal was in desperate need of political legitimacy, financial support, and prosecutorial direction. As it turned out, the new prosecutor was just the person for the politics and the fundraising, although less so to formulate and implement a prosecutorial strategy. Critics of the Goldstone Commission noted that it had produced just one trial in three years. "He could have been much tougher and wiser from the beginning," another South African political analyst said. "By the time he got into the investigations, much of the evidence had been shredded."[3] A more admiring associate at the commission noted that Goldstone's administrative style was to delegate internal work, while himself taking primary responsibility for the external politics of the commission. His point was that this was how Goldstone was able to juggle the immense responsibilities he assumed, first at the commission and now at the tribunal.

THE TRIBUNAL AS A LOOSELY COUPLED SYSTEM

Heath and the British press were hardly the only ones skeptical about the prospects of the tribunal making a difference in the Balkans. The sociologists John Meyer and Ron Jepperson seriously question whether UN institutions such as the tribunal and the human rights movement can reshape the real world in the ways they promise.[4]

Meyer and Jepperson incredulously describe the human rights movement and the new field of international humanitarian law as a modern attempt "to create and elaborate global conceptions of 'human rights' and to implement them in legal systems."[5] The Hague tribunal is probably the most visible contemporary expression of these aims. They note, as I have in the opening chapters of this book, that the concept of agency, with its reference to the role of individuals in making a difference as independent and autonomous actors, is central to the human rights movement and to international humanitarian law. Their concern is that this reliance on agency is unrealistic.[6]

They explain that structures such as the ICT expect actor-based charisma and agency to produce unlikely goals and are too deeply rooted in unrealistic Protestant and Anglo-American beliefs. "Imagine," they propose, "a Third World country trying to maintain a broadly legitimated stance toward women's rights in a traditional peasant economy."[7] They argue that the expectations accompanying human rights norms and international humanitarian law produce a "loose coupling" or "decoupling" of the words and deeds of modern institutions and actors. The implication is that the initiating principal, in this case the UN, lacks sustaining principles to guide the principal-agent relation, and therefore the tribunal and its chief prosecutor will tend more toward ceremonial form than real-world substance—promising to do things that cannot be accomplished. From Meyer and Jepperson's perspective, the lofty ideals of the tribunal will be only loosely coupled to its actual operations— a political institution with little legal impact—or, again in the words of the British press, "a fig leaf for inaction."

GOLDSTONE'S ARRIVAL

Richard Goldstone soon found himself in front of UN-arranged press conferences in New York and The Hague. "Both conferences proved a difficult start to my new relationship with the international media," he observed, "which effectively had written off the International Criminal Tribunal for the Former Yugoslavia as the 'fig leaf' of the international community established to hide its shame for inaction in the former Yugoslavia, particularly in Bosnia. There was little I could say to change that negative attitude." These press conferences were quick reminders that Goldstone had his work cut out on the political and financial fronts that awaited him.

As he had at the commission on political violence in South Africa, Goldstone realized that he could concentrate better on the external relations of the tribunal if he delegated internal organizational matters to his office staff. From Meyer and Jepperson's perspective, this was a recipe for loose coupling. An admiring article in the *American Lawyer* noted, "Upon arriving in The Hague in mid-August of 1994, Goldstone recognized that his was a big-picture diplomatic role and that the hands-on prosecution work could be pushed down to experienced prosecutors and investigators like [Graham] Blewitt—at least for the time being."[8]

When Goldstone arrived Blewitt already had been at work for six months assembling a prosecution office that included forty employees. Blewitt met Goldstone's plane in Amsterdam. They got on well from the start and became firm friends, which was a relief for both of them. "I had the distinct impression," Goldstone recalled, "that Blewitt was concerned that I might wish to reorganize the Office of the Prosecutor." He needn't have worried, because Goldstone confided that "nothing was further from my mind."[9] What was on his mind was the interview he had promised to do with Mike Wallace for *60 Minutes* on his first morning at his new office in The Hague.

Wallace wanted to know how Goldstone was going to bring the Balkan war criminals to justice, noting, "You've got to get them here on trial." Goldstone's uncertain answer, which began, "The members of the international community and—and—the media," was an acknowledgment of his acute dilemma and of his understanding that political pressure aroused by the media was his only real resource.[10] At the moment, the media were not helping Goldstone's cause but instead underlining the inadequacy of the tribunal.

THE ANGLO-AMERICANS ARE COMING

The Office of the Prosecutor began with an allocation of 126 positions and no one to fill them or sustaining funds to pay them. When Graham Blewitt arrived in February 1994 he nonetheless found hundreds of résumés awaiting him. He sorted them by area of expertise and soon realized that almost none showed courtroom experience. "So I just pushed all those [without court experience] aside," Blewitt recalled, "and I looked at what I had left and I virtually had nothing." He realized that a more personal approach to recruitment would be necessary. "I just picked up the phone and I called people that I'd been working with."

The concern initially was less with the prosecution side than with investigations, since the process had to begin with building cases as the foundation for indictments. Blewitt chose an Australian colleague as his first chief of investigations. "He was a guy I had known for years . . . , he had worked on my team on the Australian National Crime Authority . . . he was effectively the driving force behind the whole thing. . . . I phoned him up and asked him if he was interested and he said yes."

Blewitt also pursued the transnational network he knew from his work on Nazi war crimes in England, Scotland, and Canada. "I phoned . . . Scotland. That's how I got Gavin Ruxton. . . . The British, let's see, I got Mike Blaxill." The trail then led back to Australian colleagues: "That's how John Ralston and Bob Reid got here. And Grant Niemann as well. . . . Indirectly through Bob Reid, that's how we got Anne Sutherland. Anne was working for the defense in Australia." Steven Upton was recruited from New Zealand, where he had done work on international drug crimes and money laundering.

Another source of Anglo-American recruits emerged when the United States sent twenty-two lawyers and investigators to work in the OTP. These included individuals such as Clint Williamson, who had been very proactively involved in the U.S. Department of Justice. The next chapter describes the role that Williamson played with indirect help from the United States in developing the first arrest for the tribunal with a secret indictment. His experience with undercover work in the United States exemplified the kind of expertise in the field and the courtroom that Blewitt ideally wanted to recruit into the tribunal.

The American secondees were appreciated for their energy and enthusiasm as well as their experience. Brenda Hollis was an Air Force lawyer, Terree Bowers was an assistant U.S. attorney in Los Angeles, Nancy Paterson came from the sex crimes unit of the district attorney's office in Manhattan, Patricia Sellers prosecuted sex crimes in Philadelphia, and Pat Treanor worked as a historian of Nazi war crimes in the Department of Justice. These were the sort of skilled professionals Blewitt needed, "people who have a lot of experience in prosecuting complex cases, but also . . . in the context of working with police and other disciplines in the investigative process."

An early and extremely important American recruit who stayed was Mark Harmon, who was also a Department of Justice lawyer. California-born, athletic, and assertive, few who see Harmon in the courtrooms of the tribunal would mistake him as anything other than American. Yet he also had a unique and long-lasting childhood memory that linked his southern California upbringing to a more distant and menacing past.

> When I was a kid I grew up near a survivor family who never recovered from the camps where they had been interned. I didn't get it

at the time; I knew there was something that had happened to this family that I couldn't at six or seven years old understand. They were very nice people, wonderful people. But they were physically broken people and as I grew up I learned, as I started to read books on the Holocaust . . . I saw pictures . . . of people who had perished, who were stacked like cord wood, piled high, white, naked, emaciated bodies. I was stunned. I was literally stunned. The historic event that made the most significant impression on me; maybe I was like one of Lorenzo's little ducks who was imprinted with some image, but that was the image that was imprinted on me, and then I could put it together with my people who lived down the street from me, who were wonderful people, and who were human and were alive; it was incomprehensible to me. . . . And that's the motivation that brought me here in the first place.

This motivation infused Harmon's initial interest in justice in the United States, but it would take some time for a more direct link to the tribunal to develop.

Harmon began his career as a public defender in Santa Clara, California, and found his way to the Department of Justice in Washington, D.C., where he worked on civil rights and environmental law cases. He was one of three lawyers in charge of prosecuting the *Exxon Valdez* case. During this period he also joined with Peter McCloskey, who came later to the tribunal, in a successful suit against the department for imposing mandatory drug testing on its employees. Harmon was fascinated by his work in Washington, but the politics of the city and the department disturbed him. He was ready for a change of work setting.

Alan Tieger, a lawyer involved in the Rodney King case and also in the tribunal's first prosecuted case, was the connection that led Harmon to Blewitt and the tribunal. This recruitment illustrates how large a role social networks played in the early life of the tribunal.

Alan and I were friends from the old days. Alan came to the Department of Justice as a result of my recommendation. . . . After Rodney King and Exxon had finished, I was walking down Pennsylvania Avenue. . . . So I run into Alan and I hadn't seen him since the Rodney King case; we were talking and I asked Alan what life was like after a big case, because life changes in a certain sense. He told me he was coming here, so I . . . asked him what this job was about, and I said, "I'd like to apply," and he said, "It's too late, the applications are in, they're going to make a decision." . . . Unfortunately, my section never got the solicitation. . . . So I thought about that. It was the kind of job that I didn't think was possible and would ever come up again after

Nuremberg, but lo and behold it did. I'm not somebody who is easily
discouraged, so I picked up the phone and called Graham Blewitt. I
asked Graham if they were still accepting applications for prosecutors
and he said they were. I needed to submit a résumé to him the next
day, and I did that and then I actually got the job.

Joining the tribunal was an easy decision, and the experience confirmed Harmon's motivation for coming. "Having now met many victims . . . only confirms what I think; what happened in Bosnia, and in
Croatia, those were great wrongs that should not have happened in the
first place, that should never be repeated again. . . . So that's the motivation."

The challenge was finding lawyers and investigators with the right
mix of motivation and experience. One lawyer who was among the first
hired for the OTP described the recruitment strategy this way: "Graham
Blewitt was responsible for the shaping of the office. . . . Especially in
the first three years he was extremely concerned to get people who have
law experience from domestic investigation and prosecution, and to get
well balanced people, to get reliable people, not to get 'political animals';
not to get too many persons who are more human rights activists than
professional criminal justice lawyers and investigators."

The above account of recruitment to the tribunal matches answers
to questions about recruitment that I included in a survey I conducted
with more than one hundred employees, a one-third random sample of
those working in the OTP. One question asked whether the respondents
had found their jobs with the tribunal through referrals, applications,
or being personally asked to apply (for example, by Blewitt).[11] I then
grouped the responses by the chief prosecutor (Goldstone, Arbour, or
Del Ponte) at the time the employee was hired.

Referrals accounted for about one-half of the hires in all three periods. Although being asked to apply accounted for about one-third of
the additional hires in the Goldstone era, when Blewitt was exploring
his personal networks for talented investigators and lawyers, this route
to the tribunal became almost nonexistent by the Del Ponte period. In
contrast, cold applications grew from about 14 percent to more than
one-third of hires from the Goldstone era to the Del Ponte era, as increasingly talented persons began to seek out employment at the tribunal on their own. More specifically, another survey item indicated
that whereas nearly 50 percent of the respondents reported that they
had help from someone at the tribunal in getting their jobs during the
Goldstone era, fewer than one-quarter had by the Del Ponte period.
These figures reveal the extent to which Blewitt and Goldstone were

able to make use of personal networks to recruit employees in the early years of the tribunal.

A result was that when Goldstone arrived in July 1994, the tribunal already had a distinctively Anglo-American atmosphere. By Goldstone's account, Blewitt "had already assembled about forty people in the office, twenty-three from the United States, five from Australia, and the others from an assortment of other countries."[12] Blewitt said, "There was a nucleus of about 12 people that I knew and they arrived here in fairly quick order, and those people together with the American secondees gave me about 40 people upon which to get started."

The OTP survey helped further locate the Anglo-Americans in their relationships to others who have come to the tribunal. The survey asked respondents to rate nineteen different sources of satisfaction in their work. Of these factors, the highest ranked is the opportunity to work with a team of people. So there is considerable agreement about the satisfaction teamwork brings at the OTP, but there also is interesting variation in the ranking of this and other sources of satisfaction between the Anglo-Americans and others.

Compared to others who work at the tribunal, the Anglo-Americans tend to place significantly greater emphasis on the opportunities to play leadership roles with respect to important issues that involve public service, and they place slightly less emphasis than do others on teamwork. This does not mean that Americans are not team players. The point is that the Anglo-Americans are distinctive in their interest in leading as well as joining and following in the team experience.

The emphasis on leadership among the Anglo-Americans is especially striking, because as indicated in the survey, leadership ranks second lowest among all OTP employees in their evaluation of job satisfaction. Nancy Paterson expressed a clear sense of satisfaction about the early American leadership role, saying that "the Americans who were here in the first two or three years were the real backbone of the tribunal. I mean, not exclusively by any means, a lot of people contributed, but there were some very key Americans here who were the real pushers behind the scenes and made a lot of things happen."

It was striking how much the OTP had already changed in the first six months, not only with regard to recruitment but also in spatial terms. The judges of the tribunal were housed in several rooms of the World Court until the UN leased part of the four-story building owned by the Aegon Insurance Company in the suburbs of The Hague. Gavin Ruxton recalled that when he came to the tribunal to meet with Blewitt in February 1994, Blewitt had one room on the ground floor. The employees of the OTP shared a cafeteria with the insurance company employees, which prohibited any work-related luncheon conversations. However, the installation of a ten-foot wrought iron security fence and cameras around the entire building seemed to create a symbolic turning point. Ruxton noted that "when they put up the fence they [the insurance company] started to think this isn't a good place to be and we expanded as they contracted." By mid-summer of 1994, the OTP had taken possession of the third floor of the building, and the desks and computers were starting to arrive.

GOLDSTONE BEGINS

Goldstone's first several months as chief prosecutor were a blur of media appearances and financial negotiations. During the first month alone, Goldstone reported, he gave two dozen interviews and news conferences. At the same time he learned more about the financial squeeze the tribunal was facing and its quarterly budgeting process. At one point the UN funding problems threatened to halt all travel by investigators to the Balkans. Aryeh Neier, as head of George Soros's Open Society Fund, stepped in with a three-hundred-thousand-dollar grant for the first year of operations. Meanwhile, Goldstone was also able to solicit more than eight million dollars' worth of voluntary contributions from thirteen countries.

The key to the annual budget from the UN was its extraordinarily powerful ACABQ committee—the Advisory Committee on Administrative and Budgetary Questions. "We had to defend the budget for the first time in November of 1994," Goldstone recalled. "It was at that meeting that I was advised, 'You have to have an indictment out, otherwise you're not going to get any money, and you'll get no sympathy from the ACABQ.'" Goldstone and Blewitt now needed to quickly identify the targets for their first indictments.

The obvious place to look was in the work already done by Cherif Bassiouni's commission of experts. Bassiouni clearly relishes telling the story of traveling to the tribunal when Goldstone was first appointed, having previously shipped them the commission's database. Bassiouni recalls his meeting in The Hague with Chief Prosecutor Goldstone: "He arrived in The Hague on a Friday; I arrived in The Hague on Sunday. I walked into his office. The office was absolutely bare. And he said, 'I'm at a loss, I don't know anything about the subject matter, I don't know anything about the conflict. I have nothing to go on.' . . . So I said, 'I'll tell you what, let's start from A, let me put up a map of Yugoslavia somewhere and let me try to brief you on the conflict.' He said, 'We don't even have a map of Yugoslavia.' And so I brought in my two assistants. We gave him his first map. And 65,000 documents,

300 hours of tapes, hundreds of maps and charts and what not. There was enough to fill a container the size of this room [Bassiouni's ample office]." Justice Goldstone appreciated Bassiouni's contribution and good will, but he remembered the transfer of material slightly differently. "Cherif was extremely cooperative. And generously so because he'd been . . . more than badly treated by the UN. At the same time he didn't want to see all his hard work and many hours and a great deal of courage simply wasted. . . . Graham Blewitt had already gone through Cherif Bassiouni's reports. . . . There's a lack of appreciation . . . of the fact that Cherif's report is nothing more than pretty much a beginning of prosecutions . . . but it was a huge help because it was a compass. . . . It pointed Graham Blewitt in the direction of the massacre and the death camps in the Prijedor region." At a minimum, the commission report provided a place to start. Meanwhile, Goldstone and Blewitt were also busy simply getting the office equipped.

THE CADILLAC OF COMPUTERS

Simply getting the infrastructure of the tribunal in place was a challenge. One thing that strikes any visitor to the OTP who is familiar with law firms is the absence of printed material and the rather sterile feeling, reflected in its sparsely furnished offices and often empty desks. Blewitt explained that "right from the outset the idea was to have a paperless office. So that all the information that comes into the place would be on a computer on a server somewhere, so that if you had the authority you could gain access to the documents with different ways of searching for it." The database transferred by Bassiouni was a potential starting point for this computerized operation.

From Bassiouni's perspective, the UN legal affairs office once again impeded the tribunal's progress in this area, and on this point Goldstone and Bassiouni probably would agree.[13] Bassiouni felt that UN legal officers were initially responsible for disparaging the value of the commission's database to Goldstone and the tribunal. He reported that they "basically told him that the database that we had developed here was not very useful." The question again arose as to whether the UN was attempting to slow the progress of the tribunal to leave time for political negotiations.

Bassiouni knew the limits of his database all too well. "It was a database that was designed to handle 100,000 documents. If you say, 'Can you handle 1,000,000 documents?' the answer is 'no.' This is, or was, a Ford. You want a Cadillac." Blewitt had the foresight to realize the scale and longevity of the tribunal and wanted a computer system to match. Unfortunately, the original British computer expert who was commissioned to develop a system worked for many months without producing a useful product. Ultimately the United States came though with a three-million-dollar contribution that allowed the tribunal to develop the computer system Blewitt needed.[14] Now they had the Cadillac, and they needed somewhere to drive it.

A COURTROOM IN WAITING

The Aegon Insurance building had to be retrofitted not only to accommodate the computer system but also to provide a state-of-the-art courtroom. The UN was sensitive to the formal face the courtrooms would give the tribunal and budgeted nearly a million dollars to complete the first courtroom renovation by December 1994. The courtrooms are still the only parts of the tribunal that are open to the public.

The original courtroom has a decidedly modern appearance that has become the tribunal's dominant motif. It is bathed in tones of UN blue and populated by legal actors dressed in somber black gowns. The courtroom is located at the front of the building. Visitors pass through the security entrance, where cameras and tape recorders are left behind and belongings are passed through a metal detector. A second security person and metal detector are located at the base of the staircase leading in a semicircular ascent to the next level and the courtroom. At the top of the stairs is a third security person who familiarizes the visitor with the handheld translation device that when attached to waiting headphones provides simultaneous audio interpretations in English, French, and Serbo-Croatian.

The courtroom is separated from its visitors' gallery by bulletproof glass and shade-like curtains that can be dropped to shield the identity of witnesses. Several elegant columns stand just outside the glass partition and provide the only softening of this austere division between the court and the observation gallery. Courtroom observers are further distanced from the immediacy of the legal drama that is played out before them by the translation of an interpreter whose delivery necessarily lags behind that of the speaker and is often different in gender. Camera images of the court hover on monitors suspended from the ceiling on each side of the partition.

The overall feeling of the courtroom is one of sleek efficiency, with the teak and metal look of an IKEA showroom. It is sensible, even elegant, yet somewhat spartan and decidedly modern by classical courtroom standards. The English barristers who represented the first defendant, Dusko Tadic, added a pre-modern element when they insisted on wearing their wigs, but this practice has since disappeared. The three judges sit on bright blue chairs, wearing black robes with red collars, on a raised dais with UN flags to each side. Slightly curved defense and prosecution tables stand to each side of the judge's bench, and the opposing counsel are similarly dressed in black robes with white collar pieces. The defendants are located to one far side of the room, behind their counsel, with armed security guards alongside them. Across the room, behind the prosecutors, are located their aides and assistants. The interpreters are positioned in a glass booth behind them. There is a table in front of the judges' dais for the clerks and representatives from the registrar's office, who are responsible for matters such as the distribution of documents.

The judges, witnesses, defense counsel, and prosecutors have computer screens before them to view exhibits. Side rooms are available for the accused, judges, and witnesses to prepare themselves before appearing in court. The defendants are swept in and out of underground security areas of the building on their way to and from the UN detention facility, a twenty-four-cell unit specially created inside a prison in the nearby coastal town of Scheveningen. Each unit provides its detainee with a television, radio, and shower, and provisions are made for conjugal visits. These essentials were in place by the end of 1994, and the tribunal now needed defendants to put its hastily created infrastructure to work.

DECIDING ON A DEFENDANT

Goldstone notes that in the fall of 1994, the ACABQ committee was at least indicating that it wanted something to happen, certainly indictments if not a trial, to make use of the resources it was allocating for the building renovations, personnel, courtroom, and detention center in The Netherlands. Bassiouni's view was that the tribunal should indict the generals who were responsible for the siege of Sarajevo, whom he believed could be pursued using the strategy of command responsibility outlined in his report from the commission of experts. "Go after the commanding generals of the Romanija corps," Bassiouni reportedly told Goldstone. Goldstone chose to go neither that far nor that fast.

Instead he decided to go after Dusko Tadic, who was mentioned numerous times in the commission's Prijedor reports. In Goldstone's view it was a case of Hobson's choice: "We had an empty prison. There was a great deal of frustration. The judges were frustrated. We were all frustrated." Investigations of the Omarska detention camp and of ethnic cleansing in Prijedor, where Tadic was involved, were already under way in the office. Goldstone reported, "I didn't mull it over. It seemed an obvious thing to go get him."

Ironically, when Tadic had been at risk of being drafted into the

Bosnian Serb army, he had moved to Munich and was recognized by camp survivors in a government registration office and subsequently arrested. Bassiouni reported that he helped make the arrest happen. "He was seen by one of the victims of the Omarska prison camp who we had interviewed. In fact, a journalist to whom she reported it came to see me in Geneva. I picked up the phone. I happened to know the director general of the ministry of justice for criminal affairs. . . . I said, 'I have in my office a woman' and so on. He said 'Let me call you back.' He called the police, called back and said, 'Well, can you have the woman come?' She came, swore an affidavit, and they arrested him." Bassiouni nonetheless dismissed the importance of Dusko Tadic, saying, "He was a nothing."

Goldstone obviously understood that Tadic was not a leadership figure. Tadic, a police officer, was more a participant in than an instigator of the sadistic acts that made him infamous in Prijedor. Against the proposal to begin at the middle or upper level of command responsibility, Goldstone argued publicly that "our strategy includes the investigation of lower-level persons directly involved in carrying out the crimes in order to build effective cases against military and civilian leaders."[15] Yet before the Tadic case went to trial, Goldstone himself acknowledged that the tribunal's success would have to be judged "by the degree to which the most guilty are adequately punished." Tadic clearly was not among the most guilty, and Goldstone therefore further acknowledged that "if in two years' time Tadic is all we have to show, then clearly we will have failed."[16] This proved to be a troubling timetable.

Goldstone assigned a team of twenty OTP investigators and lawyers to the case in the fall of 1994. He then asked the tribunal judges to hold a hearing to order Germany to transfer Tadic for prosecution. The judges also raised the question of whether Tadic was too minor for the tribunal's attention. Goldstone's response, that "the Tadic case relates to an important investigation which was in any event under way in the prosecutor's office,"[17] seemed unconvincing, but the judges nonetheless granted the application. Germany took its time in complying, so that Tadic did not become the first occupant of the tribunal's detention facility until the following spring.

It had taken nearly two years from the creation of the tribunal in the spring of 1993 to get the first defendant into custody, and it would be another full year before Tadic would actually go on trial. Since Goldstone would leave the tribunal in the fall of 1996, it took most of his entire term as prosecutor to begin the first trial before the tribunal, and the defendant in this trial was of dubious significance.

DANCING ON THE GRAVE

Acutely aware that Tadic remained the only defendant in custody, Richard Goldstone made what seemed a desperate effort to kick-start NATO's Implementation Force for the Dayton Accords (IFOR) into making arrests for the tribunal. His effort came as Richard Holbrooke was arriving in Sarajevo on February 11, 1995, to make plans for a summit concerning implementation of the Dayton Accords, which had been signed the previous November.

In the dead of winter, just before Holbrooke's arrival, two senior Bosnian Serb officers, General Djordje Djukic and Colonel Aleska Krsmanovic, made a wrong turn into Bosnian-controlled territory outside of Sarajevo and were taken into custody by the Bosnian Muslim army. Goldstone hoped that these senior officers could be part of a leadership case of the kind Bassiouni had favored, leading up the chain of command to General Ratko Mladic, whom the tribunal had indicted on charges of genocide. He regarded the officers as likely "building blocks for bigger things." The weak link in this strategy was that neither Djukic nor Krsmanovic had been indicted in advance by the tribunal. The tribunal was reacting to events more than planning to make them happen.

Slobodan Milosevic immediately demanded that Djukic and Krsmanovic be released, insisting that in addition to being unindicted both were simple soldiers and that Djukic was dying of cancer. Holbrooke flew to Belgrade to deal with this unexpected threat to his fragile Dayton agreement and then returned to Sarajevo the following morning. Blewitt recalled that "there was a great deal of negotiation taking place at the time, between me and . . . Goldstone and people like Holbrooke who had just negotiated Dayton and they were, of course, very keen to make sure it stuck together and didn't unravel." Holbrooke was worried that General Mladic might order Bosnian Serb forces to storm the Sarajevo prison to rescue their officers.

The IFOR troops responded by outlining a plan of action to Holbrooke: "With the prior knowledge of the Bosnian prison authorities, a special group of specially selected French soldiers would move into the jail at night, grab the two prisoners, and move them quickly to American helicopters for transport to The Hague. The greatest danger . . . was that the Serbs would get wind of the operation and try to block it on the roads or shoot the helicopter down."[18] Neither threat materialized, although an enterprising television crew managed to get into position to film the entire event.

Once Djukic and Krsmanovic were installed in the Hague prison unit, Goldstone issued a statement noting that the detention was "temporary" and would not extend beyond "a number of weeks" and that the Serbian officers would be provided their choice of counsel. A little more than two weeks later, Djukic was indicted by the tribunal for committing a crime against humanity as the assistant for logistics to General Mladic when his Bosnian Serb forces "deliberately or indiscriminately fired on civilian targets that were of no military significance in order to kill, injure, terrorize and demoralize the civilian population of Sarajevo."[19]

Yet within two months, Djukic and Krsmanovic both were released. Blewitt explained that "the case we had against him [Djukic] was not particularly strong. He was in charge of logistics, sort of supplying the military hardware." He continued, "Our biggest problem would have been, had it gone to trial, establishing a level of his knowledge that what he was doing was supplying material and weapons to be used specifically for criminal activity as against military activity." Djukic refused to cooperate in any way, and since he was near death from cancer, there was no time or leverage to build a case around him. Goldstone said simply, "I didn't see any good point and neither did the judges in having him die a couple of weeks later in prison. . . . It would have made a martyr of him." There was little choice but to let him go. Meanwhile, Krsmanovic was never charged. "It was a fuck-up," one UN official surmised. "They had nothing on him [Krsmanovic], but they arrested him anyway."[20] Major General William Nash of IFOR agreed that "Judge Goldstone made a very serious mistake in having a nonindicted individual brought to The Hague."[21] All sides in Bosnia subsequently agreed not to apprehend someone as a war criminal unless he or she had previously been indicted.

Back in Belgrade, Mladic was unable to contain himself. When Djukic died in a Belgrade military hospital in late May, Mladic dressed up in full military uniform and paraded before the television cameras at his loyal subordinate's graveside. The event was covered not only by the Serbian media but also in the Western press. American officials claimed that they protested Mladic's appearance to Milosevic, who reportedly explained that "funerals are very important to Serbs."[22] Goldstone held the Americans and NATO as well as Milosevic accountable for not arresting the indicted Mladic.

The NATO military commanders were the essential but unwilling partners for the purposes of collecting evidence and making arrests in the Balkans. On this front, Goldstone had almost no success. "It was all mission creep and not wanting to assist," he reports. He was unable to establish productive relations with NATO military commanders during the remainder of his time in The Hague, and he is resentful to this day of their lack of support for and cooperation with the tribunal.

WITNESS FOR THE PROSECUTION

What Goldstone and the tribunal were unable to make happen in early 1996 soon showed some signs of happening for them: a potential star witness fell into their hands. His name was Drazen Erdemovic, and in early March he wanted to confess to his role in the Srebrenica massacre. He tried to turn himself in to the American embassy in Belgrade, but an embassy telephone operator told him nobody could speak with him.[23] Instead he confessed to a freelance television reporter for ABC who also could not interest the American embassy in the story. Erdemovic said he had murdered about a hundred Muslims the previous summer in Srebrenica.

This was eyewitness evidence of participation in the most murderous event in Europe since the Holocaust. More than seven thousand persons from Srebrenica were reported missing and presumed dead by the International Red Cross. General Ratko Mladic claimed that no massacres had occurred in the Srebrenica area and boasted, "They can't arrest me and they should not even think of that. I am going to travel whenever I feel the need to travel."[24] This boast was accompanied by a thinly veiled threat. Referring to the Somali warlord Mohammed Farah Aidid, whose guards killed eighteen U.S. troops in a failed raid, Mladic suggested, "I believe they have learned something from Aidid in Somalia."[25]

Erdemovic spoke in greater detail with a reporter for *Le Figaro*. He told of being a member of an eight-man execution squad in which he personally shot and killed seventy Muslims, adding that the squad murdered at least twelve hundred people in less than six hours at a state farm near the village of Pilice, outside of Srebrenica. When the reporter from *Le Figaro* went to meet Erdemovic the next day, he was told that a police unit from Belgrade had arrived at three o'clock in the morning and arrested Erdemovic with a fellow soldier and taken them away. The fellow soldier was Radoslav Kremenovic, and the situation was further complicated by the fact that Erdemovic was suffering from a bullet wound to his stomach resulting from a shootout with another soldier involved in the Srebrenica massacre.

Erdemovic and his colleague had been arrested by the Belgrade police when the latter realized he was talking to reporters about Srebrenica. Graham Blewitt recalled, "It started on a Saturday night. I had a frantic telephone call from one of our investigative staff who had been contacted by a journalist in England who in turn had a journalist friend in Belgrade who was in touch with Erdemovic. Erdemovic wanted to surrender to the tribunal. He wanted to speak to us and through the process of getting him out of the country for the purpose of coming to the tribunal, he was arrested by the police." Blewitt knew immediately that Erdemovic was in grave danger. "The London journalist in contact with the Belgrade journalist was very nervous about this man's safety, because at that stage this was . . . a major breakthrough. It was the first witness we had encountered who could inform us about the events in Srebrenica."

By Sunday morning, Blewitt was in his office putting in motion the paperwork to demand the transfer of Erdemovic to the tribunal. This was not simply a bureaucratic task. Blewitt explained, "My first . . . priority was to preserve this man's life, because we didn't want him to disappear into the system. So on Sunday I came here and drafted several orders that I signed and then faxed immediately to Belgrade, indicating that we wanted to interview this man." The point was to "put them on notice that the tribunal knew that he was in their custody and as a consequence would be held accountable if something happened to him."

Goldstone next publicly demanded that Erdemovic and his colleague be turned over to the tribunal. The press statement by Goldstone emphasized that on the same date Erdemovic was taken into custody by the Yugoslav police "the prosecutor requested the Belgrade authorities to serve summonses on both men ordering them to appear before the tribunal,"[26] later explaining that "the reason I went public with Erdemovic was to save his life." As it was, he points out, Erdemovic was probably only turned over because he was a Croat citizen who had served in the Yugoslav army, rather than a Serbian.

The following week Blewitt traveled to Belgrade to question Erdemovic. John Shattuck, the U.S. assistant secretary of state, was on hand and pressed the Belgrade authorities to grant access to Erdemovic and Kremenovic for questioning. "They were brought from wherever they were being detained," Blewitt recalled. "We conducted a brief interview with these two in the presence of a lot of other officials. We established for ourselves that 'yes, these people were important and relevant,' and having established that we then indicated to the Serb authorities that we would be seeking their transfer to The Hague." Under the glare of publicity and accompanying pressure from Shattuck, the Serbs agreed that they would transfer Edemovic to The Hague in the following weeks.

Blewitt announced in a Belgrade press conference that "the tribunal and in particular the prosecutors' office has reached a new beginning in cooperation" with the Serbian leadership. Meanwhile, "Erdemovic was cooperating. . . . In the course of events we couldn't get enough evidence against Kremenovic so he was . . . ultimately released, whereas Erdemovic . . . wanted to plead guilty. So we indicted him and then . . . [initiated] the first guilty plea process before this tribunal."

Within a week of Blewitt's visit to Belgrade there were reports that U.S. officials had located remarkably precise pictures of the Pilice massacre site from U2 spy planes flying over Bosnia on July 17, 1995. The photographs showed bodies strewn over a field about five kilometers northwest of Pilice. Earlier photos released by Madeleine Albright had shown evidence of disturbed earth, but these images now showed bodies actually grouped together in a location and manner that matched the details of the Erdemovic confession.[27] As March ended, Serbian officials handed over the tribunal's newly validated star witness, Drazen Erdemovic.[28]

In early June, Erdemovic entered his guilty plea. Mirko Klarin, who had covered the tribunal from its inception, found the Erdemovic courtroom confession the most extraordinary experience in his time at the ICT. Five times Klarin recalled him repeating, " 'I am guilty, I am guilty.' " The prosecution now had a key witness, but it was not until the Tadic trial was well under way that they figured out how they could begin to use him.

GETTING TADIC TO TRIAL

A unique feature of the Tadic trial was that it brought three American women lawyers—Patricia Sellers, Brenda Hollis, and Nancy Paterson— together in an investigation team that became a trial team. Goldstone reported, "Soon after I arrived in The Hague, I was besieged by thousands of letters and petitions signed by people, mostly women, from many countries, urging me to give adequate attention to gender-related war crimes." These letters were stimulated by the systematic mass rapes reported by the media. Goldstone realized that the human rights and women's groups could provide badly needed political support for the tribunal. He sought their input, saying later that "it led, among other things, to my appointing Patricia Sellers, a thoughtful international lawyer from the United States, as my special advisor on gender."[29]

Sellers came to the tribunal in July 1994 and "turned on the lights with Graham Blewitt." She is quick to acknowledge that before her arrival much useful work had already been done on sexual assault, and this included work on the case of Dusko Tadic. Sellers recalled taking her initial direction from the commission report and the materials

Bassiouni had transferred to the tribunal. "I remember the first time I . . . spoke with him was calling his assistant on the phone to see which of those boxes held crucial information for sexual violence."

Nancy Paterson, who had led much of the work on rape and sexual assault for Bassiouni and the commission, joined the tribunal at about the same time as Sellers. Sellers recalls that "in the spring and summer of 1995, I was working with Nancy Paterson and we were trying to get together, what should our investigation strategy and legal strategy be given our resources, given which events had been most pronounced, given what the commission of experts had alluded to as the pattern, and given the prosecutor's mandate."

It was clear from the commission report that rape and sexual assault were key parts of ethnic cleansing in Bosnia, as exemplified in Prijedor. Speaking from her new vantage point as a lawyer for the tribunal, Paterson commented, "They put together a good dossier, a good starting point, but so much of their information was hearsay, second hand, was not anything we could corroborate. We didn't know who the source of much of the information was. You can't use information if you don't know where it came from."

It soon became clear that the interviews with the rape victims in Prijedor would not only have to be done again but would also need to be done in greater length and detail to more fully connect individual cases into a more complete picture. In the interviews for the commission, Paterson noted, "We were lucky if we could see a witness for three hours; a whole day was unheard of." With the tribunal the interviews were protracted: "It was not unheard of to do three or four days, with one witness, to have a 40 page statement."

For example, in the commission report on Prijedor it became known that the police chief, Simo Drjlca, played a central role. Paterson reconstructed the more extended forms these detailed interviews now took: "I'd say to the woman, 'Well, who was in charge of the camp?' She might answer, 'I don't know. Well sometimes we'd see the guy who used to be the police chief. . . .' Well, if I go in knowing . . . that it's the police chief, you can ask more direct questions, ... you can focus more on the issues you know are important." This was the kind of interviewing that now had to be done to build the case against Tadic around the events in Prijedor.

Brenda Hollis came to the tribunal from the Air Force. She became co-counsel with Grant Niemann and was increasingly important in developing courtroom testimony as the trial progressed, finally taking over the concluding stages of the trial.

TRIALS OF A TRIAL TEAM

The Tadic prosecution team was entirely Anglo-American in composition. The lead prosecutor was the Australian Grant Niemann, and in addition to Brenda Hollis he was assisted by Michael Keegan of the Marine Corps and Alan Tieger, Mark Harmon's colleague from California. There was some sensitivity about the American prominence on this prosecution team. Keegan explained that "the United States was the first country to provide lawyers to the tribunal, and we were immediately assigned to the Prijedor/Omarska investigation, which was the first investigation undertaken. Since the Tadic case flows out of that investigation, it just made sense that we would be the trial attorneys."[30]

There is no question how hard the prosecution worked to develop this case. There was tremendous pressure, given the skepticism about the low position of Tadic in the ethnic cleansing operation in Prijedor, to find ways of making the case significant. Brenda Hollis was in Bosnia through much of 1995 and 1996, working with interpreters who helped her interview prosecution and defense witnesses. The conditions were difficult and dangerous. "When I first started going there, shelling and sniping were still going on. . . . We didn't have radios. . . . We were traveling through areas that were held by people that would very much like to have taken away from us the statements . . . we had with us. And we would have had to be very seriously harmed before we would have let them." Hollis continued, "It was quite a harsh period to be in Bosnia because a lot of the infrastructure was gone. Food was still in short supply. . . . The hotels and places that we stayed would have electricity and water intermittently, if at all." The vehicles they used were often unsafe. They even had trouble getting their interpreters paid. "We had interpreters saying, 'I'm not going again because they owe for three missions already and they haven't paid me.'"

The interpreters were crucial to the success of the interviews concerning sexual assault and rape. These interviews were particularly difficult, both for the interpreters who had to process the accounts at first hand and for the lawyers and investigators who had to press for the detailed information that would be necessary in court. Hollis emphasized the traumatic quality of much that she heard. "Many of the people still had not had any sort of distance between what had happened to them, and they hadn't received any sort of treatment. And so it was pretty raw stuff."

The prosecution team was able to win a major point on a pretrial motion to protect the identities of the victims and witnesses. The judges ruled that three victims of sexual assault could testify anonymously, identified in court only by letter of the alphabet, in order to protect their families from retribution. The granting of anonymity allowed testimony about rape and sexual assault that otherwise would not have been given. Unfortunately, as the case went to trial the rape charge against Tadic was abruptly dropped. The key witness, who was placed in a witness protection program, became too frightened to testify. This was a major loss because this charge could have distinguished the Tadic case as the first conviction for rape as a war crime and could have laid the groundwork for recognizing rape as a weapon in the larger campaign of ethnic cleansing, if not genocide. Still, testimony about rape and sexual assault was a part of the trial.

The loss of the rape charge from this case was only the first of a number of instances in which investigators and lawyers invested heavily in developing witnesses, only to see their cases come apart as they approached trial. Nancy Paterson, who pursued many of these cases in Bosnia, described the disappointment and difficulties involved in a case of this kind. "We tried, she tried, nobody to blame, can't help it, you just have to move on. I mean this happened in the middle of the . . . trial. We had to drop the rape counts because one witness was unwilling to testify. . . . I was the one that spoke to her, and tried to talk her into testifying, and she agonized over this. She desperately wanted to do the right thing, and all of her reasons for not testifying were perfectly legitimate. And I would have made the same decision had I been her. . . . You know, finally, I had to say, 'Okay, . . . look, it's your decision to make and we will respect that.' We went out for a long walk for an hour, we went for a coffee, we came back and she said, 'Sorry, I just can't do it.' " Paterson added that in many of these cases, even if the witnesses had been able and willing to testify, they were so fragile psychologically that they would have been "ripped apart by the defense."

The initial Tadic indictment consisted of thirty-four counts. The most graphic charges included the castration and murder of Fikret (Hari) Harambasic along with the torture and murder of other detainees at Omarska and the rape of a female prisoner at Omarska identified in court as "F." Yet since Tadic ultimately was not found guilty of personally castrating and killing Harambasic (but rather of being present and involved when these events took place) or of raping "F" (because this charge was dropped), the charge that proved most consequential was that of persecution. This count held Tadic responsible for subjecting Muslims and Croats inside and outside the camps to a campaign of terror that included killings, torture, sexual assaults, and other physical and psychological abuse. Persecution on political or racial grounds is a crime against humanity. Thus, this first trial in an international criminal tribunal since World War II sought to establish beyond reasonable doubt that Dusko Tadic was guilty of acts of political or racial persecution constituting a crime against humanity.

TRIAL OF THE CENTURY?

The specialty cable channel Court TV is co-owned and managed by the *American Lawyer* magazine, so when the former decided to offer gavel-to-gavel coverage of the trial of Dusko Tadic, it is perhaps not surprising that both decided to bill this legal event as "the trial of the century." *American Lawyer* reporter William Horne urged that the trial would be "more important than the treason trials of Ethel and Julius Rosenberg and of East German spymaster Markus Wolf. More important than the Watergate trials, the Rodney King case, the Chicago Seven Trial, and yes even O.J." Nuremberg, of course, was the more telling comparison, and here Horne again found the Tadic trial more significant, because "while Nuremberg came too late to help the Nazis' victims, the Tadic trial and those that follow at least have a chance of deterring Serbs and others from continuing to commit war crimes."[31]

The first day of the Tadic trial attracted the largest collection of television and print journalists the tribunal had yet seen, with the news corps spilling beyond the courtroom and entry area out onto the lawn in front of the building, where tribunal officials had set up several tents. This coverage did not actually equal that of Nuremberg, where three hundred reporters arrived along with Howard K. Smith and later Edward R. Murrow for CBS radio and television, but it did reveal an appetite for the story.[32] Unfortunately, the early witnesses in the Tadic case did not hold the attention of the media. By the time a succession of witnesses were called whose personal accounts more successfully and dramatically depicted the horror of the Prijedor detention camps, the television cameras had left. This testimony now included the kind of eyewitness accounts and video footage that a half-century earlier had made the depictions of the Holocaust so chilling at Nuremberg. The journalist Edward Vulliamy, who visited and reported on the camps at their peak, provided disturbing eyewitness descriptions that translated the experience into the language and experience of the judges. Yet five weeks into the trial the judges had still not heard testimony personally linking Tadic to these horrific events.[33]

An array of witnesses followed who convincingly made the point that Tadic was in the detention camps and that he participated in beatings and sadistic torture of men and women, including former friends. Yet the prosecution repeatedly was disappointed in its efforts to produce eyewitness testimony that Tadic personally engaged in acts of murder or the infamous castration incident that attracted so much attention to the case. In closed session witness H provided a horrifying description of the way in which the castration incident occurred, including being forced himself to hold down the victim's arms. However, to the astonishment of those observing, when Michael Keegan asked H if Tadic was present during the castration, he answered no. Keegan later reported that "the witness said Tadic was not the man."[34] This was clearly not the testimony the prosecution was seeking.

The prosecution's case concluded with what promised to be their star witness, referred to as witness L and later identified as Drago Opacic. Again, in closed session, L testified that he was a guard at Trnopolje and that he was ordered by Tadic to kill ten Muslim inmates in November 1992. When L refused this order, he said, Tadic shot two of the men and then ordered him to kill the remaining eight, which he reportedly did.

It would soon become apparent that Opacic was a confessed liar. He was exposed when the defense team located his family, which he had claimed was dead. In turn he recanted the rest of his story, now claiming that Bosnian authorities had imprisoned him and on threat of death forcibly trained him to present his story to the tribunal. It was left to Grant Niemann, who had advanced the testimony of Opacic, to inform the court on behalf of the prosecution that the testimony of this witness should be disregarded.

Brenda Hollis had increasingly taken the lead of the Tadic prosecution team, and with Niemann now associated with witness L, she was clearly the person to pull the prosecution case together. The defense took the position that Tadic also was a victim—"an ordinary little man caught up in the great whirlwind of war"—who had simply served as a member of the traffic police reserves.[35] Hollis made the opposing argument that Tadic was beyond a reasonable doubt individually responsible for the crime of persecution by virtue of his "repetitive and significant presence" at many crime scenes in the Omarska, Keraterm, and Trnopolje camps. He was seen at Omarska by thirteen witnesses. The evidence was compelling that Tadic was present in these camps when a great deal of violence occurred.

The argument that Hollis needed to make in concluding the prosecution's case was that Tadic was a "significant presence," not a "mere presence," in the camps, especially Omarska. The defense responded by insisting that Tadic was not actually in the camps, but that if he was, his presence was not significant enough to constitute participation in the active sense required by the operative statutes. After eighty-two days in court, 115 witnesses, more than five hundred exhibits, and more than six thousand pages of transcripts, this argument about when "presence" is "participation" became the legal point on which the case finally turned.

TADPOLE IN A SEA OF SHARKS

The trial concluded in November 1996. Another half-year passed before the verdict was delivered, followed by sentencing hearings and appeals, so that altogether the trial lasted almost four years. The initial verdict found Tadic guilty of nine counts, partially guilty of two counts, and not guilty of the remaining twenty counts. The sentencing judgment recorded that "the crimes consisted of killings, beatings, and forced transfer by Dusko Tadic as principal *or* accessory, as well as his *participation* in the attack on the town of Kozarac in Opstina [municipality,] Prejidor, in north-western Bosnia."[36] So participation was the criminal act for which Tadic ultimately was found guilty. The judgment included the charge of persecution, which as a crime against humanity carried the greatest sentence exposure.

The prosecution maintained at the pre-sentencing hearing that Tadic committed his crimes "out of greed, hatred, jealousy, bigotry and intolerance" and recommended that the judges consider a life sentence.[37] The original verdict surprisingly concluded that the conflict could not be considered international in that the armed forces of Republika Srpska could not be regarded as an extension of the Yugoslav military. The presiding American judge, Gabrielle Kirk McDonald, dissented on this point, arguing that the Bosnian Serb forces were very much under the influence of the Yugoslav military.

When she announced the Tadic verdict, McDonald placed two dimensions of the Tadic case in bold relief. She began by dramatically addressing Tadic, saying, "You committed these offenses intentionally and with sadistic brutality using knives, whips, iron bars, the butt of a pistol, sticks, kicking the victims and tightening the noose around the neck of one until he became unconscious. Why?" McDonald then launched into her own explanation, concluding, "You embraced the extreme principles of Serb nationalism and you played an increasingly major role in the SDS [Serbian Democratic Party]." The former assertion was more solidly grounded in the facts of the case than the latter, in that it was never convincingly established that Tadic played a "major" political role. Still, he was clearly a brutal participant in murder and in the poisonous Serb politics, and "this awareness and support, manifested in his actions, gave rise to Dusko Tadic's liability for crimes against humanity rather than just war crimes, and is a significant factor in the imposition of sentence." The original sentence was twenty years' imprisonment.[38]

Both the defense and the prosecution appealed the Tadic verdict and sentencing, and the case continued into the new millennium. The most important of the appeal decisions established that the Bosnian conflict of which Tadic was a part was an international conflict. This reversal of the original verdict made Tadic accountable for additional murders, but more significantly confirmed the role of the Milosevic-led Yugoslav forces in the Bosnian conflict. This decision affirmed McDonald's earlier dissent in concluding that there was a close personal, organizational, and logistical interconnection between the Bosnian Serb army, paramilitary groups, and the Yugoslav military.[39]

Because Tadic was now found guilty by the appeals chamber of the additional international counts under the Geneva conventions, including involvement in five more murders, he was again sentenced, this time to twenty-five years of imprisonment. The defense again appealed, now describing Tadic as a "tadpole in a pool of sharks" and following with the question of what sentence the "sharks" could expect to receive if they were ever sentenced. Judge McDonald responded that she did not believe that the victims of Tadic would have seen him as a tadpole.[40]

The appeals chamber ultimately agreed that the sentence needed to consider the position of Tadic in the command structure, which, "when compared to that of his superiors, or the very architects of the strategy of ethnic cleansing, was low." His sentence was therefore reduced to the original twenty years, including the provision that he serve at least ten years from the time of his custody in Germany, making him available for release as early as 2007. This seemed to confirm that Tadic was indeed a tadpole. The prosecutor's spokesman, Paul Risley, looked for closure by expressing the hope that "this is the last the tribunal will hear of Tadic" and that "he will be able to start serving the sentence."[41]

JUSTICE IN ABSENTIA

In the summer of 1996, Richard Goldstone's tenure as chief prosecutor was coming to its conclusion, one year after the massacre at Srebrenica. The Tadic trial had not sustained the attention of the media, and meanwhile NATO, the United States, and Britain were not helping the tribunal arrest Karadzic, Mladic, or others under indictment. The courtroom and prison, not to mention the judges and prosecutors, were underutilized. Goldstone decided to move ahead with a Rule 61 in absentia hearing—a hearing designed essentially to get around the inability to apprehend defendants.

The concept of an in absentia hearing is controversial because it is a variation on a trial in absentia, which the UN Security Council statute creating the tribunal explicitly prohibited. Martin Bormann was tried in absentia at Nuremberg, and French law permits trials in absentia for persons charged with crimes against humanity.[42] Yet Guest points out that "such trials are prohibited by the International Covenant on Civil and Political Rights, and there is wide agreement that they would have undermined the authority and credibility of the tribunal."[43]

Nonetheless, the first president of the tribunal, the Italian judge Antonio Cassese, was anxious to have an in absentia capability. His successor, McDonald, fought but eventually accepted the Rule 61 procedure when the rules of the tribunal were adopted in February 1994. Scharf explains that "the purpose of the hearing is to allow prosecutors to convince the tribunal judges to issue an international arrest warrant when the authorities in the area where the initial arrest warrant was have refused to cooperate with the tribunal."[44] Only the prosecution presents evidence at this hearing; there is no provision for representation by defense counsel.

Some members of the prosecution staff voiced strong reservations about the Rule 61 procedure. One senior prosecutor put the matter starkly: "Rule 61 was essentially a way of circumventing the UN ban on trials in absentia. No matter what the judges say, no matter what you hear, that's all it was. . . . The whole thing was just a mechanism to have trials in absentia . . . to make it look like the tribunal was doing something." In contrast, Goldstone believed that a Rule 61 hearing on Karadzic and Mladic would pull together ongoing investigations and put pressure on international authorities to arrest these indictees. The seven-day hearing was convened in the end of June 1996, with one Swede (Eric Ostberg) and two Americans (Mark Harmon and Terree Bowers) as co-counsel. As in the Tadic case, Goldstone did not appear in court.

The prosecution did not repeat the mistake of the Tadic trial—opening with obscure expert testimony—but instead moved quickly to dramatic videotape evidence of the involvement of Mladic and Karadzic in the Bosnian genocide. First Mladic was seen directing the attack on Srebrenica, and then Karadzic was shown overseeing the shelling of Sarajevo. The evidence about Srebrenica to follow was described as consisting of "scenes from hell, written on the darkest pages of human history." More specifically, the evidence of fifteen witnesses during the week of testimony would "describe scenes of unimaginable savagery: thousands of men executed and buried in mass graves, hundreds of men buried alive, men and women mutilated and slaughtered, children killed before their mothers' eye, a grandfather forced to eat the liver of his own grandson."[45]

During the first days of the trial the mayor of Sarajevo, Tarik Kupusovic, testified about the siege of his city, and the Dutch lawyer from the commission of experts, Christine Cleiren, described the use of rape as a war crime in the ethnic cleansing of Bosnian towns and cities. Kupusovic testified that twelve thousand people were killed in nearly four years of besiegement of Sarajevo, including sixteen hundred children. "It was inconceivable how anyone could attack a city with no military targets," he observed. "We considered it to be madness. Only lunatics could do that."[46] Cleiren described camps detaining victims of and for serial rape and identified thirty locations in northern and eastern Bosnia where rape often occurred in detention. Her testimony was followed by that of tribunal investigator Irma Osterman, who detailed gang rapes and torture in the southeastern town of Foca in April 1992. Just two days earlier the tribunal had announced its first indictment defining rape as a war crime and charging eight Bosnian paramilitaries with rape, torture, enslavement, and inhuman treatment.[47]

By the fourth day of testimony, the hearing was building toward its peak. Mark Harmon, who would later lead the case against General Krstic for genocide in Srebrenica, now took over the presentation of four hours of testimony about the Srebrenica massacre. His key witness was the intense young French investigator, Jean-René Ruez, who had been working on the Srebrenica case from its discovery almost a year earlier, organizing the exhumation of bodies found near Srebrenica.

The American lawyer and the French investigator were a compelling combination. Harmon is tall and commanding in his courtroom presence. Ruez is smaller, with a wiry build and a tightly wound personality. Ruez knew he had crucial evidence to offer and felt that his superiors at the tribunal had underestimated its importance. He would later say that the way in which Harmon led his testimony "made it a really powerful thing. It was really a 'hit in the stomach' for many. No one had a clue that in one year we had gained so much information on what had happened there."

Ruez began by explaining that Srebrenica was located near the Drina River, which divided Bosnia from Serbia. Over time, as ethnic cleansing proceeded through surrounding areas and as the town was designated by the UN as a "safe area," its population had grown to forty thousand, with an added three to six thousand armed Muslim fighters who sometimes made raids on surrounding Bosnian villages. In the early days of July 1995, Bosnian Serb troops began to move in on Srebrenica, making a mockery of the Dutch peacekeepers assigned to monitor their activities. By the middle of July, Serb forces had taken the town, separated the men from the women, and executed about six thousand of the mostly male civilians they had taken prisoner.

Ruez was able to introduce as evidence records of exhumed corpses, shreds of clothing, footwear, and aerial photographs indicating that the Serbs had tampered with mass graves in an effort to conceal the massacre. Harmon asked Ruez to place black stickers on a map of the Srebrenica area to identify seven sites where General Mladic had appeared and where prisoners were later executed. Ruez was able to document that Mladic had left one site only fifteen minutes before executions began. During this testimony, another event attracted attention beyond the tribunal: Radovan Karadzic announced that he would comply with the Dayton Peace Accords' ban on his seeking the presidency of Republica Srpska as an indicted war criminal.

The final day brought the Rule 61 hearing to its intended climax with the testimony of a victim, identified only as witness A, who lived through the Srebrenica massacre, and of Drazen Erdemovic, the confessed murderer and now star witness. Witness A told of seeing Mladic six times during a three-day period in which he was herded from place to place before finally being taken to the site of his intended execution. He was driven to the last site in a truck. His group was ordered to climb down from the truck to be shot. By a stroke of luck, he was knocked to the ground as the men behind him were shot, and he lay there beneath a growing pile of bodies. At one point he recalled that Mladic arrived in a small red car. "Ratko Mladic watched as people were being forced out of the truck and lined up. Ratko Mladic stood and watched until all the people had been killed and were silent. Then he returned to his small car."[48]

Erdemovic seemed to be a broken man when he appeared. His arm twitched, his eyes remained shut for long intervals, and by the end of his testimony he was in tears. He had seen Mladic only once at Srebrenica and had heard him give no orders. However, he estimated that his unit shot twelve hundred men and described hand grenades being tossed into a building crowded with prisoners. After he had already killed seventy to one hundred men, he was ordered to continue. He said that he and three others in his unit finally refused: "I said that I didn't wish to kill anyone, that I was no robot for the extermination of people." Erdemovic reported that at a later point in time he himself was shot in the stomach by a fellow soldier who surmised that "I might do what I'm doing today—that is, testify."[49]

It was now nearly exactly a year since Drazen Erdemovic had participated in the killing spree he described on this day to the tribunal. Mark

Harmon brought the Rule 61 hearing to a close by remembering the victims and the justice their memory deserved, adding, "What should be remembered as well is that the world had the ability to bring these two alleged architects of genocide to justice and did nothing. It will haunt the victims and it will shame us all." Several days later, the trial chamber decided unanimously to issue the international arrest warrants for Karadzic and Mladic and went on to call for an investigation of the role played in these crimes by Slobodan Milosevic.

TRIALS AND TRIBULATIONS

As the Rule 61 hearing came to an end, and the seemingly unending Tadic case continued into the fall of 1996, there was a sense that Goldstone had done all he could for the tribunal. He was anxious to assume his seat on the new Constitutional Court in South Africa. His pursuit of Karadzic and Mladic had made his own life more difficult. He was now traveling in an armored car with two bodyguards, and a mobile police post had been constructed outside his apartment building in The Hague. His wife and children had hoped that the time away from South Africa would be a respite from security concerns, but as Goldstone noted, "here they were again, with a vengeance."[50]

There were other irritants. The previous spring, Boutros-Ghali had berated Goldstone for being away from The Hague so frequently. Boutros-Ghali also noted that he agreed with complaints that Goldstone was spending too much time in the United States. Goldstone insisted that his travel and political contacts were essential in establishing the tribunal, both financially and institutionally. Even one of his harshest critics in the prosecutor's office acknowledged that "Goldstone was somebody who was an effective political symbol and front person in the initial stages of the tribunal, . . . to get some monetary contributions and that sort of thing." Then this observer dropped the other shoe, adding, "He had zero criminal background."

The concern was that there was no coordinated prosecutorial strategy to guide the work of the office. The Office of the Prosecutor was largely operating in the manner that the sociologists Meyer and Jepperson describe as a loosely coupled system. The problems were most visible in the form of indictments. There were now more than seventy indictments. A senior prosecutor argued, "It was the product of having a prosecutor who did not have a familiarity with criminal law and who was much more willing to go on a flier with certain indictments which later proved to be inappropriately grounded." When Louise Arbour succeeded Goldstone, she dismissed a number of these indictments. Inside the tribunal, the view was that "it's the only thing that saved the credibility of the institution. Had we gone forward on some of these trials it would have become painfully clear that they were not indicted on sufficient evidence and in at least two occasions, we actually had the wrong person."

There is the further question of why Goldstone choose to indict and try Tadic as his first case. The answer is that from his perspective he had little choice. As Cherif Bassiouni, his rival for the position, observed, when the UN and United States said to go fast, Goldstone had to go fast. The commission of experts had already done some of the groundwork on the Tadic case, and he was in custody in Germany. There was also a rape charge in the initial Tadic indictment, and Goldstone was sensitive to the wishes of women's groups. When Goldstone tried to aim higher, with the two Bosnian Serb officers, the first officer turned out to be dying of cancer and there was insufficient evidence to indict the second. Since NATO forces had cooperated at Goldstone's insistence in removing these suspects by cover of night to The Hague, and since both suspects were shortly released, this initiative only aggravated an already troubled relationship between the NATO military leadership and the tribunal. The tribunal remained not only loosely coupled internally but disconnected from any outside forces who could exercise an arrest power. The empty courtroom and prison made Tadic the only obvious option.

At least one prominent legal historian of the tribunal, Michael Scharf, has argued that the Tadic case was actually extraordinarily important. He supports his contention by saying that "just as the Nuremberg trials following World War II launched the era of human rights promulgation fifty years ago, the Tadic trial has inaugurated a new age of human rights enforcement."[51] Nuremberg, of course, is remembered as the trial that brought Hermann Goering and other high-ranking Nazi figures to justice.

Geoffrey Robertson voices the widely shared view that "Dusko Tadic was no Hermann Goering."[52] Instead, Tadic was a more ordinary person swept up in the wake of higher-level demagogues and the events they orchestrated. As such, Robertson argues, Tadic "takes on a symbolic capacity, a scapegoat almost, for the community of which he was part. His punishment is less an example of individual responsibility than collective guilt."[53] Goldstone had responded to critics of the Tadic case by saying, "Anybody who regards it as just symbolic has got it wrong. What has been created is a serious international criminal justice system."[54] However, this symbolic or ceremonial quality, which Goldstone accentuated by using his judicial title and being photographed in his judicial robes, is exactly the concern that Meyer and Jepperson express in their depiction of human rights institutions as loosely coupled. Their point is that the lofty goals of such institutions are often only weakly reflected in their real-world operations and accomplishments.

The Rule 61 hearing of Karadzic and Mladic in the closing months of the Goldstone period was the most significant effort to aim tribunal resources at more highly placed targets. A star witness, Drazen Erdemovic, had fallen into their hands. Yet if prosecuting Tadic was aiming too low, then the Rule 61 hearing risked aiming too high. The procedure itself was flawed. The statute that created the tribunal explicitly forbade trials in absentia, because without a defendant and a defense, the procedure risked the appearance of a theatrical performance, or worse, a show trial. The absence of defendants or their legal representatives in the Rule 61 proceeding gave the tribunal a "virtual" quality.

Yet there may still have been value in Goldstone's use of the procedure. A critic in the prosecutor's office argued that on one hand, "most Rule 61 hearings were a complete waste of time; they diverted very limited resources towards the dog and pony shows which had no real impact whatsoever and took away from the ongoing investigation at a very critical time." On the other, this same observer conceded, "the Karadzic and Mladic one was probably beneficial. It forced us to develop our theories, get our evidence around, and it did show that we were making some progress in our investigations." The Srebrenica investigation headed by Jean-René Ruez was displayed to considerable advantage in this hearing.

These comments make a larger point about the Goldstone period. This was the time when the first investigation and trial teams were forming and individuals were beginning to work together toward their shared goals for the tribunal. We saw early in this chapter that of nineteen different sources of satisfaction rated by the employees of the prosecutors' office, working in the team setting ranked highest. These data further revealed that employees who came to the tribunal during the Goldstone period continued to rank working with a team most highly as a source of their work satisfaction. The teams that were formed during the Goldstone years featured Anglo-Americans in leadership roles, including Brenda Hollis, Nancy Paterson, and Patricia Sellers working on the Prejidor investigation and the Tadic trial and Mark Harmon working with Jean-René Ruez in developing the presentation of evidence on Srebrenica for the Rule 61 hearing. These and other teams formed during this period continued to be driving forces in the tribunal for many years.

Graham Blewitt was the deputy prosecutor who played the managerial role in helping to form such teams, and Richard Goldstone had the foresight to let Blewitt and these individuals get on with their work while he sought the political backing and resources that were necessary to allow this to happen. If they made mistakes, especially in the Tadic trial, they were learning from them, and they were building well-led and powerful investigation and trial teams that would serve the tribunal effectively in the future. Many of these individuals were personally sought out, and they were choosing to invest important years of their professional lives in this new transnational institution. Goldstone felt in retrospect that they had "a common sense of ownership of this new institution" and that "going through the hard times made the institution all the more valuable to them."

Michael Scharf probably provides the most optimistic assessment of the Goldstone years. His view is that "In retrospect, Goldstone was perfect for the job. A compact, quietly charismatic man with a resonant voice, the 56-year-old Goldstone effused a sense of deep commitment and had a nose for international politics. Through his unwavering persistence during his two years in the post of prosecutor, Goldstone would expertly navigate the minefields of the U.N. bureaucracy and lead the Yugoslavia tribunal to international recognition and influence."[55] The indictment and vilification of Karadzic with the Rule 61 hearing helped drive him from elective office, leading Richard Holbrooke to acknowledge that "the tribunal emerged as a valuable instrument of policy that allowed us, for example, to bar Karadzic and all other indicted war criminals from public office."[56] Scharf added that "perhaps his [Goldstone's] greatest challenge, and most notable success, was obtaining funding for the fledgling tribunal."[57] In my interview with Goldstone his own assessment was modest: "My task was merely getting it on its feet from very difficult circumstances. A lot of people thought the tribunal was going to be killed by lack of resources and lack of interest and fighting and all the rest of it. So my period unexpectedly became a diplomatic mission. I think I spent more time on diplomacy and pushing and talking and screaming and shouting for the tribunal than on the simply prosecutorial work. I was very lucky to have Graham [Blewitt,] who had tremendous experience in the area." A different way of saying this is that Goldstone was more of a political advocate than a prosecutorial strategist. His sense of politics is instinctive, and he served the tribunal well in this regard.

That left the question of who should succeed Goldstone. Few knew who Louise Arbour was when she was selected for the job. When Michael Scharf met Arbour he was dubious: "Where Goldstone had been tenacious in his quest to launch the prosecutions and obtain resources for the tribunal, Arbour struck me as somewhat more cautious in her approach, though no less personally committed to the success of the tribunal. Only time will tell whether she will be able to insure that the tribunal maintains momentum at a critical period in its history."[58]

CHAPTER FOUR

The Real-Time Tribunal

Richard Goldstone knew better than anyone what he had achieved and what remained undone when he left his position as chief prosecutor at the tribunal. The tribunal for the former Yugoslavia was now up and running and the funding was more secure, but when it came to the actual prosecution of cases, he was clearly frustrated. One of the senior prosecutors described a two-day meeting held late in the summer of 1996 before Goldstone departed to assume his seat on South Africa's constitutional court. They met around a large conference table. Colleagues took turns outlining obstacles in their respective cases. Goldstone was noticeably distracted. Although he would continue as the ICT prosecutor for another month, he would spend most of this time in South Africa, and his interests were obviously shifting.

For all the attention Goldstone had gained for the ICT with interviews and fundraising efforts, it remained an institution without teeth, unable to arrest and prosecute the very persons it was designed to punish. The judges were especially restless. They wanted to move beyond minor figures such as Dusko Tadic. Some also were weary of the publicity, sensing that the ICT had become known as "Goldstone's tribunal."

Goldstone realized that his successor needed to be skilled in the strategic use of criminal law. His successor should probably also be a woman who could effectively address rape as a war crime. She should be fluent in French, to deal with Rwanda. And he knew that his successor would have to be veto-proof in the UN security council. Goldstone and his wife, Noleen, had actually already met this person at international law conferences. When they sat down to dinner one evening and speculated about his replacement, they both immediately came to the name of the Canadian jurist Louise Arbour.[1]

Arbour has been described as "feminine, Quebecoise, amusing, worldly-wise and business-like without appearing relentless."[2] She is said to radiate self-confidence and further "she enjoys the limelight."[3] The more prosaic terms *enterprising* and *determined* also describe Arbour, beginning with her early struggle to leave her Francophone childhood to become a successful legal scholar in Anglophone Canada. This ascent included learning to speak English on the fly while clerking at the Canadian Supreme Court, during her rapid rise to the appeals bench of the Ontario Supreme Court, and during her leadership of a highly publicized governmental inquiry into human rights abuses in Canadian womens' prisons.

At the tribunal, Arbour would be quoted in the style that would become her trademark, commenting, for example, that "here we eat adrenaline for breakfast."[4] In social science terms, Arbour was an entrepreneurial source of agency,[5] a person with charismatic qualities who could get things done by and with others. But there remained the issue of exactly whose agent she might become.

ANGLO-AMERICAN DOMINANCE

When Slobodan Milosevic appeared at the ICT in July 2001 to face his May 1999 indictment, he stated, "I consider this tribunal a false tribunal" and said that "this trial's aim is to produce false justification for the war crimes NATO committed in Yugoslavia."[6] Similar views about NATO and American domination of the tribunal often have been offered by others. For example, the author and journalist Michael Parenti writes: "The International Criminal Tribunal for the Former Yugoslavia was set up by the United Nations Security Council in 1993 at the bidding of Madeline Albright and the US government. It depends on NATO countries for its financial support, with the United States as the major provider, and it looks to NATO to track down and arrest the suspects it puts on trial. . . . It hardly qualifies as any kind of independent judiciary body."[7] In chapter 3 I noted Meyer and Jepperson's related assertion of Anglo-American influence in the conception and institutionalization of international human rights law enforcement.[8] If any of these commentators are correct, then the ICT is an unlikely setting in which to find agency operating in the sociological sense, that is, with any significant independence from NATO and American wishes.

One way of assessing this attribution of influence is to examine the hierarchy of the prosecutor's office that Arbour inherited and further developed at the ICT. The survey of OTP employees introduced in the previous chapter provides a way of going beyond national origin and other personal attributes to identify the hierarchical structure of the OTP, as reflected in responses to questions about actual influence in office decision-making, autonomy in the workplace, personal investment of time at work and, perhaps most persuasive, income. The results of this survey confirm that the OTP has a hierarchical structure in which Anglo-Americans in particular, rather than NATO appointees more generally, predominate.

For example, the responses from the survey show that, with other relevant factors statistically held constant, being Anglo-American consistently predicts which employees determine their own work responsibilities (that is, have occupational autonomy), influence office decision-making (that is, exercise workplace authority), work the longest hours, and earn the highest salaries. As expected, having advanced degrees also is a consistent predictor of these things, but for earnings in particular being in this group is the strongest determinant, with group members at the tribunal on average receiving nearly $15,000 per year more than other employees.[9] The Anglo-Americans also work on average about five hours more a week than do others.

These statistical indications of Anglo-American dominance in the prosecutor's office are consistent with the fact that although during the period of our research the former Swiss attorney general, Carla Del Ponte, became chief prosecutor, her predecessor was the Canadian Arbour; the deputy chief prosecutor, Graham Blewitt, and chief of investigations, John Ralston, both were Australian; the chief of the Trial Division was Canadian; and the two most prominent prosecutors in press reports of cases were American and Canadian.

It is difficult to assess whether it is the common-law experience, national backgrounds, or networks of these employees that is the cause of their prominence, but it is clear that they form the dominant recognizable elite of the OTP. As we will see below, the United States also is by far the largest national financial supporter of the ICT, having made throughout its history more than 40 percent of the voluntary contributions, with Britain the only other country contributing more than 10 percent. By this account, the Anglo-American countries are the source of the most financial support as well as of the employees who work the hardest and in turn are given the most autonomy and authority and paid the highest salaries at the tribunal.

On one hand, these data suggest that Anglo-Americans dominate the tribunal. On the other, they indicate that these employees also have autonomy in their everyday work, which may or may not translate into agency in a larger sense. Obviously, Slobodan Milosevic denies that tribunal officials and employees have any real autonomy or agency.[10] Yet we will see that the issue of autonomy and the agency it might allow is more nuanced than this, in part because the Anglo-Americans who dominate the tribunal are not a homogeneous group.

THE FORTY-NINTH PARALLEL

To understand the energizing and strategic role Louise Arbour played at the tribunal, it is essential to appreciate her Canadian origins and ambitions. From the early 1990s, when she was still in her early forties, Arbour was regularly identified as a candidate for the Supreme Court of Canada, to which she was appointed on her early departure from the tribunal in 1999. It often was suggested that Arbour's position as chief prosecutor at the ICT was a natural springboard for her appointment to the court.[11]

Although the United States joined Canada in giving early support to the tribunal, the American commitment was always more ambivalent[12] and couched in expectations of special protection. For example, although Madeleine Albright was one the tribunal's strongest American advocates, she also argued, as the Bush administration would later do even more adamantly, that the United States was "the indispensable nation" and that therefore its military personnel and politicians could not be liable to international criminal prosecution. This assertion reflected ambivalence in Clinton administration circles about the competing principles of universal jurisdiction and national sovereignty, and insider accounts further emphasize just how ambivalent the Clinton administration was throughout most of the 1990s about addressing human rights abuses in the Balkans and about supporting an activist tribunal.[13]

In contrast, throughout the 1990s Canada's foreign affairs minister, Lloyd Axworthy, advanced a Human Security Agenda, which involved a declaration that Canada must do whatever is possible to defend the rights of world citizens, wherever and by whomever their security is threatened. "He has a romantic progressivist vision of Canada," one columnist observed, "but . . . he has forgotten that Canada is a part of the West."[14]

Axworthy set a foundation for Arbour's pursuit of an independent agenda by expressing Canada's view that "things can happen without the United States being a participant."[15] The difference between the Canadian and the U.S. positions was a significant one, and it presented a choice of channels along which the principal-agent relationship involving the chief prosecutor of the tribunal could be developed.

Moreover, Arbour anticipated that she herself was likely to have what has been described in earlier chapters as an alternation experience—a change of perspective growing out of a transitional life experience—in becoming chief prosecutor of the Hague tribunal.[16] She realized that encountering the atrocities of war was likely to be an experience that would intensify her commitment to the human security agenda that came with her Canadian background. Once installed at the ICT, Arbour traveled extensively to Rwanda, Bosnia, and Kosovo to increase awareness of the atrocities she was prosecuting. She witnessed fresh evidence of the slaughter of eight hundred thousand Tutsis in Rwanda and observed, "I'll never forget it . . . the cruelty is on a scale that is completely mind-boggling." She returned to the tribunal, where she reported that she "worked 15 hours a day, sleeping little and not very well."[17] More than a year later she was asked, after climbing from the grisly depths of an exhumation site in Kosovo, if there wasn't something cruel about the expectations she must raise among relatives and still-living victims when she visited places like these: "She thinks about this, hands on hips, head down, and then says fiercely, 'We have no choice. . . . If there are expectations, we just have to meet them.' "[18] Arbour was expressing a sense of agency that she would later call the "exhilaration of action."

THE MISSING STRUCTURAL LINKS

Before leaving for The Hague, Arbour attended a Duke University conference where she listened with others as Richard Goldstone summarized his experiences as chief prosecutor. Goldstone's last major initiative had involved the seven-day in absentia public hearing of the indictment of Bosnian Serb leader Radovan Karadzic and his military chief, General Ratko Mladic. The frustration of the hearing was that it underlined that of seventy-six people charged by the tribunal, only six were in custody, with the remainder, including Karadzic and Mladic, still at large. "If the situation continues for much longer," Goldstone remarked, "the credibility of the international tribunal is going to suffer."[19] The nature of the Karadzic-Mladic hearing made the decoupling of the ICT from its enforcement goals all too apparent and evoked the image of a "virtual tribunal."

Arbour traced the virtual unreality of the ICT to the lack of foresight with which the ICT began by hiring judges before having prosecutors or defendants to place on trial. "Anybody with half a brain would know that you don't launch an investigative and judicial tribunal the way the ICTY was set up. You don't start with renting a building, hiring 11 judges, including a full complement of appeal court judges before you've even hired the first investigator, let alone the prosecutor. . . . Isn't it clear that something is wrong with that picture?" Arbour's own approach was to start with the evidence and the arrests, and the issue became whether and how this would unfold.

Before officially assuming her duties in the fall of 1996, Arbour made a fateful trip to an exhumation site Clint Williamson was supervising at the Ovcara farm, near Vukovar, Croatia. Williamson was a lawyer still in his thirties who came to the ICT from the U.S. Department of Justice. His subsequent work at The Hague involved high-level contacts with the Croatian government regarding prosecutions of Serbs for crimes committed in the area of Vukovar.

Williamson briefed Arbour shortly after her arrival at the tribunal and urged her to visit the exhumation at the Ovcara farm, where the two hundred Vukovar hospital patients had been taken, murdered, and piled into graves. Arbour flew to Vukovar on a UN cargo flight with a group that included the forensic expert Clyde Snow, known for his cigar-smoking cowboy manner. She was relieved to find Williamson waiting. He picked up the account: "So she flew to Zagreb and then over to Vukovar and we met her. . . . I rode with her in the vehicle and we went all the way through the region around Vukovar. . . . I was able to give her a background chronology of what had occurred there and that this was really the first battle of the war. Vukovar at that point [was] . . . devastated—it's the most destroyed large town anywhere in Yugoslavia, the destruction is just amazing, probably 90 percent of the buildings were destroyed. And we went all the way through and then we went down to the grave site." Despite the fact that Vukovar was called by some "Croatia's Stalingrad,"[20] the account of Ovcara farm that unfolds next received only fragmented press attention, for reasons that will become apparent.

Williamson understood that this was Arbour's "first introduction to Yugoslavia as prosecutor and just everything that she had encountered in the course of this day . . . was overwhelming." She later observed, "I was blown away. It was like a B movie from World War II. I remember it as though it were in black and white."[21] Yet Arbour, like others interviewed for this study, also described this and other field experiences as having an impact that was so exhilarating it engendered a compensatory feeling of guilt.

> You feel guilty that it's at times so much fun, because people say to you all the time, "We admire so much what you do, it must have been so depressing and so hard," and in fact, you have a lot of ambivalence, because you understand that that's the way you should feel, although very often on a day to day basis the excitement of being there and feeling very alive and that you're making a difference, and the excitement; it's a bit dangerous, not always in a typical sense, but it's risky, you're putting the project at risk, it's risky, it's a war zone, less so now, but at times, so all that, in fact, very often makes you oblivious to the human suffering that you're dealing with and it is replaced with this kind of exhilaration of action. And then, of course, you're ashamed for

having felt that way, as though you had forgotten your mission in all the excitement of getting it done.

The present point is that such experiences can have an alternation effect, in this case further spurring Arbour into action.

Going into the field, "on mission," also created a sense of camaraderie between the chief prosecutor and the larger investigatory team. During the day she met Jacques Klein, a retired U.S. Army general and a UN administrator for the area who would assume great importance in engineering a crucial arrest described below. In retrospect, she felt that the visit gave her "great confidence in the players and I now knew Klein, so it made everything . . . easier to happen." As the day came to an end, Williamson asked Arbour if she wanted to stop and get a cold drink. She answered, " 'I could really use a beer,' . . . so we went to this place that was near the river in Vukovar, called Tower Pizza, and we got beers for everybody and just talked about it a little bit and then took her back to the airplane."

The evidence from the hospital massacre and burial at Ovcara ultimately would constitute a turning point in Arbour's reorganization of the tribunal's agenda. Before this could happen, however, Arbour first confronted the frustration that Goldstone expressed at his Duke Law School talk: the tribunal had no arrest powers or police to enforce them, and Western and NATO leaders were providing little or no help in undertaking arrests. The view in the American military command of NATO was that "we are not globocop" and that assuming this role would constitute "mission creep."[22] The absence of an arrest capability made the ICT, in the sociologists Meyer and Jepperson's terms, the ultimate decoupled system.[23] Michael Ignatieff put the matter even more cogently: "Without arrested indictees the tribunal would be out of business."[24]

FINDING A SECRET SOLUTION

Arbour concluded that the tribunal had to radically change its mindset and devise a new strategy that would be more surreptitious than the highly publicized practices of the past. She recognized that you can't publicly give warning that you are seeking to arrest a particular person and expect to have much success. Nor did it make sense, she concluded, to place so much blame on others for the absence of arrests. "The general mode of the place," she observed, "was permanent whining. 'Ah, isn't that terrible, nobody helps us, nobody loves us and they're not arresting anybody.' . . . There was an atmosphere . . . of dependency."

She nonetheless was shocked at the solution to the arrest problem that was being proposed: "The big topic when I arrived there was [whether] to start trials in absentia. Well, if that passed, I would have left. I didn't go there for theater purposes." Arbour did not want to participate in a media-created "virtual" tribunal. She believed that the tribunal was potentially far more powerful than was understood and that the answers to its problems could be built from its mandate. "It had a mandate from the Security Council of the United Nations with the provision that said 'All states must cooperate with the tribunal and all states must obey its orders.' I thought this was a dream. . . . I've always believed in the legal process. I wouldn't have gone here if I hadn't believed in this." She thought the legal power was there to make the necessary events happen.

Arbour nonetheless realized that she must devise new structural linkages that would result in arrests and persons to prosecute. She developed a plan that she believed required at least three things: time and patience from the judges, withdrawal of attention from the NGOs, and the use of secret indictments. "I had to plead with the judges to give me a little time, to try to think of a way to make these arrests happen; that was the first thing. And they agreed to give me a chance when I got there. I had no particular plan, but I had to work on it. The second thing was that I became absolutely persuaded that if we were going to make it happen, we had to stop talking, we have to stop talking to the NGOs. We're not going to make arrests if we spend our time talking to the press. And it had to move and to be a more secretive issue, and that's why we started issuing secret indictments." By the fall of 1996, Arbour had made it known within the OTP leadership that secret indictments were going to be an important proactive resource. As Clint Williamson put it, the understanding was that "If they're not going to turn people over, this is our only chance at getting at people." Arbour stressed that arrests were essential for public relations reasons as well as legal reasons. "There were just too many people trying to work the arrest issue, journalists and so on. Just everybody was talking about it and I really believed our only chance was to seize the agenda and make it happen."

The secret, or "sealed," indictments were attractive because they promised an element of surprise that reduced the risks of injuries and deaths during arrests. The arrests would also solve her problems with the restive judges who wanted to proceed with trials. "I was absolutely determined, arrest was so clearly the key, because I thought if we start getting arrests, then everybody will be busy." Arbour also believed more generally that successful engagement in field investigations and court work would lift the tribunal's collective morale by building a shared commitment to its goals.

Sealed indictments also presented another key benefit that could provide Arbour—and the office of the prosecutor as a whole—with increased influence and therefore independence. As a prosecutor in the office noted, the sealed indictments held the potential of ultimately being unsealed in a way that could embarrass NATO authorities into action. The implicit threat was that "if something doesn't start to happen at some point we will unseal these indictments and reveal [that] you're not meeting the responsibility of arrests."

"THE PUCK STARTS HERE"

The new strategy began with the evidence collected at the exhumation site at the Ovcara farm. A secret indictment was confirmed by an ICT judge for the arrest of Slavko Dokmanovic, the Serb mayor of Vukovar who had participated in beatings and was present at the killings at Ovcara. The challenge was to arrest Dokmanovic. The leadership of NATO had taken the position that arrests were dangerous to peace in the region, not to mention to the safety of NATO military forces.

Arbour needed a way to force the enforcement hand of the NATO leadership. To make her point, she appropriated the Canadian colloquialism "the puck starts here," saying, "This is our game . . . we will take the initiative, we will decide what's going to happen and we're going to make it happen and they're just going to have to follow." A legal advisor in her office observed that "at the time we had a complete log jam, no arrests and the credibility of the place was very dangerously low, and I remember her saying one day, 'You have to make your own luck,' and the Dokmanovic thing was the first."

The specifics of the plan were developed by Williamson and three members of his investigation team, including one Czech and two British investigators, with input from the chief of investigations, John Ralston, and the deputy prosecutor, Graham Blewitt, and final approval from Arbour. Two factors made Slavko Dokmanovic a promising target. First, ICT investigators had made contact with Dokmanovic during the fall. He had moved into an area of Serbia not far from Vukovar when the Dayton Accords gave formal control of the area back to the Croatians. "He was obviously not prepared to sit around and wait for the Croatians to come back," an investigator reported, "because he saw himself as one of the first people that would probably get locked up as soon as the Croatians took over." Yet Dokmanovic was known to be willing to talk: "He was very much a nationalist and wanted to try and put his side of the story to people who he thought might be able to take some action as far as the Serbs were concerned."

This led to the second element in the emerging plan: the former American general Jacques Klein, whom Arbour had met on her visit to

Vukovar. Klein was the head of the UN authority in Eastern Slavonia (UNTAES), where Vukovar is located. Williamson had first met Klein at the U.S. embassy in Brussels on his way to become the transitional administrator for eastern Slavonia in late 1995. He had talked with him about his plans to undertake the exhumation at the Ovcara farm. "Klein was very supportive of this and said, 'Of course, we'll make this happen.' And he also said if any war crimes suspects were found under his command he would arrest them."

In effect, Williamson now had a perpetrator, a policeman, and an enthusiastic prosecutor. Still, turning these assets into a successful arrest was hardly a given. The risks were well demonstrated when Goldstone was forced to release two Bosnian Serb suspects. Arbour saw the tribunal as now having the advantage of a proactive strategy instead of having to be, as Goldstone was, reactively opportunistic. "Early on you've got to seize the moment," she explained, "to seize the opportunity." Now she believed time was on their side, giving the tribunal the opportunity to be strategically proactive. "I think these two cases' scenarios are symbolic," she insisted, "of a maturity in the institution, where all of a sudden it had the capacity—that's all it takes—it had given itself the capacity to take the initiative and to be in charge."

MAKING THE ARREST HAPPEN

Williamson began to put together a plan that would involve luring Dokmanovic back to Vukovar. The authority of Klein's UNTAES office then could be used to make the arrest. Williamson met with Ralston, and together they took the tentative plan to Arbour. She was supportive from the beginning. Williamson recalled, "She saw this as the chance to get something moving, but at the same time was, I think, very careful in her approach. She asked me, 'What's the worst that can happen?' I said, 'Well, it's possible that he can get killed, I said it's possible that one of the soldiers can get killed or a civilian in the area could get killed. And then you could have some destabilizing things happening there.' But she weighed everything and then said, 'It's a chance I want to take.' So she gave us the go-ahead and then basically left it up to me to work it out with Klein how was the best way to do it." He noted Ralston's perhaps characteristically Australian appraisal of Arbour's decision: "We were walking back up the stairs and he turned to me and he said, 'That little lady has balls.' "

The secret indictment of Dokmanovic was confirmed, and the leadership of IFOR was informed. No arrest followed from this loosely coupled and still ineffectual linkage with NATO before the end of 1996. Arbour was anxious to move ahead.

Williamson met again with Klein, who said that he would make a Polish special forces unit available. Williamson also made contact with a U.S. Army intelligence officer who participated in the operation. One of the British OTP investigators then made contact with Dokmanovic in January 1997 and tried to get him to come to Vukovar for a meeting about Croatian crimes against the Serbs. "Although he was more than willing to talk to us," Williamson recalls, "I think he was not willing to cross into Croatia, and we tried several different options, and at one point it looked like he was going to come but in the end he did not."

Several months passed before the second British investigator reestablished contact with Dokmanovic. The Czech investigator and Williamson found a location from which the house could be watched. They then scouted out the routes that could be taken to Vukovar. The idea was to get a conversation going with Dokmanovic. The investigator visited him in his home on a Tuesday, and Dokmanovic brought up his desire to see Klein about obtaining compensation for his unsold house. Williamson called Klein, who was then in Washington, to ask whether he was willing to let them use his name to draw Dokmanovic over, "and he said, 'Yes, of course.'"

The British OTP investigator returned to see Dokmanovic the following day, Wednesday, and an assistant for Klein set up a promised meeting with Klein for Friday, June 27, 1997. A vehicle was sent Friday afternoon at 3:00 to pick him up at a bridge crossing into Croatian territory that was under Klein's authority. The vehicle was driven by a Polish special forces officer with his commanding officer seated alongside. Williamson was waiting at the base, where he ran the operation with a Klein associate from the U.S. State Department and the U.S. intelligence officer. Williamson recalled: "Five minutes later he was at the Polish base and as the vehicle pulled in they just hit the brakes very quickly, and within three seconds there were Polish soldiers on each side of the car. The soldiers had already searched, handcuffed and hooded him. . . . The Czech investigator advised Dokmanovic of his rights and told him what the charges were and he started protesting and saying, 'I had a meeting with Klein on this.'" Klein had previously authorized a Belgian Air Force plane under his command to fly Dokmanovic to The Hague, and with little delay they departed.

FRAMING THE ARREST

Few details were released to the press of this first arrest under a secret indictment on formerly Yugoslavian territory. A week later an AP writer offered a theatrical framing of the "hooded snatching" as "Hitchcockesque," and it was.[25] Williamson explained the hooding of Dokmanovic, which seemed to dramatize the danger and intrigue involved in the operation. "If you're driving along, and if somebody on the side of the road looks in and sees him in there, they can alert other people and say, 'Oh my God, I just saw the mayor of Vukovar being taken away by UN forces or something.' You want to do everything you can to protect the secrecy of the operation until you get in the air, and this was our major concern. We wanted to be safely out of the region, in the plane, before anyone knew." The larger point the ICT wanted to make was that this kind of arrest could be made without losing lives or risking peace. Blurring the line between exactly who was responsible for this arrest and the details of its occurrence was essential to making it happen and to minimizing its destabilizing consequences.

There were no violent reactions to the arrest, and the tribunal sought to avoid unnecessary provocation by publicly releasing few details. Williamson recalled, "There certainly was no violent reaction, but at that point no one knew what was going to happen." Another legal advisor observed, "We'd been fed all these arguments, if you do this, there will be sniping, the war will break out, massive disruptions and problems, and it didn't happen."

The tribunal, apparently with American cooperation, had succeeded in making it unclear exactly who made this arrest. Although the ICT itself has no arrest authority, the *Observer* reported that "in a daring undercover operation, a snatch squad sent by the International War Crimes Tribunal has captured the former Mayor of Vukovar,"[26] and the *International Herald Tribune* quoted Jacques Klein as saying that "it was the tribunal, rather than UN peace-keepers, that carried out the arrest."[27] The *New York Times* insisted that the Clinton administration had not been consulted in advance,[28] and this point later was reiterated in an interview for this study with the administration's U.S. Ambassador for war crimes, David Scheffer, who said, "Arbour did this on her own." At the time, President Clinton issued a statement through his press secretary saying, "I congratulate the ICTY and UNTAES on their successful apprehension."[29]

Three days after the event, Arbour simply said in a public press statement, "I'm determined to continue to use this method for as long as I believe it will be a successful strategy for providing us with the accused." A new kind of structural linkage was emerging in the arrest area, but its form wasn't being made clear, at least in the public domain. This was in large part because Arbour still needed to persuade the NATO leadership to start playing in other areas of the Balkans the linking role that UNTAES had played in Vukovar.

It was nonetheless plain to those who needed to know that Arbour and the ICT had taken a bold risk. She herself has noted elsewhere, "I love gamesmanship, I love to play all kinds of games: cards, board games, whatever. Games of strategy where you have to plot the next seventeen moves. I think, If I do this, he'll do that." She extended this to the tribunal, confiding, "I calculated my moves in so many ways."[30] She had confidence in Klein and Williamson and concluded that "the plot, if I can put it this way, wasn't dead easy to execute, but it was very clean, and we knew that legally we had a very good chance of making it all stand."

When the arrest was successfully completed, she could engage the NATO officers who had refused earlier to countenance a serious arrest policy. "She pushed the military—she was a women of small size, and the soldiers, the big tall guys in uniform, were not used to dealing with that, and they found it challenging and sort of a game." Williamson certainly recognized that the first round in the arrest game had been played, noting that the Dokmanovic arrest "gave her an ace in the hand to go to NATO and say, 'Look, this can be done, they just did it in Vukovar and this wasn't a well armed UN force up there. You've got all the might of NATO behind you, certainly you can do the same in Bosnia.' And I feel certain that this is what prompted NATO to start moving with the arrests in Prejidor that happened two weeks later." As one prosecutor put it," Once they pulled that off, this developed some peer pressure for the people inside Bosnia; they said, 'Well, if they can do it, we can certainly do it,' and as one national group succeeded another, then people realized that World War III wasn't going to break out with the arrest of some of these thugs. And so each subsequent nation decided they'd do their part, and so it just snowballed."

A GAME THEORY OF NORM ENFORCEMENT

Arbour had in effect begun a process known by sociologists as esteem competition. The goal of this competition was the enforcement of the norms of international criminal law. This beginning of norm enforcement in the former Yugoslavia held the potential to at last launch the ICT as the flagship institution of the UN, representing the ideals of international humanitarian law and more generally what the political historian of international criminal tribunals Gary Bass has called liberal legalism.[31] However, while Bass saw such tribunals as expressing liberal legal ideals and the associated "power of the legalistic norm," he was pessimistic about the Hague tribunal and Louise Arbour's leadership more specifically, concluding that "the overall story of The Hague will be largely a dispiriting one."[32]

A larger literature on norm enforcement draws more optimistically on sociology and is flourishing in the fields of law and economics and international relations. The potential of this literature is signaled most clearly for the present purpose in Richard McAdams' elaboration of William Goode's sociological classic, *The Celebration of Heroes*.[33] The significance of McAdams's work for our interest in liberal legalism and the ICT is that it formalizes a process by which competition for social esteem, when combined with the agency of Goode's metaphorical "hero," can institutionalize a norm that has no prior regularity—exactly the kind of decoupled, standardless, ineffectual institutional state that sociologists such as Meyer and Jepperson correctly suggest the ICT (with its lack of an arrest power) previously had come to represent.[34] McAdams articulates a way out of this impotency that Arbour had clearly recognized and had begun to counteract with her secret indictment and arrest gambit. He describes the situation Arbour confronted: "Suppose that there is a newly expressed, idealistic consensus in favor of some behavior that no one has yet been willing to undertake, because while it benefits the group, it is costly for the individual."[35] Raised to the level of nation-states, this is the situation that confronted the ICT, which began under Goldstone with idealistic principles or standards of international criminal justice that all the major Western powers endorsed—but with little space, inadequate funding, and no defendants. Goldstone made notable progress on the first two problems from 1994 to 1996, but the ICT still had few defendants to prosecute. The powerful Western allies agreed that the tribunal should prosecute war crimes, but little or no strategic action was being taken to make this happen.

In Goode's and McAdams's framework, the tribunal needed a moral agent or norm entrepreneur to initiate a status competition, and Arbour was this person. This initiation involves a moral agent or norm entrepreneur who will bear the potential risk costs (for instance, that her actions will be ignored) to undertake the idealized behavior that may result in obtaining the status of "hero." The phase *primary norm enforcement* also involves the actors (described below) who respond to this behavior with their own norm enforcement efforts with the goal of obtaining similar esteem, albeit in reduced amount, though still an amount large enough to offset their investment of resources, since they are early followers but not initiators of this sanctioning behavior. The next stage, called *secondary norm enforcement,* begins as those who followed earlier in this "norm cascade" are encouraged, often by the media, to impose external costs of *dis*esteem on others (also identified below) who have not yet joined in support of the sanctioning behavior. These are the primary and secondary processes proposed by McAdams as having the potential to structurally transform social and legal norms by means of their effective enforcement.

THE GAME UNFOLDS

Arbour's initiative involved the ICT and three of the major NATO powers: Britain, the United States, and France. All three endorsed the enforcement of norms of international criminal law, yet when Arbour became Chief Prosecutor none of these nations had invested their political capital by involving their own troops in making arrests, and they would feel no necessity to do so unless one of the others acted first. This is the starting point of non-enforcement that McAdams describes and Arbour encountered—with NATO declining to make arrests when she took over from Goldstone.

McAdams's game theoretic logic more specifically asks that we assume, for example, that taking an active arrest role in norm enforcement would cost three million dollars per country per time period and that each NATO ally values its esteem ranking per time period as follows:[36]

Esteem from being the only enforcer:	+ $4 million
Esteem from being one of two enforcers:	+ $2 million
Esteem when all or none are enforcers:	+ $0 million
Esteem from being one of two non-enforcers:	− $2 million
Esteem from being the only non-enforcer:	− $4 million

McAdams then reasons that if any one or more of the three allies becomes an enforcer, then all of the allies are better off if they join in as enforcers, in the sense that they will at least not lose esteem. If any one of the allies does not become an enforcer for a period of time, there is a gain for the allies who do become enforcers for that time period. The challenge is therefore to get one or more of the parties to become an enforcer, for example, by demonstrating that the costs are not too great. Arbour took Goode's heroic gamble of initiating the competition and demonstrated the low apparent costs of enforcement when she authorized the Dokmanovic arrest.

Her deputy prosecutor, Graham Blewitt, said that overall "it took about three months for SFOR [the NATO security force] to finally accept that Louise Arbour was not going to back down." When SFOR resisted, Blewitt reported, she said simply, "No, it's the only way to go and I insist that you arrest [Simo] Drljaca [the target of her next pending indictment], and if you don't, well, we're prepared to give you enough time to do it. But when it becomes apparent to me that there is no real intention to apprehend anybody and that your mandate is just a fraud, then I will expose it."

British troops under NATO command were the first to heed Arbour, and they did so with American help. A new American general, Wesley Clark, had taken command of NATO, and Tony Blair had been elected prime minister in England. Less than two weeks after the Dokmanovic arrest, a British SWAT team under NATO command descended on the city of Prijedor and arrested Milan Kovacevic for his role in administering the neighboring Omarska and Keraterm prison camps. Simo Drljaca, the former police chief and brother-in-law of Kovacevic, was shot dead after pulling a gun and shooting a British soldier in the leg during the same raid. Both Kovacevic and Drljaca had been secretly indicted by Arbour. They were continuing to harass Bosnian Muslims in the Prejidor area and had interfered recently with witnesses in the Tadic trial. Aside from the injured soldier's leg, the costs of the shootout and arrest to the British were low, especially compared to Tony Blair's political gain for his early and highly visible role as a primary norm enforcer. Since the press had barely noticed the arrest of Dokmanovic, Blair received enormous credit, which Arbour was happy to encourage. Although General Clark received a verbal warning from Milosevic that "trying to seize these 'war criminals' is like holding a lighted match over a bucket of gasoline,"[37] ultimately the repercussions were not significant.

There was speculation that Drljaca's death would stimulate other publicly indicted figures to surrender. "The accused got the message that there was an easy way and a hard way to come here," a legal advisor in the prosecutor's office observed. Within a few months a planeload of ten Croats who had been indicted by Goldstone turned themselves in at The Hague. Arbour concluded that "all the tribunal had to do, it seemed to me, was to show its ability to deliver and . . . it would become a self-fulfilling prophecy in the same way that I think I was persuaded that arrest would then trigger a few voluntary surrenders and then more arrests—a momentum for making it happen and bringing the more reluctant partners into the fold." In the closing month of 1997 Dutch SFOR soldiers arrested two more Bosnian Croats with British support, and in the first month of 1998 American SFOR troops arrested Goran Jelisic, a self-proclaimed "Serb Adolf." More arrests followed, including the arrest on a secret indictment by American SFOR troops of Radislav Krstic, a Serbian general whose conviction for genocide for the Srebrenica massacre is the focus of the following chapter.

Arbour and her advisors also used the evolving experience in the field as an opportunity to change the formal procedural rules of the tribunal and to create a more tightly coupled system of arrest. For example, "the rules that made it look as if you could only send a warrant to a state, so that Republika Srpska eventually had to do the arrest, were changed so that warrants no longer have to be addressed to states, so that they could be addressed to the person on the envelope," a legal advisor noted. In this way the SFOR troops could more directly take on the arrest role that the local Serbian authorities in this region would not. "We tried to take out all the rules that were limiting our flexibility in arrests, and we pushed these proposals through plenary sessions of the ICT . . . , to put the legal framework in place so the secret indictment process would run through consistently and do things in Bosnia with muscle provided by SFOR and keep the local authorities out of it."

The transfers that followed these arrests are shown in figure 4.1, with Dokmanovic indicated toward the left side of the figure. The arrest and transfer of Kovacevic followed, and the line spikes upward with the arrival of the planeload of Croats. Then arrestees began arriving at a more stable rate of about one or two a month, until by June 1998 about thirty defendants were under detention in the tribunal's twenty-four-unit facility. The result was that the ICT was now underbudgeted and beyond its physical capacity, allowing Arbour to initiate an intensified campaign for increased funding, which is discussed further below.

Arbour had succeeded in what at first had seemed an impossible task, especially from Meyer and Jepperson's perspective: to structurally link NATO forces to the tribunal as the enforcement arm and to thereby couple the discourse of human rights enforcement with actual arrests. It was, of course, still true that neither Karadzic nor Mladic was in custody. Karadzic was believed to be in the Pale area, which was in the French zone of Bosnia, and only France among the NATO allies was not participating in the new arrest regime, remaining decoupled from these enforcement obligations. So Arbour initiated the next phase in her prosecution plan with a visit to France, for the purpose of stimulating what McAdams calls secondary norm enforcement.

ARBOUR FINDS HER VOICE

McAdams writes that "a secondary norm arises when individuals lower their opinion of those who fail to censure primary norm violators."[38] To engender this disesteem it is necessary to make sure others notice that the party in question, in this case, France, is not engaging in primary norm enforcement. Arbour went to France in December 1997 to make its nonparticipation fully apparent. Her goal was "to generate an atmosphere of compliance," which would involve using "enough coercion to make things happen." This involved "going public," a role that Arbour had at first resisted.

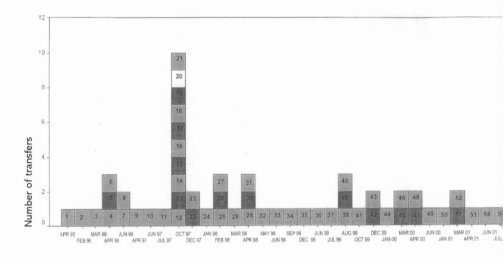

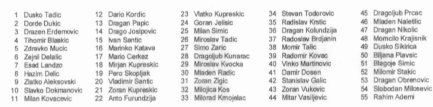

1	Dusko Tadic	12	Dario Kordic	23	Vlatko Kupreskic	34	Stevan Todorovic	45	Dragoljub Prcac
2	Dorde Dukic	13	Dragan Papic	24	Goran Jelisic	35	Radislav Krstic	46	Mladen Naletilic
3	Drazen Erdemovic	14	Drago Josipovic	25	Milan Simic	36	Dragan Kolundzija	47	Dragan Nikolic
4	Tihomir Blaskic	15	Ivan Santic	26	Miroslav Tadic	37	Radoslav Brdjanin	48	Momcilo Krajisnik
5	Zdravko Mucic	16	Marinko Katava	27	Simo Zaric	38	Momir Talic	49	Dusko Sikirica
6	Zejnil Delalic	17	Mario Cerkez	28	Dragoljub Kunarac	39	Radomir Kovac	50	Biljana Plavsic
7	Esad Landzo	18	Mirjan Kupreskic	29	Miroslav Kvocka	40	Vinko Martinovic	51	Blagoje Simic
8	Hazim Delic	19	Pero Skopljak	30	Mladen Radic	41	Damir Dosen	52	Milomir Stakic
9	Zlatko Aleksovski	20	Vladimir Santic	31	Zoran Zigic	42	Stanislav Galic	53	Dragan Obrenovic
10	Slavko Dokmanovic	21	Zoran Kupreskic	32	Milojica Kos	43	Zoran Vukovic	54	Slobodan Milosevic
11	Milan Kovacevic	22	Anto Furundzija	33	Milorad Kmojelac	44	Mitar Vasiljevic	55	Rahim Ademi

Figure 4.1. Transfers of individuals to the International Criminal Tribunal for the Former Yugoslavia, November 1993–July 2001 (International Criminal Tribunal for the Former Yugoslavia, 2001)

"When I first came to it," Arbour explained, "I had been a judge for many years. I had no media experience and I had all the wrong instincts. Judges don't talk to the press." Gradually her views changed: "It took me a while but eventually I started appreciating that the fundamental premises of criminal law, traditionally, were that it's public and local. . . . When I applied that internationally it became apparent that the only way we could even remotely be public and local was through the use of the international media. We had to be out there." Ultimately, Arbour knew the issue was one of making the case for resources, "and when I started being more proactive and media friendly, the public displayed interest and support, which encouraged politicians to fund the work appropriately."[39]

The specific incident that pushed Arbour into action was a remark made in early December 1997 by the French defense minister, Alain Richard, in *Le Monde*. In addition to being asked to participate in NATO arrests, Richard had been asked to have French military officers testify at the tribunal. France had sustained far greater losses in the Balkans than any other NATO country, including seventy-five deaths, and its politicians were worried about the political consequences of reliving these events in the press. Richard's strategy was to say that French officers would not under any circumstances testify at The Hague, which he then called a *justice spectacle*. This translates roughly as "show trial."

This was the worst kind of public relations nightmare for the ICT— calling into doubt the tribunal's institutionalization of the rule of law and liberal legalism. Arbour felt an instant necessity to respond. She coincidentally had planned to attend an early December conference in Paris on Rwanda and then meet with French officials. She decided to use this occasion to make France's nonparticipation in the tribunal's work fully apparent. When she arrived in Paris the French press asked her about Richard's remarks. She began with the issue of arrests, answering archly that "the vast majority of the indicted [war crimes suspects], including the most important ones, are in the French sector. We have an opportunity to take sizable actions [to arrest suspects] in the French sector. Yet we're in the face of total inertia." She added that war criminals felt "absolutely secure" in the French sector. Then she turned to Richard's "shocking" remark about the tribunal being a "spectacle," saying that it showed a "contempt for witnesses . . . who have come to tell us about the atrocities they suffered." The culmination was a pointed evocation of secondary norm enforcement, noting that generals from Britain and the United States had already testified at The Hague and that these nations were joining others in contributing financially to the tribunal. "The French failing," she concluded, "is therefore pretty remarkable." These words were broadcast not only locally but internationally, through a detailed report by the Paris bureau chief for the *Washington Post,* Charles Trueheart.[40]

Arbour insists that she was very uncomfortable in this encounter. She had no press person to travel or work with her. "There was enormous resistance inside to giving the prosecutor what I believe was the appropriate support for media work. . . . I wasn't very interested in doing it and, worse, nobody in my office, I had no spokesman, there was nobody to do it."

The Paris experience brought Arbour's first clear awareness of how essential the communication of her message through the media was, and indeed how unexpectedly good she herself could be as a messenger: "I found myself in the eye of a huge political storm . . . and I had to go on instinct." It helped that in France Arbour could launch her counterattack in her first language. Still, as one of her senior colleagues noted, she was taking an enormous risk. "It was a high wire act. Because remember you're taking on a government with an incredible staff behind it, and I mean she didn't have any public affairs people or political strategists, so she's up there performing without a net."

The immediate French response was outrage. It would take a while before international and domestic opinion began to provide secondary support. First reports indicated that a French military official had foiled a planned arrest of Karadzic, and relations between France and the United States were now more strained. By April 1998, things had deteriorated to the point where the *Washington Post* quoted a senior U.S. official as saying that "no trust" remained between Washington and Paris, a quote then picked up by *Agence France Presse;*[41] by June, the *European* was reporting that "U.S. anger with the French is so great that Pentagon planners are now believed to be contemplating a snatch in the French sector without informing Paris."[42]

Finally, French president Jacques Chirac, who had been a central figure in the Dayton Accords, began to cooperate in arrest plans. French military officers also began to testify at The Hague. In early 2000, the French SFOR forces made their first successful arrest, and that April the French arrested the Bosnian Serb politician Momcilo Krajisnik, the most important figure taken into custody before Milosevic.

Arbour had now found her voice beyond the tribunal. One of her advisors joked that "she had learned to speak in short sentences." In any case, she now began to use her knowledge of the cultural or normative themes of international criminal law to argue for the financial resources the ICT needed to prosecute the indictees waiting in the tribunal's detention unit. Arbour approached her task as one of persuasion, pointing out publicly that "what's needed is the political will, but this is never achieved spontaneously: it is created by public opinion,"[43] while also acknowledging more privately, "I became persuaded that life is all about these perceptions." The result was a new awareness that she was in a symbolic framing contest, which Sewell describes as involving a crucial element of human agency, "the actor's capacity to reinterpret and mobilize an array of resources in terms of cultural schemas other than those that initially constituted the array."[44]

THREE CULTURAL SCHEMAS

The first of these cultural schemas, or interpretive frameworks, pitted the traditional concept of national sovereignty against the international norm of universal jurisdiction for crimes against humanity. Arbour warned in written pieces and also in the press that there was an "international culture of state immunity and sovereignty" and asserted her intention to "ensure 'state sovereignty' is no longer an excuse to get away with murder."[45] She emphasized that the work of the tribunal involved "constantly struggling to overcome the international culture of state immunity and sovereignty, even in the face of the most outrageous violations of international law." The ultimate test of these competing frames of reference would, of course, involve the indictment of Slobodan Milosevic as a sitting head of state. Her argument was that Milosevic "benefited from a convenient confusion between heads of states and the states themselves, between personal criminal responsibility and state sovereignty and immunity." The key for Arbour was that the Security Council mandate creating the tribunal had given it extraterritorial jurisdiction over the former Yugoslavia, so there was no cover of national sovereignty.

Arbour's first theme was closely related to the second framing contest she entered between the worlds of international law and criminal law. She emphasized that these worlds are different culturally as well as institutionally. Arbour called the former the world of limousines and striped-pants diplomats and contrasted it with the work of the armed and uniformed look of criminal law enforcement. She stressed that this had everyday implications and consequences, so that "when I arrived there was this perception outside and inside that we had to be really nice to be effective, that we had to beg for witnesses and documents and be quite deferential and polite." The consequence was that "we had to be in this cooperative mode. This struck me as totally incompatible with our mission."[46] Instead Arbour emphasized that the criminal law is a coercive instrument and that its mechanisms, such as the secret indictment, have to be imposed with the force this law was intended to have. "I thought we were operating too much in the political, diplomatic, cooperation mode, when in fact all we had to do was start playing the only cards we really had, which were the legal kind of coercive compliance cards. We represented the Security Council, you obey. Here is the card, now what do you say. Which is very much the criminal mode. Criminal law is coercive and it's not deferential to states, and in fact criminal law is highly suspicious of state power, particularly of abuse of power by the state. International law is very consensual and is very deferential to states." Arbour used the tough-talking cultural schema of criminal law to publicly overcome the polite protections of sovereignty her adversaries sought through the habit of deference to a more consensual international law.

Arbour recalled going to a London meeting of the Peace Implementation Council as a follow-up to the Dayton peace agreement. She was confronted by the Bosnian Serb politicians Momcilo Krajisnik and

Biljana Plavsic, who would later directly experience the coercive criminal power of indictment and arrest. When Arbour was asked to address the group, she took the opportunity to stress the coercive power of international criminal law. She first acknowledged that "you are here to discuss many issues, strategies and policies about the implementation of the peace process in Bosnia." She then drove home her point: "the question of the arrest of indictees, war crimes, indicted war criminals, I hope you understand, is not a matter of debate, it is the law." In this context, Arbour wanted the criminal law to be understood as "rough street stuff" capable of overcoming the cloak of state sovereignty.

Finally, Arbour waged her most publicized effort to bring her prosecutorial regime from what she called "historical time" into "real time." By this she meant that international criminal law had for too long been consumed with righting historical injustices, evoking the associated imagery of aging Nazi hunters, and needed to move into the present, where war crimes and crimes against humanity were being committed now and could be pursued before the trail grew cold.

The immediate point was that as events unfolded in Kosovo, the world was seeing war crimes committed on its television screens. Arbour could see the stark challenge these events presented to this tribunal, which was authorized to deal with current as well as past events in the former Yugoslavia. She publicly posed rhetorical questions that were in reality calls to action: "Would we be a real-time prosecution outfit during wartime? Or would we always be sort of an historical prosecution unit?"[47] The answers to these questions pointed to getting her investigators and legal advisors, if not herself, into Kosovo. When forty-five people were found murdered near the Macedonian border in the Kosovo town of Racak in January 1999, Arbour quickly put together a small group of three investigators, two bodyguards, and one legal advisor with the goal of entering a war in progress.

THE PROSECUTOR IN THE FLAK JACKET

For much of the preceding year the Serbian- and Yugoslav-dominated government had been killing ethnic Albanians or driving them out of Kosovo. This was an organized program of war crimes, and the tribunal had UN Security Council authority to prosecute these actions. However, Milosevic's government was refusing to give it access to Kosovo, and the NATO leadership had rebuffed Arbour's efforts to assist her entry. When Human Rights Watch reported a massacre of male adults in the town of Racak, Arbour decided to go to the Macedonian border city of Skopje to engage the media in publicizing the massacre.

Clint Williamson was the legal advisor who accompanied Arbour and wound up acting in part as her de facto press secretary. The ICT admin-istration was still resisting the assignment of a press person to the OTP, and so when Arbour's party of seven went to Racak the

> inadequacy with respect to media relations and press was obvious and pathetic. I suspected there would be some press attention. "Do you need someone?" Well, after a lot of back and forth and so on, the United Nations decided they would release a guy who was their press person in Macedonia. He met us at the airport. The only equipment that he owned and had with him was his own mobile phone, and nobody had that number. That's it. He didn't have a pen, a piece of paper, didn't know anything. He was a wonderful team player, but in the circumstances he couldn't do much. The seven of us each had our own cell phones, and that's the extent of the communication we had with the rest of the world. The number of my cell phone—my office in The Hague had it, General Wes Clark and Richard Holbrooke had it. That's it. They were the only people who could speak to me directly.

Arbour vowed that this would be the last time she did her press relations without advance work and assistance; but for the moment she would have to make it up as she went along.

Arbour and her team arrived at the border on January 17 and gave the crossing guards her UN papers amidst a swirling crowd of interna-tional journalists armed with cameras that carried this image around the globe. Her bodyguards had wanted her to stay in their vehicle and hand her papers through the window. Instead she stepped out into the road with only a bright yellow flak jacket as apparent protection. When the border guard refused her entry on the basis that she had no visa, Arbour angrily demanded, "Do you know who I am?" When he con-firmed that he did, Arbour asked whether he was acting on orders from Belgrade. He denied this, and their party was turned back.[48]

By presenting her credentials at the border, Arbour was playing what she earlier called her "UN Security Council card." Her team had known that rejection was a likely scenario, but they nonetheless felt compelled to follow through with it. Arbour held a short press briefing reiterating what had just happened in a small clearing in the no man's land be-tween the Serbian and Macedonian border posts. Now they could only return to Skopje to plot their next move.

LOSING THE BATTLE AND WINNING THE FRAMING CONTEST

They had assumed that they might simply return to The Hague, but as they were sitting at the hotel having a beer and recouping, Arbour's cell phone rang. It was Richard Holbrooke, and he told her, "Just stay where you are, you're putting incredible pressure on them, don't give up, just stay there." Williamson recalled that it seemed like "being the visiting team, down by thirty points, and the coach telling you that you have them exactly where you want them."

Now Arbour's cell phone really came to life as a round of negotiations began between Clark, Milosevic, Arbour, and intermediaries. Williamson was screening the calls:

> We were just constantly getting these phone calls, and it was one of Clark's aides, and he would say, "General Clark for her," and I would hand it to her, and we had four or five of these calls. I mean Clark called the first time and it was something to the effect that Milosevic was saying that the only thing that could happen was that she could come to Belgrade and talk and possibly be escorted down there [Racak]. And she said, "Well, I want my legal advisor to come with me as well" and that "I want the investigators to be able to go on the ground." So I think we started off with going to Belgrade, just me and her. Then that they would take us to Racak with the minister of justice escorting us. . . . And then she countered and said fine, o.k., but then they get to stay. And then they were like "no." And that's sort of where it ended, but Clark would go in, he would talk to Milosevic for an hour or so, and then he would come out and he would call and say, "O.k., this is what they're offering," and in the end it was just unacceptable.

Clark's account of this marathon phone exchange is much the same but is further complicated by the other issues he simultaneously was pursuing with Milosevic.[49] However, the phone calls with Clark were only half the story.

The other half involved the crowd of journalists that had followed Arbour's party to the hotel and the calls from the press that were coming on the cell phones. The pack of journalists followed every step they took. Arbour gave on-site interviews, and Williamson handled the incoming phone calls on her colleagues' cell phones, which were not designed for this intense use. Arbour recalls, "I spent the evening, my phone was actually hot. I had to take it away from my ear, it was getting so hot, while giving interviews to the CBC and the BBC and the newspaper from Tokyo. All on this pathetic instrument, on the cell phone of my bodyguard who kept saying, 'You've got to get off the phone. This is my security equipment.' . . . It was just pathetic."

The group with Arbour wound up awaiting further developments in Skopje for three days. There was no way they could know how this event was seen from the outside world, much less the lens or cultural schema through which it was viewed. The unexpected televised reality was that the media were watching a prosecutor from the International Criminal Tribunal being turned away from a real-time crime scene by a sitting head of state using claims of national sovereignty to conceal evidence in what seemed a transparent concession of guilt. Arbour explains that this was the period of time in which she fully realized the significance of media-conveyed images, because while the above was the story the world was seeing, she was experiencing something different. She was ready to just go home, quit, and concede failure: "I was completely discouraged and I started drafting my letter of resignation. This was the only time I've done that, because what was very clear to me as an experience was that I could not do it. I had taken it physically to the end of the road and in a real sense: when I turned around, there was nobody behind me. NATO wasn't there, the Security Council wasn't there, and I thought, 'Get one of the boys,' they're all chums, maybe if you get a great big boy on the front of the line, maybe you'll come with him, but you're not coming with me, so get somebody else, I can't do this." She went back to The Hague ready to throw in the towel.

When Arbour arrived at her Hague office the next day, she encountered a completely different reality focused around her picture in the *New York Times* confronting the border guards.

> When I came back to The Hague I realized that what I had lived, and that what in reality was a failure, had been lived differently in The Hague, because they weren't there, they were seeing it only in the press, as the greatest success story of the tribunal. Therefore, it became clear to me that reality is never as real as the media makes it. The only thing that counts is the image, because what became the conventional wisdom of the reality of those three days was not what I lived but what the tribunal, the bad guys, NATO, the politicians, the world, my mom, everybody in the world perceived—which was that I had singlehandedly put the tribunal on the map, that we were on a roll, it was absolutely surreal. How did they get this notion? How did they get this phoenix to rise from the ashes of defeat, which is exactly what happened: I went to the border and I didn't get in. But the spin, the images—as my assistant put it, 'We made the *New York Times*,' she said, 'above the fold!'

Her assistant was referring to the picture of Arbour in her yellow flak jacket. The imagery was charismatic: the crusading prosecutor, dressed for combat, who had faced down the tyrannical head of state. Arbour had lost the border battle and won the media war, without even knowing it.

Did *Arbour herself* win the war? "For granted," the anthropologist Martin Sahlins answers, "that persons may have historical effect—that is, as expressions of their individuality rather than functions of the totality—still, they have to be put in a position to do so."[50] Arbour occupied a *position* in a set of occupational, institutional, national, cultural, and international relationships that I have described and that allowed her to win by losing, while not even knowing she had done so.[51] Arbour and her enactment of liberal legalism and the Human Security Agenda were authorized and empowered by the structural position she occupied and by the media event she provoked, and in which she unknowingly prevailed.

TEMPORAL CONTROL

As if to reestablish that this Canadian cultural schema (the Human Security Agenda) was still very much in play, within a day or two of Arbour's return to The Hague the first official announcement appeared that Canadian Supreme Court justice Peter Cory, whom Arbour, it was now rumored, might replace, would retire in June.[52] This meant that somebody must assume his seat by September, which would require a spring or early summer appointment. On the return flight from Racak, Arbour had confided to Williamson that her time at the tribunal was likely coming to a close. "We were on the airplane coming back and it was just me and her going back and . . . I think there were some security people, but I mean she had said even then that she was probably going to be leaving."

To some of those close to Arbour at the tribunal, the prospect of her Supreme Court appointment began to feel like an accident waiting to happen. A colleague commented that "it was like there were two trains on a collision course—and I can not tell you how close they came." The larger world was not at this point aware that the prospect of Arbour's court appointment was in imminent danger of competing for attention with the development of an indictment of Slobodan Milosevic. For those who knew Arbour and the ways of Supreme Court appointments in Canada, it was not difficult to foresee the drawn-out scenario that awaited her. "Beforehand, it's very mysterious, because there's no formal process. You don't apply for it. So it's very amorous, gossipy stuff that's going on. Some of that gossipy stuff was going on, even though she was thousands of miles away." There was reason to worry that the two trains headed Arbour's way would collide and that all could be lost in the wreckage.

Yet from this point forward, Arbour gained increasing influence over not only the events she sought to control—the Milosevic indictment and the supreme court appointment—but also over the timing of these events. The sociologists Mustafa Emirbayer and Ann Mische emphasize how important controlling the timing of events and relationships is in achieving agency.[53] For her part, Arbour was acutely aware of her need to simultaneously orient herself toward the prospect of the Canadian court appointment and the growing possibility of a Milosevic indictment.

Arbour now finally acquired an important new resource to assist with the timing and shaping of her fast-moving agenda: the UN authorized a public relations person to help handle the press from the OTP. Arbour selected Paul Risley, a young but already experienced handler of politicians, who had had an early stint with Al Gore. Risley arrived in The Hague on April 10, 1999, and four days later was sent to Tirana, Albania. The mass deportations from Kosovo and the NATO bombing of Serbia and Kosovo had begun, and the refugees were streaming across the borders into Albania and Macedonia. Risley's first task was to screen reporters who were vying and often interfering with ICT investigators interviewing the refugees as crime scene victims and witnesses.

RACING THE CLOCK

Well before the bombing started, and more so after, it was clear that Kosovo was the place to most effectively develop the Milosevic indictment. Because Kosovo, as contrasted with Bosnia, was still part of Yugoslavia and events were unfolding in what Arbour liked to call real time, it would be easier to establish the chain of command that led back to Milosevic. This is why Arbour wanted to enter Kosovo with her investigators at Racak before the bombing began and why as events unfolded she wanted to enter Kosovo along with the NATO troops after the bombing stopped. Meanwhile, Arbour reorganized her investigators and legal advisors into special teams that began interviewing the refugees in the Albanian and Macedonian refugee camps.

Arbour felt that a clock was ticking on the Milosevic indictment, because as negotiations took place to end the war and the NATO bombing, there would be pressure to include an immunity clause in the agreement. When Risley began working with Arbour on this, "we were literally racing . . . to get an indictment public and on the table before any negotiations began. . . . Louise felt very strongly that 'I've got to have a public indictment out there.'" To do this Arbour worked personally with a small team of "people who are 'doers'" that included her deputy prosecutor, Graham Blewitt, and two of her closest legal advisors, Clint Williamson and Nancy Paterson.

Arbour emphasized that "there was a relatively small group of people who actually worked on this. And I told them from the time, essentially from the beginning of January, 1999, when it looked really promising, that we could actually get this guy on Kosovo, because then he was in the right line of command juridically." She had to pull the members of this team away from other important work they were doing. "That was very hard to do internally, because people were all involved in other things and they were very committed to their work. It was a bit at the beginning like pulling teeth, . . . but it finally gelled."

After the mass deportations and bombing began, Williamson took responsibility for the refugee camp work around Tirana, Albania. "I went down the week after the bombing began in March. . . . We had to take a ferry across from Italy because there were no flights." He set up an office in Tirana. "The Albanian government gave us a villa which had been the residence of the former prime minister in the communist regime, so it was a large building. . . . I was basically running the operations on the ground in Albania and we were sending our investigators out to the refugee camps."

To impart her sense of urgency, as well as to stay informed, Arbour met almost daily with the core group in The Hague. Toward the end, the group was expanded to collect advice about the specific charges, for example, whether Milosevic would be charged with genocide. The core group worked together intensively. "I met with them daily and I think that helped. It helped me. Even on some days we didn't have that much to report, but it also gave a sense of urgency, that my message essentially was an expectation that every day there would be something new. So it generated a lot of momentum."

In the beginning Paterson handled the writing: "He [Williamson] was collecting the evidence and funneling it back to us and I was organizing it and drafting the indictment." After his organizational work in Tirana, Williamson headed back to The Hague to help with the writing. "Nancy and I just really split the indictment in half. I did most of the background sections of the indictment, the factual scenario of everything, and Nancy had done the criminal responsibility section, and then we split the crimes." The charges largely involved the persecutions and killings that led to and accompanied the deportations of the Albanian Muslims from Kosovo. "She did most of the writing on the deportations and I did the writing on the persecutions and on all of the killing incidents. . . . Then there were three or four people from the leadership research team . . . who did some of the editing and contributed to it." Paterson found that "it was a little crazy the first couple of weeks, but once we actually got going, . . . I actually thought it worked quite well." The daily meetings were essential, and Williamson and Paterson both commented on the amount of contact they maintained with Arbour during this period.

There were days that Arbour would necessarily miss, usually to travel to Germany, Britain, France, or the United States to pursue essential pieces of the evidence that would form the indictment. Paterson worked closely with Arbour: "I can remember for a while there we were having pretty much daily, or twice a day meetings, when we were putting the indictment together. It was great. I would come in each day with a new chart, 'Here's where we are and here's where we need to get to,' and she would basically say, 'What can I do to help?' And I could literally say to her, 'Well, you need to go to such-and-such a country and talk to so and so,' or 'We need to get this intelligence information, call up whoever you need to call to make it happen,' or whatever, and she'd go off on her assignments, just like one of the investigators, and come back and have her own part to contribute. That also contributed to that feeling of a team. She was included along with everybody else." In one ten-day period Arbour traveled to Bonn, London, Washington, Paris, and Brussels. Tony Blair's foreign secretary, Robin Cook, made a public appearance in London on April 20 to complete what he described as "the biggest handover of British intelligence to an outside agency in history."[54]

A further sense of the core and expanded group dynamics involved in the creation of the indictment is provided in Arbour's description of how decisions about its specific content were finally made: using a process that empowered Arbour with the authority to finally alone make difficult decisions, for example, about whether to charge Milosevic with genocide. "I was better informed about that investigation than about any other that had taken place ever since I was there. And we kept it quite close, but then when it came to critical decisions, for instance, about whether we have enough evidence to charge him with genocide or not, then we expanded. We brought in all the legal talent we could. So let's have all the lawyers look at the materials, and let's have it out, let's debate it. And I participated but I didn't lead. I just kind of listened. I said, 'Just talk and I'm going to take it all in.' Eventually I knew I'd have to call it, but they were very talented people there. Very helpful for me to do it that way." The entire indictment, start to finish, was written in fifty-two days. When pressed to summarize her sense of this collective process, Arbour said, "I take a lot of my own energy from other people and I suppose I share it too."

The planning that went into the timing of the announcement of the indictment ultimately rivaled the attention paid to the drafting of its content. Risley had seen in the run-up to the Milosevic indictment in

Kosovo that each of Arbour's cultural schemas—involving the real-time triumph of international criminal law over sovereign immunity—could be powerfully communicated with effective press coverage. "Kosovo made that very simple and made it very easy because each of those themes is really a sound bite in a way. . . . Kosovo was the vivid picture of those themes."

Risley saw a clear connection in Kosovo between the communication of these cultural schemas and increasing the resources of the ICT. By the time he arrived on the scene, he could report that "this sort of thing was pretty clear to Louise Arbour. . . . She knew that the *Washington Post* and the *New York Times* were the kinds of papers that she needed to be a part of." He then hammered the point home: "In the U.S., if you want the Security Council and if you want Kofi Annan and the other ambassadors to know what the tribunal's doing, you've got to be in the *New York Times,* you have to be there in the morning."

In the end, Arbour and Risley knew it would come down to planning the final days and then the hours of the morning of May 27, when the indictment was to be announced. "Ten days before hand," Risley recalls, "the prosecutor told me of her intentions—that she thought on a particular day [May 27] she would be prepared to make public an indictment. She wanted to take it to a judge [on May 22] and get it confirmed [by May 23]." Arbour's plan was to use the three-or-four-day period to "take care of the diplomatic necessities" that followed from her earlier trips to collect essential evidence in the capitals of Western Europe and the United States. "In each case," Risley explained, "the secretaries of defense of ministers would say to her, 'please inform me when you are to indict Milosevic.' "

THE DIALECTICS OF AGENCY

Arbour was at this point deeply engaged in a dialectical process of give and take involving the final authority to make the indictment decision. The decision might ultimately be hers, but the secretary-general of the UN, Kofi Annan, also had major input, along with the leaders of the NATO nations who were now committed to the bombing campaign. Her agency derived from their authorization, even though the indictment decision was formally hers as chief prosecutor.

To preserve her autonomy, Arbour devised the plan of signing the indictment in the OTP on the evening of Saturday, May 22, with judicial confirmation on the twenty-third, followed by four days of consultation that she regarded as notification. She reasoned that the dating of her signature was a crucial point of no return that would haunt any effort by others to stave off the indictment by intervening in her process. A pretext for the four-day pause was protecting a humanitarian group in Belgrade that would be concluding its mission by the twenty-seventh: the timing would protect them from the unlikely risk of being taken hostage in revenge by Milosevic.[55] An alternative explanation of this delay was that it was an effort to protect a secret UN team of fact finders at work in Kosovo.[56] However, Risley put the real reason this way: "She didn't want to give them the chance to co-opt or slow down the indictment, because that would really get at the heart of her independence as a prosecutor. So she was very careful to have Judge Hunt confirm it and then hold it under wraps, under seal—as we say—for four days, and in that period she made phone calls to each of these foreign ministers, and you know they all called her back and said, 'Good, we support this.'"

Rumors were now rampant about the indictment, as well as about her prospective appointment to the Supreme Court. Risley figured that about fifty people in the tribunal knew precisely when the indictment would occur. The international press was watching Risley intently, and he especially did not want to be blamed for an inadvertent leak. "So with Deputy Graham Blewitt's blessing I went down to Tirana (where he had been traveling frequently) and spent that whole weekend before the biggest story of this building." By the time he left on Saturday, the tension was mounting.

The core group worked through Saturday so that the indictment could be confirmed internally on Sunday, and on Monday Arbour could begin making the external contacts that would lead up to the announcement on Thursday. Arbour arrived late Saturday afternoon to see the penultimate draft of the indictment. Clint Williamson picks up with the beginning of what proved to be a long and taxing evening.

So she arrived and we were still working on it and making changes and doing little things with it, and so we kept pushing it back, and we were working in Nancy's office on her computer. . . . I took it down, I think shortly after six and gave it to her and Graham to read. Then Louise called back and said, "Well, I've read through it and I have a few changes." . . . So I went back up and Nancy was typing in the changes. Every time we'd take a new draft down and then she'd find something else or whatever. This went on and on, so it's already getting to be like eight o'clock. . . . I was sitting down and I was typing and then all of a sudden it just went to like these symbols on the computer, on the monitor, instead of the letters. And we were like "Oh no," and so I ended up calling this guy that was one of the senior computer technicians. It's Saturday evening at eight o'clock and "Yeah, I'm out at the beach, just having a beer, whatever," and I say, "Can you come quickly, this

is really important." And he said, "Yeah, I'll be there in five minutes."
And I told him, I said I can't tell you what this is about. . . . He walks
in and sits down and he sees "Prosecutor vs. Slobodan Milosevic"
and he goes, "Oh shit, I see why this is important." He was able to re-
trieve it for us, thank God. I think we finally got it down to her maybe
around nine o'clock in the final form and she signed it.

This dated signature on May 22 was crucial to Arbour, because, she
reasoned, this locked the sequence of events in place.

Nancy Paterson sensed that the event should be recorded in some
suitable way, so she found a UN flag and prepared a signing ceremony.
Williamson described the event: "We got a picture actually . . . it was
me and Nancy and Graham standing as she signs the thing, with the UN
flag behind and sort of draped across." Nancy later had the photograph
framed with the inscription, "Those who say it can't be done should get
out of the way of those who are doing it." The plaque hangs on the wall
of Justice Arbour's Supreme Court office in Ottawa.

Judge Hunt read the indictment on Sunday, and although the following Monday was a UN holiday, Hunt signed the indictment, adding the
necessary further source of dated authorization. Williamson described
"dropping it off with him and explaining to him what was in there and
just walking him through how to find everything in the supporting material." After the judge had signed, Paterson and Arbour retreated to
their offices and, though exhausted, savored an interim moment of closure. "Several of us had come upstairs," Paterson recalls, "and were kind
of mingling around, and then Judge Arbour and I were just standing
there looking at each other rather exhausted, and she said to me, 'This
is a good thing, right?' And I said to her, 'Oh, yes, Judge, this is a very
good thing.'"

While they were having celebratory drinks afterwards one of their
cell phones rang. It was Judge Hunt saying, "I have a question." Williamson was thinking, "Oh God, what is it?" He simply wanted to know
the official name of Switzerland because the orders they were asking for
had to be directed to all UN member states. That was the only question
Judge Hunt asked of the prosecutors. A dinner in an Asian restaurant
followed, and this time it was a phone call by Arbour that punctuated
the moment. "We were sitting around this Chinese restaurant and I
guess the indictment may have just been confirmed within the hour or
something; she picks up her cell phone and calls Kofi Annan . . . , informing him, 'I promised you I'd let you know the deed is done' or whatever their code word was.'" A colleague noted that the following day,
Tuesday, Arbour "flew to Stockholm, spent an hour in the VIP lounge at

the airport, and then she flew back" and added, "The secretary-general for the UN was on vacation in Stockholm at that time." This was Arbour's opportunity to deliver and discuss in person the signed and dated indictment.

THE DIFFERENCE A DAY MAKES

Risley and Arbour were both back in The Hague by late Tuesday with two announcements looming before them: the public unsealing of the Milosevic indictment and, known only within Arbour's inner circle in The Hague and in the Canadian prime minister's office in Ottawa, her appointment to the Supreme Court. By now Arbour knew that the prime minister's phone call was coming.

Arbour worked with Risley and Blewitt to gain control over the final days of these intertwined events, focusing first on the indictment. The goal was to make sure the public announcement of the Milosevic indictment had maximum exposure. Risley followed a simple premise: "In American political reasoning it is very important [to have] . . . a two-day story, not a one-day story. You want to make sure that it sinks in to peoples' minds what's happening." The larger logic of the two-day story was that "one, reporters would take it seriously and they would be here, and two, it would mean that the *New York Times,* the *Washington Post,* the London papers, the papers that I take most seriously, would run two sets of stories. They would run one story Thursday morning, saying an indictment is likely today, according to CNN, and another story the next day reporting that an indictment was issued yesterday in The Hague."

Risley began his work on the two-day scenario from Tirana. He called about five reporters who he wanted to make sure would cover the story, including Christiane Amanpour, and without explaining exactly why, told them to be within two hours of The Hague on Wednesday. He reached Amanpour in Washington, D.C., and she immediately asked, "Is that because there will be an indictment on Thursday?" He responded, "I can't tell you that but you have enough good friends, you can check it out, you can talk to people." He knew that Amanpour's husband worked as Madeline Albright's spokesman at the State Department and that Albright would receive Arbour's notification of the coming announcement. Amanpour shot back, "You know that I can't use my husband as a source." Risley retorted, "I'm sure you can find somebody who can be your source for this." His goal was to get the story out early with CNN to give it visibility, and then make sure it was a surprise for the rest, with the exact charges and the number of persons who would be co-indicted coming out Thursday morning as the "real" news story.

True to her news-breaking reputation, Amanpour phoned Risley on landing at Heathrow Airport on Wednesday afternoon just before four o'clock.

> She was standing at Terminal 4 at the airport, calling me on her mobile phone, saying, "Can you now, definitely, can you tell me that the indictment is tomorrow?" And I said, "You know I can't tell you that, but I can assure you as I did before that you are in the correct spot and that we will hold a press conference tomorrow at nine o'clock here." And she said something like "I need to just say something like sources have confirmed that we have an indictment." I said, "Well, I can't tell you that but if you read me your story, read me the first two lines of what you intend to say, I'll listen to it and if I don't have a problem I'll still be on the phone, I'll listen to it." So she read basically just that, a couple of short sentences that she'd thought of and they sounded fine to me. . . . So maybe ten minutes later from the airport she did a live newscast for CNN, so I was able to watch her minutes after talking to her on the phone, and she sort of blurted it out to the world.

They now were assured that the front-page story in the morning papers would be that the indictment was coming.

When the Thursday morning press conference began in The Hague there were more than ten satellite trucks and a hundred reporters waiting to report the indictment. Thinking of the impact on the investigation and trial teams, Arbour called a meeting of the two hundred OTP employees who were "in house." A colleague remembered that "you could see out the window the cameras and the trucks that were starting to roll in for the press conference." The gathering lasted about twenty minutes. "I just made a little speech," Arbour recalled. "I said I felt that even those who hadn't been directly involved in it, that we had sucked all our energy internally, that everybody was in agreement that this was one of the good things we had done collectively." She later added, in explaining the importance of this gathering for herself, "I felt good and confident and positive that the thing had been thought through and that we had to be all in this thing together." An hour later Arbour delivered the announcement from Courtroom Three of the tribunal, with reporters watching from the public gallery and on monitors in the downstairs lobby. Amanpour followed with an interview from Arbour's office. The tribunal had its two-day blockbuster story.

CLOSELY TIMED TRAJECTORIES

The other side of Arbour's story occurred almost simultaneously, out of view of the watching press. Arbour was at pains to find a way to keep this side of the story separate from the indictment, but she also knew the prime minister's call was coming, and it was a call whose invitation she wanted to accept. What Arbour and those around her did not want to happen was for her to announce the indictment of Milosevic in The Hague at the same time the prime minister was announcing her Supreme Court appointment in Ottawa.

Risley was intimately aware of the looming appointment and resented the problems the prime minister of Canada, Jean Chrétien, was creating. Risley thought the conflict in timing made no sense in the context of the Canadian Human Security Agenda. "They were shooting themselves in the foot because here's the most visible Canadian in the whole world, leading this crusade for justice, and they instead decided to take her home to what is an important national role, but just removing her from the world stage." Chrétien wanted to make his call on the twenty-sixth or the twenty-seventh and immediately announce her acceptance. Risley and Arbour realized that "were she to indict Milosevic and then announce six hours later that 'I'm quitting now to go to the Supreme Court' it would look like some kind of conflict of interest, or that she had been pressured out, or that the indictment wouldn't really stand, that it had been political—that the NATO countries had told her to do this and then we're going to make you a Supreme Court justice." Risley concluded, "the Canadians were just crazy, they were thinking 'We have to get this done quickly' for some reason. It made no sense. They weren't thinking."

Arbour took the prime minister's call and accepted the offer of the Supreme Court appointment but insisted that it not be revealed until the following month. The Canadian Federal Cabinet Order in Council confirms that the appointment was approved but undisclosed on May 26, 1999, the day before Arbour's announcement of the Milosevic indictment.[57] Normally appointments are announced in the week they are made, with the prime minister publicly announcing Supreme Court appointments. In this case the official announcement was withheld for two weeks and reported in the press on June 11, 1999. When the press caught up with Arbour and asked about the implications of leaving the tribunal a year before the end of her term, she joked that she had actually done the work of four years in three. She then insisted that the ICT had developed a momentum that would not be stopped. There is monetary evidence for this conclusion.

Financial data reveal that annual UN operating funds for the tribunal had more than tripled from about thirty million to nearly one hundred million dollars during Arbour's tenure. This figure remained relatively stable for the next several years. In addition, annual voluntary U.S.

funding for dedicated projects at the tribunal increased from less than one to more than eight million dollars during Arbour's tenure.

Finally, when the percentage of total voluntary contributions from all countries is disaggregated by year, these contributions track in a lagged fashion the disaggregated yearly percentage of total arrested persons transferred to the tribunal. This pattern again illustrates how responsive contributing countries have been to the success of the tribunal in making arrests, especially during the Arbour years.[58] Arbour put it this way: "Arrest was the issue, and it was clear that if we got people arrested then everybody inside the tribunal would be busy. We would be starting to do what we were set up to do, the United Nations would have to continue to support us financially and politically, and that's when we arrived at the point of no return."

EMPOWERING LIBERAL LEGALISM

There is little doubt among those surrounding Louise Arbour that she possesses a genuine charismatic quality. In the more than one hundred interviews conducted at the tribunal, nearly everyone expressed admiration, from her closest co-workers to clerical staff and drivers. However, the most poignant expressions were from relatives and victims she encountered in her trips into the field. To pick only one example, a co-worker who accompanied her into a small village off the beaten path in Kosovo remarked about "just seeing the reaction of people to her and seeing how she was able to convey to them that she really did care about what had happened to them." Yet there is also skepticism about the significance of such charisma and the agency and accomplishment that can flow from it.

I began with the hopes of the political historian Gary Bass for the institutionalization of liberal legalism in international criminal tribunals. These hopes, however, were followed with his prediction that the history of the Hague tribunal would be "dispiriting" and that Arbour personally encouraged this fate by "jumping ship" to take up her Canadian Supreme Court appointment. The sociologists Meyer and Jepperson were even more pessimistic, arguing that the human rights agenda and its expression in transnational organizations such as the ICT are products of Anglo-American religious convictions that encourage unrealistic ideas about charisma and agency and result in loosely coupled systems with standardless, ineffectual results. The initial failure of the ICT to generate arrests and bring defendants to trial during the Goldstone years seemed to validate the early fears of these and other scholars.

Yet Richard McAdams's theory of primary and secondary norm enforcement based on status competition suggests a more optimistic set of possibilities. Sewell's theory of structural agency further suggests how resources and cultural schemas reinforce one another in ways that allow charisma and agency to produce enforcement of norms that derive from frameworks such as liberal legalism.[59] These contributions combine to suggest the possibility of legal empowerment, even in settings where norm enforcement is previously absent or sporadic. These contributions explain how institutions such as the ICT can become functioning realities with real-world, intended consequences. A goal of this chapter has been to open up the black box of agency and reveal more precisely how this can occur.

This chapter suggests that there are three important tactics of agency that can enable successful norm entrepreneurship. These tactics involve structural linkage, cultural legitimation, and temporal control.[60] Louise Arbour's began with the structural linkages she formed to obtain arrests for the ICT, gained momentum through the cultural schemas she used to legitimize this institution in the media, and then sustained this momentum through the temporal control she imposed on events surrounding the Milosevic indictment.

The crucial first instance of structural linkage and primary norm enforcement came with Louise Arbour's use of the secret indictment procedure and the first arrest based on this strategy in Vukovar. This arrest stimulated subsequent arrests by British and U.S. NATO forces based on similar secret indictments. The result was a more tightly coupled norm enforcement process in which British and American NATO troops took on necessary arrest roles. When France conspicuously refused this role, Arbour went to Paris and used her public voice to initiate a secondary norm enforcement process that ultimately shamed the French into active cooperation.

The success of Arbour's Paris media exposure encouraged her to publicly advocate an interconnected set of cultural schemas that further legitimated the coercive use of international criminal law to overcome the defense of national sovereignty in the "real-time" context of Kosovo. This mission reached a preliminary climax with Arbour's attempted border crossing at Racak, which was broadcast worldwide by the media. Although Arbour was denied entry to Kosovo, this rejection served to underline her assertion that the cultural schema of national sovereignty was a legal conceit used by Milosevic and others for protection against criminal prosecution and punishment. Arbour's success in gaining arrests and media exposure led in turn to the initiation and carefully timed confirmation and announcement of the Milosevic indictment. This indictment then was synchronized with the timing of Arbour's appointment to the Canadian Supreme Court.

There are at least six junctures in this account when Arbour engaged in explicit acts of agency that advanced the tribunal's normative goals: by authorizing the first arrest using a secret indictment, demanding that NATO forces make arrests based on these indictments, speaking out in Paris against French policies that threatened to undermine the tribunal, demanding access to Kosovo at Racak, securing the first indictment of a sitting head of state, and influencing the prime minister of Canada to reschedule her Supreme Court appointment. Yet agency and charisma have essential social as well individual components—and in this case, the Canadian aspect of Arbour's tenure at the tribunal was central to the agency she exercised. The difference between the Canadian and U.S. positions on national sovereignty and human security highlighted perhaps subtle but nonetheless significant divisions between these Anglo-American co-principals in their sponsorship and development of the ICT. This distinction gained importance and presented a choice of channels along which the principal-agent relationship involving the chief prosecutor of the tribunal could evolve.[61] In many ways, Arbour's agency at the ICT lay in knowing just when, and how, to call on members of the NATO alliance and the Western press—giving the issue of who is the "principal" and who is the "agent" a dialectical dimension.

Of course, the most visible of the instances of agency noted above involved the initiative taken by Arbour in the Milosevic indictment. The Clinton administration was ambivalent about indicting and prosecuting Milosevic, with strong voices in the administration still arguing that Milosevic could be manipulated to advantage in the peacemaking process, perhaps with the promise of an amnesty from prosecution. An official in the administration offered the following description, in an interview for this study, of a difference in judgment that was expressed even by Madeleine Albright on the eve of the Milosevic indictment: "One particular moment was the actual timing of the Milosevic indictment when people like Albright and others in the administration would say, 'Gosh, is this exactly the right time, May, 1999, in the middle of the Kosovo campaign, to further enrage this man with an indictment? We have to first defeat him on the battlefield and maybe this would make him more belligerent on the battlefield. . . . There was some angst in May about 'Is this exactly the right time to indict this fellow?'" Arbour responded to this problem by choosing not to ask representatives of the Clinton administration if the moment was right.

The U.S. general and NATO commander Wesley Clark also reported that right up to the May 27, 1999, announcement of the Milosevic indictment, "some in the Pentagon and the White House were unhappy about this." He explained their concern was that "an indictment on war crimes charges would rule out the possibility of conducting direct negotiations with Milosevic."[62] When Christiane Amanpour asked Arbour about this on the day of the indictment, she answered that justice should take priority over politics, rather than the reverse, and that in any case Milosevic was demonstrated by the indictment to be a dubious person with whom to reach political agreements.[63] By initiating the indictment, Arbour in effect "called the bluff" of the American commitment to international humanitarian law and the tribunal.

The account presented in this chapter provides a detailed analysis of how norms relating to international criminal law were successfully instituted and implemented at the Hague tribunal, through interconnected processes of structural linkage, cultural legitimation, and temporal control. Each of these mechanisms, however, also involves a further nuance that is central to successful norm entrepreneurship—namely, that a charismatic individual rarely if ever acts alone but rather acts in interaction with others. In particular, although the decision to *initiate* the indictment of Milosevic lay with Arbour, the secretary-general of the UN, Kofi Annan, also had input into (which is different from control of) the process, along with the leaders of the NATO nations who also had committed themselves to supporting the tribunal. The authority that backed Arbour's agency derived from the process of consultation she pursued in seeking internal and external support for the indictment. Her control over the timing of this process, including the dating of her signing of the initial indictment, established a turning point that would have been difficult to reverse. Yet without the interactive involvement of others that stretched back to the first arrest on a secret indictment and that included essential figures on her staff as well as beyond the tribunal, Arbour's agency could not have prevailed. Louise Arbour's charisma was socially organized and used dialectical authorization and teamwork to make it a productive source of agency.

CHAPTER FIVE

The Srebrenica Ghost Team

The office of Jean-René Ruez was a scene of singular purpose. Next to his desk was a chart identifying more than thirty burial sites with the bodies of thousands of persons executed at Srebrenica. Ruez explained that the vertical axis of the chart gave the location of the grave, while the horizontal axis recorded the evidence each contained: "bodies, body parts, documents, chemical and human residues, bullets, shell casings, blindfolds, ligatures, watches." Ruez paused to light another cigarette and then pointed to a framed picture of a Seiko wristwatch.

The watches tell the story of when time stopped for victims of Srebrenica. Ruez learned from the manufacturer that the watches keep time for twenty-four to thirty-six hours after their movement ceases. This information was joined with the numbered day of the month on the watches to estimate the timing of executions. This is one of the ways in which the evidence collected from the exhumations allowed the victims of Srebrenica to speak from the silence of their graves.

Jean-René Ruez has the brooding intensity of actors such as Steve McQueen and Jean-Paul Belmondo. He was still in his mid-thirties when he arrived at the tribunal from France. Srebrenica changed his life. Today he has a dark and ironic wit, an obvious and quick intelligence, and an artistic flare that may seem surprising in a police investigator. A colleague remembered seeing him before Srebrenica took over his life and thinking, " 'Who is this happy kid in the hallways?' I wanted to know who he was."

Ruez was a police superintendent for ten years and has a master's degree in law. His family is German as well as French; he speaks German, and this was a source of his early interest in war crimes. We saw in the previous chapter that France had a troubled relationship with the tribunal, and Jean-René also had his difficulties during his work with its prosecutor's office.

He arrived in the spring of 1995. When he received my survey four years later, he phoned from The Hague to say he had things he wanted to report in person. We met several times, and the interviews lasted for hours.

Louise Arbour recalled Ruez as "an amazingly engaging guy, passionate about his work, extremely knowledgeable." She also said working with him was challenging. "If anybody or anything stands between him and advancing the work," she remarked, "he will denounce it." Arbour was pleased to have Ruez lead the Srebrenica investigation, adding, "I had so much confidence in his integrity." Yet even as the appreciation of him and his working conditions improved during Arbour's tenure, Ruez had trouble sleeping, and the combination of anger and stress was devastating to his health.

Ruez had extraordinarily strong ties to the members of the Srebrenica investigation team that he led for more than five years. But his experience clearly also illustrates how embedded in transnational organizational arrangements the charismatic agency of lower- and higher-level leadership figures can be at the tribunal.[1] His story is an account of organizational and transnational intrigue as well as cooperation, for Ruez quickly discovered that without internal and external ties there could be no effective Srebrenica investigation.[2]

THE GHOST TEAM

The massacre at Srebrenica began in mid-July 1995, just as the tribunal was issuing its first indictment against Karadzic and Mladic. The timing of the massacre was an unmistakable reminder of how little thought the Bosnian Serb leadership gave to the ICT. Jean-René Ruez already was in Srebrenica collecting preliminary evidence within days of the killings. In Arbour's terms, this was real-time investigation work, even though the trial of General Radislav Krstic would not begin for nearly another five years.

Dutch soldiers had been unsuccessful in monitoring Srebrenica as a UN "safe area," while a French commander who had authority over NATO planes had failed to authorize air support. It was against this backdrop that the tribunal's Srebrenica investigation was headed by a Dutch team leader, with the newly arrived French investigator, Ruez, as his subordinate. It was never an effective working relationship, but rather a short-lived example of a tribunal team that had no chemistry from the start.

Ruez knew how important the Srebrenica massacre was, but he could not get his Dutch superior to assign anyone else to work with him on the case. He felt that his superior was palmed off on the tribunal by the Dutch police, saying, "They found a golden cage for him here." Ruez was unable even to get proper office space. In October 1995, the Dutch government issued a report on the Srebrenica massacre that was widely criticized as "an exercise in obfuscation."[3] Ruez complained that for months he was unable to access an English-language translation of the report. He finally located the report in a filing cabinet. Ruez remained without much assistance or space until his Dutch superior left the tribunal more than a year later.

Yet there were also early signs of transgovernmental support for the tribunal and its Srebrenica investigation. Surviving refugees from Srebrenica fled to Tuzla, where Bosnian Muslim police began taking witness statements that were passed on to Ruez. He also began his own interviews. Within weeks of the massacre, the U.S. assistant secretary of state, John Shattuck, traveled to Tuzla and met with survivors. Based on these accounts, the U.S. State Department asked the CIA to begin scanning aerial photographs for evidence.[4]

The CIA search produced preliminary results on August 3. Photos from the previous July 13 showed several hundred prisoners gathered on a soccer field near Srebrenica. The prisoners had disappeared from photos taken several days later, and there was evidence of freshly moved soil nearby. These photos were revealed to the UN Security Council on August 10.

The Serbs finally were driven by NATO bombing as well as losses on the ground to negotiations leading to the Dayton Accords in November 1995. Worried that the Dayton Accords might provide amnesties for the Bosnian Serb leadership, Goldstone worked with Blewitt to push through a new indictment of Karadzic and Mladic for Srebrenica. Blewitt remarked, "We wanted to make sure that we were going to be part of the Dayton solution."[5] The accords put little pressure on NATO forces to arrest indicted war criminals, but they at least guaranteed the continued role of the tribunal and the prosecution of war crimes as a recognized part of official Balkans policy.

Goldstone hastily traveled to Washington for meetings on November 15 and 16. A letter he had written complaining about delays in getting intelligence information was leaked to the *Washington Post*.[6] David Scheffer, the US ambassador for war crimes, arranged appointments for Goldstone, including one with the CIA director, John Deutch, who was outraged by Goldstone's letter. Scheffer deflected this issue, and the results of the meeting included two clear signs of progress: the establishment of a secure telephone link between Washington and

The Hague and the immediate expansion of a CIA unit to process requests from the tribunal. Goldstone said simply, "I got everything I was seeking."

The U.S. embassy in The Hague became the transfer point for Ruez and others at the tribunal to receive crucial information. Scheffer described how "a team of experts would fly over to The Hague and . . . present the summary to them so that there could be some discussion. Eventually a great deal of information was made available to the tribunal, especially aerial imagery. . . . Sometimes we gave them so much that it would pile up at the U.S. embassy in The Hague, where it was archived and the tribunal had access to it." This transfer of intelligence may have been Goldstone's greatest contribution to the Srebrenica investigation.

When Shattuck returned to the area of the massacre in January 1996, he went with Ruez to the Kravica warehouse where men had been taken to be executed. Hand grenades had been tossed into the warehouse while Serb soldiers had sprayed the building with machine gun bullets. David Rohde wrote that "bodies were pulverized. Blood and crimson bits of flesh were spattered across the gray cinder-block walls."[7] Six months later, while Shattuck roamed the site, Ruez discreetly scraped blood samples from the walls and placed them into a film canister. Shattuck used the opportunity to call for the exhumation of mass graves adjoining the site.

Ruez spent the early period of the investigation in Tuzla establishing contact with the local Muslim police and conducting interviews in the big tent city that was constructed for the thousands of refugees at a UN air base. Working alongside Ruez was a young crime analyst, Stefanie Frease, whose mother's parents were Serb and Croatian. "When the war broke out," Stefanie recalled, "I just knew instinctively that was where I should be." After this brief initial time in Tuzla, however, she was reassigned to document work back at the tribunal.

By January of the new year, boxes of witness statements collected by the Bosnian Muslim police were accumulating at the tribunal. Ruez continued to complain about the lack of attention being paid at the tribunal to the Srebrenica massacre. He ran into Frease in the hallway of the OTP and asked what she was doing now. After hearing about her document project, Ruez insisted with deadpan sarcasm, "I think Srebrenica is a little more important." Frease convinced John Ralston, who was now in charge of investigations, to assign her to the case. This meant that there were now two people to investigate a massacre of thousands.[8] Ruez and Frease called their pairing "the ghost team."

THE TEAM EXPERIENCE

The ghost team added several members and over time shared a kind of field experience, "on mission," that also motivated and sustained many other employees in the office of the prosecutor, developing long-term organizational commitments to this work and the transnational field of humanitarian law. This kind of commitment was suggested in the finding from the OTP survey discussed in chapter 3 that work as a member of an investigation or trial team is the most prominent source of satisfaction at the tribunal. Members of the Srebrenica ghost team clearly developed intense commitments to their work and to one another.

Thus there is a shared sense of purpose that comes out of the kind of work that Jean-René Ruez and Stefanie Frease, among many others, do as members of teams at the tribunal. This shared purpose is further reflected in responses to six closely correlated items among the sources of work satisfaction measured in the OTP survey. These involve teamwork and the importance attached to this work and connected measures involving the people the respondents help and the significance they attach to their efforts, as well as feelings of independence and of doing public service. These items form a hierarchical, second-order factor model displayed in the appendix that is reflective of a collective sense of purpose.[9]

This model is the basis of a scale that can be further incorporated into a causal model that is also presented in the appendix. The purpose of the model is to document the ways going on mission, as described in several forms in this chapter by ghost team members, can be a part of an "alternation experience" that builds a sense of shared team purpose and intense as well as long-term feelings of work commitment. In addition to these features, this model also includes measures of having been "on mission" in the Balkans in the past year, as well as national background, type of work, and the total number of weekday, night, and weekend hours the respondents reported working in an average week. Anglo-Americans, lawyers, and investigators at the OTP were most likely among respondents to have gone "on mission" during the past year in the Balkans.

As noted in earlier chapters, alternation experiences are changes of perspective that grow out of life transitions. Alternation experiences can be as common as advancing from high school to college, moving from school to work, and making a career change[10] or as potentially unique as participating in a social or political movement.[11] Some alternations can emerge as key turning points in life and thereby produce powerful and enduring changes.[12] Arbour herself had this kind of turning-point field experience (described in the previous chapter), and she made it an organizational priority during the Kosovo period to get as many OTP employees into the field "on mission," as possible. The causal model estimated with regression equations in the appendix suggests that the experience of going into the field for the tribunal in the Balkans had an alternation effect on the work commitment of many OTP employees.

About two-thirds (67 percent) of the OTP respondents reported that they had been on mission in the Balkans in the past year. The model presented in the appendix indicates that having been on mission is a significant and relatively strong predictor of developing a sense of shared purpose at the tribunal, and that this in turn leads to longer work hours and a commitment to future work in this field. The breadth and intensity of this work commitment at the tribunal is reflected by the fact that more than half (51.7 percent) of the surveyed employees report that they work on average more than fifty hours a week. Furthermore, nearly half (42.2 percent) indicate they expect their work in this field to still be *very* important to them in ten years, with most of the remaining half (47.7 percent) also indicating that they believe this work will continue to be important to them in the future. It seems clear that among the most committed employees in the OTP are those who have developed a shared sense of purpose through team experiences.

This chapter further illustrates with the example of the ghost team and the Srebrenica investigation how internal team ties at the ICT and linkages to external governmental and nongovernmental organizations are overlapping and reinforcing factors in the formation of a transnational field of international humanitarian law. A partial and summary picture of how this happened in the Srebrenica investigation is provided in figure 5.1. This figure portrays the leadership hierarchy at the ICT in squares, the members of the investigation team in circles, and external organizations in triangles. The remainder of this chapter describes how these linkages emerged and developed during the Srebrenica investigation, which led to the first trial of a genocide charge at the tribunal.

A PLEA FOR INFORMATION

In early March 1996, Drazen Erdemovic had surfaced in Belgrade and confessed to his role in the Srebrenica massacre. General Mladic was still insisting at this time that no massacre had occurred. This denial became more difficult to sustain when Erdemovic described an eight-man execution squad in which he personally shot and killed seventy Muslims at the farm site near Srebrenica. He reported that more than twelve hundred Muslim men were executed around him and that bull-dozers plowed the bodies under a light covering of topsoil.

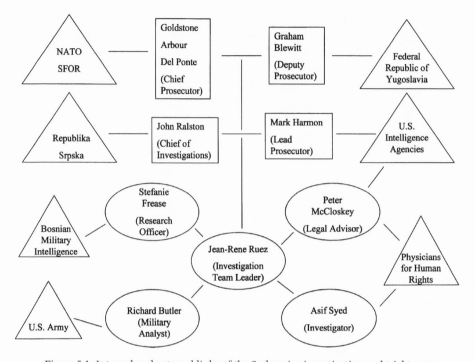

Figure 5.1. Internal and external links of the Srebrenica investigation and trial teams

It soon became apparent that Erdemovic was an invaluable eyewitness. He not only had participated in the shooting deaths, he also had witnessed a mass execution in a nearby warehouse and could locate mass burial sites and describe the structure of the killing operations. These were the ingredients for a plea bargain.

Much has been written in the American criminal justice literature about plea bargaining as a tool to build cases in areas of organized criminal activity, especially with regard to drugs and white-collar crime.[13] Yet plea bargaining is not as well accepted in other jurisdictions, it is not mentioned in the tribunal statute, and Justice Robert Jackson explicitly rejected plea bargaining at the Nuremberg trial.

Nonetheless, Jean-René Ruez was already using the information Erdemovic was providing to help launch the exhumation process, to confirm details of how the massacre unfolded, and to chart the organization and chain of command that led to the massacre. Richard Goldstone, like his predecessor Jackson, resisted the idea of rewarding such cooperation with a plea bargain. If Erdemovic was going to plead guilty, he insisted, it would be to an indictment that included the charge of a crime against humanity. Goldstone maintained that "it wasn't a plea bargain in the American sense. . . . He was charged with the most serious crimes to which he confessed. There was no bargain." Erde-movic continued to be cooperative, and Ruez developed an effective relationship with him. Stefanie Frease remarked that "Jean-René was brilliant with him. . . . He knows his business very well and he is able to identify with people. . . . Some of it was maybe chemistry as well."

Erdemovic's moving and effective appearance at the in absentia Karadzic and Mladic hearing was described in chapter 3, and his "vol-untary, brave, and public testimony" was duly noted at his sentencing hearing in late November 1996. He was described as "remorseful" and note was made of his cooperation with Ruez and the OTP lawyers. A sentence of ten years' imprisonment was imposed for his confessed crimes against humanity—one-quarter of the potential exposure un-der such charges. Louise Arbour, now the chief prosecutor, took the opportunity to say that she regarded the sentence as a message: "It should send a very strong signal that the court is very fair and balanced and that the prosecutor will support the expression of remorse and the coming forward of those who wish to cooperate." Still, Erdemovic was visibly disturbed by the sentence, and although his lawyer was careful to say he was not displeased, he also said that he would file an appeal.[14]

The appeal was filed just before Christmas, and the following fall the appeals chamber announced a decision that Erdemovic was "not sufficiently informed" about the "meaning and consequences" of his earlier guilty plea and allowed him to plead guilty to war crimes instead of crimes against humanity.[15] The appeals court was signaling this as an opportunity for Erdemovic to receive further compensation for his cooperation by pleading to a lesser charge and reduced sentence, and he did so.

The resulting judgment now took explicit notice that a plea bargain agreement had been reached between the prosecution and defense in this case, for the first time in the history of the tribunal. In addition, the appeals chamber outdid the prosecution's and defense's recommenda-tion of a seven-year sentence by imposing a sentence of five years, with credit for two years of time already served in detention. The message taken by one observer was "Come forward, confess your crimes, coop-erate with the prosecutor—all will be taken into consideration."[16] It was a message that reflected a new level of cooperation not only between a defendant and the prosecution but also between the prosecution and the sentencing judges. This internal linkage was essential in reward-ing Erdemovic for the information about burial sites that could now be used in developing linkages with external state and nonstate agencies and actors.

BRINGING OUT THE DEAD

Ruez called 1996 "the year of finding the crime scenes." He recalled the spring and summer as a blur of feverish activity, "finding the graves, continuing to interview people, . . . finding the locations that the people were talking about and finding the graves." His consuming legal fear was that "without bodies, no crime." Ruez was haunted by the insistence of Mladic that no massacre had occurred.

The process of finding the first grave sites and exhuming the bodies was much more challenging than it would later appear in the newspapers. Without Erdemovic, finding a specific site from CIA aerial photos was like looking for the proverbial needle in a haystack. As Ruez put it, "You might have all the evidence in the picture, you just don't know where to look." Forming an effective working relationship with the CIA personnel required giving them enough information to narrow the search.

For example, a survivor of the massacre at the Grbovci school told Ruez there were two important burial sites on each side of a railroad track. Ruez had to first travel to the area and then find the site from the verbal description. "The only thing we could do with [him as] the witness was narrow down the area where he believed the execution happened by a ground search." This search was made more complicated and threatening by the lack of IFOR protection, the hostility of Serbians residing in the area, and concerns about land mines. An IFOR commander complained, "They were very difficult to work with, because they were not well coordinated in their efforts. They didn't know exactly where they wanted to go, they wanted to kind of explore. They would hear a rumor and suddenly decide they wanted to go check out an area."[17] In short, the IFOR leadership regarded Ruez and his colleagues as a pain to work with.

Of course, Ruez had an interest in knowing where he was going as well. After he located the general site that Erdemovic described, he communicated this more precise information to the CIA. Some of the initial results included remarkably precise pictures of the Pilice massacre site taken from U2 spy planes that had flown over Bosnia on July 17, 1995. The photographs showed bodies spread over a field.[18] "The site matched the description that the witness told us," Ruez noted, "how the bodies are lined up, and the bodies are still visible in these photographs." However, this was only the first step. Before IFOR would provide security to begin digging, it was necessary to determine as exactly as possible where these bodies were buried.

The process required moving between the eyewitness accounts of Erdemovic and others and the CIA photos. Ruez also persuaded survivors to go back to identify execution sites. Frease explained the challenge of getting the survivors to do this: "It was extremely powerful and it took persuasion. . . . I mean, imagine, they're going back into enemy territory—it's still enemy territory to them—persuading them to go in there—to go to the place where they were supposed to die."

It was an iterative, back-and-forth process. "We had witnesses who had walked by and smelled the mass grave a day or two after it had been dug. 'Where is it?' 'It's up. . . .' You'd try once; can't find it. We'd go back to the witness. We'd drive by, take videos, reconstruct the situation, and then weed through the area and would find it." Some of the match-ups of witness accounts and aerial photos provided remarkable cross-validations. Frease described an important match-up: "We had a witness who talked about being at the Kravica warehouse and who drew a sketch . . . of the warehouse complex and how the buses came around and that they parked in front and there was an aerial image of exactly his sketch." They were making progress, but there also were puzzling aspects of what they were finding.

HIDING THE BODIES

Ruez now began to piece together what happened after the massacre. There were four major execution sites with mass burial pits located nearby, showing that the victims were "killed and buried on the spot." Several months later, in the fall of 1995, it became apparent to the Serb military that there was going to be an agreement reached at Dayton, and they began to worry about the ease of finding the poorly disguised burial sites.

At the Dayton talks, Richard Holbrooke placed pressure on Milosevic to support John Shattuck's trips into Republika Srpska. "A few days later, this request produced a strange sight: Milosevic's special military security forces escorting Shattuck into Banja Luka, which no American official had visited in several years, as he sought access to mass grave sites of massacres committed by Serbs."[19] A new cat and mouse game was beginning that involved the missing Muslim men of Srebrenica.

The Serb military had responded to the threat of looming exhumations by organizing a large-scale reburial operation. Ruez put it starkly: "The excavators came and dug up all the dead bodies." Some of the first evidence of this operation was discovered from aerial photos taken on September 29, 1995, showing heavy equipment being used at the Pilice farm site, where Erdemovic had said one of the mass executions had occurred. In late October, more digging was observed. The operation was organized with new, smaller, and more distant graves dug for the reburial of the bodies. Ruez eventually discovered about thirty secondary sites. Many of the reburials were done under the cover of night, and they left bodies, in whole and in part, behind. In addition, they often moved incriminating evidence along with the bodies. For example, one execution site was located near a glass factory, and identifiable pieces of glass were moved with the bodies to the secondary site.

Ruez made the telling point that the reburials were incriminating in additional ways, for example, in the disregard they showed not only for the dead but also for the living who were exposed to this operation.

> Killing the people in the way they killed them, that's one thing. But then disposing of their bodies like trash—I think this is a crime on top of a crime. The disturbance of the graves is an unbelievable crime. Moving the bodies is an incredible thing. A great deal of calculation was involved. . . . You have to imagine these dozens of trucks carrying tons of dead people. The bodies were rotting. This went on for two to three months. Going through towns where people must have smelled the dead bodies. Seeing the limbs sticking out. You have things falling out of the trucks. Just completely crazy. . . . All of this is a part of the crime. . . . This was a further crime against humanity in the sense that it was a crime against everyone who became aware of it.

It was only as these primary and secondary grave sites were discovered and exhumed that it became possible to confirm the stories of the Srebrenica massacre. The chief of investigations, John Ralston, observed, "If we hadn't dug up thousands of bodies in Srebrenica, then the revisionists would be in there saying, 'Well, they weren't really killed, they're just missing.' "

The importance of the relationship that Ruez established with Drazen Erdemovic was recognized and reinforced by the plea agreement and the sentencing decision of the appeals chamber. This linkage within the tribunal was an essential step toward establishing following linkages with outside agencies who could undertake the exhumations of the bodies. Influential individuals, especially John Shattuck as a U.S. State Department representative, used their international political capital outside the tribunal to champion this cause. No one had anticipated the scale and cost of the exhumations, and they could not have begun without a wide-ranging transnational, governmental, and organizational effort that was linked to the tribunal's ghost team, which at this point still had only two members.

RAISING THE DEAD

The planning of the exhumations began in April 1996, but the digging did not begin until July. As they went into the field in the spring to locate sites, Ruez was assigned one more team member, Asif Syed, who came from Pakistan and had experience as a human rights police officer in Africa. Pakistan was an early supporter of the tribunal, and Syed was one of the first appointees. When things did not work out well on his first team assignment, Syed requested a change. He was reassigned to work with Ruez, who reported that he was not told this for the first three months. However, Syed then became an essential part of the team.

The ghost team was now a threesome, the absolute minimum needed to maintain an essential ongoing presence at the exhumation sites. At least one member of the team had to always be at the exhumation to maintain the "chain of custody" of the evidence and represent the tribunal. Another team member had to be doing the day-to-day work back in The Hague. Ruez explained that this meant "in reality you have to have three people to make sure you can cover these rotations."

Before the exhumations could begin they had to deal with the continuing problem of inadequate security. Syed described the vulnerability the team sensed. Serbians now fully occupied the area that they had ethnically cleansed. "They know what's happening there—what *had* happened there and what is happening now." Land mines were a major concern. Ruez grimly noted that he did not want to return to his wife and child with missing limbs and that he felt a responsibility for all who worked on the exhumations. "I'm a reserve officer in my country," he explained. "I know . . . what kinds of injury they create. . . . You generally regret not being dead after that." Goldstone, Scheffer, and others pushed hard to get the demining done.

In July Ruez was finally able to lead the team to the initial sites he had identified. The final preparation involved driving a heavy Y-shaped British vehicle over the site to set off and divert the explosion of any mines that had been missed. As the last sweep was completed the entourage arrived with three armored personnel carriers at the front and back and a convoy of six Land Rovers in between. Heavily armed soldiers were placed in the surrounding forest by IFOR. "I don't know how many soldiers were in those woods," a team member remarked, "but I know that if you went for a piss, some American serviceman would pop his head out and say, 'Don't piss over here, please.'"

The site was cordoned off with yellow tape. The investigators began by poking a five-foot steel probe into the soggy soil. They sniffed the end for the stench of decaying bodies. Frease called this their "scratch and sniff test." During this first summer, four sites were excavated in Bosnia (Cerska, Nova Kasaba, Lazete, and Pilice) and one in Croatia (Ovcara).

The bodies were placed in a refrigerated container and taken to a makeshift morgue in Kalesija to establish causes of death. Overall, 450

bodies were recovered by the Bosnian operation in 1996.[20] The farm
site that Erdemovic had described was one of the early exhumations
of that summer. Rainstorms overwhelmed the work on this site and
turned the grave into a muddy swimming pool from which the water
had to be pumped daily. The grave itself was about one-third of a foot-
ball field long, ten yards wide, and about fifteen feet deep. The backhoe
used in the digging constantly threatened to fall on the workers, and at
one point a wall of the grave collapsed. "And then there were the bodies," Elizabeth Neuffer observed from the grave side, "gelatinous, ooz-
ing corpses, hardly skeletalized at all." The workers found themselves
slipping and sliding among the bodies they were trying desperately to
preserve: in "mud to their knees, it was difficult to discern where one
body ended and another began."[21]

Clint Williamson was simultaneously leading the exhumation of the
Vukovar hospital massacre victims at the Ovcara farm site in Croatia.
The two hundred bodies recovered there provided corroboration for the
sealed indictment and arrest of Dokmanovic described in chapter 4.
Arbour's prosecutorial strategy was gaining momentum. As fall set in
and the exhumation season was coming to a close, however, the primary sites identified by Erdemovic and other witnesses were largely
exhausted. The team would next have to look for the secondary sites
where bodies were reburied.

FINDING MORE BODIES

Peter McCloskey joined the tribunal staff at about the time Louise Arbour became prosecutor in the fall of 1996. McCloskey was in his mid-
forties and had been working for more than a decade in the U.S. Department of Justice's civil rights division with Alan Tieger and Mark
Harmon. Like Harmon, McCloskey had grown up in southern California. His father served for ten years in the U.S. Congress and in 1972
challenged Richard Nixon for the presidential nomination, later urging
Nixon's resignation during Watergate. While at the Department of Justice, Peter had supervised civil rights investigations in Mississippi.

McCloskey was drawn to the importance of the Srebrenica case and
was comfortable mixing his legal background with the investigative
task. He instinctively liked Ruez. There were neither the ego problems
nor the defensiveness that sometimes complicated collaborations of investigators with lawyers on investigation teams. McCloskey said, "I had
a team leader and investigator that was very open to having me there,
and while there's always a bit of a tension, it worked out very posi-
tively." He confirmed that Ruez was "a very impressive, charismatic,
magnetic figure."

By the fall of 1997, Ruez and Frease had worked out a routine for finding the grave sites, and Peter McCloskey now added his experience as a lawyer. He recalled, "We would go over to the embassy, we'd review the photographs, we'd see where it was on the map." The challenge was that although they could view the aerial photographs at the embassy in The Hague, they could not take the photos away with them. "So we'd get a sketch of the disturbed area, and the roads and the houses nearby, and Jean-René is a pretty good artist, so his sketches were fairly accurate, and then we'd have a map grid coordinate, down to . . . maybe 25 yards of accuracy."

The ghost team would then take their maps and sketches to the Srebrenica crime scenes. "We'd have the map and we'd have the point on the map where the grave was believed to be, and we'd have this little sketch, and we'd get in the truck and we'd drive out." McCloskey's job as legal advisor was "to make sure they were doing it the way it would be appropriate for trial."

There originally had been five principal graves. The bodies were then relocated to about thirty smaller graves spread throughout the countryside. The aerial photos steadily increased the team's enumeration of the graves and their knowledge of each grave's history. "Sometimes we could see [in the photos] the actual holes sitting there waiting to be filled, sometimes we'd come in a couple of days later [with the photos] and see the dirt had been filled in . . . that was important because we didn't have any witnesses for the trial that could talk to us about that," McCloskey explained. In other cases it was the evidence found in the grave that made the connection, "artifacts in the grave that helped us tie it to a particular incident, Dutch newspapers, Srebrenica letters." Gradually the pieces fit together, "and then we would have these photographs that show exactly when these things were created, or within a time frame of days. So that's why these [photos] were so valuable."

The IFOR leadership was becoming more cooperative in providing security, but not without occasional prodding. A British member of the forensic team appreciatively recalled how Jean-René could make his presence felt. "One day the security decided that they weren't going to cover us. There was a problem. And he goes 'strange' at some five star general, poof, as only JR could. Whereas we might say, 'Can I make an appointment for a week next Thursday?' JR said, 'I've got 10 guys sitting there and this is costing so and so and your country's provided all this bloody money, why aren't your men out there?' And four hours later we've got our security back! So he was right. Sometimes you need JR's approach."

THE GHOSTLY SCIENCE

Notwithstanding the progress made on exhumations in 1996, it was still possible to question whether the time, money, and effort were well spent. The bodies necessary to make the most basic case were still mostly in the ground. Before the expense of further exhumations could be justified in 1997, Ruez had make to make the case for them: "You had to identify a lot of sites and then build an argument for the exhumations taking place." Furthermore, as the plans went forward, a new challenge emerged. The chief pathologist at the morgue had modified some statements on the reports made at the burial sites. "The chief pathologist at the time was a kind of guy who never believed this thing would one day see the courtroom and took it upon himself to just change some of the causes of death without ever asking the people who were doing the autopsies."

There were additional complaints about procedures used at the exhumation sites. There were charges that some bodies and their parts had been misidentified. It is difficult to doubt this, since despite extraordinary efforts to sort out the bodies, as recently as March 2001 there were still 694 body bags in the morgue containing parts of two or more people.[22] "There were allegations that evidence was compromised," Graham Blewitt conceded, "and we didn't know what the truth was."[23] He concluded that an investigation could remove these doubts. A result was that Peter McCloskey was assigned the tedious task of making certain that every pathology report from the first year of exhumations was complete and authentic. As Ruez put it, McCloskey spent much of 1997 "revisiting every single pathologist wherever they were on the planet," to have them all reexamine their reports and confirm or modify them so that they were correct. A result of these problems was that only seventy bodies were exhumed in the summer of 1997.[24]

Perhaps it was some compensation, albeit belated, that Ruez was formally named the team leader for the Srebrenica investigation in 1997. Frease had to push Ruez to insist on being named team leader: "I talked to him a lot about getting his butt in line and in gear and getting the job." Finally Ruez had the recognition of the title team leader, which was descriptive but also meant far more than its organizational rank and salary implied.

SEARCHING AND SEIZING EVIDENCE

The opportunity emerged in the winter of 1998 to take another major step. Jean-René Ruez was intensely frustrated that the exhumations had not progressed in the area of Srebrenica, but he also sensed that this lack of progress had led the Bosnian Serb military to let down their guard.

There was reason to think that well-executed search-and-seizure operations could produce uniquely useful information. The targets were Bosnian Serb brigade headquarters in Zvornik and Bratunac.

This phase of the investigation involved tracing the logistical work and chain of command from the ground-level operations, already exposed by Erdemovic, up through the as-yet-unexposed hierarchy of authorities responsible for the planning, preparation, and execution of the massacre. The operation again involved transgovernmentalism, but now of a more strategic and complicated kind associated with a search-and-seizure operation in hostile territory. This required the enforced acquiescence of Bosnian Serb authorities in the Banja Luka area, as well as protection from UN and NATO forces (SFOR).

Stefanie Frease played a crucial internal bridging role between tribunal teams in launching this initiative.[25] She had heard in the hallways that a search-and-seizure operation was being planned for Banja Luka. "I went back to our guys . . . and I said, 'Why aren't we doing this?' " The Srebrenica investigation required information about the planning and chain of command that made this massive operation possible, and this information was likely in the brigade headquarter files. Frease knew that the Banja Luka operation would require a significant number of experienced professionals. She explained that "we piggy-backed on to that one [the Banja Luka operation] because . . . you need people who know the subject matter, you need people who know the language, you need to come up with a procedure for how you are going to process all the material. You have to know what you're looking for . . . and so we assembled a big group of people."

The overall operation was overseen by John Ralston. Investigations at the tribunal were organized around eleven teams, each with a leader, who with two or three other leaders then reported to investigation commanders, who in turn reported to the chief of investigations. Ralston had worked with Graham Blewitt for five years on war crimes in Australia and had risen through the investigation hierarchy to the level of chief before leaving soon after Carla Del Ponte became chief prosecutor. He spoke sparingly and with a reserve that understated his hard-nosed determination.

Ralston had great respect for Ruez and McCloskey, noting that when the investigation teams work best "the team leader and the legal advisor are sort of joined at the head." Ralston recognized that Ruez was a dynamic leader and emphasized that he had carefully picked McCloskey to work with him. Frease played the bridging role between Ruez, McCloskey, and Ralston, a point that Ralston seemed to recognize when he again emphasized, "I never had a lot of people I could put in there, so we made sure everybody we did put in there was excellent and . . . they all clicked pretty well." Ralston continued by stressing the selflessness of McCloskey as an experienced lawyer in a long-term investigation. "For the first couple of years Peter was here, he was never in court. He didn't have anybody charged, there was an investigation cooking, he was heavily involved in the investigation and that's what we wanted. That changed when Krstic got arrested." The search-and-seizure operation was a key to locating General Radislav Krstic as a key target in the Srebrenica investigation.

The first operation was orchestrated by Ralston for the tribunal in 1997 in Prejidor, and Banja Luka came about ten months later, in February 1998. The Srebrenica team's searches and seizures were conducted in Zvornik and Bratunac about a week after the Banja Luca operations. In each instance the plan was to send a representative of the tribunal with authorizing documents to a high-level authority, such as the office of the president and the ministries of justice and defense of Republika Srpska, immediately before the tribunal team went to the site. Two members of the team, the leader and the legal advisor, entered the site first and negotiated access on the basis of a warrant from the tribunal. If access was refused or (more often) delayed, the person in charge locally was asked to call the higher-level authority. Ralston recalled saying on at least one occasion, "I suggest you ring your president." The office of the high representative of the UN mission in Bosnia as well applied political pressure to secure cooperation.

Ralston and his teams gained access to all the sites they pursued in Bosnia: "We sought and got cooperation in each of the locations, although it took some negotiation." The emphasis was on a strategic use of authority, force, and speed. "We had escort forces providing backup and ensuring a secure environment for us to conduct the missions—we seized the materials and came out." An exhibits officer was appointed in each room searched in each site. Each item of evidence was taken to the officer; "he logs it, bags it, tags it, and then he's got custody of it until you actually get it to secure premises." The documents were taken away by the truckload, with Ralston estimating that as much as half of the evidence connected to charges against General Krstic in the Srebrenica case came from the search-and-seizure operations.

Frease recalled a specific instance when they found the exact kind of document needed by the military analyst on the team, Rick Butler. Butler was seconded from the American military. Normally Butler was the most closed-lipped participant in the entire Srebrenica undertaking. Ralston wanted Butler as a part of the operation because he knew exactly the documents required for his military analysis, but Ralston was also concerned about someone inexperienced in this kind of operation "drawing attention to what it is you're looking for." Just as Ralston feared, Butler was the one who lost his customary detachment when he found exactly what he was seeking in the Bratunac military brigade office, summarizing his gleeful surprise with a very audible "Bingo!" Frease recalled saying, "Rick, could you not say bingo when you find something good, you know, we're trying to be discreet."

Ruez was certain that the Serbs had hidden or destroyed all the most obvious documentary evidence before their arrival. However, he also observed that "we found all our golden nuggets in departments where they never thought we would find things." These units included the engineering department that maintained log books recording the allocation of fuel and movements of security personnel, which revealed, for example, that "the day before they installed these people in the detention sites, you have the movement of all these guys going to these sites." This information also cross-validated the investigation team's identification of the detention and execution sites and confirmed that the selection and use of these sites was planned in advance. Ruez surmised, "They didn't know what they needed to hide."

He emphasized that "before this [operation] we . . . had all the material that enabled us to reconstruct the events through the eyes of the victims, but not through the actions of the perpetrators, and the two should be overlaid." This was the difference between knowing of the crimes and knowing who at the higher levels planned, prepared, and executed them. With only the victim reports, "you have a good reconstruction of what happened but you don't know who did it." The search-and-seizure operation altogether trucked away more than thirty thousand documents from Zvornik and Bratunac, including Butler's prize evidence.

INTERPRETING THE INTERCEPT EVIDENCE

Stefanie Frease took a particular interest in the interception of radio and telephone communications. Her language skills and cultural background in the Balkans stirred her interest in what the Serbian military figures were saying in their communications. The intercepts captured "the conversations of what was happening . . . [on] those days, and that kind of evidence was extraordinary." As the case progressed, her interest in the intercepts kept increasing, "so I wanted to take it up—I wanted the project."

When she began to work on the intercepted communications, she confirmed for herself how unusual and challenging it would be to develop this form of transgovernmental cooperation. In her words, these intercepts were "the crown jewels" of the Bosnian Muslim intelligence operations. Frease had to coax the Bosnian authorities into releasing the intercepts. Ruez saw the resistance as involving a longer view of the potential threat they could later pose. He noted that "these people were victims. In another investigation they could be perpetrators."

As the intercept investigation moved forward it kept expanding in size and scope. At first, Frease had difficulty understanding what all the material was and why, in particular, it often appeared to repeat itself. This turned out to be crucial, because it reflected the fact that there were multiple sources of the same intercepted conversations that could be used to cross-validate one another and establish the veracity of crucial conversations. There were two recording sites on different mountaintops, and there were also multiple units within the same site recording the same conversations. The challenge was to sort out what was in the intercepted materials, what it meant, and why it was there. Frease did not assume that the content of these materials could be taken at face value. "There were just all these questions . . . what does this mean and is this stuff real? That was always in my mind too. Are they bullshitting us or is this stuff real?"

Frease hired translators to work at the tribunal and began to narrow the range of material. She traveled back to Bosnia to interview the inter-cept operators who would later testify in court. Much of the translating and matching up of materials was done by a small group who worked on the intercepts at the tribunal. The movement back and forth between the various versions of the materials was tiresome. "Very tedious, very, very tedious. But it mattered that it was done with precision, and I knew that it was going to have to be as close to perfect as we could get it." When the electronic intercepts were translated, the attention shifted to the other sources. "We extended out with a base and then went from looking at the printed matter and the handwritten matter and . . . the other way. . . . So you had handwritten, you had printed, you had tapes, you had those three, and then you had three or four different sources. So getting all that . . . to match up was a lot of effort."

Finally, the essential bits of conversations began to emerge, for example, discussions of fuel that were needed and persons who had to be moved. "I remember getting so excited when I found the fuel conversation." The challenge was to find and understand what was being said, some of which involved understanding euphemisms and code words. As John Ralston also observed, "Generally speaking, people don't use plain language in communications over electronic media, so you have to work out what it is they're saying and how it relates to what's going on." The work continued throughout the investigation and on into the period of the trial itself. Frease stayed on at the tribunal until after the testimony on the intercepts was given in the Krstic trial by her and others.

A TRANSGOVERNMENTAL SHIFT

The problems associated with subcontracting the 1996 exhumations were one more indication to Louise Arbour that the tribunal was too dependent on human rights organizations such as Physicians for Human Rights. Arbour felt it was now necessary for the tribunal to take greater responsibility for this work. She made a special appeal to the member states of the UN to contribute to a special exhumation fund, and she set out to raise more than two million dollars. In the middle of July she called the diplomatic corps of The Hague together for what amounted to a fundraiser. The event included a slide show about the exhumations completed the previous summer, and Arbour announced that the tribunal had now received about half of the two million dollars she sought.

Arbour found herself excited by this fundraising effort, and this again illustrated her sense of the "exhilaration of action." She said, "You know, in a criminal investigation it's the forensic stuff that tells the story so compellingly . . . , the science in it is frankly quite spectacular. I mean assembling teams of anthropologists and geologists and pathologists, and you can tell where the money had to be spent, refrigerated containers, teams in the field." Arbour made her presentation on several occasions. Ruez played a key role in these events, and Arbour concluded that "we raised the money very effectively, with Jean-René, you can imagine, like a movie star: put a couple of slides up there and he would just tell the story."

The response to Arbour's plea included sizable contributions from Austria, Canada, Denmark, Malaysia, The Netherlands, Saudi Arabia, Sweden, Switzerland, the United Kingdom, and the United States. This was a movement from transorganizational to transgovernmental relationships that Arbour later described as a wholesale shift: "When I arrived in The Hague, all the commentary—the praise, the suspicion, all of it—came from a circle of humanitarian organizations, from Human Rights Watch and others. . . . When I left The Hague, all the evaluations and assessments came from the politicians, the military, the national security thinkers. . . . The tribunal was inside a new circle."[26]

Ruez was determined that these new resources would now move the Srebrenica case from investigation to prosecution. All of the resources in 1998 were focused in Republika Srpska. The work began on April 20 at the plateau of the dam at Brnice, near Zvornik, where a thousand

Muslim men were reported to have been executed. Peter McCloskey recalled that "by the time the spring came we were very energized and very anxious to get the process moving."

McCloskey and Ruez began at the spot where the aerial photographs had shown signs of burial activity and where after four hours of their own previous digging they had located a skull. They knew there were bodies to be found, but they had hardly begun to dig when they encountered problems: "First the bulldozer broke and then the backhoe," McCloskey noted. By this point, they had reached an understanding that there were occasions when there was "the UN way" and "the ghost team way." Kelly Moore, a press representative, was along on this mission with McCloskey: "We were driving back discussing this and we drove by a backhoe that was sitting next to a gas station. We inquired whose it was, found the Bosnian contractor, arranged that night for a deal that he rent it to us . . . , and the next day or two we had that guy's backhoe, and it was a lousy, dangerous backhoe, but it worked. . . . And there were other incidents where Jean-René had to jump start people for the same kind of thing, not just because of somebody who was being incompetent, but that it helped to have people being there who were seeing the bigger picture and who cared about the final product in the end." Once the digging at this first site began, and pieces of human skull and shell casings began to appear, even the Russian army personnel assigned for security, who had at first joked about creating another mass execution, grew silent at the sides of the grave.

McCloskey noted that as the exhumations moved forward they created their own momentum. "It definitely motivates you to see a large hole with many people in it, usually 20 to 30, sometimes 100, 150." With the succession of sites, the systematic effort that had gone into hiding the bodies was unmistakable. The primary and secondary sites could be distinguished. The next challenge was to begin to think of how to organize all that they were finding as evidence so that it could be presented most meaningfully in court.

DEATH IN FOUR LAYERS

Ruez liked to think of the final product of the exhumations as a four-layered glass box. The layers were reflected in the photographs that recorded the grave site: "the U2s are flying close to outer space, then we have the helicopter views, then we have ground views, and then we have the views from under the ground." The vision Ruez had of this photographic evidence was shared by Clifford Smith, who first joined the Srebrenica exhumation for six weeks in the summer of 1998. Smith was an important one-man example of transgovernmentalism. He was a criminal investigator for thirty-two years with the London police, specializing in crime scene and mass disaster coordination for the past twenty years.

Smith realized that working with Ruez would be no ordinary experience when he asked him one night in a hotel in Tuzla to tell him about the Srebrenica case. "He gave me a lecture which lasted an hour and a half . . . never looked at a reference, he just went through it all—names, dates, amazing man . . . very, very intense." Ruez and Smith soon recognized that they shared nearly identical views about what they wanted to bring from the exhumation sites to the courtroom. They wanted to reveal to the court the feeling as well as the history and content of the mass graves. They concluded that this required a careful opening of each grave site in combination with a systematic sequence of photographs.

Exhumations customarily began by individually removing the bodies from the grave and separately photographing each. Smith proposed that rather than immediately removing the bodies, they instead begin by digging around them. "We took a grave out down to about three feet without moving a single body. We 'mushroomed,' where you just leave all the bodies exactly as they are, and you just extract a sculpture. Very macabre. People thought I was a little bit bizarre at this, but what you do is then take a picture of it, so that when you start a trial you project it, and you say 'That's why we're here.' " His view was that unless one did this, the effect of the creation of the grave, as part of the crime against humanity, is not communicated.

Then there was the more direct evidence of who these victims were and how they were killed. "We're not talking here about victims of fighting. Because the defense would be that 'it was warfare and we put them in mass graves.' But then you start finding the ages, young, old, their arms are tied, sometimes behind their backs, their feet are tied. They're not soldiers. . . . They've got close quarter bullet holes to the head with the burns, this sort of thing, clothing burns." Often they would find tins in which the Muslim men would carry their cigarettes. "These tins in which invariably they'd scratch their names and the date—and the date wasn't the date of birth . . . you'd find it was the killing date." Smith continued, "Then you find an ID document, you open it . . . you have 'This man is from Srebrenica, his name is so and so, it's in his jacket which he was wearing,' it's game, set, match as to where the people are from. You then have got witnesses waiting, you know that other officers have got witnesses as to what happened, it all goes together. It's satisfying. It's bizarre, isn't it? But there is a satisfaction in it."

This fieldwork often seemed all-consuming, in contrast with the eight-to-ten-hour days back at the tribunal. "Out there, there's nothing else to do. So you start at eight in the morning and it's common to work through ten at night, every day, for three, four weeks." But there were also breaks that underlined the recurring point that the entire experience was not grim and that the dark quality of the exhumations was not alone the defining feature of this work. Smith explained that "somewhere in the middle, you take a day off and have a barbecue all day, and the sun is shining and the hell stops."

GENOCIDE ON TRIAL

The 1998 exhumations ultimately involved hundreds of people, most volunteering their time, from thirty-seven nations. The result was the removal of the remains of 650 to 800 victims and the collection of more than twenty thousand photographic images and the positive identification of many of the victims. All together, more than one thousand bodies had now been exhumed in Croatia and Bosnia. The crime base for a Srebrenica trial was in place and growing, making the timing right for an arrest and trial. As the exhumation season came to an end, Louise Arbour presented the tribunal with a sealed indictment of Radislav Krstic, the Bosnian Serb general charged with genocide in Srebrenica. The indictment was presented on October 30 and confirmed on November 2, 1998. Arbour sensed that the time was ripe for an important arrest.

Exactly one month after the tribunal's confirmation of the secret indictment, on December 2, 1998, American commandos swooped down on a car in northeastern Bosnia and arrested Radislav Krstic.[27] *Newsweek* concluded that "the fact that Washington OK'd Krstic's capture signals a deep shift in U.S. policy toward President Slobodan Milosevic, whom Krstic could implicate."[28] Krstic was only the tenth indictee transferred to The Hague and the first with major command responsibility. The charges against him included genocide. By the time the trial began in March 2000, investigators had exhumed nearly two thousand bodies from the Srebrenica massacre, and they knew where another twenty-five hundred bodies remained.

Nearly four years after Jean-René Ruez first testified for Mark Harmon in the Rule 61 hearing concerning Karadzic and Mladic, Ruez and Harmon were going back to court to prosecute Krstic. Stefanie Frease remembered Ruez saying the first time he encountered Harmon, "I'm going to have a lot to do with that guy." Harmon had recently finished prosecuting a Croatian general, Tihomir Blaskic, in another notable case involving command responsibility. The Blaskic case, however, was different. Andrew Cayley, a co-counsel on both the Blaskic and the Krstic cases, recalled that working with Harmon on the Blaskic case was "like watching him work . . . [with] a thousand pieces on a table . . . [and] putting this thing together without any plans." This was a comment on the poor state of the Blaskic file when Harmon received it. Frease insisted that the Krstic case was a dramatic contrast. "The Srebrenica case . . . was built on a really strong foundation. We started at the beginning and we built it up. It was a rock."

GOING TO COURT

Srebrenica had taken a toll on Ruez. He had suffered a leg injury, had bouts of pneumonia, and was developing an ulcer that by the summer of 2000 left him hospitalized. He was also in the midst of doing interviews with other high-ranking suspects and potential witnesses in Banja Luka. A particular problem in the Srebrenica trial was the volume of photographic material Ruez had assembled. There were about thirty thousand pictures, of which Ruez had taken a large portion himself. He was the only person who knew what he had. "That's the problem—it's like you are supposed to be the head of the orchestra, but you also have to play the trumpet and the violin."

These weren't just single shots in specific settings; there were combinations of pictures to be assembled in thematic as well as chronological order. "We took, let's say, the best photographs of all the blindfolded bodies that were coming out of the graves, to put them on a big board, so you have a huge photograph composed of a mosaic of, let's say, 150 photographs, all of them being blindfolds. Then you have the same kind of board, all of them ligatures. Wrist ligatures, ankle ligatures, stuff like that. Hundreds. I don't know how many." Ruez ordered a private lab to process three thousand photographs for presentation. He lamented, "I had to summarize in the extreme." The photos came back from the lab in complete disorder. The result was that "the days before I was on my knees here with 3000 photographs. . . . I spent three days on my knees in the corridor putting together the exhibits." The order was still in doubt when Ruez left for his first day in court. He barely arrived in time to hear Mark Harmon make the opening statement in Europe's first genocide trial.

THE TRIUMPH OF EVIL

When it came to the Srebrenica trial, Louise Arbour said simply, "Srebrenica was the biggest case in the house, . . . the case that carried the history of the war the most dramatically. Mark Harmon had been there—it was his." Jean-René Ruez couldn't have been more pleased. He finally began believing that his investment in this investigation was going to produce the results the case deserved.

Harmon's hour-long opening statement was a passionate, detailed, and extraordinarily disturbing outline of the case of genocide, which Harmon called "a case about the triumph of evil."[29] He began by tracing the background and involvement of Krstic in the "Operation Krivija 95" attack on Srebrenica in July 1995, noting that Krstic was trained in the former Yugoslavian army and had moved with many others during the Bosnian conflict into the army of Republika Srpska (the VRS). Krstic was a middle-aged career soldier who walked with a noticeable limp that made him look more like a weary high school principal than a brutal Balkan warrior.

Krstic rose to the post of chief of staff and deputy commander of the Drina Corps before stepping on a land mine and losing much of a leg in December 1994. He returned to service less than six months later, in the spring of 1995, and was promoted to the rank of major-general during the summer. By the time of the attack he had assumed the de facto responsibilities of commander of the Drina Corps, and during the attack, on July 14, 1995, he was formally appointed commander by Radovan Karadzic. General Mladic was his superior, but Krstic issued orders as commander of the Drina Corps, with specific responsibility for the Zvornik and Bratunac brigades. The charges against Krstic held him accountable for two categories of crimes: the deportation of twenty to thirty thousand Muslims from Srebrenica and the genocidal murder of thousands of male Muslim civilians.

Harmon anticipated that the defense would be that Mladic created a separate chain of command that went around Krstic. Harmon's response was the Nuremberg principle that it is criminal to "merely stand by" when subordinates commit crimes against international law, so that "by doing nothing, he cannot wash his hands of international responsibility."[30] Harmon emphasized from the outset the scale of the genocidal massacre.

First, it involved the issuing, the transmitting, and the dissemination of orders to all units that participated in the movement, the killing, the burial, and the reburial of the victims. It involved the assembling of a sufficient number of vehicles and buses, trucks, to transport the thousands of victims from the location of their capture and surrender to detention centers that were located near the execution sites. It involved obtaining fuel for these vehicles, and one must bear in mind that at the time there was a fuel embargo and that fuel was extremely precious. This operation involved providing guards and security for each of the vehicles that moved north toward the killing sites. It involved identifying detention centers that were secure enough and in close proximity to the execution fields. It involved providing secure routes for prisoner convoys. It involved obtaining sufficient numbers of blindfolds and ligatures so these prisoners could be bound before they were executed. It involved obtaining sufficient men to secure the actual detention facilities themselves, to guard the prisoners for the days or for the hours that they were kept there before they were executed. It required obtaining transportation to take the prisoners from the detention facilities to the killing sites themselves. It required obtaining the killing squads, organizing the killing squads, and arming the killing squads. This operation required, as well, the requisitioning and transportation of heavy-duty equipment necessary to dig the large mass graves, and it required men to bury the thousands of victims who we were later to discover.[31]

Harmon then described the cover-up of the deportation and massacre. He paused to introduce as evidence a picture of an exhumed grave where bodies were severed and left behind in the rush to move and rebury some of the dead.

The point was that the events at Srebrenica were planned and highly organized in ways reflective of systematic genocide. This was the outline of the military analysis later to be presented by Richard Butler using the documents seized at the Zvornik and Bartunac headquarters and the intercept evidence developed by Stefanie Frease. Harmon finished his opening statement by introducing a number of the execution and burial sites whose stories would be told by Ruez using exhumation evidence, seized documents, and intercepted communications, along with the testimony of surviving witnesses and Drazen Erdemovic, the confessed participant. As mid-morning of the first day arrived, the court still was coming to terms with the horror of a modern genocide. The picture that was emerging of Krstic was of a mild-mannered military bureaucrat—but a well-armed and organized bureaucrat—a middle manager of mass murder.

DEATH AND DESTRUCTION IN SREBRENICA

Harmon followed his opening statement by calling Jean-René Ruez as his lead witness. There was no mistaking the respect in the trial chamber for this French investigator, now hardened by five years of work on the Srebrenica case. Presiding Judge Almiro Rodrigues introduced Ruez to the court by encouraging him to "be at ease" and remarking, "You're a master of sorts."[32]

Harmon first directed attention to a map of the military operation "as seen by those who did it" that had been seized from the Zvornik brigade in the raid of early 1998.[33] The map included the farm site where Drazen Erdemovic participated in the killing of more than one thousand Muslim men. A second map with colored symbols identified the execution and burial sites where Ruez and his team had worked for nearly five years to locate and exhume bodies. Harmon asked Ruez to introduce the map. His introduction reflected the detail and complexity involved in depicting this crime scene: "The triangles represent areas where prisoners were concentrated. The red triangles mark execution sites, but small-scale execution sites. In reality, what we consider small-scale execution sites in this environment is roughly under 100 individuals. At the red circles, we have mass execution sites. Then we have yellow circles which indicate the locations where mass graves can be found, those that we call primary mass graves, undisturbed mass graves. The ones which have a cross in it are disturbed mass graves, because, as you know, there was a robbing operation of all these graves."[34] Rodrigues at several points interrupted to ask Ruez to slow down so that the interpreters could catch up.[35]

As the first morning of testimony was coming to a close, Harmon asked Ruez to introduce his video material. This material drew heavily from the propaganda work of a Belgrade journalist, Zoran Petrovic, whom Mladic had brought along to record the fall of Srebrenica. Ruez had convinced the VRS to turn over Petrovic's work, parts of which Petrovic had sold to the international press.

The Petrovic video recorded Krstic accompanying the triumphant Mladic on his entry into Srebrenica on July 11, 1995. There was an untranslated segment which Ruez explained was Mladic announcing that "the time has come to wreak vengeance on the Turks in this area."[36] The term *Turks* was often used in a derogatory way to describe the Bosnian Muslims. The video showed the detention of Bosnian Muslim men in crowded settings and Bosnian Serb soldiers posing as blue-helmeted UN forces to mislead the Muslims into surrendering. In another segment the commander of a unit called the Drina Wolves, identified by their blue patch armbands featuring a wolf, gave instructions to his troops to yell like wolves to terrorize the Muslims. Next the Muslim men were separated and crowded into what was called the White House. From here they were transported to staging points and to their executions and burials.

Another segment of the video cut to the long column of Muslim men who had fled from Srebrenica. The video showed shelling with anti-aircraft weapons that showered the fleeing column with deadly shrapnel. A Muslim man was asked why he looked so scared. He asked in return why he wouldn't be scared with a dead body shown nearby him on the roadside. These individuals were also taken to execution sites, where they were shot and buried. The video shifted back to Srebrenica to show a destroyed town that was empty except for stray animals and human bodies. The darkened court sat in stunned silence before it adjourned for a twenty-minute mid-day recess.

When the court returned for an afternoon of testimony, Ruez resumed the stand and began an account of the execution and burial sites. Again he moved between maps and photographic materials to identify the locations and to briefly describe how they were found. The photographic material included helicopter footage and land-based shots, as well as the CIA aerial images. Ruez moved through the "chain of executions" in their various locations, ending with the village of Pilice and the military pig farm in Branjevo, the scene of Drazen Erdemovic's killings.[37]

Krstic looked on impassively during this testimony. An occasional tic briefly distorted his bland face, but he otherwise seemed emotionless. While Krstic seemed numbed, Ruez was clearly exhausted by the recreation for the court of his last five years' worth of work. The hearing was adjourned in mid-afternoon. Ruez worked the rest of the afternoon and into the night reordering the exhibits, preparing for testimony that would last another two days.

The enormity of the massacre that Ruez spent so much time and energy unraveling became steadily more apparent. Judge Patricia Wald asked Ruez to provide summary figures to organize the court's comprehension. He estimated that fifteen thousand men had formed the column that headed in panic toward Tuzla. Of these, he estimated that six thousand had broken through and reached Tuzla. He further estimated that three thousand men had gathered in Potocari with the women and children. When Wald asked how many of these men were able to get on the buses that deported the women and children, Ruez answered that "we only know about one man who survived after having gotten on board a bus."[38] When asked by Rodrigues about the organization of what happened to the rest, Ruez responded that the execution squads "were already waiting for their victims at . . . predetermined site[s]."[39] One of these predetermined sites was the farm near Pilice that Drazen Erdemovic, the confessed executioner, would soon describe to the court.

BACK FROM THE DEAD
The first damp days of April provided a drizzly backdrop to the next round of testimony in the Srebrenica case. In the days and weeks that followed the court heard from UN observers and Dutch soldiers who were present during the fall of Srebrenica, as well as from the few

survivors who had been taken for dead but clawed their way back to rejoin the living in the days following the massacre.

The Dutch officers described how their small group of soldiers was easily overwhelmed by the Serb forces. Their command structure collapsed. Krstic was visibly present and active in this early phase of the operation.[40] A UN observer, Colonel Joseph Kingori, occupied a perhaps uniquely neutral vantage point from which to report events. Kingori was a Kenyan soldier assigned to monitor violations in the Srebrenica ceasefire agreement. One Colonel Vukovic was his Serbian contact. Even before the Serbian assault, Kingori reported Vukovic as saying that "the Muslims have to leave Srebrenica enclave in total." Vukovic later said that "if the Muslims do not leave, he is going to kill all of them."[41]

Kingori was in Srebrenica when the shelling of the community began. He reported that "there were no military targets in that area" and that "at times we could count over a hundred shells landing in the same place." The shelling was not only concentrated on civilians in the area, but also was timed to maximize its effect, by "waiting for the people to come out to pick [up] the injured."[42]

Harmon turned attention next to the movement of the civilian population from Srebrenica to the UN compound at Potocari on the eleventh of July. "Inside the compound there were about 5000 or so refugees, and outside there were actually more than that. It could have been even up to 7000, 8000 or even up to 10,000."Kingori described the scene as Mladic arrived in Potocari with his photographer Petrovic to record the unfolding events. Mladic was filmed giving children candy and soft drinks. However, "I saw . . . [that when] the camera turned to a different direction, some of the soldiers would pick the candies back . . . from . . . the children. . . . That forced me to conclude that this is just a PR . . . thing . . . just to show the international community."[43]

The following day Kingori saw Mladic near what was called the White House, where men were taken and kept apart from the women. Kingori asked Mladic to take him to the house. "We went there with him . . . and when we arrived there, they started distributing beer, soft drinks to the men now. And he asked me, 'Can't you see that they're o.k.?' . . . I requested him to allow me to enter the house, and he personally told me no, there is no point in going inside there."[44]

Later in the day Kingori saw Mladic again, this time with several Serbian officers, including Krstic, in the area of the White House. Muslim men were being forced to leave their belongings. "By that I mean even the money they had, the pocket knives they had, their wallets, and any other belongings."[45] This included leaving their identification cards behind. The pretext often given for separating the men from the women was to search for "war criminals." Yet the removal of identification cards contradicted this purpose. The Muslim men were now placed on buses, and it was clear that they were fearful. "This was an emotional time . . . because some of the men are people we had lived together with in that village, and they were being put into these buses . . . when they were lined up beside the road, they could cry and shout to us. . . . They could shout and say, 'You know these people are going to kill us, and . . . you are not doing anything about it.'"[46]

The Dutch deputy commander in Srebrenica, Major Robert Franken, subsequently was asked by Judge Fouad Riad whether what he at first described as an "evacuation" was actually a deportation, "a planned deportation approved by the U.N."[47] He agreed. Krstic had boasted on camera that this operation was being conducted "very successfully" and would continue "to the end."[48]

Five survivors of the firing squads at the various execution sites testified that they were lined up to be shot in groups, some with their eyes covered and their hands tied behind their backs. They survived by lying motionless underneath piles of corpses and then fleeing hours later. The testimony of this kind of firsthand witness and victim was an intense experience for the prosecution trial team, as well as all others involved. Andrew Cayley remarked that "[they are] all extraordinary people. It makes you feel very humble when you speak to them. Tremendous sort of poise these people have, because they're often represented to you as peasants from some remote part of Bosnia, but they come here and they have a sense of strength about them as people, they've been through harrowing experiences, which never ceases to touch me." He continued, "I'm not here for sentimental reasons, but that is something—the way you feel that you can actually serve. That's very important to me."

Cayley noted that the British practice is to keep the pre-court contact with a witness to a minimum, so that the courtroom exchange seems spontaneous and unrehearsed, whereas the American practice adopted at the tribunal will often involve a day or two of preparation with the witness. He concluded, "I find particularly with witnesses who have suffered intense trauma that by actually establishing a rapport, establishing a trust with them, say, over a day of proofing, it makes the quality of their evidence much higher when you actually get into court." The point for our purpose is that for prosecution lawyers, this experience in proofing the witnesses and conducting the courtroom testimony can be a highly compressed version of the alternation experience that the investigation team members have over a longer period of time when on mission.

Cayley concluded that "Krstic was a case which actually I think represented the real—the true reasons—why this place was established. It represented the best of what we can do as an office." He continued, "Anybody who was involved with that case has been touched. They call it the Srebrenica effect here. But it's interesting, it's definitely true, it changed us all, that case."

EVIDENCE OF GENOCIDE

With credit for time served, Drazen Erdemovic was again a free man when he testified in the Krstic case in late May 2000. Before being drawn into the war, Erdemovic was a married twenty-three-year-old Bosnian Croat living in Tuzla as an unemployed locksmith. He was pressured into joining the military after crossing over from Tuzla to Bijeljina. Their unit became the Tenth Sabotage Detachment of the army of Republika Srpska. Erdemovic had no personal knowledge of Krstic and took most of his orders from Milorad Pelemis, a first lieutenant.

Pelemis told his group that they would be joined by the Drina Wolves, who were part of the Drina Corps, during the assault on Srebrenica that began on July 11. They helped move the limited number of persons still in the town toward its center. Pelemis ordered one of the men to slit the throat of a civilian they encountered, and he did so.

Harmon led Erdemovic though his account of the massacre. Erdemovic recalled that as they drove to the farm they were told that buses would soon be bringing civilians from Srebrenica. "I and some of the others started objecting," Erdemovic reported, "saying, 'What are we going to do there?' And he said we would have to execute those people." Erdemovic said he protested, " 'I cannot do that, that is not the task of our unit.' He reported being told, 'If you don't want to do it, stand up with them or give them your rifle, and you will see whether they will shoot you.' "[49] When the first bus arrived, the initial group of ten blindfolded Muslim civilians was brought from the bus with their hands tied, and Erdemovic and his group were told to form a line in an open field. "The men in front of us were ordered to turn their backs. When those men turned their backs to us, we shot at them." This is how the executions progressed in groups of ten through the morning, punctuated only by a failed experiment with a malfunctioning machine gun that left the half-dead Muslim civilians pleading to be "finished off."[50]

In the early afternoon a group of soldiers, dressed in Republika Srpska army uniforms and reportedly from Bratunac, took over the executions. The Bratunac replacements apparently knew some of the Muslim civilians and used the opportunity to settle old grudges. Erdemovic estimated that by the end of the day fifteen to twenty busloads of Muslims had arrived and that between one thousand and twelve hundred Muslim civilian men had been executed. He was able to identify on aerial photographs where they were told the bodies were going to be buried.[51]

Erdemovic and his group were subsequently taken to the nearby village of Pilice, where Muslim civilians were awaiting execution in a warehouse. Erdemovic reported that "four of us said that we wouldn't go there to do that, that we'd had enough, that we were nobody's killing machine."[52] The men from Bratunac apparently were willing to do the job, because Erdemovic and his group could hear the killings taking place from a café where they drank coffee across the road. Of his own volition, Erdemovic repeated that he knew nothing about Krstic, remarking, "I don't know him and I don't know that he issued any orders."[53] The challenge for the prosecution was apparent.

Harmon began to address this challenge by recalling Jean-René Ruez shortly after Erdemovic's testimony to reiterate the larger context in which the executions he described had occurred. Ruez reintroduced the array of primary and secondary burial sites, including those at the farm. He again presented the U.S. aerial photos from July 17, 1995, showing the bodies so that in addition "one can see the traces of the excavator that collected these bodies on the soil."[54] This was followed by a September 21 "before" picture that showed the area with the primary burial completed. Then an "after" picture from September 27 was presented, showing a newly excavated trench. An enlargement of this picture further revealed a backhoe and a front loader, "two types of equipment that we will constantly see again in action on these areas." The implication was that some or all of the bodies had been removed and reburied. "We cannot conclude that the excavation is completed at that moment," Ruez observed, "but it is the best frame of the date that we can have at this moment."[55]

A series of forensic experts testified next about the exhumations, including the farm site about which Erdemovic had testified. They had been able to establish that there were fifty-three complete bodies, twenty-three nearly whole bodies, and 170 body parts. This was only a fraction of the Muslim men Erdemovic reported had been killed at the farm, but their appearance as the grave was unearthed was consistent with his description of them being led to their deaths with their hands tied behind their backs: "We see, looking down into the grave, the top of an assemblage of approximately 130 persons. We can see, for instance, the individual labeled number 3. He's lying sort of on his side with his face facing towards the upper part of the picture, so you can see his hands are bound behind his back. . . . All told in this group of remains, 77 people had their hands bounds behind their back."[56] The implication was that this was a primary grave site and that although some of the Muslim men were still in this location, the others had been moved. An example of this demonstrated linkage involved 283 people who were identified as having been executed by Erdemovic and others at the farm site and reburied at a secondary grave site called Cancari Road 12.

INTRODUCING THE INTERCEPTS

The next phase of the Srebrenica case was built around intercepted communications from the period of the executions, reconstructed by Stefanie Frease with the help of the Bosnian army. Seven Bosnian participants in the interception of these communications testified about their collection and content.[57]

The names of those communicating were sometimes indicated before the tape began. However, "they would sometimes give their names themselves, and then the orders; judging from the orders, one could gather who was ordering whom, and from that one would know who was the most important participant. Then came the voice, then the other code names used, and all these little pieces are put together like a jigsaw." Witness V added that "if we couldn't hear something, then a couple of colleagues would come and then we would try to decipher it together, and if we didn't succeed, then we would put dots to indicate that that part of the conversation was unintelligible." Three large volumes of transcribed conversations were introduced into evidence. The importance of the intercepted communications was clear from the start. An early intercept, for example, reported an operator at Drina Corps saying, "I can just put you through . . . to General Krstic. He's in charge of this attack."[58]

Witness Z was a Bosnian intelligence officer who transcribed an early but crucial intercepted conversation between General Krstic and Colonel Ljuba Beara. The naming of Krstic, the date of the communication, and the subject of this intercept were all argued after its presentation. The communication involved thirty-five hundred "parcels," which is the euphemism introduced in Mark Harmon's introductory statement as referring to the Muslims of Srebrenica who were being deported and executed. The urgency of the communication included the problems Beara had with completing the executions Drazen Erdemovic described. Erdemovic had testified that his group refused to continue the executions and that replacements were brought from the Bratunac brigade. Beara complained on the tape that he had been asking for help for three days. The Bosnian Serbs used unsecured lines of communication in urgent circumstances like this. Krstic warned Beara at the outset, "Ljubo, this /line/ is not secure." Beara answered, "I know, I know."[59]

The intercepted conversation involved Beara ([B), insisting that Krstic, or Krle, as he often was called, provide him with fifteen to thirty desperately needed men.

B: Krle, I don't know what to do any more.

K: Ljubo, then take those MUP /Ministry of Interior/ guys up there.

B: No, they won't do anything. I talked to them. There's no other solution but for those 15 to 30 men with Indzic. That were supposed to arrive on the 13th but didn't.

K: Ljubo, you have to understand me, too, you guys fucked me up so much.

B: I understand. But you have to understand me, too, had this been done then, we wouldn't be arguing over it now.

K: Fuck it, now I'll be the one to blame.

B: I don't know what to do. I mean it, Krle. There are still 3500 parcels that I have to distribute and I have no solution.

K: I'll see what I can do.

There was little doubt that the "parcels" were Muslims and that "distribution" referred to their impending execution. An earlier reference to Krstic and Beara in the opening of the conversation, and several subsequent references to Krle, further helped identify the parties involved.[60]

It was now mid-summer in The Hague and the prosecution was beginning to narrow its focus to Krstic. He was emerging as a less than enthusiastic but nonetheless active participant in the Srebrenica deportations and massacre.

A MILITARY ANALYSIS OF GENOCIDE

The prosecution began the final and most elaborate part of the case in the last week of June. This involved nine days' worth of testimony by Richard Butler, the U.S. army military analyst. All three prosecution lawyers—Mark Harmon, Andrew Cayley, and Peter McCloskey—were involved in the questioning. Their combined purpose was to provide a comprehensive analysis of Operation Krivija 95, the assault that led to the massacre.

The intercept evidence that Frease developed was crucial in pulling together and giving life to the military analysis of the Krivija 95 operation. The defense objected that the notebooks in which the intercepts were transcribed were not always consistently stamped, paginated, dated, and signed, questioning in particular the names of those conversing. The defense insisted that "[we therefore] will have to request an expert analysis regarding the authenticity of these exhibits."[61] This would prove to be important.

Harmon responded by emphasizing that each notebook had been identified by the witness who had originally produced it, by noting that conversations such as that between Beara and Krstic about the "distribution" of the "parcels" had been recorded from three different locations, and by reasserting that the transcriptions had been done with care because they could "potentially save lives" and "even change the course of a war." The judges agreed to accept the intercepts into evidence,[62] but the issue was revisited throughout the trial.

The stage was now set for Richard Butler, the prosecution's military analyst. Butler had been working on the case since April 1997. His expertise was based on his training as well as experience working on the former Warsaw Pact, on Soviet army operations in Afghanistan, on the Gulf War, and in southwest Asia. His detailed testimony was built on his analysis of the thirty thousand documents seized from the Zvornik and Bratuanc brigades.

Butler outlined the command structure of the Bosnian Serb military as it related to the Krivija 95 assault. He explained that the directive for this assault came from Radovan Karadzic, as president of Republika Srpska, and called for creating "an unbearable situation of total insecurity with no hope of further survival or life for the inhabitants of Srebrenica and Zepa." Butler introduced a video interview of Karadzic giving Krstic explicit credit for carrying out this attack with Mladic, who had already received much public attention. Karadzic explained in the interview that "we wanted to turn Mladic into a legend. . . . We failed, however, to bring up the successes of individual corps commanders. Now Krstic, for instance, who planned it in front of me and I approved that task for Srebrenica. . . . It should be known that Krstic is a great army commander."[63]

One of the most persuasive aspects of Butler's testimony focused on the mobilization of buses, trucks, and digging equipment for the operation. He commented that fuel in East Bosnia was a precious commodity, "the equivalent of liquid gold," and had to be requisitioned for sixty to seventy buses from the state-owned transportation company in the area.[64] Krstic was in charge of this well-planned operation.[65]

The defense disputed the timing of Krstic's assumption of the role of commander of the Drina Corps. Butler presented evidence that Krstic moved to this command between July 13 and July 14. An illustration of the detail Butler could provide was the evidence that a truck made ten trips along the Zvornik-Pilice-Kula-Zvornik route with approval by Krstic while dredging was being done at the farm site where the massacre in which Erdemovic participated took place.[66]

As the ninth day of Butler's testimony ended, McCloskey introduced a video of a Serbian army ceremony in which Mladic addressed a gathering of troops. Mladic thanked Krstic, saying, "You who fought under the leadership of your Chief of Staff or Corps Commander who although severely wounded made a tremendous contribution to the victory of the Serbian army."[67]

The court in the Krstic genocide case had now heard fifty-five days' worth of testimony and seen about one thousand exhibits and sixty witnesses.[68] As the end of July approached, the prosecution began to summarize its case, in part by presenting witness DD, a woman who could give a sense of the damage done to the living as well as to the deceased in Srebrenica. When the attack on their village outside Srebrenica began, DD and her family hid in the nearby forest. When the assault intensified, it was decided that "the adult men should go through the woods and women and children to UNPROFOR" in Potocari. "So we parted," the witness explained. "My husband left with my eldest son." She never saw them again. She and her remaining three children spent two days in the crowded heat of Potocari, without food and water. On what she called "black Thursday," they were lined up to get on buses. "We walked for about 50 meters, and then from the left column one of their soldiers jumped out, and he spoke to my [fourteen-year-old male] child. 'Young man, you should go to the left side.' And he said, 'Why me? I was born in 1981.' But he repeated what he said, 'You people should go to the right-hand side.'" When DD resisted, the soldier dragged her protesting son to the left side. "That was the last time I heard his voice."

When DD regained her composure she went on to describe her current life, five years after the Srebrenica massacre, still living in a squalid refugee camp with her troubled remaining children and without hope for the future. She concluded, "I would have stayed in front of our house together with my whole family and let them kill us together if I had known what would happen."[69] The courtroom was in stunned silence as she then turned to the defendant: "I would like to appeal to you to ask Mr. Krstic, if you can, whether there is any hope for at least that little child that they snatched away from me, because I keep dreaming about him. I dream of him bringing flowers and saying, 'Mother, I've come.' I hug him and say, 'Where have you been, my son?' and he says, 'I've been in Vlasenica all this time.' So I beg you, if Mr. Krstic knows anything about it, about him surviving some place."[70] Apparently shaken by this witness, Krstic silently held his head in his hands.[71]

Jean-René Ruez was the prosecution's closing as well as opening witness. He had interviewed Krstic for three and one-half hours the month before the trial began. In the interview Krstic laid out the defense the prosecution anticipated at the beginning of the trial, namely, that Mladic had masterminded the deportation and massacre in Srebrenica and carried it out with a select group of officers and units who were "the main order-makers and executioners of everything that took place between 12 and 20 July 1995."[72] These officers were individuals such as Ljubo Beara who were prominently featured in the intercepted communications and the units including the Tenth Sabotage Detachment in which Drazen Erdemovic served. Meanwhile, Krstic claimed that he and the Drina Corps were ordered to move on to another area of operations.

Harmon and the prosecution team clearly hoped that the contradictions between Krstic's assertions and the evidence they had already presented would undermine the development of this line of defense. As the prosecution rested its case and the court adjourned for an August recess, Krstic and the defense had much to think about.

"KILL THEM ALL"

Krstic appeared on his own behalf as the first defense witness. He described himself as a family man and a career professional soldier, with "the best years" of his life spent in Sarajevo, where he married and became the father of a daughter. He invoked his concerns about his family later when he was cross-examined about his responsibilities to take action in response to violations of international laws of war. He insisted, "I was afraid . . . for the security of my family and myself and my relatives and the relatives of my wife." When asked who he was afraid of, Krstic responded, "General Mladic was responsible for the crimes. . . . I feared him as well as his security services."[73] He further maintained that he knew little of what happened in Srebrenica before the proceedings. When confronted with intercepted communications, he denied his role in the conversations.[74] Peter McCloskey asked him whether he had ordered any killings of Muslim men between the dates of July 11 and November 1. Krstic insisted that he had not.

As McCloskey built to a climax in his cross-examination, there was a visible change in the appearance and demeanor of Krstic. He began to tire under the persistent questioning. His answers grew vague and were often mumbled. He bent down repeatedly to rub the stump of his lost leg, which reportedly was causing powerful phantom pains.[75] The presiding judge called breaks in the testimony to allow Krstic relief. But McCloskey continued to press him about his whereabouts and actions in the final weeks of July 1995.

After a series of denials by Krstic, McCloskey dramatically introduced a tape recording from August 2, 1995. The transcript was accompanied by copied pages from two notebooks with handwritten accounts of the recorded conversation. McCloskey indicated that the foundation for this submission would be laid in rebuttal.[76] The defense countered that ultimately the identification of the voice of Krstic would have to be confirmed by an expert. McCloskey moved ahead and reminded the court that Krstic had denied giving orders to kill Muslim men between July 11 and November 1. Yet, McCloskey now told the court, in the recorded conversation he says, "Kill them all. Not one should be left alive. Kill them all."[77] McCloskey told the court that this evidence was introduced to impeach the statement of Krstic that he had given no such orders.

Judge Wald intervened: "Just one second. I don't quite understand. You've had this for a while or you just got hold of it yourself recently?" McCloskey acknowledged that they'd had this for a while and the judge responded, "But for strategic reasons or whatever, you have not laid the same kind of foundation yet for this document that you did for all those other intercepts, right?" McCloskey agreed and volunteered that the recording was already in the hands of voice identification experts from whom the prosecution had yet to receive an official report. With that, the court adjourned for a fifteen-minute recess.

The trial resumed in mid-afternoon in dramatic anticipation of hearing the alleged conversation between Krstic (K) and his chief of staff for the Zvornik brigade, Major Obrenovic (O):

K: Is that you, Obrenovic?
O: Yes.
K: Krstic here.
O: We've managed to catch a few more, either by gunpoint or in mines.
K: Killed them all. God damn it.
O: Everything, everything is going according to plan. Yes.
K: [Not a] single one must be left alive.
O: Everything is going according to plan. Everything.
K: Way to go, Chief. The Turks are probably listening to us. Let them listen, the motherfuckers.
O: Yeah, let them.[78]

McCloskey went on to quote from Bosnian Serb reports that described Muslim "stragglers" in the Zvornik brigade area being captured and killed in early August 1995.[79]

Krstic vehemently denied ordering the killings and insisted that the conversation was a complete fabrication. He stared back at McCloskey and declared, "This is 100 percent montage. On that day I didn't talk to Obrenovic at all. Second, I did not recognize the other participant in the conversation, and especially not my own voice, myself. I repeat: this is a montage, 100 percent, rigged. I never would have done that on the phone or physically, had he been in my presence. I would never have done that."[80] The verifiability and timing of the introduction of this intercepted conversation would continue to be an issue through the closing phase of the Srebrenica trial.

CLOSING IN ON KRSTIC

All three judges engaged Krstic with questions that kept him on the stand for most of two days.[81] The American judge, Patricia Wald, posed a series of pithy questions that cut to the core of the Krstic defense. Wald was well known at the tribunal for her "American-style informality."[82]

Wald asked Krstic whether after finishing his work in Zepa he heard anything at all about graves and reburials. He insisted that "everything that happened later on the grave sites and digging . . . was done in far greater secrecy than the killing itself of the war prisoners."[83] As Wald moved to her concluding questions, she inquired about visits that Krstic reportedly made to his own and his wife's family in the area near Srebrenica and Zepa on the evening of July 12, in the midst of the fall of Srebrenica. Wald wondered whether he would have heard something about the massive scale of the events in Srebrenica from family members. "I went to spend the night with my wife's family, and at the time nothing was talked about for the simple reason that nobody knew anything about it. It was between the 12th and 13th of July. . . . There was nothing."[84]

The defense presented its own military analyst, a Yugoslav army general, Radovan Radinovic, to bolster the claim that Krivija 95 was "a hastily prepared and provoked military action with limited aims," that is, until "a crazy plan to capture Srebrenica crossed someone's mind." Radinovic attached more blame to Karadzic than to Mladic, but also joined Krstic in attributing responsibility to an "independent chain of command within the security services. . . ."[85] Andrew Cayley noted for the prosecution that the Radinovic analysis, which was drawn out over seven days, relied on a variety of dubious sources.[86] The most astonishing of the unsubstantiated assertions involved a secret plot for the massacre of Muslims, using mercenaries and organized by French intelligence services, that Radinovic said was unknown to the Bosnian Serbs and therefore could not be prevented. This remarkable testimony occurred as the year was coming to an end. The court was adjourned for the Christmas holiday, to resume with the prosecution's rebuttal in the new year.

CONFIRMING THE SREBRENICA INTERCEPTS

The collusion of Krstic in the massacre remained the issue in the closing days of March in the Srebrenica trial. The defense had insisted that ultimately voice experts would need to confirm the authenticity of the tape that allegedly recorded Krstic ordering his chief of staff to "kill them all." A British expert said the poor quality and short duration of the tape made it impossible to confirm whether it was Krstic on the tape or not, whereas an American expert was at least able to confirm that the recording was of two "speakers of ethnic Serb background."[87] The prosecution now introduced the evidence that the Krstic conversation had been recorded and identified independently at two separate Bosnian Muslim listening sites.

Harmon first reintroduced Witness BB, who confirmed that he had heard the taped conversation and transcribed it into the notebook introduced as evidence. He also insisted that he had no doubts about the identification of Krstic, saying, "I had heard him certainly several tens of times." The defense counsel asked why this evidence had not been introduced earlier.[88] Judge Wald came back to this point by later asking defense counsel, "Putting authenticity aside, you are still objecting that they shouldn't have come in on rebuttal . . . ?"[89] If this point was not previously clear, with the assistance of Wald, defense counsel now agreed that timing was at issue.

In cross-examining the following witness, Z, defense counsel returned to the issue of the timing of the intercept evidence. Witness Z confirmed that Stefanie Frease had brought this conversation to his attention in November 1999.[90] The prosecution then introduced more tapes and witness testimony to further confirm the activity of Krstic in the Srebrenica massacre, leading Wald to at one point comment in apparent bewilderment about "so many intercepts floating around here." The issue again was the late entry of these tapes into the case. The following day the prosecution again came back to the issue of timing with regard to a particular tape, and Wald asked McCloskey, "Just to pin this down, at the time you were cross-examining General Krstic, you didn't have this tape?" McCloskey answered, "Actually, during the cross-examination, this tape was sitting with, probably with 30, 40 others in a locker. Eventually, we were able to find the Bosnian log that went to all those tapes, and by reviewing the log, though they misspelled General Krstic's name, we were able to find it in early November, after the cross-examination of General Krstic."[91]

In the final days of the trial, the court heard from Frease about her work as the member of the Srebrenica team who oversaw the intercept project. Frease testified that she was "absolutely certain"[92] about the dates attributed to specific conversations and that, more generally, the intercepts were "absolutely reliable."[93]

THE KRSTIC VERDICT

More than six years after its demise, Mark Harmon summarized in the late summer of 2001 the fate of the Muslim community of Srebrenica. In restrained tones that purposefully contrasted with the enormity of the alleged crime, he somberly concluded that "what was once a vibrant community is no more. What remains are only the memories." He noted that it had taken only five days to destroy this community in eastern Bosnia. Meanwhile, it had taken a five-year investigation, a trial more than a year and half long, the exhumation of more than two thousand bodies, the testimony of 128 witnesses, and eleven hundred exhibits to re-create the crime. "Is there any sentence," he asked rhetorically in recommending eight life terms of imprisonment, "that can be appropriate?"[94]

General Krstic appeared gaunt and pale as he entered the courtroom on crutches to hear the verdict on August 3, 2001. The courtroom was again crowded with reporters. Presiding Judge Rodrigues introduced his judgment after taking the unusual step of acknowledging the work of Jean-René Ruez and the Srebrenica investigation team, saying, "I wish to pay tribute to the work of the Office of the Prosecutor in the broadest sense and, in particular, to Mr. Jean-René Ruez, the former team leader in the Office of the Prosecutor." These remarks reflected the impossibility of sitting through the Srebrenica trial without taking notice of the scale and intensity of the investigation that made this trial possible.

Rodrigues then offered a condensed version of the 250-page judgment. In the end, he directly addressed the defendant as he said that "in July 1995, General Krstic, you agreed to evil. This is why the Trial Chamber convicts you today and sentences you to 46 years in prison." The judgment held that what had begun as a plan for ethnic cleansing had become genocide: a deliberate decision was made at a critical point in the cleansing operation to kill all the Muslim men of fighting age, with an awareness of the fatal impact this would have on the entire group. The key was that by first deporting the women and children and then deciding to kill all the men of Srebrenica who were of fighting age, "a decision was taken to make it impossible for the Bosnian Muslim people of Srebrenica to survive."[95]

The judgment was also careful to note that although the evidence from intercepted communications was "meticulously weighed" and played an important role in its verdict, the taped conversation that most disturbed Krstic was excluded on the procedural grounds of its late introduction. Rodrigues emphasized that "the Trial Chamber did not admit a recording in which a voice alleged to be that of K. is heard saying: Kill them all! I emphasize this point because it might have appeared that this exhibit was part of the case-file whereas it has NOT been admitted and is not an exhibit."[96] It is nonetheless important to recall that this recorded conversation was played repeatedly in the trial for the purposes of authentication. Wald helped formulate for the defense the grounds on which it was ultimately disallowed, but the damage to the Krstic defense may already have been done.

Two paragraphs drawn from the decision and read directly to Krstic focused specifically on the events of the four days in July when the massacre occurred:

On the evening of 13 July, I repeat—13 July—you took command of the Drina Corps and signed your first order as the corps commander around 20:30 hours. On 14 July, you launched the attack on Zepa. Nonetheless, you remained perfectly well informed of what was going on in the area to the north of the town of Srebrenica. In the night of 14–15 July, troops from the Zvornik Brigade moved up from Zepa toward Srebrenica, and you knew why they were doing that. On 15 July in the morning, the security chief of the Main Staff called you and asked for your help in dealing with "3500 packages."

You knew exactly what was meant by "packages," General Krstic— Bosnian Muslims who were to be executed. You expressed your displeasure. That same officer told you that the MUP forces, the Interior Ministry police, did not want to do it. You said you would see what you could do. On 16 July, some of your subordinates, men from the Bratunac Brigade, participated in the mass executions at the Branjevo military farm. On 16 July, the security chief of the Drina Corps whose commander you were, continued to keep you informed about the situation. You asserted to the Trial Chamber that, subsequently, you wanted to take measures against that officer, but out of fear of reprisals against yourself or, more specifically against your family, you decided not to. The Trial Chamber, however, found nothing to confirm your assertions. . . . Nothing makes it possible to establish that you participated in the activities designed to conceal the massacres and, to this end, in the operations of digging up and reburial of the corpses. But how could anyone think that you would not have known about work requiring the use of such large machines? In any case, General Krstic, you were seen being congratulated for the action you took in Srebrenica. You were seen right next to General Mladic when in December 1995 a ceremony was organized for the Drina Corps. Finally, General Krstic, you supported General Mladic against President Karadzic when he tried to remove General Mladic.[97]

Krstic showed little emotion as these paragraphs were read.

The *New York Times* took its cue from the judgment's introduction and included an extended quote from Jean-René Ruez about the trail of evidence that he and his team had pursued. Ruez recalled that "the Serbs went to great lengths to hide the evidence of the crimes." He then explained that "they did a sloppy job. They moved bodies from mass graves, but left behind many. They erased records and cleaned out archives. Binders from 1995 were missing. But they left some things. They did not remember to destroy the engineering logs showing how they used heavy equipment to dig the graves. We found timetables of the military police guarding prisoners."[98]

The presentation of the judgment concluded with the chilling observation that Krstic was in some ways simultaneously a "good soldier" and a genocidal killer, saying that "the trial chamber does not dispute that you are a professional soldier who loves his work." The court conceded that the decision to move from an ethnic cleansing operation to genocide was probably not his and that "someone else probably decided to order the execution of all the men of fighting age."[99] Krstic's crime was to have agreed to help. Krstic agreed to this evil, and this agreement was the grounds of his conviction and sentence to forty-six years in prison for genocide and other crimes. To the end, Krstic seemed more like a harried bureaucrat than a general. However, he had now gone from being an armed bureaucrat to being a bureaucrat behind bars.

GRIM BUT REWARDING WORK

One of the most striking features of the tribunal experience is the juxtaposition of the horror of the violence and victimization that is its day-in and day-out focus, and the shared sense of purpose and energetic determination that sustains the commitment of those who persist in its work. Mark Harmon, awaiting the outcome of the Srebrenica trial, easily conceded that "this is a grim business that we're in. We're not dealing with material that is joyful or that elevates the spirit here. It'll wear you out . . . these crimes are so horrific that they weigh on your mind." Still, Harmon had no doubts about staying with this work, and he has a good sense of why he continues to find it important and rewarding.

Harmon finds the power of the tribunal in what it is able to communicate, often most eloquently through the voices of the victims of the assailants it prosecutes. For Harmon, this point was vividly illustrated by a survivor of the massacre of twelve hundred Muslim men that Drazen Erdemovic helped execute. As the survivor of this horrendous event came to the conclusion of his testimony, he was asked whether there was anything else he wished to say. Harmon recalled his answering that "from all of whatever I have said and what I saw, I can only come to the conclusion that this was extremely well organized; it was systematic killing and that the organizers of that do not deserve to be at liberty. Yet if I had the right and courage in the name of all those innocents and all those victims, I would forgive the actual perpetrators of the executions because they were misled." Harmon found this an extraordinary statement "from someone who should be in normal expectations, somebody who was grievously wounded himself, barely survived, somebody who should be extremely bitter but has a spirit like that, an expression like that is elevating. That's what gets you through the day. People like that." This was a courtroom version of the alternation experience associated with teamwork on mission and described throughout this book. The consolation and motivation that Harmon found in his work with colleagues such as Jean-René Ruez in the courtroom paralleled the motivation that many others found while on mission, working with team members and with victims in the Balkans.

CHAPTER SIX

The Foca Rape Case

$\mathbf{A}$nother historic trial—the Foca rape case—began within a week of the Srebrenica genocide case in mid-March 2000. The tribunal now had nearly one thousand employees, and its annual budget was approaching one hundred million dollars. Three courtrooms were in simultaneous operation, and there were plans for expansion. Louise Arbour had moved onto the Supreme Court of Canada and Carla Del Ponte had inherited a full docket of cases, as well as the nagging priority of apprehending the still-unarrested indictees—Karadzic, Mladic, and Milosevic. The challenge was to maintain a sense of momentum.

The Srebrenica and Foca cases broke new ground in crucial areas of international criminal law that the Tadic case initially raised but failed to successfully address in the ICT's first trial. Dusko Tadic was to have been tried for genocide in Germany, but this was not contemplated at The Hague. Tadic was instead to be tried for rape, but a key witness was unable to appear. The tribunal tried on several later occasions to prosecute genocide and rape charges, but without success. The tribunal needed to give life to the international laws of genocide and rape, and the Srebrenica and Foca cases took on this challenge nearly simultaneously from the neighboring courtrooms of this increasingly busy international courthouse.

More than case law and the defendants were at stake. These cases also promised to provide important lessons about the roles of investigation and trial teams and their leadership in providing measurable signs of justice using international criminal law. In addition, the two cases combined to reflect the gendered realities of war, namely, that whereas men tend to get killed, women and children more often are forcibly detained and deported, and young women in particular are at risk of sexual assault and rape. Women also are more often left with the challenges of rebuilding the lives of their devastated families.

The similarities between the Srebrenica and the Foca cases were more than superficial. Both trial teams were led by highly skilled and experienced North Americans, and both investigation teams were led by determined and effective Europeans who had training in law and who had worked in highly committed teams to develop their cases virtually from the time they arrived during the first days of the tribunal. But although these were noteworthy similarities, the differences were as large or larger.

In fact, the dynamics of the two trial teams probably could not have been much more distinctive. The principals in the Srebrenica team had known each other for years and had developed great respect for one another. Structuring the Foca trial team was a more difficult matter and an instructive case for comparison. In the language of social science, the Foca trial team was a negative case[1] that seemingly contradicted a major thesis of this book—namely, that tribunal investigators and lawyers are joined in team efforts by shared purposes that produce long-term commitments to the field of international humanitarian and criminal law. The Foca team was seriously split along a gender divide potentially as challenging as the defense that formed the prosecution's more visible opposition. In the end, however, I argue that it was still a strong sense of shared purpose, in spite of gendered disagreements, that allowed the Foca team to overcome and move beyond its differences.

A TEAM DIVIDED

The two principal prosecutors in the Foca case, Hildegard Uertz-Retzlaff and Dirk Ryneveld, knew next to nothing about one another when they were assigned as co-counsel in the Foca rape trial. Uertz-Retzlaff is a middle-aged German lawyer with a quick smile and a disarming cheerfulness that belie her determined sense of moral purpose. Known to most by her first name, Hildegard came to the tribunal with a background in the prosecution of international white-collar crime. She had investigated and prosecuted a German investment fraud that involved losses of several hundred million dollars to twenty thousand victims spread across Europe. Philosophically as well as more pragmatically, Hildegard is guided by postwar Germany's strong sense of the tribunal's historic and international significance. In addition, her husband comes from the former Yugoslavia, and they "were both very upset with what was going on" in his former country. Hildegard came to the tribunal in the spring of 1995 and headed the Foca investigation, which led to the arrest of Dragoljub Kunarac in 1998.

Tejshree Thapa, known to her friends as Tej, arrived at the tribunal on the same day as Hildegard, and they were both immediately assigned to the Foca investigation. From Nepal, Tej also is trained as a lawyer and was hired as a crime analyst. She is a small woman in her thirties with dark eyes and a serious demeanor. Tej was the lead investigator on the Foca case and conducted most of the preliminary interviews with the rape victims. She also handled the supporting documents and developed the database that was used to organize the prosecution of the case.

Tej and Hildegard worked extensively with a Croat interpreter named Nina, whose manner and success with the victim witnesses was a lesson in the demands of this kind of work. Hildegard emphasized that "she was important for everything because she had a very good rapport with the witnesses. . . . She was a very calm person and that made it easier for them." Nina was also a lesson in the toll taken by field work with rape victims. "For her it was harder than for the rest of us, because she was a filter. So now she works as a secretary. . . . She can't work here anymore. She says, 'No way.' She had to get out."

Hildegard was further assisted by Peggy Kuo, an Asian American lawyer still in her mid-thirties. Kuo is an American success story. She was brought at the age of three by her immigrant parents from Taiwan to New York City. She grew up in the ethnically diverse Washington Heights neighborhood, where she excelled in school. She had an intense interest in racial and ethnic problems and went on to study hate crimes in Germany before graduating from Harvard Law School. Kuo was a key addition to the team, in part because she had gained early trial experience in the civil rights division of the U.S. Justice Department.

Tej remarked that "Hildegard and myself were the core, and Peggy came in at a very good time, when we had to go to trial and we really needed the help. We were under a lot of pressure and she became a part of the core team." She added that "Peggy is brilliant and very articulate, and very, very important for us at that time was that she was natively English speaking, because Hildegard felt very uncomfortable [with German as her first language]." The three women developed the Foca case largely on their own. Patricia Sellers and Nancy Paterson provided legal advice and help in writing briefs for the trial.

Hildegard and Tej did not want to prosecute single individuals for isolated rapes but rather to build a case that reflected the organized way in which rape was a part of the ethnic cleansing that occurred in Foca and elsewhere. As Hildegard observed, "We didn't want to indict a person who raped once; . . . we wanted to have a leading person raping many, many times." While the war was still going on, nongovernmental organizations and journalists such as Roy Gutman had begun interviewing rape victims in the Foca area. Hildegard and Tej were able to interview rape victims from a variety of such sources.

Between fifty and sixty rape victims were interviewed from the Foca area, producing a combined total of about 150 witness and victim statements and nearly another 100 statements for subsequent Foca prosecutions. Tej continuously monitored the database, looking for patterns. "We decided on the basis of this information," Hildegard recalled, "that a certain person, Kunarac, was mentioned very often as being a leader of a group of rapists, and so we made a decision to investigate this person."

By 1997 the investigation was nearly complete, and Hildegard and Tej had to move on to other work while they awaited an arrest. "I mean if I was in Sarajevo on other business," Tej noted, "there were a handful of people I would call and just say, 'Hello, how are you,' and there are some witnesses who are more special than others, and you remember them better. For them I always made an effort. But there were large numbers of people who I couldn't keep in touch with." Hildegard felt the same frustration, although she remembered several instances in which she had to become reinvolved with witnesses and victims with special problems, some of which could jeopardize the prosecution of Foca cases. "For instance, . . . sometimes a witness called and said, 'I am supposed to go back to Foca, I'm afraid to go there and, of course, I will not testify. I would be killed.' So then we had to do something."

It took several years to get Kunarac into custody, but ultimately he voluntarily surrendered to French SFOR troops in Foca. Two other defendants, Radomir Kovac and Zoran Vukovic, also were apprehended later and charged with multiple rapes. Kunarac was a commander, whereas Kovac and Vukovic were subcommanders, and the indictment charged Kunarac with responsibility for his subordinates and the acts he knew or had reason to know they had committed. Their alleged activities included a regime of gang-rape, torture, and enslavement of Muslim women and girls in Foca from April 1992 to February 1993.[2]

After being brought to the tribunal, Kunarac made four "initial" appearances in which he entered a confusing series of pleas. He was described as "a rather short man in his forties, with two strong vertical lines marking deeply sunk cheeks. His face is hard, as if carved out of wood. He looks dried out, a type of skinny but tough man one often finds in the mountain villages. His curly dark hair is receding at the top and looks untidy, as though it doesn't get washed too often."[3] Kunarac's nickname was Zaga, the Serbian word for a carpenter's saw.[4] Uertz-Retzlaff reported that during early court appearances, "he kept on saying I have a bad conscience, I have done something wrong, but when you asked him, [he said] *he* was raped—that it was all happening against his will." The court finally entered a not guilty plea on his behalf.

Peggy Kuo displayed her courtroom talents from the first day of the trial, and *Time* ran a profile calling her "the war-crime fighter."[5] Yet Kuo was clearly too young to lead the Foca case. In Germany, Hildegard Uertz-Retzlaff would have led the case from investigation through trial. Yet she was not familiar with common law courtroom procedure, and this combined with difficulty with English, made the prospect of Hildegard leading the case doubtful. Nonetheless, it was easy enough to understand why she sought this challenge. In her words, "Here I was in the field, doing everything, making all the decisions, and suddenly when it starts in the courtroom, there is a new person on it, not knowing the facts actually, and suddenly in charge."

The person placed in charge of Foca was Dirk Ryneveld, and having just arrived at the tribunal, he too was surprised. About the same age as Uertz-Retzlaff, the Canadian Ryneveld had spent the last twenty-five years of his life in the attorney general's office of British Columbia prosecuting murder cases. He is a large man with a courtly demeanor and a care and respect for words. He is unflappable and verbally astute and has a talent for seeing both a broad legal picture and the specific details of a case.

A Canadian colleague who had worked at the tribunal suggested to Ryneveld that he might enjoy international law at this stage of his career. Ryneveld felt that in Canada, he'd "sort of reached that plateau or milestone where I had done just about everything there was to do, there was just more of it. Same files, different names, if you know what I mean." He was an admirer of Louise Arbour, saying, "I had great respect for her and believed she was making a difference." He applied to the tribunal but didn't think much about it until a telephone interview was hastily arranged with Arbour, Graham Blewitt, Bill Fenrick, and others. A formal letter of offer came from the UN in late December 1999. He was already committed to a murder trial in British Columbia, but two days after the trial ended he left for The Hague. He was placed in charge of the Foca case almost immediately.

Ryneveld recognized the awkwardness of the situation for his two fellow lawyers. "I get parachuted in and they are told that they are now subordinate to me, and it's clear that I'm still trying to find out where the cafeteria is and, you know, not up to speed on the file at a time when we had to get going. So there were some initial dynamics that were a problem in the sense that they had to learn to accept me as their boss, being fully cognizant of the fact that they knew the file and I didn't. And that did cause some difficulties at the outset." This was an understatement of a fundamental problem that continued to confront the team as the trial developed.

PIECES OF A PICTURE

The Srebrenica and Foca cases represented two different parts of the effort to achieve a Greater Serbia by means of the ethnic cleansing of strategic areas in Bosnia and later Kosovo. Daryl Mundis, who became a member of the Foca team shortly before it went to trial, came to understand ethnic cleansing and the pursuit of a Greater Serbia in his own introductory encounter with the case files from this Balkan conflict. Mundis was a lawyer in his late thirties with degrees from Harvard and the London School of Economics.

As the father of young daughters, Mundis struggled to understand the Balkan wars and especially the use of rape as a terror tactic. He came to the conclusion that the various cases he was learning about were pieces of a larger picture. "The farther you step back the more you see that all the smaller cases fit into a bigger picture," he observed. "The same types of things were happening throughout these areas where the Serbs were the alleged perpetrators. I think you can certainly draw inferences that there might have been, or that there was, a common purpose or plan behind these events that were happening all over the place in very similar patterns and very similar types of progressions."

The smaller pieces forming the larger picture involved similar scenarios described by independent witnesses from different places. "I started reading what the witnesses said happened in the first couple of days of the conflict and . . . it was amazing the similarities between what had happened up in the Prejidor region in terms of, the armed attack unfolded like this, and the civilians were rounded up in this way, and the men and women were separated this way, and most of the men when this fighting took place took off into the hills, leaving behind the children and the women. . . . It's very, very similar." The challenge was to decide which parts of this picture of ethnic cleansing to pursue, because with hundreds of thousands of persons killed and raped, and millions more terrorized and deported, all of the victims' cases could not be pursued and all of the perpetrators could not be punished.

This is the dilemma that provoked the drawing of distinctions between kinds of cases. The leadership cases, as illustrated by the Srebrenica genocide case, were obvious candidates for prosecution, but they were also among the most difficult to pursue in terms of making high-level arrests and assembling necessary kinds of evidence to achieve convictions. The thematic cases involving notorious but lower-level perpetrators, as illustrated by the Foca rape case, also required careful investigation and involved difficult problems in the handling of witnesses. There was the further concern that witnesses from communities featured in thematic cases might become further traumatized by reliving their experiences, making it difficult to bring them back later as witnesses for the leadership cases. The leadership and thematic cases therefore to some extent have competed for the resources of the tribunal.

Nonetheless, those who work on the thematic cases with notorious perpetrators are emphatic about their importance. Just having completed work on the Foca rape case, Daryl Mundis insisted, "I think clearly this is a piece of the puzzle . . . because we had numerous women from all throughout Bosnia that said this type of thing was happening, and this is clearly one of the stronger cases where we got the actual perpetrators. Again, they're relatively low level, we're never going to find anything from Karadzic telling his soldiers 'Go out and rape all the Muslim women,' we're not going to find that kind of evidence. But clearly this is the type of thing that again fits into the bigger picture of persecution . . . [of] trying to intimidate and drive out the non-Serb population from certain areas in Bosnia."

This is the backdrop against which the Srebrenica and Foca cases both came to center stage in the Hague courtrooms in March 2000. Mark Harmon, acting as lead counsel in the Srebrenica case, and Dirk Ryneveld as lead counsel in the Foca case made the opening statements that set the stage for these two historic trials. Looking over Ryneveld's shoulder as he presented the opening statement in the Foca case were Hildegard, Peggy, and Tej, the threesome who had developed the victims and witnesses and were now seeing this case of rape and sexual enslavement presented by a male lawyer whose belated presence they understandably resented, but whose purpose they nonetheless shared.

THEIR WORLDS COLLAPSED

The week after Mark Harmon gave his opening statement about the Srebrenica genocide, Dirk Ryneveld rose in the neighboring courtroom to make his introductory remarks in the Foca rape camp trial. The three defendants seated across the room were a decade younger and decidedly less professional in their bearing than Srebrenica's middle-aged General Krstic. Ryneveld wasted no time in describing their alleged crimes:

> This is a case about rape camps in eastern Bosnia, whose uncovering in 1992 shocked the world. This is a case about the women and girls, some as young as 12 or 15 years old, who endured unimaginable horrors as their worlds collapsed around them. Before their very eyes, their family members were killed and their homes were destroyed. They were then brutalized, sexually assaulted, and dehumanized by

their captors, including the three accused who sit before you today. This is a case about justice and international laws that seek to proscribe the atrocities committed during the armed conflict. In this trial, you will see the human face of the atrocities, both of the perpetrators and the victims. The victims will testify about what happened to them. They will identify these three men as being among those who raped and tortured them.[6]

The prospect of the victims coming face-to-face in the courtroom with those who years earlier victimized them added a crucial element and chilling intensity to the unfolding trial. Ryneveld noted that because the three defendants were only a few from among a larger number of indicted persons who were still at large, the identities of many of the victims and witnesses in the case would have to be protected, for their own safety and that of their families.

The tribunal's statute, Ryneveld explained next, specifically enumerates rape as a crime against humanity. There could be little question why this should be so when he advised that "the trial chamber will hear that women and children, some as I said earlier, as young as 12 years old in Foca, were detained and raped vaginally, anally, and orally; subjected to gang-rapes, forced to dance nude with weapons pointed at them, and even enslaved."[7] Ryneveld emphasized that these were not simply isolated acts of individual depravity but rather crimes against humanity; that is, these were organized activities within a larger program of ethnic cleansing undertaken across Bosnia in 1992.

The success of this ethnic cleansing operation was reflected by the fact that prior to the spring of 1992, the population of Foca was more than half Muslim. By the following fall there were almost no Muslims in the area, and the Serbs had renamed the town Srbinje to reflect its newly purified Serbian population. The point was that this was not just a trial about rape but also about "an organized campaign of rape and sexual assault upon various women at various locations over a prolonged period of time" and about the role this played in "a policy of ethnic cleansing unleashed by the Bosnian Serb leadership on the non-Serb civilian population."[8]

Much of the trial would consist of witness testimony to establish the involvement of the three individuals in the incidents and patterns of alleged rape. To provide an overall sense of the organization of these events, Ryneveld asked Daryl Mundis to present two schematic diagrams, one that placed the detention site locations on a timeline and another that summarized the interconnections between the locations, victims, and perpetrators. As an example, these charts identified a location that was formerly a Muslim family's home known as "Kara-man's House." This site served as a holding center where many of the victims were kept. Ryneveld observed that "this was the place where, by Mr. Kunarac's own account, his men rested between missions and spent their time off. Kunarac himself has acknowledged being there . . . this house also served as a rape house." This was only one of three houses and additional detention centers.

Ryneveld turned finally to a significant part of the case: the culpability attributed to Kunarac, not only as a perpetrator of rape himself but also for "his failure to either prevent or stop the offenses committed by his subordinates or by his failure to report or to punish his subordinates who committed rapes and other acts of sexual violence." Kunarac was charged with command responsibility that derived from his rank as a corporal and his role in commanding a mine-clearing and reconnaissance detachment that bore his name.[9] The question was how this related to his responsibilities when off duty in Foca. He was personally charged not only with rape but also with being "physically present when his men divided the women up amongst them and raped them."[10]

As Ryneveld brought his opening statement to a conclusion, he addressed the concern of some that this case did not pierce the leadership level of ethnic cleansing in Bosnia. He conceded this point and then responded, "But make no mistake about it: there would have been no ethnic cleansing if there were not individuals willing to turn on their neighbors, to unleash terror and hatred, to turn multi-ethnic communities into homogenous communities and to leave scarred victims. Unlike the policymakers who dealt in theories and plans, these were the individuals who rounded up innocent women and girls, then raped them, or sexually assaulted them, tortured them, enslaved them, and then, in some cases, exchanged, sold, or transferred them to other soldiers. These accused are the individuals who gang-raped these women, while boasting that the women would give birth to Serb babies in order to further humiliate them." Ryneveld closed by quoting from an interview with a victim who had summarized her feelings of dehumanized despair by saying, "I was out of myself, like a machine in their hands."[11]

Much of the remainder of the day and the week that followed involved establishing the setting of the case. Mundis reported that "in the Foca trial the judges . . . wanted to see a lot of the testimony . . . in graphic form, so we simply had the graphics people upstairs create summaries of the evidence." These summaries largely took the form of pie charts. Tej Thapa was called to introduce this documentary material, which was followed with video material about the conflict in Foca.

Ryneveld had traveled to the Foca area so that he would be familiar with the locations of the events. The visit also served the function of bringing home how tense the situation remained in such areas in the Balkans. He recalled that "it was an unusual trip in the sense that we had the French army, about 250 men, with tanks and armored vehicles at every side road where we went. . . . We also had three van loads of Italian military police with us in these motorcades, and every time I got out of the vehicle, they were looking around for snipers."

Ryneveld thought the security might have been excessive but had to give the authorities the benefit of the doubt in light of the behavior of Dragan Gagovic, the first co-accused in the Foca indictment, who the previous year had driven his car directly at SFOR soldiers before being shot.[12] There also was the story of Janko Janic, who had more recently blown himself up with a hand grenade while being pursued by SFOR troops.[13] Only three of the original eight co-accused in Foca had been apprehended, and two others were now dead. These were clearly dangerously violent people.

Krstic was described in the Srebrenica case as a middle manager of mass murder and genocide; Kunarac would emerge from this account as a lower-level leader of a gang of serial rapists who completely dehumanized their victims. Command responsibility was attributed to both, albeit at very different levels, but in ways that contributed to a comprehensive program of ethnic cleansing that led to an alleged genocide in Srebrenica and crimes against humanity in Foca. Ryneveld concluded that in Foca, as elsewhere, "there's usually a leader and people who follow, so that's one of the legal issues in this case."

THREE GENERATIONS OF RAPE

As Dirk Ryneveld planned testimony for the Foca case, he realized that he needed to make his co-counsel, Peggy Kuo and Hildegard Uertz-Retzlaff, central to the presentation of the evidence. This followed from their respective roles in developing the case and the witnesses. Ryneveld emphasized that he was comfortable giving his co-counsel prominent roles in the trial, saying, "I like working with teams." He was also anxious to move beyond the initial awkwardness of being parachuted into the case. "It's very difficult to give instructions with confidence," Ryneveld dryly noted, "in a situation where you may have the top rank . . . but you realize you're the least informed."

Beyond their familiarity with the witnesses and the case, Hildegard, Peggy, and Tej insisted that their roles with the victims also would be essential in getting them through the ordeal of testifying. Tej commented that "there was a moment about six weeks before the trial came when I thought none of them were coming. It took a lot of effort . . . just to get them to come." She gave a lot of credit to the victim witness unit for smoothing out potential problems. Tensions increased as the preparations for the testimony of the first rape victims built toward the first appearance in court. When the day finally came, Tej remembered, "I was just amazed that the witnesses showed up at all."

The division of the courtroom labor was an early turning point in the case. Hildegard insisted she handle the testimony relating to Kunarac—both his own cross-examination and all the testimony by victim witnesses against him. She further insisted that Peggy handle the testimony of the remaining rape victims. Hildegard was uncompromising. She put the issue as starkly as she felt it: "We didn't want a man. We were a woman team. Of course, we had some male investigators. But we found it all a disturbance."

Hildegard had reason for her feelings. She began by insisting, "I think the witnesses . . . have to trust you. . . . They have to know you and build a kind of trust relationship." Some of the rape victims also would need confidentiality, which would involve testifying anonymously and sometimes in closed session. The victim witnesses needed to trust an advocate, such as Hildegard, to provide and protect these arrangements. She explained, "The rape victims need confidentiality for two reasons, not only because they have to fear retaliation, as a usual witness has to fear, but they also have to fear retaliation in their own group. . . . They're treated like someone who needs to feel ashamed, and that is why they all, most of them want protection. They don't want their own families to see and hear. Therefore we had [to arrange] a lot of cases in closed session. . . . There are victims who say, 'My husband doesn't know.'"

Hildegard wanted to be certain that she could control the arrangements for these witnesses and be able to assure them that they would be treated with care and sensitivity. She was blunt in making clear that she didn't trust men, perhaps especially North American men, to do this. Meanwhile, she felt she understood the Balkans through her husband's family and her field work. "I can understand when the people speak, I know what they're talking about culturally, you get a feeling for it in ways that others don't. . . . That helps me . . . because I know how it has to go. And that's sometimes a problem with the Americans because they're always so direct, and . . . this is not a culture where that is allowed."

Dirk Ryneveld agreed to this strategy, saying, "We had a meeting in advance and decided in terms of what would the witnesses be most comfortable with, especially in light of their unique cultural sensitivities, and we felt that since many of them are very young women, very young, some girls, that they may feel more comfortable discussing these things with women. That is not to say that I didn't take some rape victim witnesses, I did, but I took some of the older women, I took some of the mothers." He added, "There were a lot of witnesses to do, so we decided in advance what would be the best way to divide up these responsibilities. I also cross examined the experts." This division of labor was crucial to keeping the team together, and once this bridge was crossed, Ryneveld felt that "the working relationship changed to the point that . . . we . . . [became] a good team." Hildegard simply said, "It was decided who would take the rape victims and then it was okay."

The wisdom of this approach quickly became apparent with Uertz-Retzlaff and Kuo's early and seamless presentation of four powerful witnesses—a grandmother, father, mother, and daughter. Uertz-Retzlaff led with the grandmother (witness 62) and mother (witness 51), and Kuo followed with the daughter (witness 50). Ryneveld handled the father. This set of witnesses graphically made the point that rape was a means of humiliating and terrorizing Muslim families, with the goal of setting examples and getting Muslim residents to permanently leave the area.[14]

Ryneveld drew the connection between the goals and tactics of ethnic cleansing in Srebrenica and Foca this way: "The obvious way is to kill a bunch of people. The other obvious way is to make life so unbearable that they not only want to move out temporarily, but they never want to come back. They just leave en masse. . . . So you murder a portion, you beat the heck out of a portion, and you rape the women." The three generations of women in the Muslim family the chamber heard from early in the Foca case fully illustrated this scenario.

The grandmother had lost her husband when he was taken away and never returned. They presumed he had been killed and thrown in the Drina River. Hildegard Uertz-Retzlaff asked the mother to describe to the court their experiences in the fall of Foca. She responded by recalling that in the spring of 1992 they had begun to spend their nights with other Muslim families in the nearby forest. They were afraid they would otherwise be trapped while sleeping as their houses were burned to the ground. In early July they were captured by Bosnian Serb forces, who promised they would be safely transported from the area. Instead, this began a period of captivity in which the mother was raped once and the daughter innumerable times.[15] Tej Thapa watched this testimony with an initial anxiety that was finally tempered by her relief that "once the first witness went on and she didn't collapse, I really didn't have any concerns about the case. The evidence was really compelling."

Peggy Kuo introduced witness 50, the sixteen-year-old daughter. Witness 50 was singled out the first night by one of the co-accused, Zoran Vukovic, and taken to a separate room where he raped her. "He had a pistol. He threatened. And even had I risked my own life there, I was afraid for my family's lives. So I didn't dare do anything." She didn't even tell her mother what had happened when they were back together. Three years later, when she was interviewed by an investigator from the tribunal, she still did not mention this first incident: "Those words could not leave my mouth." She added in court five years later that "it's not easier for me to talk about it today, but nevertheless, I wanted everyone to hear about it."[16]

Soon after this incident the daughter and mother were taken by bus to the high school in the center of Foca. On the second day at the high school a group of soldiers arrived and picked the daughter and other women to go with them. She was taken to another classroom and was raped. She could only describe the event as "awful. There are no words in this world that could describe my feelings. It is the worst thing that is happening to me."[17] She was kept at the school for ten or eleven days. Each night soldiers would come and select her and other women. Next they were taken to the Partizan Sports Hall, where they were kept on and off for about a month.

Witness 50 was raped repeatedly for much of the next month, sometimes at the Partizan Sports Hall and other times at places where she and others were taken away from the hall. On one occasion she tried to hide in the restroom, but her mother was forced to find her and make her go with the soldiers. On another occasion she was taken by a former neighbor, who was married and twenty years her senior. "It was terrible. He laughed. I had the feeling that he was doing this precisely because he knew me, to inflict even more evil on me." Dragoljub Kunarac also took her from the hall and raped her. "Eight years later and after so many rapes . . . I only know that he was very forceful, that he wanted to hurt me as much as possible."[18]

The hall served as a brothel, with soldiers coming regularly and repeatedly to select whom to rape and how. The soldiers seemed to treat the visits as recreation following their time in battle. Witness 50 described a group of soldiers who "said they had just been at the front line, that they had just returned from the front line, that they had vanquished the Muslims."[19] The rapes were vicious and the ordeal lasted until mid-August 1992, when the rumor spread that the International

Red Cross would be coming for inspections and they were given permits to leave Foca.

RAPE AS A CRIME AGAINST HUMANITY

The story of a twelve-year-old rape victim referred to as AB may be the most disturbing of the succession of accounts the court heard in the Foca trial during the month of April. Ryneveld introduced the story of AB by asking her mother to identify her picture and tell how old she was. An observer in court at the time reported that "instead of an answer, her mother cried. But this was not really a cry. . . . It lasted half a minute, a long, deep, whining sound of somebody, a human being or an animal, so deadly wounded that it can make no other sound but a howl."[20] The court abruptly adjourned to allow the mother to regain her composure.

The mother's husband, AB's father, had been taken away in early June 1992 with about thirty other local Muslim men to the local prison and was never heard of again. The following September another person came and demanded that her daughter go with him. "We cried. She cried too. Then he threatened to kill all of us, and he took her away in a car." Her daughter was returned two days later. Her mother recalled, "I just heard there was this house, Karamen's House, where my daughter was taken. They said they had opened a brothel there . . . and they took children there."[21] The mother had heard that "Zaga," as Kunarac was locally known, ran the house.

Later in September, the mother and daughter were bused with two hundred other local Muslim families to the Partizan Hall in Foca. After spending the day at the hall, they were driven to the Drina Bridge, where the bus was stopped by a police car. "They got out of the car and came to the bus . . . and called us out by name and—called her out by name and surname. We cried and screamed and I tried to see. . . . I didn't see her anymore, and he pointed a gun to my forehead and said he'd kill me, and he told me to keep quiet. And that's how they took her out of the bus." The indictment charged that AB had been sold to a soldier for 200 German marks.[22] The mother never saw her daughter again.

Witness 95 recalled the beginning of the war in April 1992 and her retreat with a group of about twenty persons to a nearby forest. Hildegard led the testimony. Witness 95 explained that they could see a Muslim village across the river in flames and reasoned that if one had to die it would be better "to die by a bullet than [to be] burnt in one's house."[23] About twenty-five members of her family were killed in the war. Her village also eventually was burned, and she was taken with her two young daughters and others to the high school in Foca, where she described being among a number of young women who were individually interrogated and raped.

"The first night . . . one of them came and said, 'You, you, and you, come with me.' And . . . they took us off to another classroom, and there were four men there . . . each of them took one girl or woman." This scenario was repeated daily for about three weeks, but the memory of the first day remained distinct. "[He] told me to take my clothes off, but I refused, and he said 'Take your clothes off,' harshly. And I said, 'I won't.' And he slapped me twice. And as I saw there was no way out for me, then of course I had to take my clothes off." She was raped vaginally and reported afterwards, "I just withdrew into myself." Over the course of about twenty days at the school, she thought, she was raped about 150 times. "You, you, and you, come out." The order echoed through her testimony. "I was taken out every night and every day."[24]

By the beginning of May, the Foca rape case was focusing more specifically on Kunarac's role and the issue of his command responsibility. Witness 48 described being raped about one hundred times and identified Kunarac as saying that "we [Muslim women] would no longer give birth to Muslim babies, but to Serb children."[25] Witness 205 was kept in the house Kunarac controlled and said that "the soldiers always asked Zaga [Kunarac] for everything," including permission to go to the Partizan Hall to collect girls.[26] At the end of May, the prosecution called a former officer in the Yugoslavian and Bosnian army to testify about command responsibility for the behavior of subordinates in the military. He answered that if subordinates were known to have engaged in sexual assault, there was a responsibility to "report it to his superiors and request the dismissal and criminal prosecution of those soldiers."[27] Not doing so is a war crime, if not a crime against humanity.

HOW WIDESPREAD OR SYSTEMATIC?

The presentation of the prosecution's case was coming to an end by early June. The prosecution argued that it had by now established with witness testimony that a crime against humanity was committed in the Foca area that included a widespread or systematic pattern of sexual assaults. The prosecution remained concerned, however, with exactly how widespread or systematic this pattern had to be demonstrated to be in order to meet the requirements of this charge. Peggy Kuo argued that it would be useful to hear from an expert witness, Christine Cleiren, the member of Cherif Bassiouni's commission of experts who had helped prepare a report on the occurrence of rape in Bosnia.

Kuo noted that "what we are concerned about, and the reason we're bringing in somebody like Dr. Cleiren, is that the law may require—and we're not exactly sure how this Trial Chamber will rule on this—may require that there be a larger geographic scale [for it to be considered] . . . widespread or systematic." She continued by suggesting that "rather than bringing in witnesses from all over Bosnia to come in and tell us what happened to them, we believe that it would be more expeditious to bring in an overview witness, someone who could testify as to the pattern of allegations that has emerged."[28] In effect, Kuo was arguing that at this point in the trial it would be useful to see how this case fit as one piece in the larger picture Daryl Mundis described earlier of crimes against humanity in Bosnia.

Dirk Ryneveld also stressed that the case law defining crimes against humanity was not extensive and that there was a problem being sure what the court would regard as meeting the standard of "widespread or systematic" attacks on civilians. "We didn't have a clear indication what a trial chamber would find to be 'widespread or systematic.' . . . We were wondering how much of the rest of Bosnia we might have to prove." Ryneveld continued, "You don't know the limits and you don't want to be the person who fell short. So we thought that what we had to do was to show that in addition to what we could prove in our three or four municipalities that were represented, that this was a representative sample of what was going on in the rest of Bosnia. And since there was a body of evidence that had been collected by the commission of which Tina Cleiren was a part, we thought that that evidence should come in."

Judge David Hunt was concerned that Cleiren would be introducing a collection of unsubstantiated allegations that the court itself would be unable to examine. "What you are asking us to do," he said, "is to accept that there was a pattern of allegations of widespread rape, and to jump from that into accepting that it was much more widespread than the evidence which has been given in this case." Kuo answered that this was where the expertise of the witness and the nature of her evidence became relevant, "because that's where the expertise comes in . . . to say, 'Well, individually, any given allegation may not be true, but if you look at the pattern of it, the fact that they were so specific, that they were occurring at the same time, that the people making the allegations couldn't have communicated with each other . . .'" Hunt interjected, "What sort of expert is this witness? In some form of inference or statistics, or what?" Since Professor Cleiren was a legal scholar, Kuo was obliged to give a simple "no."[29] It eventually was agreed that Cleiren could be called the following day to set the historical context of the case, as she had earlier in the Karadzic-Mladic Rule 61 hearing. The women members of the team felt strongly that Cleiren's testimony should be heard.

When court was called into session the following morning, Ryneveld rose to say that "we have decided, out of an abundance of caution, to cancel the witness we had proposed to call today, Dr. Cleiren."[30] He explained that "we'd had the benefit of thinking about it overnight" and "I made a prosecutor's call, basically." Judge Hunt responded by saying that "article 5 does not require you to prove that the rapes were widespread, it only requires you to prove that the *armed conflict against the civilian population* was widespread."[31] Ryneveld was quick to concur, saying, "Absolutely. Rape is *one* of the constituent ingredients in the widespread *or* systematic attack." Thinking on his feet with this deft and cogent phrasing, Ryneveld had synthesized and summarized the core jurisprudence of this case. Hunt reiterated that "we do have to be satisfied beyond reasonable doubt that the *attacks* were widespread."[32] Ryneveld later concluded that "the bottom line is that they did find that we had proved 'widespread or systematic' with a very much smaller representative sample" and with rape as the key constituent element in this case.

DEFENDING KUNARAC

The beginning of the defense phase of the Foca case coincided with the promotion of Hildegard Uertz-Retzlaff to the position of senior trial attorney. She was ambivalent about this promotion. "I actually didn't want it at the beginning because I liked the investigation stage of the proceedings very much and the senior trial attorney is not so much involved in the investigations anymore. . . . But it was obvious to me that with my role and experience I would continue to be in court and in all sorts of cases. So I thought . . . I should be a senior trial attorney." This was a timely event, since Hildegard knew more about Kunarac and his prospective defense than anyone else, and she now could handle his cross-examination with new authority.

There also was a looming set of major prison camp trials that had important implications for the membership and dynamics of the Foca team. Dusko Sikirica, the alleged commander of the Keraterm detention camp in Prejidor, was arrested and was scheduled to go on trial as early as possible in the new year.[33] It was now apparent that Uertz-Retzlaff and Kuo were more than capable of handling remaining responsibilities in the Foca case, so it made sense to extend their roles while assigning Dirk Ryneveld new and added responsibility for the Sikirica case.

A further indication of the quickening pace of the court was the setting of an early trial date for Milorad Krnojelac, the former warden of a Foca prison that was turned into a detention camp where many Muslim men were tortured and killed.[34] This would be the second in a series of expected cases related to Foca. Uertz-Retzlaff would soon be assigned as lead counsel for this case, with Kuo as her co-counsel and Thapa as their crime analyst. First, however, they would have to finish their work on the defense portion of the original Foca case. Asked how the rest of this case went, Tej answered in a way that focused on the other women of the team, saying, "It worked because . . . we had a history of working very well together, we are good friends, and I think that's the primary bond that pulled us through it."

The defense's opening statement, offered jointly on behalf of the three accused during the first week of July, seemed to carry all the historical baggage of Robert Kaplan's *Balkan Ghosts.*[35] It began with the settlement of the Foca area in 1363. Judge Hunt quickly responded, "We are not concerned with what happened in the 14th century." The defense team went on to argue the ensuing political grievances of the Serbs in Bosnia, leading Hunt to insist again, "We are not here to determine who was at fault in starting the conflict."[36]

The first defense witness was Kunarac himself. His appearance was an extension of his perplexing behavior at the initial hearings of his case. Kunarac said the confusion regarding his guilt dated back to when he surrendered to SFOR in 1998: "I said that I felt guilt and had a guilty consciousness for [protected prosecution witness DB]. I surrendered in order to prove my innocence in relation to everything else."[37] In his testimony, he explained that he had become concerned about a story associated with a journalist, Gordana Draskovic, who had interviewed witness DB and been told that he and others were raping women held in detention in Foca. Kunarac indicated that he had had sexual intercourse with only one of the women indicated in the Foca indictment, the protected witness DB.

He maintained that to investigate this story he went first to the Partizan Hall to make inquiries and then by car with DB to the house at 16 Osmana Djikica to investigate the charges of rape and to elicit from DB or others the names of those who might have been responsible. He reported that he spoke with DB for an hour or two in a room of the house. "She was sitting next to me. . . . Then she started kissing me on the mouth, on the body. . . . After that I accepted this behavior of hers and we had full sexual vaginal intercourse, although I did nothing to give her reason or pretext for this."[38] Judge Florence Mumba asked

Kunarac, "Is it your position, accused, that DB seduced you?" He answered, "I had sexual intercourse with her against my will."[39] He insisted that his persistent intent was to investigate the journalist's rape charges. "I wanted to clear all this up. . . . I had the sincere intention of bringing criminal charges . . . so that the authorities could take the appropriate measures."[40]

Notwithstanding Kunarac's description of the lengths to which he went in pursuing the culprits in the charges of rape, his defense counsel sought to dispel the assumption that Kunarac had this responsibility as part of his military role or functions. These points were made by describing the voluntary nature of the reconnaissance work that he periodically undertook with groups of four or five fellow soldiers. "Once I completed my assignment and they returned from the assignment, they would go back to their basic units and carry on the tasks that they were doing before they went on assignment with me. And I had no means of controlling them, nor was it my duty to do so. So I did not know their whereabouts."[41]

Hildegard Uertz-Retzlaff conducted the entire cross-examination of Kunarac. Her initial questions were designed to establish his command responsibility. He insisted that his role was focused on individual assignments, but he conceded, "I was the leader of this assignment and in charge of seeing that the assignment was carried out at that particular moment." Hildegard focused intensively on the encounter Kunarac reported with DB. Her questions elicited a view of this encounter that mixed issues of gender, power, fear, and nationality. He reported that "she herself started to physically excite me and to engage in sexual relations; that is to say, she was a Muslim, I was a Serb, but the sexual relationship that I had with her at the time was not a relationship." He acknowledged that he could sense the feelings of fear of DB and other women at the house. Hildegard then read back to him from a statement he had given in an interview with a tribunal investigator. "I realized that there was fear. By their behavior, I felt fear. They were disheveled; they were dirty. At that time they hated me because I was the enemy of their people. I was the enemy of their side in the conflict. She was crying." Kunarac then retreated into his protests that "I was confused" and "she caught me unaware."[42]

RYNEVELD VERSUS RADINOVIC

The defense challenged the prosecution charge that the alleged rapes constituted a crime against humanity in the sense of being a systematic or widespread attack on civilians. The defense argued that because a majority of the witnesses who testified to being rape victims were from the same village, the pattern of assault was neither systematic nor widespread.[43] The defense also presented the retired Yugoslav general and now professor Radovan Radinovic, who subsequently testified in the Krstic case. He testified here that Kunarac had no authority over soldiers from his unit when they returned to Foca, maintaining that Kunarac's command responsibility only included the time when they were "functionally" engaged in a mission.[44] In this sense, Radinovic argued that Kunarac had only a functional command responsibility.

Ryneveld resumed a lead role in several days of cross-examination of Radinovic. Drawing from the previous experience of Mundis as a military lawyer, Ryneveld and Mundis designed a sequence of questions designed to expose the implausibility of positions taken by Radinovic. In retrospect, Ryneveld remarked that "I think that was an extremely interesting cross-examination where he more or less was led down the path of the scenes of *A Few Good Men*." Mundis explained, "Look at what he [the military prosecutor] did with Nicholson, where he just boxed him in, because . . . the character that Nicholson portrayed is the same personality [as Radinovic]." Ryneveld continued, "I'm not saying that this is an exact adaptation . . . I'm just saying we boxed him into a position from which he ought not to be able to escape."

The questioning of Radinovic began by establishing his knowledge of military regulations:

Q: General, you are familiar with all these regulations, are you not?
A: Yes. . . .
Q: And these regulations provide that the responsibility of a commander for the conduct of his subordinates "begins the moment he had failed to undertake all the necessary steps within his powers to prevent and obstruct the perpetration of war crimes or crimes against humanity"; is that right?
A: Yes, yes.
Q: Now, Professor, are there any exceptions to those regulations?
A: No.
Q: Well, then, Professor, can you please point to the section in the regulations that says that functional commanders are not responsible for the actions of their subordinates?
A: I did not say that, nor can I point that out, but the function of commander has responsibility only for as long as that function lasts, his function as commander. And I stated that the function of Kunarac was temporary in nature because the group itself was established ad hoc. That is the fine distinction.
Q: So there's no exception in the regulations that says a function—

A: No.

Q: —commander doesn't have responsibility for his subordinates, correct?

A: No, there is not.[45]

As the exchange continued, Radinovic sought to reestablish his distinction between a restrictive functional responsibility and a more comprehensive command responsibility. Ryneveld countered by leading Radinovic back into a series of affirmations of the importance of maintaining good order and discipline at all times and then asked for a luncheon recess.

When cross-examination resumed in the afternoon, Ryneveld focused on the contact that Kunarac maintained with his men at the detention centers and houses where the women were kept. Ryneveld reminded Radinovic that Kunarac had told investigators that he conducted his own investigation of an incident in which he believed someone had posed as him at one of the detention centers. Ryneveld continued:

Q: He said in his statement, "I lined up my men and told them that whoever did this, that I personally was going to execute them, and they knew me well." There's a reference to "my men," and he's lined them up. Is that consistent with the actions of someone who is in charge?

A: No.[46]

Turning to a later part of the statement, Ryneveld recalled Kunarac having taken witness DB to one of the houses, presumably to identify men who attacked her.

Q: He [Kunarac] said, "And I then issued a military order for all men to leave, and I only left one at the entrance of the house. I issued him an order to not allow anyone to enter the house." Fairly clear language, is it not, sir?

A: That can be interpreted in different ways. You are interpreting it that way, but I interpret it as the position of a man who has a reputation and authority, and when his authority was smeared, then he wanted to confront the people knowing that he did not do that. That is how I interpret it. Everything that he says is derived from his reputation, his personal reputation as an asserted soldier for combat tasks, and he is doing that on the basis of that reputation, not on the basis of command function.

Q: Sir, if those men obeyed that order, would you not agree that it appears that Mr. Kunarac believes he is their commander and they

believe he is their commander, and everybody acts in accordance
with that belief; isn't that true?

A: It doesn't seem that way to me.[47]

The day's testimony was coming to an end, and Ryneveld found his
opportunity to close on the theme he had begun with twenty-four hours
earlier—that this was a witness of dubious objectivity—in this closing
exchange:

Q: Well, sir, we also see in the balance of the statement that Mr. Kunarac
      was aware of the allegations that were made by various detainees,
      including these women, both against himself and against the sol-
      diers under his command and control . . . If that is, indeed, so, by
      his failure to take proper action, was he not in violation of his duty
      and thereby would render himself criminally responsible for the
      violations?

A: If that is your question, my answer is in the negative. No. Kunarac
      was not commander of a unit but of a group that is disbanded the
      very moment they return from an assignment. From that moment
      onwards, he has no authority whatsoever over the members of
      groups that he headed, and he also has no obligations towards them
      either.

Q: And that is your objectively held view, is it, sir?

A: Yes.[48]

Ryneveld concluded that Radinovic had "built this house of cards and
then we blew it over and he's still trying to pick up the pieces and put it
back together, but by then . . . it became an issue of affecting credibility,
so you couldn't lose."

CLOSING PHASES OF THE FOCA TRIAL

The Foca rape case resumed in the early fall, and the court heard first
from physicians who had been called as witnesses from their practices
in Belgrade. The first said that she was "shocked" that no medical evidence was presented to confirm the problems that would have followed
from the violent rapes that had been described in court, claiming that
"without a file, it's as if the rape did not happen." Another asserted that
rape charges "must be medically proven because half of the women
who report have not been raped at all."[49] Peggy Kuo answered that there
was no opportunity to receive medical attention in Foca at the time of
the rapes.

Prosecution witness 87 reappeared to deny a claim that she had been
romantically involved with Kovac, although she was kept at his apart-

ment and may have received some protection from being raped by others: "For me, it was the same, but if you wish one could say that there is a difference between being raped by one or two, and being raped by twenty soldiers."[50] Hildegard Uertz-Retzlaff emphasized how difficult it was to recall witnesses to refute Kovac, saying, "This was really a very bad experience for them. They were very, very angry about this situation."

When the time for closing statements finally arrived, Uertz-Retzlaff spoke first for the prosecution, reflecting her new prominence in the case. She reminded the court on this cold and gray November morning that Foca was unlike any rape case heard in a national jurisdiction, in that the thirty-one prosecution witnesses, including sixteen rape victims, had testified about a program of ethnic cleansing. In legal terms, the rapes were part of a crime against humanity that involved a widespread and systematic attack on the non-Serb civilian population of the Foca area. It was a program of expulsion through terror, with rape used as an instrument to instill this terror. Uertz-Retzlaff underlined the inconsistencies and implausibilities of Kunarac's defense and then emphasized that the testimonies of the rape victims in particular were "reliable, convincing and corroborate each other."[51]

Next, Kuo specifically addressed all of the elements that are required to establish rape as a war crime and a crime against humanity. In particular, she addressed the widespread and systematic nature of the attack on civilians in Foca, noting that all five thousand Muslims who had lived in Foca itself were now gone and that "the repeated and continuous nature of the attack was evidence enough that it was systematic."[52] She emphasized that the three co-accused were "right in the middle of the attack" and that not only were they responsible personally for their individual sexual assaults on the victims but also that "whenever the accused acted in concert or as part of a plan, all the accused must be held responsible for each other's actions."[53] Kuo singled out Kunarac for his superior responsibility as commander of the detachment to which these individuals belonged and turned to Dirk Ryneveld to address this final charge.

Ryneveld argued that there was much evidence not only that Kunarac received and gave orders in ways that reflected his de jure command authority over his detachment, but also that when not in the field or on ordered missions, he also exercised clear de facto command authority over his men. He reasoned, for example, that the court had heard evidence that a group of mostly Serb soldiers from Montenegro spent their time in a house at 16 Osmana Djikica and that "whenever Kunarac was in the house, No. 16, he was the one issuing orders, and the other soldiers would listen to him." He concluded that "from this evidence, it is safe to draw the inference that these men who raped the victims at the house were men under Kunarac's command."[54]

Ryneveld's closing remarks emphasized how terrified the victims in Foca were before, during, and after the rapes. He noted that "one told you that what she suffered at the hands of Kunarac still hurt her soul; another experiences fear to this day every time there is an unexpected knock on her door; yet others talk about recurring nightmares to this day. Not one of them will ever forget. They are but representative samples of the suffering inflicted upon these girls and women."[55] It was in this context that Ryneveld asked the court to sentence Kunarac to thirty-five years in prison and his co-accused to thirty and fifteen years' imprisonment, respectively.

The defense asserted in response that Kunarac should be imprisoned for no more than five years and that his co-accused should be released. The defense held that there was no widespread or systematic attack on civilians and that there were no detention centers or rape camps but only places where the "refugees were temporarily situated" as a result of "the outbreak of a spontaneous conflict."[56] Defense counsel Slavisa Prodanovic insisted that the prosecution "did not prove that the alleged victims of rape were exposed to any severe physical or psychological suffering." He drew an audible gasp from the gallery when he concluded that "the rape itself is not an act that inflicts severe bodily pain."[57] As the Foca trial was declared closed in the end of November, there seemed good reason to expect convictions, but uncertainty remained about the charges for which convictions would result and the sentences that would follow.

THE FOCA VERDICT

The usually sparsely attended courtroom gallery at the tribunal was packed and overflowing on a Thursday in the third week of February for the announcement of the Foca judgment. The defendants seemed to almost beam with confidence as they entered the court and shook hands with their defense counsel. One stopped to kiss the hand of his female attorney.[58] Reporters and observers watched from the gallery and from elsewhere in the building on large overhead monitors. The defendants grew somber as they assumed their seats. A hush swept over the courtroom as Judge Florence Mumba of Zambia prepared to present the verdict.

Mumba's summary of the three hundred-page judgment found that the Bosnian Serb army had especially targeted Muslim women and used rape camps along with expulsion as "instruments of terror" in the early phases of its attack on Foca. After identifying ways in which the terror was imposed, Mumba returned to the issue of leadership, acknowledging that "the three accused are certainly not in the category of the political or military masterminds behind the conflicts and atrocities." Yet, she emphasized, "political leaders and war generals are powerless if the ordinary people refuse to carry out criminal activities in the course of war," adding that "lawless opportunists should expect no mercy, no matter how low their position in the chain of command may be." In this way, the court addressed the point made so often in the aftermath of the Holocaust that genocide and crimes against humanity require the willing involvement of ordinary people.[59]

Two key features of the court's verdict were its explicit conviction of two of the accused for rape as a crime against humanity and its depiction of the organized and sustained nature of this crime as a form of enslavement. Peggy Kuo commented after the trial that "this case . . . makes clear that slavery is not only forced labor but can also be sexual in nature." Rape had never before been recognized as a wartime form of enslavement, and the definition of rape in this case as a crime against humanity moved this offense to a newly elevated level of seriousness despite the relatively low rank of the accused. The acts were recognized as crimes against humanity because they were part of a campaign of systematic attacks against a civilian population across a geographic area and because the acts included elements of enslavement.[60] Dragoljub Kunarac was singled out by the court for special attention. Although he was not found guilty for violations of command responsibility, this responsibility was treated as an aggravating factor in his sentence. Mumba addressed Kunarac directly, saying, "You were a soldier with courage in the field, someone whom your men undisputably are said to have held in high esteem. By this natural authority you could easily have put an end to the women's suffering. Your active participation in this nightmarish scheme of sexual exploitation is therefore even more repugnant."[61] He was sentenced to twenty-eight years in prison.

The court elaborated its use of the concept of enslavement in sentencing Radomir Kovac to twenty years in prison. Kovac was sentenced not only for raping and selling the twelve-year-old child who permanently disappeared but also for holding three other girls who, Mumba explained, "you kept as your slaves, to be used whenever the desire took you, to be given to whomsoever you wished to show a favor. You relished the absolute power you exerted over their lives, which you made abundantly clear by making them dance naked on a table while you watched. When they had served their purpose, you sold them too."[62] Although the final co-accused, Zoran Vukovic, was acquitted of the majority of the charges against him, his brutality and abuse of young girls was emphasized, and he was found guilty of crimes against humanity and sentenced to twelve years in prison.

Patricia Sellers, who has worked on sexual assault cases in Bosnia and Rwanda for the tribunal from its inception, called the Foca judgment "monumental jurisprudence," noting that in conjunction with other cases "now we say rape is a crime, a crime against humanity, or a war crime, or a constituent part of genocide." While acknowledging the expansion in this legal attention to rape, Kelly Askin has argued that the judgment could have more explicitly made the point that the enslavement in this case was primarily for the purpose of making rape regularly available to those who took advantage of the women who were victimized. Askin emphasizes, however, how important the Foca case is for rejecting the impunity commonly granted rape in wartime.[63]

Ordinary men had become the subjects of extraordinary jurisprudence. "They look no different," a court observer noted, "from the next man, just like three guys who like to hang out in the bars." There was no indication as they filed from the court that they felt remorse. They had pled not guilty, and there was no apparent sense of guilt in their demeanor. Their defense in the end was that they had not killed those with whom they had sex and that therefore these acts should not be taken seriously as crimes. The impunity experienced by soldiers who raped in many other wars was probably especially taken for granted in the patriarchal context of the Balkans. The three men sentenced for their involvement in the Foca rape camps were probably not very different from many others around them. Slavenka Drakulic observed from the courtroom gallery that "hundreds of thousands of normal people simply believed they were right in what they were doing. Otherwise such big numbers of rapes and murders can hardly be explained. The idea that normal men, and not monsters, committed such crimes is even more frightening."[64]

MOVING TO MILOSEVIC

It would be a mistake to conclude this account without emphasizing the sense of shared purpose and commitment that emerged from the work of this divided but determined investigation and trial team. The division was in part an inevitable result of Ryneveld's being parachuted into an investigation that Kuo and Uertz-Retzlaff had already largely completed and probably could have concluded through the trial phase by themselves. Yet the division also probably resulted from the different orientations that Ryneveld and the women on the team brought to their work.

Ryneveld focused on the world beyond Bosnia, especially on those watching the tribunal in the rest of Europe and in North America for its historic jurisprudence. He wanted, as much as the women who preceded him on the case, to make constructive contributions to international humanitarian and criminal law, and he did so by assisting the court's understanding of rape as an instrument of terror, a form of enslavement, and a crime against humanity. Of course, none of this could have happened without the witnesses on whose testimony the case was built. The women members of this team focused as a tightly coordinated unit on the needs of these individuals in Bosnia, who would never have been successfully brought to the tribunal to testify without this care and attention. Yet the gender division of roles on the Foca trial team threatened to pull it apart. The women on the team had lived with both the personal and the political dimensions of the case from its inception, and they were intensely protective of both. It took all of this team's collective social skills to find the right way to share their courtroom roles and to develop a workable relationship that responded effectively to the demands of the case and to the needs of the victims.

In the end they succeeded in drawing on their respective strengths to make the Foca trial team work. They all shared the goal of obtaining convictions that would recognize sexual enslavement and rape as war crimes and crimes against humanity, and they all relished the fact that these convictions and sentences emerged unscathed in the subsequent appeal process. When Ryneveld moved on to form a new team with Daryl Mundis and Julia Baly for the Prijedor prison trial, he found himself fully at home with his work at the tribunal. "This is an extremely difficult case, but we're having fun," he reported. Although the case was then still in transition from the investigation to the trial phase, Ryneveld was fully engaged and enthusiastic. "Everyone is getting along. We're friends. . . . If you thought the morale was good with the strained relationship, you ought to see this one. This one is just excellent."

Hildegard, Peggy and Tej were just as enthusiastic about their own new team. Tej remarked, "I respect them and I respect their commitment to the work . . . it's a good working relationship. They know what I can do, I know what they can do—there's a good division. We don't tread on each other and we're not fighting for little pieces of this and little pieces of that, for praise or glory, or whatever it is." She went on to explain how this group had stayed together and moved on to its own role in the Milosevic case, saying, "I think what tends to happen is, because [of] the experiences like the Srebrenica team or the Foca team, because you work well, you just pull your people along with you when you go. So when Hildegard was assigned to do Milosevic/Croatia, she immediately, her first reaction was 'I want Peggy and Tej.'" Although the three-some seemed unlikely to work again with Ryneveld, they nonetheless agreed there were ways they could accommodate one another. Ryneveld and Uertz-Retzlaff today have neighboring offices and are crossing paths on the Milosevic case. Tej Thapa concluded, "They'll always work to complement each other."

Tej expressed a clear sense of her purpose in continuing her work at the tribunal, and her explanation echoed sentiments expressed by many others, including Mark Harmon at the conclusion of the previous chapter. She said of the victims and witnesses she worked with that "these are people whose lives were deeply affected by what happened and their relief and the strength that they got from coming forward and testifying was tremendous. That was very, very gratifying to me—that it made a difference to their lives. And that was something that was quite unexpected for me. I didn't know that people would feel so restored. Not that it can ever make them better or make anything go away . . . but they felt good about doing it."

Nancy Paterson similarly remembered one of the moments that captured for her the sustaining power of such experiences with her description of a small party that marked the end of a mission with rape victims and others near Tuzla in Bosnia. Smiling slightly, she recalled, "I think my fondest memory . . . will be the summer of 1996 . . . after Dayton when we could actually first go in with escort troops, and actually go in to Republika Srpska and do crime scenes. We took a three week mission, it was a very intense mission, and at the end of the mission our Bosnian friends threw a party for us in the garden of one of the people." She went on to explain why this gathering was so memorable for her. "It was just basically a cookout, nothing particularly fancy, but we were all there and invited a few other people we knew from the UN. To this day, we all swear it was the best party that any of us have gone to in our lives. The timing was perfect, the company was perfect, it'd been a long hard mission but everybody felt very satisfied with what we had accomplished. It was so nice to have the party thrown for us by the Bosnians. That they were considerate enough to do that. It was very special." The power of such experiences is reflected in the growth and maturation of the International Criminal Tribunal in The Hague and its linkages into the wider emerging field of international humanitarian and criminal law.

CHAPTER SEVEN

Courting Contempt

Within days of the opening of the Milosevic trial in February 2002, the UN announced in New York City that sixty countries had ratified the 1998 Treaty of Rome, the number required to establish a permanent International Criminal Court (ICC). An ICC office in The Hague began receiving potential cases the following July. The ICC is seen by many nations and nearly all U.S. allies as a means of enforcing the international rule of criminal law beyond the confines of nation-states and against illegitimate claims of sovereign immunity. This permanent court institutionalizes universal goals of liberal legalism, most notably the rule of law, by means of the enforcement of international humanitarian and criminal law.

The Bush administration soon sent its ambassador for war crimes, Pierre-Richard Prosper, to present its alternative conception of international criminal law to a congressional international relations committee. His remarks were provocatively titled "The U.N. Criminal Tribunals for Yugoslavia and Rwanda: International Justice or Show of Justice?"[1] Prosper advanced an argument for an *ad hoc legalism* that is intentionally impermanent and adaptive to situational demands. Its core principle is that "when domestic justice is not possible for egregious war crimes due to a failed state or a dysfunctional judicial system, the international community may, through the [UN] Security Council or by consent, step in on an ad hoc basis." Prosper continued by promising that "In the years ahead, the United States will continue to lead the fight to end impunity for genocide, crimes against humanity, and war crimes. We will help create the political will. We will continue to seek to bring justice as close as feasibly and credibly possible to the victims in order to create a sense of ownership and involvement. In our work with the Rwanda and Yugoslav Tribunals, the Special Court for Sierra Leone, and elsewhere, we will stress that all parties have a responsibility on the road to justice." Prosper followed with a mixed assessment of the Rwandan and Yugoslav tribunals, concluding that both "are on the path to success" but that "in both Tribunals, at times, the professionalism of some of the personnel has been called into question with allegations of mismanagement and abuse. And in both tribunals, the process, at times, has been costly, has lacked efficiency, has been too slow, and has been too removed from the everyday experience of the people and the victims." This was a mixed message reflecting long-term U.S. ambivalence about international criminal law.

These remarks underlined a distinction between the ad hoc International Criminal Tribunals for the former Yugoslavia and Rwanda and a permanent International Criminal Court, which are all descendants of the Nuremberg International Military Tribunal. Liberal legalism sees a historical progression from Nuremberg that the United States refutes by refusing to ratify the Treaty of Rome and its permanent ICC. Most European Union countries, along with Canada, New Zealand, and a number of African, eastern European, and central Asian countries already have ratified this treaty.[2]

When Prosper appeared before the House committee in late February 2002, he also indicated that the ad hoc Rwandan and Yugoslav tribunals should complete their work by 2008. The charge of inefficiency seemed at odds with the extended timetable. Meanwhile, he reiterated the Bush administration's opposition to the ICC, reasserting that it lacked sufficient safeguards against a "politicization of justice"[3] that could jeopardize American citizens, a position that would harden in months to follow.

Prosper is a youthful and politically astute African American. His remarks gained further credibility because he is a former prosecutor of Los Angeles gangs, he successfully prosecuted a genocide case at the Rwanda tribunal in 1998, and he has played a primary role in negotiating the ad hoc tribunal for Sierra Leone. In short, Prosper has earned a right to be heard when speaking about international criminal law. Yet many also questioned the ingenuousness of airing the Bush administration's misgivings about both the ad hoc tribunals and the permanent court using language about a "show of justice" and a "politicization of justice," language similar to the invective Milosevic was directing more or less simultaneously at the Hague tribunal. The timing was ironic, to say the least.

Carla Del Ponte responded that the ICTY already had in place an "exit strategy" for 2008, adding that "there may be people who are saying [after 11 September] the world has moved on and the issue of the day is now terrorism," but, "we cannot take that view of international justice."[4] The Council of Europe condemned Prosper's allegations as "unacceptable American pressure and attempts to interfere with international justice," and Human Rights Watch called the remarks a "smear campaign," while Kofi Annan rejected "any allegations of corruption and mismanagement."[5] Meanwhile, the president of the Hague tribunal, Judge Claude Jorda, welcomed the U.N.'s decision to move ahead with the ICC and reasoned that "the work accomplished to date by the ad hoc Tribunals for the former Yugoslavia and for Rwanda will thus be continued and amplified."[6]

It sometimes seems that Prosper is actually the more supportive member of a "good cop, bad cop" administration tag team with regard to international criminal law. The other member is John Bolton, an undersecretary of state for arms control and international security. Bolton is the point person for the administration's insistence that the ICC is a potential "rogue court" and a threat to U.S. sovereignty, as well as its politicians and military personnel. Bolton's response is an argument for *legal exceptionalism* that would grant U.S. citizens a special immunity from ICC prosecution. Such immunity is a threat to basic principles of the universal rule of law that are the core of liberal legalism.

Bolton argues for legal exceptionalism along three lines: by advocating that the United States "remove" or "unsign" itself from the Rome Treaty (a largely symbolic signature for President Clinton, with no real expectation of congressional ratification), by encouraging Congress to forbid Americans at all levels of government from cooperating with the new court (a preemptive strike at the kind of transgovernmental alliances with U.S. agencies the ICTY has pursued), and by insisting on exemptions for Americans from ICC jurisdiction (based on a possibility of prosecution that seems unlikely to most observers). Bolton began in early May 2002 by writing Kofi Annan a one-paragraph letter saying that "the United States does not intend to become a party to the [Rome] treaty" and "accordingly, the United States has no legal obligations from its signature on December 31, 2000."[7] A summary overview of liberal legalism, ad hoc legalism, and legal exceptionalism is presented in the table opposite.

Within a week of Bolton's "unsigning," the House passed a bill authorizing the president to use force to rescue any American held by the ICC. Critics wondered whether its sponsor, Tom DeLay, understood that under the rescue provision "we would be sending our troops to invade the Netherlands."[8] Subsequent efforts focused on establishing bilateral agreements with nations that they would not allow extradition of U.S. citizens to the ICC.

The Bush administration has continued to alternately use its voices of ad hoc legalism and legal exceptionalism, with the former again

Overview of Positions on International Criminal Law

Legal Regime	Signature Element	International Framework	Principal Features	Prominent Advocate
Liberal legalism	Universal rule of law	Multilateral	Permanent and free-standing	Louise Arbour
Ad hoc legalism	Law in the breach	Bi- and multilateral	Impermanent and adaptive	Pierre Richard Prosper
Legal exceptionalism	U.S. immunity from rogue court	Unilateral	National sovereignty	John Bolton

articulated by Prosper. He arrived at the Hague tribunal the week after his congressional appearance and held a press conference with ICTY prosecutor Carla Del Ponte. He now emphasized that the United States would see the tribunal through its work, including trying Karadzic and Mladic, who, he said, "cannot out-wait justice." The same press account noted that "Mr. Prosper seemed at pains to temper the criticism he delivered last week in testimony on Capitol Hill."[9] Del Ponte reemphasized her plan for the tribunal to end twenty current investigations of one hundred suspects by 2004 and finish trials by 2008. Prosper said he was "in complete agreement."[10]

He then observed the trial of Slobodan Milosevic.[11] It is impossible to know what Prosper was thinking as he watched the Milosevic trial, but he might well have been recalling just how involved he and Colin Powell had been in working with Carla Del Ponte to get Milosevic transferred to The Hague. He might also have been considering how heavily involved the United States was in laying the groundwork for this trial with NATO and the UN, its further voluntary financial support, and its representation by American employees at the ICT. By these means and more, the United States is heavily invested in the success of ad hoc legalism and the ICT. Prosper might well have been contemplating this investment as he watched this historic trial through the bulletproof glass of the tribunal's public gallery.

THE MILOSEVIC TRANSFER

The prologue to this book mentions Colin Powell's phone call to Carla Del Ponte on the day of Slobodan Milosevic's first appearance at the tribunal. This was not the first indication of interest by the U.S. secretary of state in what already was being called "the trial of the twenty-first century." Powell was seeking reassurance about the strength of the case against Milosevic. Nancy Paterson's interview with a *Boston Globe* staff writer, which became the basis of stories in newspapers around the world, had piqued Powell's concern. "If the Serbian government continues to be cooperative, especially with access to witnesses," Paterson told the *Globe*, "proving the case is going to be a lot easier. But, hey," she continued, "it's the Balkans. It can take weeks and months to get things to happen that would happen in a minute elsewhere."[12] Since she had co-written the Milosevic indictment, she knew what she was talking about. Powell, who at Del Ponte's urging had been working for months to get Milosevic to The Hague, probably already realized how prolonged and perilous the end game of this case would be.

Powell's predecessor and sometime adversary, Madeleine Albright, was previously the most highly placed advocate of the ICT in the U.S. government. She had campaigned for the ICT as the ambassador to the UN and had established the ambassador-level post for war crimes first filled by David Scheffer. Unlike their predecessor at State, Henry Kissinger, Powell and Albright had little to fear from international law, even though Louise Arbour and Carla Del Ponte both insisted that the leaders of NATO, the United States, and any other parties involved in the Balkan wars were fair game for prosecution—if grounds were found.[13] Powell was an especially unlikely target for the ICT, however, since he was widely known for his opposition to the use of NATO forces in the Balkans.[14] As secretary of state, Powell now had found a perhaps ironic monetary means of helping the ICT take Milosevic into custody.[15]

With Del Ponte's encouragement, Powell made himself the principal transnational player in a field of financial contributors to a fund to rebuild Yugoslavia's shattered economy. He led with a U.S. pledge of $181 million to be committed at a donors' conference in Brussels *after* it became clear that Milosevic would be transferred to the ICT. Fifteen European Union (EU) countries pledged $445 million, and the World Bank added $150 million. The total aid package amounted to more than $1.25 billion.[16] The scale and origins of this aid package are reminders that the globalization of the world economy as well as the end of the cold war and the media-assisted rise of human rights activism have all played important roles in shaping the political opportunity structure within which international humanitarian law is developing.

The EU was to officially host the donors' conference in Brussels, but Powell refused to participate until there was evidence that Milosevic would be transferred to the ICT. The conference was rescheduled several times as the Yugoslav government struggled to extract Milosevic from a Belgrade prison. When the transfer was accomplished, the German chancellor, Gerhard Schröder, felicitously described the reward as a "dividend of democracy." The *Guardian* reported that "donors met in an upbeat mood after Thursday's long awaited handover allowed the rump of Yugoslavia to reintegrate into the respectable European mainstream. And nobody pretended that the terms of the bargain were otherwise."[17]

The *Daily Telegraph* put the matter even more starkly, observing that "the west bribed Belgrade to hand over the tyrant, and the Serbian nation, weary of its pariah status, acquiesced in the bargain." Yet the *Telegraph*'s point was not to be critical but to praise: "that such an unprecedented extradition could be accomplished without serious bloodshed is a tribute to the courage of Zoran Djindjic, the Serbian Prime Minister."[18] Nonetheless, the *New York Times* tentatively noted that "some legal scholars are disturbed by the pressure put on Yugoslavia by rich nations, especially the United States, through threats that money needed to rebuild the country would be withheld until Mr. Milosevic was turned over."[19]

The bribery and threatening involved in the funding were the new tactics of agency and structural linkage that Del Ponte and Powell used to finally gain custody of Milosevic. The sociologist John Meyer's skeptical insights about systemic decoupling stimulated our focus on structural linkage to explain the first steps of primary norm enforcement that broke the logjam on arrests at the tribunal. Del Ponte's predecessor Louise Arbour issued secret indictments to break this logjam and to enlist NATO forces in the initiation of a cascade of tribunal arrests and transfers in 1997. Meyer further notes that when multinational corporations use monetary bribes and threats to manipulate states and regimes (for example, to seal sales and contracts), this often is seen as the height of illegitimacy, but when states and regimes use such tactics they are accepted as legitimate. States effectively have a monopoly control over legal use of such inducements, with the result that they "bribe each other routinely, and employ all the standard political manipulations."[20] In this case, the transgovernmental sponsorship of the donors' conference was used to make these monetary manipulations appear less direct and more legitimate.[21]

Unattractive tactics of apprehension have plenty of precedent in international criminal law. Israel abducted Eichmann, international sanctions forced Libya to surrender the Lockerbie defendants, the threatened loss of U.S. financial and military aid had earlier convinced Croatia to turn over General Blaskic to the tribunal,[22] and when Albright later threatened to block loans from the International Monetary Fund, Croatia followed by sending ten indictees to Arbour at the ICT.[23] Powell was following a well-traveled path in his use of financial incentives and coercion to assist Del Ponte in apprehending Milosevic, who was himself a previous obstacle to the influence of monetary sanctions and the resulting object of military and legal coercion.

THE PROSECUTOR AS PROSECUTOR

Although she is about the same height and age as Louise Arbour, the chain-smoking Carla Del Ponte is a much different person. Arbour sees herself first and foremost as a jurist, whereas Del Ponte is unmistakably a prosecutor. As a crime-fighting attorney general in Switzerland, Del Ponte was no stranger to the use of transnational financial pressure. She earned her nickname, the bulldog, because of her tenacious efforts to trap organized crime figures, white-collar crooks, and terrorists, often with the help of financial tactics. In 1989 she was nearly assassinated while helping to pursue Sicilian mafiosi who were laundering profits through Switzerland, and she has traveled with a personal bodyguard ever since.

Other targets of Del Ponte's Swiss investigations and prosecutions included premiers Bettino Craxi of Italy and Benazir Bhutto of Pakistan, Raul Salinas de Gortari, brother of the former president of Mexico, and the terrorists Carlos the Jackal and Osama Bin Laden. The *Los Angeles Times* wrote that "her diminutive stature and elfin demeanor mask a fierce determination."[24] The fact that Del Ponte was building on the momentum that Arbour had established for the tribunal might tempt one to think of her tenure as simply involving what the sociologist Max Weber called "the routinization of charisma"; however, landing a deposed head of state in The Hague and upping his charges from crimes against humanity to genocide are hardly routine, and as we will see, Del Ponte did more.[25]

Del Ponte spent two years barnstorming through Western capitals demanding the transfer of Milosevic to the ICT, while "American officials who pressed the Yugoslav government to give Milosevic up, conditioning aid on his handover to the U.N., also claimed vindication."[26] Javier Solana, the European Union's high representative for foreign and security policy, confirmed that Del Ponte insisted that the EU condition financial assistance to Yugoslavia on its cooperation with the tribunal.[27]

Yet it was the Bush administration that most adamantly insisted it would not participate in the donors' conference until Yugoslavia cooperated. The conference was rescheduled from May to June at U.S. insistence. The recently assassinated Serbian prime minister, Zoran Djindjic, recognized that with more than one billion dollars at stake, Milosevic had become "Serbia's most valuable export commodity."[28] If he did not transfer Milosevic, "the U.S. would pull out of the donor's conference," Djindjic told *Time,* and he further confided that the pressure also included threats to reschedule debt payments. He concluded with the logic that "we had to act, for the sake of our children's future."[29]

Djindjic's political rival, Yugoslav president Vojislav Kostunica, complained that the prime minister "was in a rush to deliver some unknown promise."[30] Yet it was public knowledge: Djindjic told Kostunica that he had promised Colin Powell he would carry out a decree committing the government to sending Milosevic to the tribunal.[31] The delivery of Milosevic to tribunal officials occurred on June 28, 2001, Saint Vitus's Day, the nationalist Serbian holiday on which twelve years earlier Milosevic solidified his climb to power with his infamous Field of Blackbirds speech in Kosovo.

With Milosevic on trial in The Hague, past critics have become more hopeful about the tribunal's place in history. Gary Bass, who earlier worried that Louise Arbour had "jumped ship" by leaving the tribunal for the Canadian supreme court and termed the future of the tribunal "dispirited," upgraded his assessment to say that "from its feeble beginnings, the tribunal has reached a barely imaginable milestone."[32] Still, Bass expressed concern about Arbour's successor, noting that "Del Ponte has said that she plans to indict Milosevic for crimes committed by Serb forces in Bosnia, but two of her self-imposed deadlines, the end of December 2000 and then May 2001, have come and gone without public charges."[33] The task of adding indictments of Milosevic for crimes against humanity in Croatia and genocide in Bosnia was more challenging than Del Ponte probably anticipated. The tribunal's first advocate, Cherif Bassiouni, pushed hard to set an agenda for these kinds of indictments from the outset and paid a professional price for challenging the foreign policy establishment in doing so.

The genocide charge in particular—analyzed by Samantha Power in *A Problem from Hell*—was a persistent, inherited challenge that the tribunal's third chief prosecutor was determined to meet. Power's research documents time and again how states, notably including the United States, have evaded responsibility for stopping and sanctioning genocides. The United States already had proved itself ambivalent about the Milosevic indictment for crimes against humanity. Arbour called the American bluff with the initial indictment. The charge of genocide was a bigger gamble.

First, the charge of genocide itself is more demanding, involving the *intended destruction* of a people in whole or in part, whereas a crime against humanity requires widespread or systematic *attacks* on civilians. Second, the strongest case for genocide was in Bosnia, where attacks on Sarajevo and Srebrenica and ethnic cleansing more generally claimed the largest number of lives, but the chain of command leading to and from Milosevic was clearer in Kosovo, because it was still part of

Yugoslavia. A conspiracy theory was necessary to establish command responsibility in Bosnia. Third, the events in Bosnia mainly occurred in the first half of the 1990s, whereas the events in Kosovo peaked in the latter half of the decade, leaving a fresher trail of evidence for Arbour and her "real-time" response to this conflict.

INSIDE KOSOVO

It is useful to briefly consider how the Kosovo indictment developed as a foundation for understanding how the genocide indictment followed. Brenda Hollis was one of the original American military secondees to the tribunal and witnessed the transition from the events in Croatia and Bosnia to Kosovo. She observed that "justice is always better when it's fresh because people's memories are fresher, crime scenes are fresher, . . . and it holds the public's interest." This is why Arbour pushed so hard to quickly get her investigators and legal advisors into the Albanian and Macedonian refugee camps and then to have them enter Kosovo alongside the NATO troops. This real-time involvement was also important in building the sense of shared purpose and commitment among lawyers and investigators at the OTP to the longer-term agenda of international humanitarian law, making the tribunal the successful flagship for this emerging transnational field.

One crime analyst described piecing together the information provided by the first refugees from Kosovo. "My role was to try to make sense of all this information, so we can paint a picture of what's actually going on there." More than a million refugees were streaming into the camps. "We had to think how best can we interview this many. You might have a guy who's seen one person get killed in a refugee column; now, as tragic as that is, someone else has seen ten people killed, and if you only have time to interview one person, obviously you're going to go for the guy who's seen ten." Questionnaires were used to screen the incoming refugees for subsequent interviews.

An investigator who also entered the refugee camps early similarly suggested that "we didn't know exactly at what level we were going to go, whether we were going to go after notorious criminals that committed a lot of the atrocities, whether we were just going to target at the core commander level, or whether we were just going to concentrate on the ones that had already been indicted from Belgrade, like Milosevic." The strategy was to begin with a broad sweep. "So I was trying to get as much as possible about everybody, even the guy who pulled the trigger, the local police commanders, everybody, and then let the investigative teams and the legal teams say these are important enough that we will indict here." This was valuable lead evidence that was used in the original Milosevic indictment, but it would also become secondary as the prosecution reorganized its resources to climb the chain of command.

In early June 1999, after the NATO bombing stopped, the first tribunal teams entered Kosovo. An investigator reported that "when the all-clear came . . . they went straight over the border. They'd already been able to compile a list of places to go where we had witness testimony of crimes occurring. . . . But once we were on the ground people were coming up to us with new information all the time." A senior legal advisor said simply, "evidence . . . was basically lying all over the ground."

Nancy Paterson described their arrival: "As soon as the fighting was over and we could go into Kosovo, we were there, three days after the NATO forces, on the ground. It was quite an experience. There were still dead bodies around, no food, no water, lots of destruction, interesting times." An investigator described driving into Pristina: "The only car on the road was mine, there were dogs, everything was destroyed, just like after the second world war. . . . The dogs were barking at the truck, ten, twelve, maybe fifteen dogs. It's probably the thing I will remember the rest of my life. . . . It was unbelievable to see that, such destruction in a town." The scene was bewildering, but Paterson was quick to emphasize that "from our perspective, having done all the work in Bosnia, where the crime scenes were four or five years old, to be able to get on the ground to a relatively fresh crime scene" was an advantage.

The situation was also obviously chaotic and stressful. "You had to draw on experience and be very creative. Because all the props you would have in a civilized institution to help you—cars, telephones, faxes, or whatever else you needed—you just didn't have." An investigator recalled "the challenges of finding three square meals a day, they were still shooting in the hills, . . . automatic weapon discharges, you get conditioned to that, while the domestic dogs were running in packs, reverting back to their wild instincts, . . . and initially we didn't have any places that were cleared of mines and stuff, so we had bodies lying out in the fields here and there, and we just noted them." Simply processing the witness statements was challenging: "There's no electricity, there's no water, you're living by candlelight. . . . You're trying to do statements, and you're taking statements by candlelight."

Another investigator arrived with the first NATO troops and stayed for several months. He recalled the variety of stressful tasks involved but also reported energized feelings that here, as elsewhere, at first seemed incongruous but have reappeared throughout this book: "I was in Kosovo, the week after we got access. I spent three months there, and it was the most exhilarating, fascinating time." This is what Arbour had called "the exhilaration of action," and again it appeared even in the investigator's description of the exhumation work: "Digging bodies out of the ground. Trying to find and scouting sites, helping on the sites, dealing with the local communities, crowd control, . . . finding body bags, . . . whatever needed to be done. I had meetings with generals, with aid workers. Sometimes you're just helping at a local level, sometimes you're operating at higher levels. And I found that absolutely fascinating, totally enjoyed it, very empowering, exciting on a lot of different levels." Another investigator recalled, "I was there within two weeks on mission, and it just grabs you. It's something I don't want to stop doing." For this investigator, as for others on teams identified throughout this book, the experience in the field brought a powerful sense of shared purpose. "It's something that just happens. It's certainly not something that's planned. Certainly not something that anyone would expect. If something works, it's the shared experience that bonds people. . . . It's working hard under strain, doing something for a common goal. It creates bonds."

The quantity and quality of the work product also became its own reward. "It was a smoking gun situation, you know, it had just happened. Whereas when you look at a lot of places like Bosnia and Croatia, . . . it happened ten years ago. Much more difficult to talk to people, you know . . . , once you've gone through the event; you really don't want to bring it up again, because they're trying to go on with their lives." Paterson remembered encountering the practical effects of this when she asked Bosnian rape victims to testify about past victimizations: "Tell about when you were raped back in 1992. 'Sorry, I've got four kids to raise. I don't have a house to live in, I've got no food on my table, I don't have a job, I don't know—tomorrow you want me for this case? I don't think so.' "

The investigators soon concluded that crimes similar to those in Bosnia and Croatia were committed in Kosovo, but more selectively. "Geographically," Paterson observed, "it was a smaller area; time-wise it was a much shorter period, so, of course, there are going to be less bodies. Most of the people had fled to Macedonia and Albania. There weren't that many people left behind to kill. . . . Three-fourths of the population had fled." The reasons they left were clear. She continued, "the same techniques work very effectively, no matter where you use them. You go into a village, burn down the village, and kill, even just six people, that's a pretty good motivator to get the rest of the people to leave town, pretty darn quickly. There's no rocket science to this. You want to clean out the town, come in and lay a little terror for an hour or two, and off they go. You and I would do the same thing if we were them."

Another investigator observed that "the final figure on the number of dead is around 10,000 or 12,000, which is less than how many people were killed just in Sarajevo. But they were selective killings—the end game was to expel all Albanians from Kosovo." A typical kind of event repeatedly surfaced in refugee accounts. "They had a refugee column that was moving too slowly and who didn't want to leave their homes, and so the police or the army would pull a dozen men aside and shoot them. That's a good incentive for the rest of the people to leave. Or they would raid a village and kill six or seven people, and the rest of the people would be told, 'Get on your tractors, we're serious.' . . . So the killing was pretty selective with a particular purpose in mind."

BUILDING THE KOSOVO CASE

Patterns quickly began to emerge from the accounts, and they paralleled those found in earlier cases. For example, sexual assaults and rapes, which with the preparation for the Foca case were now better recognized as an important part of the picture of war crimes, were identified and developed in the accounts. "You had a very common scenario; you'd say 'O.k., there was a refugee column and the soldiers came and picked out the youngest, best looking girls,' but then the girls themselves would give statements and they'd say, 'Yeah, they took us to the room, they made us take all our clothes off, serve them coffee, but they didn't assault us.'" A senior investigator reported that "there's a lot of reasons why they would say that, if they actually were assaulted," but rather than leave it at that, "as a result of us targeting that and using investigators that had more experience, we got information about sexual offenses fully and clearly, much as one would with a rape victim in Sydney or New York or Paris or anywhere."

The emphasis was placed on locating and understanding these crimes as events within the larger pattern of the deportation. A broader framework emerged in the following account of an investigator who focused on sexual assaults: "Very often what you had was a group or a convoy—you know, the group can be 30 people or 3,000 people, and they're moving or being moved, and in some cases literally being driven by the military. . . . And out of that, people are being killed, people are being raped, people are being tortured, and so those crimes are often—it's not the same perpetrator, but it's the same pattern of crime, occurring at the same time, under the same unit, so I mean, it's really a similar body of crime and it's repeated."

This investigator then underlined why it is important to emphasize the role of rape in the larger picture of persecution, saying, "Rape . . . became a perfect tool of persecution, because there is such a tremendous fear for any woman of being raped . . . and so they hear of women being pulled out of the convoy and being raped and people being robbed, and people being murdered, and in many cases the people become more compliant." The result was a willingness to go along with the deportation. "People who would never leave their village, people who had never been further than their own county were all of a sudden leaving with nothing because of that fear that's instilled of 'Down the road they raped forty women and killed their husbands,' and they snatch up their children and leave. So it's a wonderful persecution tool. It's a great genocidal tool if you're trying to cleanse an area. If you can instill fear, that's like the first brick, and that's what they did." The signs of genocide, as well as crimes against humanity, were already apparent in the early evidence collection efforts in Kosovo.

When the decision was made in early 1999 to focus on Milosevic as the key target for an indictment, two teams were pulled together to consolidate the evidence, the results of whose work were described in chapter 4. The core of the team in the field included six investigators and two lawyers. A key investigator on the Milosevic indictment remembered his work organizing the exhumation teams. He arrived in the Mitrovica area of Kosovo, working fourteen-hour days and staying for periods of a month and a half. "I was responsible for the pathology team and they were based in Mitrovica, the French camp, so I would go in the morning, travel from Pristina early in the morning with my interpreter, get to the camp and say, 'We're leaving, we're going to do this mass grave this morning.' It takes maybe a week, sometimes three to five days, all depending on how big the grave was." On a typical day, "I was starting at 4:30 in the morning, because we had to travel a long distance and we had to maximize the daylight. . . . I was coming back probably after 6:30, 7:30 at night and doing what we call a sitrep, a situation report. So we had long hours, no water, of course, no showers, nothing, for 13 days."

Clifford Smith, who organized exhumations in Bosnia and Kosovo, quickly established that there were once again cover-up activities like those they had seen elsewhere. "They saw what we did in Bosnia, so you have evidence in Kosovo of body removal, mass body removal in vehicles, to God knows where. Just removing evidence. Gone. Whether they've gone back to Serbia, or whether they've gone to a burning site, or whatever. You tended to find smaller graves. To find a grave of 100 was uncommon in Kosovo. Ten or twenty [bodies], possibly, but

much smaller graves. Much more of an attempt to conceal evidence."
More than a year after this interview the Serbian government revealed
that bodies had been stuffed in a refrigerator truck and hauled back
to Serbia, where the entire truck was plunged into a river. This rev-
elation emerged as the government of Serbia sought to prepare the
public for the transfer of Milosevic to the tribunal. Smith's suspicions
now were confirmed: "More care was taken in Kosovo, they were more
aware."

The Kosovo exhumation program started in June 1999, before Arbour left the tribunal and Del Ponte became chief prosecutor. By October the weather began to shut down the program, which had been
working at full speed. Del Ponte realized that she couldn't allow the
weather to break the momentum of this crucial aspect of the collection of evidence, so by December of the same year Clifford Smith was
already back in Kosovo on mission looking for likely sites for the following spring. "And then we got going again in April. . . . We had a target
to get most of these sites done [during the 2000 exhumation period],
and we mostly reached that." He explained that the exhumations had
to be finished for humanitarian as well as legal reasons. "The people,
the locals, had been waiting for the ICT to appear. And you can't say,
'We'll come the year after next to dig up your lost family member.'"
Smith's point was that most of the bodies were already buried, often by
surviving and returning relatives. Three teams were put together from
the tribunal to get the work under way. "Some people had found their
relatives dead and buried them, virtually in their gardens and things
like this, so we had to exhume them with forensic teams present. Get
the evidence. And that went as well as you can ever expect. It's all well
and good to sit and plan a protocol of exactly what will happen. Reality
then enters and you find that you can't get your vehicles up mountains
like that, and so on."

NEW EVIDENCE

The ongoing investigations in Kosovo have addressed charges by Milosevic and others that the Kosovo Liberation Army as well as NATO had
committed war crimes. An early example of these charges involved the
NATO bombing of Dubrava Penitentiary in Kosovo in May 1999. This
prison was run by local Serbians and held suspected KLA terrorists as
well as common criminals. At first, nineteen inmates were reported
killed in the bombing incident. Initially, NATO insisted that the prison
was a military barracks. Journalists were allowed to visit and reported
that they saw no military vehicles that would substantiate the claim
that this was a barracks.[34] A later report indicated that the bombing

had killed one hundred people and injured two hundred. This report said that "an investigating judge from Pec, Mr. Vladan Bojic, accused NATO of committing the most massive murder of prisoners in modern civilization."[35]

The tribunal investigation told a different story. The exhumation of bodies at the prison revealed that more than twenty inmates had been killed by the bombing. Although it acknowledged responsibility for a mistake in target selection, NATO also indicated that the prison was previously used by paramilitary forces as a staging area. The exhumation revealed at least a hundred bodies altogether; however, witness statements indicate that these individuals were shot by Serbians at the prison near the time of the bombing. The forensic examinations of the bodies distinguished individuals killed by a bomb-like explosion from those who were simply shot. Under cross-examination by Milosevic, the *Guardian* reporter Judy Rowland explained how bomb and gunshot deaths easily could be distinguished: "If I look at you now, Mr. Milosevic, I can see that you have both your arms. I can see the features of your face. I can see that your body is intact. If, however, you were hit by a bomb . . . I think I would be able to tell."[36] Since there is no indication of NATO involvement beyond the bombing that could account for wounds imposed at close range, the implication is that a massacre took place at this site and was falsely tied by Serbian authorities to the bombing incident.

The largest Kosovo grave, in Izbica, originally contained remains of more than 130 bodies. Satellite photos had shown that the Serbs had dug up the bodies on June 2, 1999, before the NATO troops arrived. "The only things that we found were pieces of bone, clothing with bullet holes in them, things like that," an investigator recalled. The body count was developed during interviews with the few surviving witnesses, such as eighty-year-old Sadik Januzi, who told his story to tribunal investigators in April 1999 and testified three years later in the Milosevic trial. His statement was introduced by Dirk Ryneveld. He explained how about five thousand Kosovar Albanian Muslims were rounded up in the village, where two elderly disabled women were summarily shot. Januzi was in a group of older men who were mowed down with machine gun fire. He survived underneath three other corpses.[37] Since the bodies had been removed from the grave by the Serbs, witness testimony was crucial. "In places like that, everyone knows everyone," an investigator recalled, "so they would say 'Well, it was John, John was born in 1927, I remember . . . his dad.' " The story of the Izbica grave was pieced together in this fashion and corroborated with the satellite photos.

Many of the exhumations involved relatively few bodies but were no less disturbing. Wells were common disposal sites for bodies. The bodies of eight women were found in one well. One woman was found with her three daughters, two of whom had been raped. The killings were most numerous and gruesome in areas where the KLA had previously been active. The scenes of the killings sometimes were preserved just as they had been left. A family of twelve was killed and buried near their house. When a surviving family member returned from Germany, he locked the door to the kitchen where the killings occurred: "So when we got there we had a [preserved] crime scene—the blood was still there, the empty shells on the floor, . . . you could see the bullet holes and the blood all over the wall."

THE DEL PONTE DIFFERENCE

As noted repeatedly in this book, going on mission was a transformative, team-building experience for many investigators and lawyers at the tribunal. The result was often an alternation of perspective about the work of the tribunal and the development of a long-term commitment to the larger transnational field of humanitarian law. These experiences were reported up and down the hierarchy of the OTP. The interviews with Richard Goldstone and Louise Arbour each involved a description of an alternation experience—an encounter in the course of doing human rights work that had a transformative kind of impact. For Goldstone it was collecting firsthand evidence from South African youth about their torture at the hands of the police. For Arbour it was encountering the evidence of genocide in Rwanda and the mass graves near Vukovar in Croatia and elsewhere in the Balkans. Perhaps unexpectedly, these experiences had exhilarating and energizing rather than depressing and debilitating effects; they were a motivational source of agency. Even the tough-talking Carla Del Ponte described such an experience. For her, the turning point was a meeting with the women of the Bosnian town of Srebrenica.

Del Ponte is not normally understood as a person of tender or compassionate feelings. Yet she freely acknowledges that meeting the surviving women of the Srebrenica massacre was a transformative moment. "When I met with the mothers of Srebrenica, that was probably the most emotional moment I have had," she recalled. "You could touch with your hands their suffering and their need for justice. They asked me to do this, to bring Milosevic to The Hague."[38] By implication, the purpose was to bring Milosevic to The Hague not only to face a charge of crimes against humanity in Kosovo but also to answer for Croatia and the genocide in Bosnia. Racak had earlier symbolized for Arbour the co-ercive potential of international criminal law to challenge the sovereign immunity of Slobodan Milosevic in real-time terms. Del Ponte's visit to Srebrenica had some of this same emotional resonance and associated social and cultural salience, and the tribunal's trial of Milosevic now promised to turn the power of this symbolism into a reality that would legally frame these events as crimes against humanity and genocide perpetrated over a decade-long period and across three theatres of military carnage.

As Paterson had forewarned on the day of Milosevic's first appearance, the case was complex and difficult to prove. Arbour had purposefully avoided the genocide charge, noting that "the evidence is neither self-evident nor easily available." Arbour went on to note that "a high level of sophistication in investigation of such responsibility is needed in order to gain an overview of the military, paramilitary and political structures, and to understand the functioning of a chain of command."[39] The challenge of this investigation, combined with Del Ponte's bruising tenacity, suggested a difficult time ahead.

The genocide charge implied that the work of the prosecutor's office would be coming full circle to the Rule 61 hearing against Karadzic and Mladic initiated by Richard Goldstone. As Del Ponte took over from Arbour the task of bringing this charge against Milosevic to court, there was a natural inclination for members of the OTP staff to reflect on the differences in the substance and style of the tenures of their three chief prosecutors. There was little doubt among staff members that it was Arbour who most enhanced office morale, but all three prosecutors were seen as making unique and timely contributions.

One staff member chose to limit her remarks to Goldstone and Arbour and to reserve judgment about Del Ponte, offering that "people had different feelings about Goldstone, but in fairness to Goldstone, looking back, in many ways he may have been the right man at the time. We needed more of a diplomat or a politician than a prosecutor, where Louise was much more of a real prosecutor—not that she wasn't a skilled diplomat as well, but the focus was very different."

Another member of the office suggested more directly a change in the organizational atmosphere of the OTP by saying, "Goldstone was absolutely right for his time because he came with moral clout from South Africa and his own particular status as a champion of human rights. . . . Arbour brought a legal involvement and a really fine legal brain to the stage when we needed it. There were legal issues, there were things that really needed some direction from someone of the caliber of the lawyer that she was, so that was excellent. And then probably as we moved on, it was right, once we began to have the problems of a functioning prosecution, with lots of cases and lots of people in court, you had to have someone who was a prosecutor by background."

As useful as these comments are in confirming the different roles that Goldstone and Arbour played in launching the prosecutor's office, they only begin to address the changes that Del Ponte brought. Without more specific attention to the current prosecutor, the overall picture is incomplete. This larger picture emerges in the following more comprehensive reflection by a staff member in the OTP:

> I don't think Goldstone had much interest or concern, nor need he necessarily have such, about the internal workings of the organization. I think what he did brilliantly was . . . public relations. If this entity was going to live, somebody had to be out there pressing the flesh, and he did that very well. As far as having an impact on how the organization was structured and ran, he probably was the main reason we pushed some of the earlier indictments a little faster than we should have. They were a little rough around the edges. But he kept us alive and he did that well.
>
> Louise Arbour was very different in personality than Goldstone. She is a very warm person. She certainly didn't have the instinctive political skills that Goldstone did, but she developed them as it came along, and I think she got us functioning on a more legal basis. It would not have been inconceivable [that this also could have happened] if Goldstone had stayed for an extended period of time. He's a very clever man; he may have developed more of an interest in the law stuff. I don't know if the transition from Goldstone to Arbour was really that radical. It was a pretty soft shift.
>
> The present prosecutor is a different kettle of fish and she's a very tough and abrasive woman. She is somebody who is not, at least in my impression, she isn't strong on people skills—either upwards, downwards or laterally—and I think she looks on herself as a person with a mission. . . . I think her approach . . . is that "My job here is to get the heavy hitting accused before the tribunal. And those heavy hitters are, preferably all three, Karadzic, Mladic, Milosevic, and if I get one or more of those people here while I'm here, it doesn't matter how much I have upset everybody, I will be a success." And she's right! At the same time it doesn't make it all that enjoyable in the process. She is certainly someone who has a hard nosed prosecutor's approach to things, . . . an approach which is something some of our prosecutors do not terribly like. She is one tough lady and sensitivity is not her middle name. But when Louise Arbour left, one of the things she said was,

"Look, this institution can live on its own, and it doesn't matter who the prosecutor is."

Several senior colleagues in the OTP added their view that in combination with the more congenial Graham Blewitt, Carla Del Ponte would be a very effective chief prosecutor.

The above interview concluded with the comment, "Look, I don't feel warm fuzzy things that I felt for Louise Arbour. . . . She [Del Ponte] does try hard on occasion, but people skills aren't her strong point. I think as long as Graham Blewitt is there as the deputy prosecutor, things will go on well. . . . He's both the momentum and the inertia, he's the element of continuity. I would think that having him go would have more of an impact on this organization than having a different prosecutor." The bottom line is that as Del Ponte pushed and Blewitt pulled, working together to advance its contingent and collective momentum, the work of the OTP moved steadily forward and then gained its own distinct urgency—perhaps a kind of urgency that the brutally tenacious Del Ponte was uniquely suited to sustain. And after a time, many if not most at the tribunal developed a clear appreciation of and affection for Del Ponte, with one investigator even insisting that "we've all come to love her."

GOING FOR GENOCIDE

It may nonetheless come as little surprise that when Del Ponte was pressed with questions from reporters about the time it was taking to develop indictments for Croatia and Bosnia, she bluntly answered, "I am putting the same questions to my investigative teams."[40] Del Ponte's colleagues likely also were not surprised to hear this public comment. One colleague remarked at about this time that "she's completely different from Louise Arbour. A very straightforward kind of woman. Not that diplomatic. Not that pleasant. But very professional. So it will be interesting to see what happens."

The atmosphere was increasingly one of respect. Another colleague observed, "To her credit, she pushes hard. Sometimes a little too hard, or at least not diplomatically enough." Yet many in the office felt something more was required than the Milosevic indictment Arbour had achieved for crimes against humanity in Kosovo. A commander of investigations who was a member of the Milosevic team put it this way: "The team working on Kosovo has done a tremendous job. A beautiful job. And my compliments for that, because it's a job very well done, but I want to see more on Milosevic, because he's the main responsible person . . . for everything that happened from '91. So indicting him for just a short period in '99 is not good enough." Thus there was support inside the tribunal, as well as pressure from outside, to move the Milosevic case forward, with indictments not only for Croatia and Bosnia but for the charge of genocide as well.

Del Ponte also raised the bar on the level of evidence required for indictments, which in the past, as in the Milosevic case, often were issued and then amended as the investigations continued. Now the standard was to be "trial ready" from the point of first indictment. I already have noted that the evidence required was more difficult to assemble in the cases of Croatia and Bosnia. The de jure command responsibility of Milosevic in Kosovo was clear, but now it was necessary to establish that Milosevic was the de facto commander. Del Ponte needed a final, court-ready indictment based on a more challenging form of evidence.

Nearly four months after Milosevic appeared at the tribunal, in late September 2001, Del Ponte announced that she had signed and passed on to the confirming judge an indictment for Croatia and that a Bosnian indictment would follow shortly. The Croatian indictment listed nearly seven hundred deaths and more than one hundred seventy thousand deportations, and it featured charges of crimes against humanity. There was speculation that Del Ponte was again using her public voice as prosecutor to place pressure on her investigators to complete the Bosnian indictment, which she indicated would now take another month and include the charge of genocide. [41]

When the Bosnian indictment came in late November, *Tribunal Update* called it "the mother of all indictments." Its sweeping charges subsumed events in Sarajevo, Srebrenica, Foca, and elsewhere and incorporated the Bosnian Serb leaders Karadzic, Mladic, Krajisnik, and Plavsic, with Milosevic centrally located as having planned, ordered, or at least inspired genocide and the full range of other crimes as the head of a "joint criminal enterprise." [42] The challenge behind this comprehensive indictment, and the certain cause of its long development, lay in the accumulation of evidence that could persuasively delineate the chains and channels of decision-making that gave Milosevic de facto command responsibility for the events already demonstrated to have occurred in Srebrenica and Foca as well as other places. Obtaining this new kind of evidence focused new attention on how the tribunal was organizing its investigative work and linking its results to subsequent prosecutions and trials. The problem was no longer simply establishing a crime base and securing an indictment that could lead to an arrest, but instead the end-game legal challenge of taking a well prepared case to court and gaining a conviction.

REORGANIZING THE OFFICE

Although the print media closely followed Del Ponte's role in developing the Croatian and Bosnian indictments, the press gave no attention to the major internal reorganization of the OTP Del Ponte initiated in March 2001. The movement of cases from investigation to prosecution, up through the command structure and ultimately to the Milosevic trial, placed new demands on the OTP and exposed some of the inefficiencies that Pierre-Richard Prosper was to describe to Congress nearly a year later. Del Ponte and Blewitt already knew of and had acted on the need to reorganize the OTP. Both the chief of investigations, John Ralston, and the chief of prosecutions, James Stewart, left the tribunal in 2001, and this presented an opportunity to rethink the top-down organization of the office. Del Ponte and Blewitt noted that problems often were resulting from a sharp separation of the investigation and prosecution functions of the OTP.

An experienced trial lawyer described this functional separation as reflecting a Queen's Counsel model in which the senior trial lawyers were "detached from the investigative component and essentially the recipient[s] of a brief that gave specific allegations against any specific accused or group of accused—as opposed to a federal prosecutor's model or public prosecutor's model that you would find, say, in parts of the British Isles or Canada or the U.S. or in the civil law countries that have investigative magistrates, or the German system with a public prosecutor." The tribunal's loosely coupled system also involved considerable variation in practices across cases and in general meant that prosecutors had too little advance preparation and analysis of materials for presentation in court.

This was one of the problems Mark Harmon confronted in the prosecution of the Croatian general Tihomir Blaskic, who was convicted in connection with a 1993 massacre of more than one hundred Muslim civilians at the village of Ahmici in Croatian-controlled western Bosnia. A colleague of Harmon's described the investigation file for the case as being like a complicated clock in a thousand disassembled pieces. Years later, new evidence of a secret command structure was discovered that seemed to at least partially vindicate Blaskic.[43] Another senior trial attorney described receiving the results of an investigation as like "getting inundated with three filing cabinets full of statements and documents" that were incoherently organized, so that in the prosecution phase "you're playing catch-up" and left asking the question, "Why do we have X number of witness statements that have to be redone or rewritten?"

Such cases may have been atypical, and in contrast Dirk Ryneveld described the outstanding work of Hildegard Uertz-Retzlaff in developing the Foca case. But Hildegard may also have been an exception that helped identify a pattern. Ryneveld explained that "she came from a civil law background where she was used to taking an active role in the investigation stage, almost like a civil law investigative judge . . . and because of an involvement at an early stage of people like Hildegard who saw it all the way through, there was a prosecutorial component to the investigation." Del Ponte had played this kind of proactive civil law role in her own prosecutorial career, and she now worked with Blewitt to bring it into the tribunal.

The first step was to appoint a new chief of investigations. Patrick Lopez-Terres emerged as a strong internal candidate. In his early forties, Lopez-Terres came to the tribunal in 1998 from France, where he was trained as a lawyer and served as an investigative judge. Although he was a senior trial attorney at the tribunal, Blewitt summarized the logic of his selection: "He had a lot of experience in France as an investigative judge, commanding and leading investigations, so it wasn't foreign to him—he was a lawyer, had investigative experience, and knew how the place worked." The last point was crucial because, as Blewitt noted, "the investigations were at a critical stage and to bring someone completely cold and put them over our investigation commanders was not the right thing to do."

Lopez-Terres was appointed on an acting basis for his first five months. He had no doubts about why he was chosen. "The real reason I was put in this function . . . was as part of the reorganization the prosecutor wanted—to try to put an end to a very strong separation that was in the house between the lawyers and the investigators. The idea was that because of my background, a kind of hybrid person, having been a lawyer dealing with investigative matters most of my career, I could be the right person." Initially there was resistance to giving lawyers a larger role in the investigations.

John Ralston was of the old school, was widely respected, and had made great strides in independently developing indictments. Lopez-Terres could see that "it was a little hard for the investigators, some of them at least in the beginning, to see that the lawyer was from now on [going to be] in charge of managing the investigation team." There was also the problem of timing. "The challenge is that we reorganized this system at the time, or very close to the time, when we are being told to complete the mandate; . . . usually . . . you are not rebuilding the place at the same time you are told to close it out." The appointment of Lopez-Terres was a bridge period: "There was a kind of period of observation, and when people realized that it was done for the benefit of the institution and for more efficiency, and not just to be a bad guy, just using a stick, the better investigators just tried to identify problems and speak together, and not just have this division which was not helpful."

During this period of adjustment in the investigation division, Blewitt and Del Ponte went on to search for a new chief of investigations. After considering internal and external candidates, they decided to proactively pursue two persons with prior experience in the office: Terree Bowers, who had worked with Goldstone and Arbour before returning to Los Angeles, and Michael Johnson, a prosecutor in New Hampshire who had worked periodically on loan to the OTP on procedural matters and fundraising efforts. Bowers turned out to be unavailable, and Johnson, after considerable arm-twisting, was persuaded to give up his elective office and become chief of prosecutions.

Johnson is an energetic, Kennedyesque figure in his mid-forties with a magnetic personality and a whirlwind manner that easily explain his movement into elective office at a young age in New England. Blewitt remarked, "I was impressed with his legal skills, impressed with his energy and his drive, his management skills and contacts. We thought he would be right for this place, so I phoned him and he said he'd think about it and in the end he said yes." Blewitt acknowledged that this appointment was actually a little harder to carry off than it sounded, because of what Johnson had already achieved in New Hampshire and because of what needed to be done in the OTP. "We had to drag him away from this job that he'd had. He was a big star there, this was a big change in his life. He came and he's had a profound impact on the place, because of his management style. I gave him . . . an open book, as it were. He could see things that were wrong, and after a period of time you aren't able to affect change, you just become part of the organization, so I said, 'Work with me but you've got an open hand to change as much as you can for the better.' So he's been very aggressively attacking different areas. And that's had a profound impact." Johnson came to the tribunal in September 2001 as chief of prosecutions and Lopez-Terres was confirmed as chief of investigations the next month. They worked together in implementing Del Ponte's reorganization of the OTP.

Decisions about sending investigators on missions now came under much closer scrutiny. This meant that Lopez-Terres had to examine "what the teams are doing [on mission] more than was ever done before and saying 'no' more often than was ever said before." Interestingly, he saw this as a move toward the civil law approach, saying, "Obviously

the background of the prosecutor is very similar to my background . . .
[and] inclines more naturally to have the lawyers in charge of decisions." Yet a North American lawyer simultaneously commented that
"we're more perhaps of an American federal prosecutorial style now."
Both were correct—there was a melding of the civil and the American
federal models of criminal investigation, which are more tightly and
proactively organized around prosecutorial goals.

From the outset, senior trial attorneys now assumed a leadership
role in OTP investigations. A prominent lawyer in the office commented that "senior trial attorneys are now assigned to a case once
an investigation has been approved by the prosecutor. And so we take
control at a much earlier stage, we're up to speed much sooner, we have
daily reporting. . . . We give direction, we focus the investigation, we're
already looking to the courtroom at the time the investigation is going
on." The aggressiveness of this leadership role generated resistance to
the reorganization.

Meanwhile, Johnson also began weeding out less productive lawyers
and investigators. Blewitt observed, "Michael has been fairly aggressive
in the nonrenewal of contracts with people who were not performing properly." Employees were given six to nine months to improve
or begin looking for other work. "So we're seeing people leave whose
performances have not been what was required in this place." Blewitt,
Lopez-Terres, and Johnson have emerged as an aggressive, tightly knit
administrative team, meeting frequently and implementing mutually
supported changes. "We all agree that if we're going to effect . . . positive
change, and change for the right reasons, then we have to work closely
together, we have to support each other, and that's what is happening.
It's been pretty traumatic for a lot of people, particularly people who are
informed in advance that their contracts are not going to be renewed
unless they can pick themselves up." So when the Milosevic trial began early in the new year, the OTP had undergone a major internal
transformation.

TRYING MILOSEVIC

The prosecution was ultimately successful in persuading the appeals
panel of the tribunal to join the Milosevic indictments for Kosovo, Croatia, and Bosnia into one case that went to trial in February 2002, with
the Kosovo part of the case heard first. Judge Richard May presided over
the three-member panel trying Milosevic. May is an experienced English judge who in the early 1970s had audaciously run against Margaret
Thatcher for parliament. No one calls him timid. "He is easily one of the
best judges," Paterson observed, adding that "he is the best at keeping

control of the courtroom and the lawyers in moving cases along."[44] He has demonstrated this capacity on occasion by lecturing Milosevic and cutting off his court microphone.

Perhaps most interesting, however, is May's role in an earlier case in which the Croat politician Dario Kordic was tried along with a military commander for attacks on Bosnian Serbs. In announcing the verdict, May told Kordic, "The fact you were a politician and took no part in the actual execution of the crimes makes no difference; you played your part as surely as the men who fired the guns."[45] This is consistent with article 7 of the UN Security Council's governing statute, which states that "the official position of any accused person, whether as head of state or government or as a responsible government official, shall not relieve such person of criminal responsibility or mitigate punishment." Still, Paterson explains that "you must show that he [Milosevic] had actual control over commanders, that he knew that atrocities were happening and that he did nothing to stop the crimes or to punish the perpetrators."[46]

Carla Del Ponte appeared in court on the first day of the Milosevic trial, making it clear that she was an engaged prosecutor and that this was "clearly the most important trial to be conducted in the tribunal." Her presentation of the case emphasized that beyond "the grandiloquent rhetoric and the hackneyed phrases," it was the search for power that drove Slobodan Milosevic to "an almost medieval savagery and a calculated cruelty that went beyond the bounds of legitimate warfare." Her statement made reference to two key sources of evidence that would be important to the prosecution's case: the testimony of Milosevic's associates and the information held by other organizations and states. She said that "the witnesses must find within themselves the individual courage to give their accounts in public" and that "organizations and governments must also find the institutional resolve to place before the chamber . . . sometimes sensitive information in their possession."[47]

These references openly sought the structural linkages required from outside the tribunal to fully demonstrate the conspiracy behind the "joint criminal enterprise" with which Milosevic and his associates were charged. After the second day of the trial, Del Ponte responded to an interviewer's question by confirming that she was negotiating with leaders in Belgrade to arrest the four co-indictees. She added, "Of course, the most important witnesses will testify about Milosevic himself. But it's important that witnesses describe the atrocities. This is vital not only for the survivors and the victims. Also the Serb people must know what crimes were committed under Milosevic."[48]

The early days of the trial seemed to draw a belligerent Milosevic into their flow, and May allowed Milosevic the latitude to become intellectually and emotionally engaged. Acting as his own lawyer, he was able to evade answering questions himself. He proved a quick study of tribunal trial procedure and, consistent with his reputation as a brilliant tactician, quickly turned his opportunities to speak into allegations that all Serbia was also on trial in this "false tribunal" that was the political tool of NATO and the United States. He portrayed himself and his government as fighting Bosnian and Albanian terrorists, just as the Americans were in Afghanistan, and that the actual crime was the violation of his sovereign right and responsibility to defend his nation from attack, while being attacked by NATO as well as the KLA.

As the trial moved on into February, pressure intensified for Yugoslavia to turn over more indictees. A March 31, 2002, deadline for U.S. financial assistance was contingent on further Yugoslav cooperation. Colin Powell refused to certify this cooperation when no new transfers of co-indictees had occurred by the end of March. On April 11 the Yugoslav parliament passed a law authorizing the handover of indictees and access to archives. Hours later the indicted former interior minister during the Kosovo conflict, Vlajko Stojiljkovic, shot himself on the parliament steps.

Carla Del Ponte arrived in Belgrade within the week to again stubbornly push her case. The Yugoslav government had just published a list of twenty-three people it said should surrender to authorities. Del Ponte protested the lack of results. Finally, two further indictees in the Milosevic case, Nikola Sainovic, the former deputy premier, and Dragoljub Ojdanic, the former army chief, turned themselves in to the tribunal.[49] Only Serbian president Milan Milutinovic remained at large among those originally indicted with Milosevic, until he, too, turned himself in at The Hague in January 2003.[50]

THREE DAYS IN MARCH

Three days of prosecution testimony in the middle of March were crucial in the Kosovo phase of the Milosevic trial. Patrick Ball, a thirty-six-year-old sociologist and statistician, presented results from a statistical study that at one point had involved his retrieving crucial data through a barrage of gunfire. His testimony poked a large hole in the Milosevic defense. Ball had identified forty-four hundred persons who had been killed. He then used a standard population sampling technique to estimate that the total dead numbered more than ten thousand. Ball presented evidence that the geographic and temporal distribution of the dead across Kosovo corresponded closely to refugee movements and concluded from this that the deaths and the refugee movements were the results of a common cause.

Milosevic's defense was that the deaths and movements were products of NATO bombing and KLA terrorism. Yet Ball was able to show that surges in refugee flows followed Serbian military activity and that NATO bombing and KLA actions followed increases in refugee movements. Ball concluded that "the findings of this study are consistent with the hypothesis that action by Yugoslav forces was the cause of the killings and the refugee flow."[51] Milosevic characteristically responded in his early cross-examination that "statistics . . . can prove anything . . . and this is done to serve the purposes of the American politics aimed at enslavement."[52] He then turned to the specifics of Ball's analysis.

Milosevic questioned how the 4,211 dead could be transformed into "the invented figure of 10,356" and then distributed across time and place in the analysis. When Ball identified the statistical procedures involved, Milosevic responded: "So you distributed the assumed dead into assumed time points by applying some kind of statistical methods. How can that be a serious way of doing it? Tell me."[53] Ball explained that he and his colleagues had used established methods to compensate for missing data, with cautionary warnings wherever noteworthy doubts arose.

Milosevic accused Ball of simplifying war with statistics[54] and asserted that if one took seriously the hypothesis that Yugoslav forces provoked the exodus from Kosovo, then there must be some unproved master plan: "So I'm asking you: if the Yugoslav authorities planned and carried out a centrally organized campaign, where is the plan? What is it called and who made it?" When Ball stuck to his hypotheses, Milosevic continued, "But you are aware of the statement of one of the NATO Defence Ministers, the German Minister, Rudolf Scharping, who said that there was a plan, the Horseshoe Operation, and this claim was later refuted. . . . Are you aware of that?"[55] May said that Operation Horseshoe was neither within Ball's expertise nor a part of his testimony. Ball had established a compelling prima facie case against the Yugoslav forces, but it was also clear that Milosevic had mastered the challenge of cross-examining a social scientist.

Ball was followed on the witness stand by Paddy Ashdown, a former member of the British Parliament, who had visited the Balkans on several occasions, including June 1998. Ashdown was on this occasion denied access to Kosovo itself, as Arbour was later, but through binoculars he could see from neighboring Albania gunfire and the torching of villages. Ashdown reported these observations to Tony Blair, and after a return visit in September 1998 to western Kosovo, he carried a letter personally from Blair to Milosevic in Belgrade. During the September visit Ashdown witnessed at first hand whole villages under bombardment and burning.

Video footage of these events was shown in court, accompanied by Ashdown's commentary, including descriptions of the subsequent deportations from these villages. Ashdown traveled directly on to the meeting in Belgrade with Milosevic. He reported that he told Milosevic that "what I had witnessed could only be described as the actions of the main battle units of the Yugoslav army in an action which could only be described as indiscriminate, punitive, designed to drive innocent civilians out of their properties, could not be explained by any targeting military operation, that this was not only illegal under international law, damaging to the reputation of the Serbs and his nation, but also deeply counter-productive." He also reported warning Milosevic, "The international community will act if you do not stop." When Milosevic initiated his cross-examination, Ashdown took the opportunity to again remind him that "I said to you, in specific terms, that if you went on acting in this fashion, you would make it inevitable that the international community would have to act, and in the end they did have to act. And I warned you that if you took those steps and went on doing this, you would end up in Court, and here you are."[56]

Milosevic did not dispute details of Ashdown's account but instead reiterated his assertion that KLA terrorism was the source of the conflict and that the Yugoslav army response was proportionate. Ashdown acknowledged that KLA attacks in Kosovo had taken Serbian lives but concluded that "none of this, none of it, justifies or excuses the use of excessive, outrageous force by your armed forces, under your control, in an indiscriminate, punitive manner, across the whole of the civilian population." Ashdown later answered a question from one of the judges about his sense of the knowledge Milosevic had of atrocities in Kosovo: "I must presume that he knew about it, but I wanted to make it explicitly clear that from the moment I had informed him and had drawn his attention to the provisions of international law, the Geneva Convention, from that moment onwards, he could not then deny knowledge of these facts if they were to continue."[57] Similar kinds of testimony were offered in June by William Walker, the U.S. ambassador and head of the Kosovo Verification Mission, and by the German NATO military commander, Klaus Naumann.[58]

CONFLICTING EVIDENCE

As compelling as this evidence is with regard to crimes against humanity in Kosovo, Graham Blewitt indicated in public the difficulties of establishing command responsibility with highly placed defendants, and he also emphasized that this case was "one of the most complicated and difficult trials in the history of criminal justice." Yet when he was asked what chance the former Yugoslav president had of eluding conviction, Blewitt answered: "You are asking a prosecutor—none."[59] Still, as the case moved into the end of summer of 2002, three years after the delivery of Milosevic to The Hague and after the appearance of two hundred witnesses, observers began to comment that no smoking-gun witnesses were forthcoming. "At this juncture," the Dutch international law expert Gerard Strijards concluded, "it is Milosevic who has the upper hand."[60]

Del Ponte responded by continuing to press the Yugoslav government for cooperation. Her chief of investigations, Lopez-Terres, commented, "We have reached a stage where because of the completion strategy we want to get results as soon as possible, so we are more involved in trying to get cooperation . . . so that these requests that we put [to the Yugoslav government] . . . are really taken care of and that we can achieve what we want." In the middle of July Del Ponte met in Belgrade with the Yugoslav foreign minister and the interior minister and head of police, as well as with President Kostunica and the government's supreme defense council. A result was that Yugoslavia freed former Milosevic associates from vows of secrecy sworn while in office, permitting them to reveal confidential information without threat of prosecution at home.[61]

The stage was set for the delivery of compelling testimony during the final weeks of the Kosovo phase of the trial. The buildup to this testimony described a Milosevic-led cover-up of ethnic cleansing operations in Kosovo and the removal of bodies to Serbia, a scenario that paralleled the reburials exposed by Jean-René Ruez in the Srebrenica trial. A Serbian detective named Radojkovic further described being instructed to dispose of a refrigerator truck that had surfaced in the Danube in early April 1999, filled with more than eighty bodies. On instructions from a district police chief, the bodies were removed for reburial and the truck was burned and destroyed with explosives.

A Serbian police captain, Dragan Karleusa, testified that Milosevic had called a meeting in his office in March 1999. "They discussed the need for a cleaning operation," Karleusa reported, "to eliminate any material that might be of interest to the Hague tribunal." The account was based on a statement taken from Rade Markovic, then the Yugoslav chief of state security, that Karleusa had obtained as head of the team that investigated the discovery of the truck full of bodies in the Danube. Orders issued at this meeting called for "the removal of all traces . . . all bodies of civilians should be dug up and transferred to different localities." Karleusa's team found additional truckloads of bodies and five mass graves.[62]

When Rade Markovic was brought from a prison cell in Belgrade, however, where he was serving a sentence for destroying police files and being held on political assassination charges, he denied his earlier statements. He acknowledged that the interior ministry and military officials reported in detail each day about their activities during the two final years of Milosevic's rule, but he answered "no" when Milosevic asked in cross-examination, "Did I ever mention in any way removing traces of crimes?"[63] Milosevic speculated that Markovic, whom he addressed by his first name, was tortured into giving his earlier statement. The trial went into an August recess with reporters again pressing the prosecution for the smoking gun that could clinch the Milosevic case.

INSIDE TESTIMONY

When the trial resumed at the end of August, the prosecution called two Serb policemen as "unwilling insiders" now released from their oaths of secrecy to confirm that the reburial of bodies from Kosovo was ordered by Milosevic and his interior minister, Vlajko Stojiljkovic. One was the district chief who ordered the reburial of bodies and destruction of the truck found in the Danube. He said that he was ordered to do this by General Djordjevic, who indicated he was acting on orders from Stojiljkovic. The other Serbian policeman had recorded the statement that Rade Markovic had repudiated before the August recess. He testified that Markovic had taken "an active part" in dictating the statement and that he had examined and corrected a draft version before signing every page.

Much of Milosevic's defense against these witnesses consisted of his insistence that Yugoslav soldiers were regularly instructed to observe international humanitarian law. In response, the prosecution next presented a Yugoslav private with the concealed identity of K-41 who testified by video link from Bosnia and confirmed testimony given in July by another private, identified as K-32. These witnesses were performing roles like that of Drazen Erdemovic in the Srebrenica trial, corroborating as confessed perpetrators the testimony of victims and other eyewitnesses.

Witness K-41 described incidents in Kosovo in late March 1999, when there were no clashes with the KLA or other provocations, in which he and others attacked Albanian villages, killed civilians, and burned houses.[64] He recalled hearing an army captain issue orders that "no one should remain alive there" and described in detail his role in killing fifteen villagers. "The people fell over, one on top of the other. What I remember most vividly, very vividly, was how a baby was shot with three bullets and it was crying unbelievably loudly."[65] Under cross-examination, K-41 held his ground, saying, "The cleansing, Mr. Milosevic, happens when the army starts killing civilians. It was something that went without saying over there. When the army moved in, the soldiers were not looking to see who is a terrorist and who is not but [cleansed] everybody in sight. . . . I know, because I was there. You should have come."[66] Milosevic was enraged, and the trial was recessed for two days when his blood pressure reached dangerously high levels.

There were those in the press who still maintained that after nearly one hundred days in court no smoking gun had been produced and that the prosecution had not sufficiently fulfilled its promise to produce important insider witnesses. Geoffrey Nice explained some of the difficulties involved in penetrating Milosevic's inner circle and especially in finding a smoking-gun witness: "Cases like this would be easy to prove in a short time if there was one member of the accused's inner circle who was able to give a fully accurate and acceptable testimony of everything that happened. Maybe the case could almost be proved by a single witness. . . . Unfortunately, life isn't like that. As regards the witnesses, the closer they were to the accused, the more difficult they are to approach and use."[67] Nice explained that Milosevic held a subtle but intimidating power to implicate, and therefore intimidate, insiders with his own inside knowledge.

Meanwhile, prosecution team members felt that Milosevic was playing more to the gallery and the television audience in Serbia than to the judges he confronted. They also felt they had effectively made their case with the collection of witnesses and evidence they had presented. The prosecution spokeswoman, Florence Hartmann, concluded that "it may not have looked spectacular, but when the mosaic is put together, we are confident we have done what we set out to do."

The prosecution resumed in the fall with the Croatian and Bosnian parts of the case. Inside witnesses from the former Yugoslavian army now testified that all significant military decisions made in the Serb region of Croatia were taken in Belgrade. One witness explained that Belgrade was "a synonym for Milosevic," turning at one dramatic point in the cross-examination to say to Milosevic, "You were Belgrade!"[68] Milosevic took ill for the fourth time in the trial after this testimony, and the judges ordered both physical and psychiatric examinations. The prosecution repeatedly asked the court to appoint a defense lawyer to move the case ahead, but Milosevic insisted that only he fully understood the evidence and that "the only reason I agreed to participate in this case of yours is because I want to be able to address the public."[69]

While testimony fitfully unfolded at the ICTY, Del Ponte simultaneously delivered a strongly worded report to the UN Security Council. The report made clear that Del Ponte felt that her investigation and prosecution teams were delivering important new forms of evidence. "We are beginning to be able to present what I might call crucial insider witnesses or sensitive sources," she explained, "but fresh hurdles are being erected and placed in the way of such people." Her point was that at the same time the Bush administration was criticizing the ICTY for inefficiency, crucial witnesses again were being threatened with prosecution by Yugoslav Federation authorities. Speaking in general terms that seemed aimed at the United States in particular, Del Ponte insisted that "if the tribunal is to meet the completion strategy targets and the deadlines that are expected of us, these other problems have to be tackled by the international community."[70]

UNVEILING A NEW STAR WITNESS

As Christmas 2002 approached, the prosecution was working through a long queue of witnesses for the Croatian phase of the Milosevic trial. When Geoffrey Nice had commented to the press the preceding summer that "cases like this would be easy to prove" with one member of the accused's inner circle, he may not have known that one member of this witness queue, Milan Babic, could be such a person. Yet as Babic's testimony unfolded, this possibility became clear. At first Babic was identified only as C-061, and his image and voice were electronically disguised, with the court moving in and out of closed session for protected periods of his testimony. He was used initially by the prosecution to identify speakers in intercepted telephone communications and then to decode the meaning of these conversations.

As in the Srebrenica trial, the court reserved judgment on the admissibility of the intercepts and then listened to them as part of its decision-making process. Witness C-061's inside knowledge of the case quickly became apparent as he explained a conversation between Radovan Karadzic (RK) and Slobodan Milosevic (SM) in which Milosevic told Karadzic about the need to use "radical measures" to force Slovenia and Croatia out of Yugoslavia in exchange for territory in the coming battleground of Bosnia. The conversation revealed that Karadzic was taking explicit direction from Milosevic in a sycophantic fashion.

SM: Three months are out of the question. I think that some things should be radically changed now, radically.

RK: Yes. . . .

SM: . . . it's time for our move now. . . . They want to separate.

RK: That's clear.

SM: That's clear and they should be allowed to separate.

RK: Yes.

SM: Now there is only one question left, to have disintegration in line with our inclinations.

RK: Yes.

SM: Nothing more . . . concerning Slovenia, I would let them go immediately.

RK: Yes.

SM: Let them go immediately, and the others as well after they have settled the issue with us. . . .

RK: Yes.

SM: You do not permit him—

RK: Yes, yes . . . you see, tonight we have them shooting, they have shot at . . . [inaudible] they have had a burst fired at his window. . . . So that what . . . should be . . . done is to do things very quickly.

SM: We should take radical steps, and speed things up.[71]

As this and other intercepts were introduced and explained, it became clear that C-061 had inside knowledge of the "joint criminal enterprise" that the prosecution had charged Milosevic with leading and that the intercepts and this witness's testimony could penetrate to the core of Milosevic's denial that he was the power and the controlling force in the Croatian and Bosnian conflicts.

It ultimately became clear that it was impossible to conceal the identity of Milan Babic by calling him C-061, and the court withdrew its protective measures and began to address him by name. Babic is a heavy-set former dentist who held a variety of government positions in the Krajina region, which was carved out by the Serbs in Croatia. He was an unindicted co-conspirator in the joint criminal enterprise and an example of what an earlier witness had called a "disposable collaborator" in Milosevic's maneuvers. Babic and the Krajina government were sacrificed in 1991 when Milosevic decided to accept a Cyrus Vance–led peace plan and a UN peace force in the Krajina region. This was one of the many instances when Milosevic suddenly reconfigured the tactical map of the Greater Serbia that he was pursuing.

Babic nonetheless continued to be involved in Krajina politics. He confirmed for the court that Milosevic had given up Serbian territory in Croatia in exchange for a reconceived share of Bosnia that would allow the establishment of Republika Srpska, under the local direction of the politician Karadzic and the military chief Mladic, with Milosevic as the outside controlling force. Four days into Babic's testimony it became apparent that he was such a strong witness for the prosecution that they were willing to bargain away the right to call fourteen other witnesses in exchange for two further days of his testimony.

With Hildegard Uertz-Retzlaff now taking the co-counsel role with Geoffrey Nice, the prosecution was able to take Babic through a detailed description of the planning and operation of ethnic cleansing in the Croatian conflict. The planning involved two lines of command, one being the JNA and territorial defense forces, and the other the local police and paramilitary groups. The terror tactics that would become common in the Balkans were planned and carried out with Milosevic's oversight. The JNA generals headed one command structure and the Serbian state security service led the other, with Jovica Stanisic as its chief. Babic was emphatic in saying that "Milosevic . . . connected these two lines of command" and that he was the "true authority, the chief, the key and most powerful political figure and everybody willingly subordinated themselves to him."

Babic was also emphatic in testifying that Milosevic imposed the Vance peace plan on the local Serbians in Croatia, removing from office local politicians who stood in his way and then using his parallel command structures in the area to ensure that the Vance plan failed. The international political elites who had sought to end the Balkan conflict by means of negotiations had ultimately been pawns in Milosevic's shifting alliances and his subversion of local events, with the Croatian part of the conflict remaining unresolved until Croatian forces finally successfully removed the Serbian forces from their territory in Operation Storm during the period leading up to the Dayton negotiations in 1995.[72]

When Babic was asked whether Milosevic knew in operational detail what was being done under his direction in the Krajina region, he answered, "Milosevic must have known. His service [DB, or the State Security Division of the Serbian police] was present there and I met the head of his Secret Service there [Stanisic]." Telephone intercepts also were introduced in which Milosevic reports to Karadzic, "You see, they want to step out and are carrying out these things exactly the way we planned it." For full measure, Karadzic echoed in response, "Exactly the way we planned it." Leaving no doubt about his own firsthand understanding of all that was happening, Babic readily acknowledged, "I participated in the formalizing and legalizing of Milosevic's practical decisions."[73]

Milosevic was able to make little headway in his cross-examination of Babic. Probably his strongest avenue of attack was to question Babic's cooperation in his testimony as a means of lessening his own exposure to indictment and prosecution. Milosevic asked, "In addition to the fact of your testifying against me are you also a suspect of this institution?" Babic answered, "I am not testifying against you, I am testifying to the truth."[74] When Babic offered his further opinion that Milosevic had funded Serbian activities in Croatia by means of his de facto control over the National Bank of Yugoslavia, Judge May interrupted Milosevic's incredulous response with a defense of the witness's right to express his view. Milosevic responded, "You are right, Mr. May. The witness has the right not to know something, but he doesn't have the right to lie." May answered, "That is a matter for us . . . [to decide] between what you assert and the evidence he gives." Inside witnesses who followed, such as General Aleksander Vasiljevic, a former head of Yugoslav army intelligence, corroborated much of Babic's account of the chain of command that linked Milosevic to early war crimes in the former Yugoslavia.[75]

In February and March 2003, Carla Del Ponte worked with the U.S. government to place new pressure on Serbian Prime Minister Zoran Djindjic to transfer more indicted war criminals and increase access to archives, threatening once again to delay or deny U.S. financial aid. Djindjic was cooperating with Del Ponte, sometimes meeting her secretly at the Amsterdam airport and in Belgrade, where an official reported she traveled incognita: "we would have to empty the whole government building so that no one could find out that she was . . . discussing the extradition of those persons she was interested in."[76] Djindjic was shot and killed while Pierre-Richard Prosper was visiting the Hague tribunal to discuss new cooperation with Serbian authorities, on the very day in mid-March when Djindjic was to sign warrants for new high-level arrests.[77] Del Ponte was discouraged from attending the Djindjic funeral but later brought flowers to his grave. Critics worried that Western leaders were pushing Serbia too hard and too fast.[78]

Yet the Serbian government responded to the assassination with wide-ranging arrests, new transfers to the tribunal, and new inside witnesses who continued to testify. These included a former casino manager, identified as C-48, who reported on meetings in which Milosevic met and discussed war plans with Croatian and Bosnian Serb leaders. Milosevic was heard discussing the paramilitary activities of Zeljko Raznatovic (better known as Arkan), asking, "Is Arkan under control?" After receiving assurances, Milosevic reportedly responded, "You just keep him under control. We need people like this now but no-one should think that they are more powerful than the state."[79] In parallel testimony, a former secretary to Arkan reported that on about ten occasions payments amounting to some $2.5 million were made to Arkan for his paramilitary operations. This witness detailed the direction and funding of Arkan's group by secret police under Milosevic.[80] This inside testimony continued to elaborate and corroborate the chain of command in the joint criminal conspiracy charged against Milosevic.

TOWARD A PERMANENT COURT

The summer of 2002 was an eventful period for the ICC, which opened an office in The Hague in the beginning of July. The Bush administration had already voiced its inclination to "unsign" the United States from the Treaty of Rome. In the past, the United States had signed without ratifying a number of treaties. David Scheffer, who signed the Rome Treaty as Clinton's ambassador for war crimes, remarked that "the only reason you would unsign the treaty is if your intention was to wage war against the court."[81] The Bush administration confirmed this intent the day before the ICC opened its office by threatening to veto a renewal of the multinational peacekeeping forces in Bosnia unless they were granted immunity from the court.[82] This was an expression of the administration's legal exceptionalist position.

When the ICC officially began its work the next day, July 1, it was an event almost as inauspicious as the opening of the tribunal nearly ten years earlier. The Dutch government was committed to providing a new building for the court on the grounds of a former military barracks on the outskirts of the city, but this would not be ready until 2007, and in the meantime the ICC would be housed in a former telephone office building next to the central train station. The court was now open to receive potential cases under terms and procedures that limited its mandate to large-scale crimes that were committed as part of a government plan or policy and that were unaddressed by a national court. Negotiators for the United States who had played the most prominent role in the 1998 conference that drafted the Rome Treaty had carefully built in safeguards against prosecuting local commanders or individuals.[83]

The head of the five-person advance team for the ICC was Sam Muller, who coincidentally had been the representative in the registrar's office who facilitated my entry into the ICT for my research three years earlier. When I tracked him down at the end of June, before the opening day of the ICC, Muller confirmed the intentionally low-key atmosphere for the beginning of the court's work, saying, "My strategy is to keep as far away from the media as we possibly can so we can get on with our work." For the first six months, until the first judges and prosecutor were selected, the main responsibility of the Hague office was what Muller called a custodial function: "That is, if on July 1 victims, witnesses and so on come in with materials, there will be a way to take possession of that, to rightfully acknowledge and receive it." The EU was providing the biggest portion of the ICC budget. The advance team was funded by the EU and the U.S.-based MacArthur Foundation. The MacArthur Foundation had played this role with the ICT, and now in the face of official U.S. government opposition, it was doing so again.

Although there is no formal link between the ICT and the ICC, Morten Bergsmo served as an advisor to the preparatory committee that is working to establish the ICC. Bergsmo's input is unique because his experience goes back to the commission of experts that preceded the ad hoc Hague tribunal, where he worked until moving to the ICC. He makes an important point not well understood in the United States: that the ICC is a vital institution in the development of the EU itself. He observed that "this is now an integral part of the European Union's foreign policy, where there has been consistent support since 1996. . . . And there is no indication that this will change."

The European press reinforced the EU position vis-à-vis the United States. The British-based *Economist* magazine reported that "the court is supported not just by Europeans but also by poorer nations where atrocities are a real danger" and that "any future compromise must . . . stop short of incorporating into law permanent blanket immunities for anyone." This is the universal premise of liberal legalism. Another *Economist* piece noted that "nearly all America's NATO allies are willing to take the infinitesimal risk [of prosecution] that this entails. So far, the Bush administration is not."[84] The Europe-focused *International Herald Tribune* concluded that "to see this court as an assault on the United States is, frankly, perverse."[85]

Support for the ICC runs deep in Europe in spite of U.S. opposition. An experienced European observer expressed "the sense that America is going against the forces of history and the overall tendency towards increased global integration and organization and that it is doing so for the wrong reasons, while the arguments that are put forward are not persuasive." He went on to say that "there is a sense of being let down on what legal counsel in the U.N. have described as the most important treaty since the United Nations was established, by the government that should lead the way." In the end, this observer noted that "the sense in Europe is that America will lose this political battle but that it will take a long time. . . . The expectation in Europe is that the U.S. is actually going to come around and that it will ultimately join the court and become maybe its strongest supporter. Maybe it will take five, ten or even fifteen years, but clearly that is what diplomats and others say when you discuss these questions with them."

This optimism was certainly at odds with the threatened U.S. veto of Bosnian peacekeepers if they were not granted immunity from the ICC. European leaders responded especially strongly to what a German government official called "almost blackmail." Britain's Tony Blair was characteristically more sympathetic to the United States, saying that he understood American concerns but felt they were met by "constraints on the international court's development."[86] In the following weeks the entire EU, Mexico, and Canada formed a common front to resist American demands of blanket immunity from ICC prosecution for its peace-keeping troops. The dispute temporarily was resolved in mid-July when the United States accepted a compromise that drew on a Rome Treaty article that extended immunity for one year to nations that do not accept the court. Still, the Canadian ambassador called it "a sad day for the U.N."[87] before nonetheless going on to say that "we must continue to work with our American friends . . . to bring their important voice to the court."[88]

John Bolton led a new initiative by the Bush administration in early August to bilaterally and individually enlist nations in pledges not to extradite Americans to the ICC for trial. Bolton initially enlisted Israel and Romania to sign such agreements, saying that the procedure was needed to prevent U.S. citizens "from falling into the potentially politicized jurisdiction of that court."[89] Later in the month the administration began warning foreign diplomats that U.S. military aid could be withdrawn if they did not enter into the bilateral agreements.[90] The EU at first protested, warning thirteen nations hoping to join its ranks that they should resist signing any agreements.

Bolton now insisted that "we're not applying any pressure on countries to sign these agreements, and we don't think it is appropriate for the European Union to prevent other countries from signing them." An unnamed "senior administration official" was quoted in the same article, however, as predicting that the European allies would eventually give in to the waiver agreements because "the reaction in Congress if they don't agree will not be good."[91] As the debate widened, the voice of Bolton became more prominent. He had written an article several years earlier saying that high-level officials such as Henry Kissinger, rather than soldiers, were his real concern: "They are the potential targets of the politically unaccountable prosecutor created in Rome." Bolton's view was that "whether the ICC survives and flourishes depends in large measure on the United States." His recommendation was to "ignore it in our official posture and attempt to isolate it through our diplomacy, in order to prevent it from acquiring any further legitimacy or resources."[92]

WITHOUT THE AMERICANS

The EU's foreign ministers met in October to find a way out of their impasse with the United States and advanced a compromise that would have its members agree not to extradite American military personnel accused of war crimes to the ICC, so long as the U.S. government would guarantee that such suspects would be tried in American courts.[93] The EU was clearly trying to find a way to minimize American objections and obstacles to the initiation of the ICC's work. Bolton responded by urging the British and the French governments to agree bilaterally to broader exemption clauses that further protect civilian leaders such as Kissinger.[94] As of this writing, slightly more than a dozen small and beholden countries have signed bilateral pledges with the United States.

Years earlier, the Canadian foreign minister, Lloyd Axworthy, had made the point that important things could be accomplished in international law without American participation. This was also the tack that the Canadian ICT prosecutor Louise Arbour took in initiating the Milosevic indictment. Knowing of reservations in the Clinton administration about such a prospect, Arbour recalled thinking to herself that "many political men thought I would not be so presumptuous, that I would consult them. But I gave myself one bit of advice: never ask for something that can be refused. So I said nothing."[95]

In a press conference about the Milosevic indictment that he held following its announcement, the U.S. ambassador for war crimes at the time, David Scheffer, also indicated the absence of American participation in its planning. He remarked that "the United States has no influence on the timing of this indictment."[96] Yet the United States and Ambassador Scheffer provided extensive information and cooperation that were essential ingredients in the development of both the tribunal and this crucial indictment. The growth and success of the ICT occurred because of transgovernmental links with U.S. agencies, as well as with many other nations' agencies and nongovernmental organizations. All of this happened in spite of American ambivalence about the development of the ICT, and this could again be the case with the ICC.

Unfortunately, there are now many skilled and highly committed Americans with ICT experience who could, along with the United States, contribute to the development of the ICC. But citizens of non-member states can not be employed by the ICC. Morten Bergsmo captured the significance of this situation with his observation that "it is unfortunate that America is not there from the beginning to help influence the construction of this organization, to help influence the establishment of its management culture." It was poignant in this context to hear Michael Johnson, who recently has played such a prominent role in the reorganization of the ICTY, say that "as an American there is no contribution that I will be allowed to make, but as a chief of prosecution of the ICTY, our office is completely committed to ensuring the success of our counterpart at the ICC, and we will." Meanwhile, when attention shifted to the American takeover of Iraq, the fact that neither the United States nor Iraq was a signatory to the Rome Treaty meant that the ICC was unlikely to play any role in the aftermath of this war.

THE LONG VIEW

I caught up with Ben Ferencz, the octogenarian veteran of Nuremberg, at a conference on international criminal law at the New School University in New York City in the spring of 2002. Richard Goldstone suggested at this conference that the success of the fledgling ICC would likely depend to a great degree on the first cases it chose to prosecute. Goldstone emphasized how far the ICT had come in its progression from the Tadic case to the Milosevic case. Ferencz had a much longer view of the progression, but both he and Goldstone seemed certain about where things were headed in the future. Ferencz moved easily among old friends and new acquaintances as he passed through the conference hall with a beaming smile and an energy that belied his years. He pressed into the hands of those he greeted a flyer with his e-mail address and a message concerning the American government's reservations about the ICC and its July 2002 start date. The message urged its readers that "Americans will have ample time to debate the merits of the new court, and to see how it works. Remaining aloof and sulking, or trying to sabotage the court, can only be counterproductive and demean our stature as a world leader supporting the rule of law."

APPENDIX

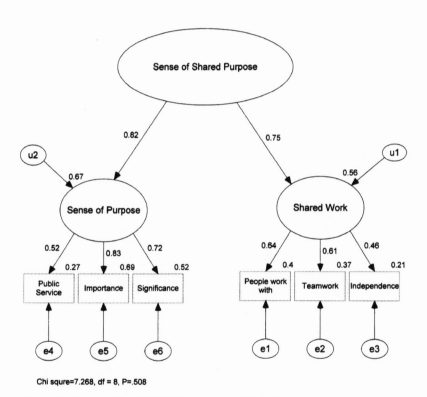

Chi squre=7.268, df = 8, P=.508

Figure A.1. Second-order LISREL factor model of shared purpose

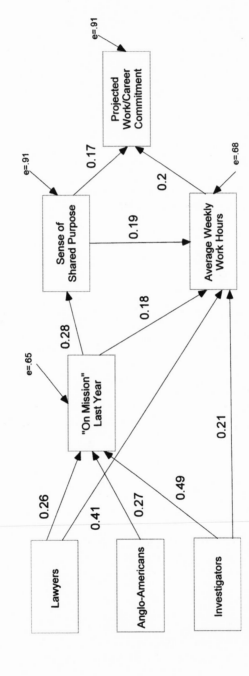

Figure A.2. Trimmed OLS regression model of alternation effects on projected work/career commitment at the Hague tribunal

NOTES

INTRODUCTION

1. For an early defense of Milosevic and a critique of the response of Western leaders, NATO, and the tribunal to his government, see Michael Parenti, *To Kill a Nation: The Attack on Yugoslavia* (London: Verso, 2000).

2. Milosevic Transcripts, p. 219, found at www.un.org/icty/.

3. See Steven Burg and Paul Shoup, *The War in Bosnia-Herzegovina: Ethnic Conflict and International Intervention* (Armonk, N.Y.: Sharpe, 1999), p. 66; Laura Silber and Allan Little, *The Death of Yugoslavia* (London: Penguin, 1995), p. 294.

4. Milosevic Transcripts, p. 9.

5. Ibid., pp. 44–45.

6. Ibid., pp. 14–15.

7. Ibid., p. 16.

8. A history of Yugoslavia from 800 to the early 1990s is provided by John Lampe, *Yugoslavia as History: Twice There Was a Country* (New York: Cambridge University Press, 1996).

9. See Valerie Bunce, *Subversive Institutions: The Design and the Destruction of Socialism and the State* (New York: Cambridge University Press, 1999).

10. Mark Mazower, *The Balkans* (London: Weidenfeld & Nicolson, 2000), pp. 128–29.

11. Milosevic Transcripts, pp. 35–36.

12. Ibid., pp. 45–46.

13. Ibid., pp. 46–47.

14. Ibid., p. 76.

15. See Sabrina Petra Ramet, *Balkan Babel: The Disintegration of Yugoslavia from the Death of Tito to Ethnic War* (Boulder, Colo.: Westview, 1996), pt. 3.

16. Milosevic Transcripts, p. 96.

17. Ibid., pp. 106–7.

18. Ibid., pp. 130–31.

19. See Tim Judah, *Kosovo: War and Revenge* (New Haven: Yale University Press, 2000).

20. Milosevic Transcripts, p. 139.

21. Ibid., p. 156.

22. Ibid., p. 162.

23. Ibid., p. 165.

24. For a vivid description of this period, see Michael Ignatieff, *Virtual War: Kosovo and Beyond* (New York: Holt, 2000).

25. Milosevic Transcripts, p. 166.

26. See also the volume edited by Alexandra Stiglmayer, *Mass Rape: The*

War against Women in Bosnia-Herzegovina (Lincoln: University of Nebraska Press, 1994); and Beverly Allen, *Rape Warfare: The Hidden Genocide in Bosnia-Herzegovina and Croatia* (Minneapolis: University of Minnesota Press, 1996).

27. Milosevic Transcripts, p. 212.

28. Ibid., p. 211.

29. Ibid., p. 178.

CHAPTER ONE

1. Olivia Ward, "War Crimes Tribunal on a Roll," *Toronto Star,* 23 March 1998, A2.

2. The Robert Houghwout Jackson Oral History, Interview conducted in February 1995 by Harlan Phillips, Oral History Research Office, Butler Library, Columbia University, p. 1204.

3. Ibid., p. 1206.

4. Sheldon Glueck, *War Criminals: Their Prosecution and Punishment* (New York: Knopf, 1944).

5. Benjamin B. Ferencz Oral History, United States Holocaust Memorial Museum Research Institute, Interview by Joan Ringelheim, 26 August 1994, p. 11.

6. Ibid.

7. Ibid., pp. 14, 6.

8. Ibid., p. 34.

9. Ibid., pp. 25–26.

10. Ibid., p. 30.

11. Ibid., p. 3.

12. Gary Bass, *Stay the Hand of Vengeance* (Princeton: Princeton University Press, 2000).

13. Ferencz Oral History, p. 44.

14. See John Laub and Robert Sampson, "The Sutherland-Glueck Debate: On the Sociology of Criminological Knowledge," *American Journal of Sociology* 96 (1991): 1402–40.

15. Sheldon Glueck, "Punishing War Criminals," *The New Republic* 109 (1943): 708.

16. See, e.g., George Creel, *War Criminals and Punishment* (New York: McBride, 1944), and more generally George Gallup, *The Gallup Poll: Public Opinion 1935–1971* (New York: Random House, 1972), 1:339.

17. Glueck, "Punishing War Criminals," p. 708.

18. Hersh Lauterpacht, "The Law of Nature and the Punishment of War Crimes" *British Yearbook of International Law* 21 (1944): 58–95.

19. London International Commission II on the Trial of War Criminals, minutes of the meeting held 12 November, 1943. Box 42, Folder 9, Glueck Papers, Harvard Law Library, Cambridge, Massachusetts.

20. Geoffrey Robertson, *Crimes against Humanity: The Struggle for Global Justice* (London: Penguin, 2000), p. 34.

21. See Samantha Power, *"A Problem from Hell": America and the Age of Genocide* (New York: Basic, 2002), p. 50.

22. Ferencz Oral History, p. 50.

23. Robertson, *Crimes against Humanity,* 295.

24. Sheldon Glueck, "By What Tribunal Shall War Offenders Be Tried?" *Harvard Law Review* 56 (1943): 1059; Sheldon Glueck, "Justice for War Criminals," *American Mercury,* March 1945, 274–80; Glueck, *War Criminals;* House Congressional Resolution 30, 79th Congress, 1st sess., February 19, 1945. See "Statement of Professor Sheldon Glueck, Harvard Law School, In Regard to House Resolu-

tion No. 93, Concerning the Trial and Punishment of Axis War Criminals," dated 20 March, 1945. Box 43, Folder 2, Glueck Papers, Harvard Law Library, Cambridge, Massachusetts.

25. "Statement of Professor Sheldon Glueck," p. 2.

26. Ibid., p. 30.

27. Glueck to Jackson, 1 November 1945, Glueck Papers, Harvard Law Library, Cambridge, Massachusetts.

28. See, e.g., Glueck to Donovan, 9 May 1945. Glueck Papers, Harvard Law Library, Cambridge, Massachusetts.

29. Ibid., pp. 5, 6.

30. Henry Stimson, *Stimson Diaries* (New Haven: Yale University Library), 48: 61.

31. Bass, *Stay the Hand of Vengeance,* p. 174.

32. Jackson Oral History, p. 1282.

33. Telford Taylor, *The Anatomy of the Nuremberg Trials: A Personal Memoir* (Boston: Little Brown, 1992), p. xi.

34. Memorandum of Meeting Held 28 June, 1945 Regarding Preparation of Evidence, 29 June, 1945. Glueck Papers, Harvard Law Library, Cambridge, Massachusetts.

35. See Digest Forms for Interrogation Reports and Documentary Proof, Glueck Papers, Harvard Law Library, Cambridge, Massachusetts.

36. Robert Jackson, preface to Sheldon Glueck, *The Nuremberg Trial and Aggressive War* (New York: Knopf, 1946), p. vii.

37. Ferencz Oral History, p. 47.

38. Ibid., p. 48.

39. Joseph Persico, *Nuremberg: Infamy on Trial* (New York: Times Books/ Random House, 1994), pp. 200–201.

40. Ferencz Oral History, p. 52.

41. Ibid., pp. 52–53.

42. Ibid., p. 53.

43. The scale of the differences between the Soviets and the British and American views of postwar justice are further reflected in the fact that the Soviets in their post-Nuremberg trials sentenced about ten times the number of Germans as did the British and Americans. See Eugene Davidson, *The Trial of the Germans* (New York: Macmillan, 1966), p. 30.

44. Glueck, *Nuremberg Trial and Aggressive War.*

45. See Laub and Sampson, "Sutherland-Glueck Debate."

46. On the role of political opportunity structures, see Sidney Tarrow, *Power in Movement: Social Movements, Collective Action, and Politics* (Cambridge: Cambridge University Press, 1994).

47. See Carol Heimer and Lisa Staffen, *For the Sake of the Children: The Social Organization of Responsibility in the Hospital and the Home* (Chicago: University of Chicago Press, 1998), p. 27n.

48. See especially Doug McAdam, John McCarthy, and Mayer Zald, introduction to *Comparative Perspectives on Social Movements: Political Opportunities, Mobilizing Structures and Cultural Framings,* ed. Doug McAdam, John McCarthy and Mayer Zald (Cambridge: Cambridge University Press, 1996).

49. See Richard Trivisaro, "Alternation and Conversion as Qualitatively Different Transformations," in *Social Psychology through Symbolic Interactionism,* ed. Gregory Stone and Harvey Farberman (New York: Wiley, 1981), pp. 237–48.

50. Doug McAdam, "The Biological Consequences of Activism," *American Sociological Review* 54 (1989): 744–60.

CHAPTER TWO

1. See Michael Scharf, *Balkan Justice* (Durham, N.C.: Carolina Academic Press, 1997), p. 41.

2. Roy Gutman, *A Witness to Genocide* (New York: Macmillan, 1993); Ed Vulliamy, *Seasons in Hell: Understanding Bosnia's War* (London: Simon & Schuster, 1994); Blaine Hardin, "Serbs Accused of '91 Croatia Massacre," *Washington Post*, 26 January 1993, A13; George Rodrigues, "Western Leaders' Timidity Aids Serbian Conquest," *Dallas Morning News*, 15 August 1993; Thom Shanker, "Missed Chances: Washington Bears Much Guilt for Yugoslav Horrors," *Chicago Tribune*, 31 January 1993, 1; John Burns, "Serbian General is either a snake or a charmer, depending on the beholder," *New York Times*, 8 August 1993, A14; Helsinki Watch, *War Crimes in Bosnia-Herzegovina*, 2 vols. (1992–93). See also Helsinki Watch, *Prosecute Now!* (New York, 1993).

3. Samantha Power, *"A Problem from Hell": America and the Age of Genocide* (New York: Basic, 2002), p. 258.

4. See also Aryeh Neier, *War Crimes: Brutality, Genocide, Terror, and the Struggle for Justice* (New York: Times Books/Random House, 1998).

5. Mirko Klarin, "Nuremberg Now!" *Borba*, 16 May 1991.

6. Quoted in Mike Sula, "On Top of the World," *Chicago Reader*, 5 March 1999, 26.

7. Cherif Bassiouni, *Investigating Violations of International Humanitarian Law in the Former Yugoslavia*, International Human Rights Law Institute (Chicago: DePaul University Law School, 1996), Occasional Paper no. 2, p. 32.

8. Carol Off, *The Lion, the Fox, and the Eagle* (Toronto: Random House, 2000), p. 264, notes that in media interviews, Bassiouni's predecessor as chairman of the commission, Fritz Kalshoven, had "let it be known that Lord Owen had actually warned him not to allow the Commission of Experts to get in the way of the peace process."

9. Tim Judah, *The Serbs: History, Myth, and the Destruction of Yugoslavia* (New Haven: Yale University Press, 1997), p. 74.

10. Sula, "On Top of the World," p. 16.

11. Patrick Glynn, "See No Evil: Clinton, Bush and the Truth about Bosnia," *New Republic*, 25 October 1993, 23.

12. Richard Holbrooke, *To End a War* (New York: Modern Library, 1999).

13. Yves Dezalay and Bryant Garth, in "Human Rights from the Cold War to Kosovo: Constructing New Universals within Hegemonic Battles" (Chicago: American Bar Foundation, 2001), draw on Bourdieu in defining the term *field* as "a semi-autonomous space of relations among individuals and groups who act in relation to each other and compete within and about certain rules of the game," p. 2n.

14. Ibid., p. 3.

15. Ibid., n. 98.

16. David Binder, "Criticized as Appeaser, Vance Defends His Role in Balkans," *New York Times*, 19 January 1993, A1; David Halberstam, *War in a Time of Peace* (New York: Scribner, 2001), p. 129.

17. Ian Guest, *On Trial: The United Nations, War Crimes, and the Former Yugoslavia* (Washington, D.C.: Refugee Policy Group, 1995), p. 104.

18. Quoted in Gutman, *Witness to Genocide*, p. 58.

19. Guest, *On Trial*, p. 57.

20. Sula, "On Top of the World," p. 22.

21. Ibid.

22. Ian Traynor, "U.S. Seeks Punishment of Bosnia's 'War Criminals,'" *Guardian*, 17 December 1992. See also Guest, *On Trial*, p. 101.

23. Carla Anne Robbins, "Balkan Judgments: World Again Confronts Moral Issues Involved in War Crimes Trials," *Wall Street Journal*, 13 July 1993, A1.

24. Quoted in Halberstam, *War in a Time of Peace*, p. 57.

25. This account is based on a Roy Gutman story published in *Newsday* and reprinted in the *Phoenix Gazette*, 4 March 1993, A12.

26. Halberstam, *War in a Time of Peace*, p. 46.

27. Blaine Harden, "Serbs Accused of '91 Croatia Massacre: U.S. Doctors Believe 200 Wounded Men Were Taken From Hospital and Shot," *Washington Post*, 26 January 1993, A13.

28. William Fenrick, "In the Field with UNCOE: Investigating Atrocities in the Territory of Former Yugoslavia," *Military Law & Law of War Review* 34 (1995): 46.

29. Guest, *On Trial*, pp. 67–68.

30. Ibid., p. 72.

31. Cherif Bassiouni, "The Commission of Experts Established Pursuant to Security Council Resolution 780: Investigating Violations of International Humanitarian Law in the Former Yugoslavia," *Criminal Law Forum* 5 (1994): 310.

32. Laura Silber and Allan Little, *The Death of Yugoslavia* (London: Penguin Books, 1995), p. 297.

33. Ibid., p. 310.

34. Fenrick, "In the Field with UNCOE," p. 49.

35. Ibid., pp. 50–51.

36. Maud Beelman, "Serb Shelling Kills 15 at Sarajevo Soccer Match," *Washington Post*, 2 June 1993, A21.

37. Fenrick, "In the Field with UNCOE," p. 52.

38. Silber and Little, *Death of Yugoslavia*, p. 311.

39. Guest, *On Trial*, p. 67.

40. Fenrick, "In the Field with UNCOE," p. 60.

41. Ibid., p. 62.

42. Galic Transcript (IT-98-29-I), Web site)cript (Major General www.un.org/icty/.

43. Patrick Bishop, "Britain 'Snubbed War Crimes Team,'" *Daily Telegraph*, 4 December 1993.

44. Bassiouni, "Commission of Experts," p. 291–92n.

45. Ibid., p. 300.

46. Ibid., p. 297n.

47. Power, *"Problem from Hell,"* pp. 277.

48. Ibid., p. 276.

49. Halberstam, *War in a Time of Peace*, p. 133.

50. See, e.g., Michael Gordon, "A State Department Aide on Bosnia Resigns on Partition Issue," *New York Times*, 5 August 1993, A1.

51. See Cherif Bassiouni, "Final Report of the United Nations Commission of Experts Established Pursuant to Security Council Resolution 780," 27 May 1994, paras. 129–50.

52. See Michael Ignatieff, *Virtual War: Kosovo and Beyond* (New York: Penguin, 2000), pp. 121–22.

53. Bassiouni, "Final Report," para. 140.

54. Halberstam, *War in a Time of Peace*, p. 83, attributes this quote to Milo Vasic.

55. Bassiouni, "Final Report," para. 158.

56. Ibid., annex V, para. 337.

57. Ibid., para. 344.

58. Ibid., para. 354.

59. The term *death camp* is used in the commission report. Power questions whether this term is appropriately used here and suggests the term *concentration camp* instead. See Power, *"Problem from Hell,"* p. 269.

60. Bassiouni, "Final Report," para. 35.

61. Ibid., p. 312n.

62. Guest, *On Trial,* p. 146.

63. Ibid., p. 148.

64. James Bone, "U.K. Blocks Choice of War Crimes Prosecutor," *The Times* (London), 4 September 1993.

65. Guest, *On Trial,* p. 148.

66. Ibid., p. 106.

67. Ibid., p. 151.

68. Halberstam, *War in a Time of Peace.*

69. Sula, "On Top of the World," p. 26.

70. Bone, "U.K. Blocks Choice."

71. Guest, *On Trial,* p. 154.

CHAPTER THREE

1. Gary Bass, *Stay the Hand of Vengeance: The Politics of War Crimes Tribunals* (Princeton: Princeton University Press, 2000), p. 219.

2. Richard Goldstone, *For Humanity: Reflections of a War Crimes Investigator* (New Haven: Yale University Press, 2000), pp. 88, 74.

3. Sudarsan Raghavan, "Richard J. Goldstone, a South African Jurist Takes on Balkan and Rwanda Conflicts, Seeking to Punish War Criminals." *Los Angeles Times,* 14 March 1995, 5.

4. John Meyer and Ronald Jepperson, "The 'Actors' of Modern Society: The Cultural Construction of Agency," *Sociological Theory* 18 (2000):100–20.

5. Ibid., p. 105.

6. "Modern actors," Meyer and Jepperson warn, "are seen as autochthonous and natural entities, no longer really embedded in culture." They argue that the agency and actorhood assumed in liberal models are very much cultural constructs with exaggerated properties rooted in unrealistic Protestant and Anglo-American beliefs. Ibid., p. 100.

7. Ibid., p. 112.

8. William Horne, "The Real Trial of the Century," *American Lawyer,* September 1995, 7.

9. Goldstone, *For Humanity,* p. 80.

10. September 10, 1995, *60 Minutes,* CBS News Transcripts.

11. See Mark Granovetter, *Getting a Job* (Chicago: University of Chicago Press, 1995).

12. Goldstone, *For Humanity,* p. 80.

13. Bass, *Stay the Hand of Vengeance,* p. 221.

14. Ian Guest, *On Trial: The United Nations, War Crimes, and the Former Yugoslavia* (Washington, D.C.: Refugee Policy Group, 1995), p. 142.

15. Press statement by Justice Richard Goldstone, International Criminal Tribunal, The Hague, 25 July 1995 at www.un.org/icty/.

16. Robert Block, "First Catch Your War Criminal," *The Independent,* 30 April 1995, p. 4.

17. Cited in Michael Scharf, *Balkan Justice* (Durham, N.C.: Carolina Academic Press, 1997), p. 100.

18. Richard Holbrooke, *To End a War* (New York: Modern Library, 1999), p. 333.

19. Djordje Dukic Indictment, Case No. IT-96-20-I, International Criminal Tribunal for the Former Yugoslavia, The Hague, 29 February 1996.

20. Elizabeth Neuffer, *The Key to My Neighbor's House: Seeking Justice in Bosnia and Rwanda* (New York: Picador, 2001), p. 175.

21. Bass, *Stay the Hand of Vengeance,* p. 250.

22. " . . . And Bring the War Criminals to Trial," *Wall Street Journal,* 29 May 1996, A18.

23. Louise Branson, "Serbian Killer Turned away by U.S. Embassy," *The Times* (London), 17 March 1996, 1.

24. William Kole, "Serb Soldier Details How Muslims Begged for Their Lives/ Tribunal Probes Srebrenica Massacre," *Houston Chronicle,* 10 March 1996, 32.

25. "Bosnia Killings Inquiry Advances, Serbs Called Willing to Surrender Two in Srebrenica Deaths," *Boston Globe,* 15 March 1996, 2.

26. Press statement by Justice Richard Goldstone, International Criminal Tribunal, The Hague, 7 March, 1996, at www.un.org/icty/.

27. Elizabeth Neuffer, "Bosnia Massacre Photo Cited U2 Pictures Reveal More Than 100 Bodies, Military Says," *Boston Globe,* 21 March 1996, 1.

28. "Serbia Delivers Witnesses to Bosnia War Crimes Tribunal," *Los Angeles Times,* 31 March 1996, 10.

29. Goldstone, *For Humanity,* p. 85.

30. Scharf, *Balkan Justice,* p. 112.

31. Horne, "Real Trial of the Century," p. 2.

32. Joseph Persico, *Nuremberg: Infamy on Trial* (New York: Viking, 1994), p. 107.

33. Scharf, *Balkan Justice,* chapter 7.

34. Edward Vulliamy, "Accused Serb 'Not Identified,'" *The Guardian,* 26 July 1996, 14.

35. "Tadic Takes the Stand," *Tribunal Update* 1, 28 October–1 November 1996, available from the Institute for War and Peace Reporting at www.iwpr.net/.

36. "The Tadic Case," *Tribunal Update,* undated, available from the Institute for War and Peace Reporting at www.iwpr.net/. Italics added.

37. "The Tadic Pre-Sentencing Hearing," *Tribunal Update* 35, 30 June–7 July 1997, available from the Institute for War and Peace Reporting at www.iwpr.net/.

38. "Tadic Sentenced to 20 years," *Tribunal Update* 37, 14–19 July 1997, available from the Institute for War and Peace Reporting at www.iwpr.net/.

39. "Tadic Case: The Appeals Chamber Judgement," *Tribunal Update* 134, 12–18 July 1999, available from the Institute for War and Peace Reporting at www.iwpr.net/.

40. "Tadic Receives a 25 Year Sentence," *Tribunal Update* 151, 8–13 November 1999, available from the Institute for War and Peace Reporting at www.iwpr.net/.

41. " 'Tadpole' Tadic's Sentence Reduced," *Tribunal Update* 161, 24–29 January 2000, available from the Institute for War and Peace Reporting at www.iwpr.net/.

42. Guest, *On Trial,* p. 126n.

43. Ibid., p. 126.

44. Scharf, *Balkan Justice,* p. 151.

45. Jonathan Randal, "Tribunal Opens Hearing on Bosnian Serbs: War Crimes Panel Uses Session to Exert Pressure for the Arrest of Indicted Leaders," *Washington Post,* 28 June 1996, A27.

46. "Tribunal Hears Account of Siege of Sarajevo," *Boston Globe,* 2 July, 1996, 5.

47. "Rape Used as Strategy, Tribunal Told," *Boston Globe,* 3 July 1996, 4.

48. Mary Williams Walsh, "Victim, Victimizer Testify to Horrors of Bosnia War; Tribunal: Survivor Says Mladic Directed Massacre at Srebrenica," *Los Angeles Times,* 6 July 1996, 1.

49. Mary Williams Walsh, "Witnesses at Tribunal Describe Bloody Fall of Bosnian City," *Houston Chronicle,* 6 July 1996, 22.

50. Goldstone, *For Humanity,* p. 104.

51. Scharf, *Balkan Justice,* pp. 214–215.

52. Geoffrey Robertson, *Crimes against Humanity: The Struggle for Global Justice* (London: Allen Lane, 1999), p. 309.

53. Ibid., p. 310.

54. Mike Corder, "No Trials Yet, But Lots of Tribulations for War Crimes Tribunal," AP Worldstream, 25 October 1995.

55. Scharf, *Balkan Justice,* p. 79.

56. Holbrooke, *To End a War,* p. 190.

57. Scharf, *Balkan Justice,* p. 79.

58. Ibid., p. 226.

CHAPTER FOUR

1. Carol Off, *The Lion, the Fox, and the Eagle: A Story of Generals and Justice in Rwanda and Yugoslavia* (Toronto: Random House of Canada, 2000), p. 276.

2. Michael Ignatieff, *Virtual War: Kosovo and Beyond* (New York: Penguin, 2000), p. 118.

3. Judy Steed, "Supreme Test for Louise Arbour," *Toronto Star,* 12 September 1999, 1.

4. Kirk Makin, "Arbour Moves from Stormy to Calm Waters," *Toronto Globe and Mail,* 12 June 1999, A3.

5. See Edgar Kiser, "Comparing Varieties of Agency Theory in Economics, Political Science, and Sociology: An Illustration from State Policy Implementation," *Sociological Theory* 17 (1999): 146–70.

6. Roger Cohen and Marlise Simons, "At Arraignment, Milosevic Scorns His U.N. Accusers," *New York Times,* 4 July 2001, A1.

7. Michael Parenti, *To Kill a Nation: The Attack on Yugoslavia* (London: Verso, 2000), p. 128.

8. See John Meyer and Ronald Jepperson, "The 'Actors' of Modern Society: The Cultural Construction of Social Agency," *Sociological Theory* 18 (2000): 100–120.

9. Anglo-Americans are estimated to still earn nearly $8,000 a year more than other OTP employees after also statistically taking into in a regression equation account autonomy, authority, and hours worked per week.

10. "Yugo Justice Minister Launches Tirade against ICTY Prosecutor," *Agence France Presse,* 24 May 2000.

11. Kirk Makin, "Potential Supreme Court Justices Lining Up," *Canadian Press,* 3 December, 1997.

12. See, e.g, Michael Scharf, *Balkan Justice: The Story behind the First International War Crimes Trial Since Nuremberg* (Durham, N.C.: Carolina Academic Press, 1997).

13. David Halberstam, *War in a Time of Peace: Bush, Clinton, and the Generals* (New York: Scribner, 2001); Wesley Clark, *Waging Modern War: Bosnia, Kosovo, and the Future of Combat* (New York: Public Affairs Publishing, 2001) .

14. Anthony DePalma, "A Canadian Rousts Diplomacy (and Ruffles the U.S.)," *New York Times,* 10 January 1999, A10.

15. Ibid.

16. Richard Travisaro, "Alternation and Conversion as Qualitatively Different Transformations," in Gregory Stone and Harvey Farberman, eds., *Social Psychology through Symbolic Interaction* (New York: Wiley, 1981), p. 243.

17. Sylvie Halpern, "Madame Justice Louise Arbour: Justice for All," *Enroute,* June 1998, 63.

18. Ignatieff, *Virtual War,* p. 117.

19. Paul Ames, "Goldstone Welcomes Karadzic's Departure, Says Arrests Needed," Associated Press, 20 July 1996.

20. Laura Silber and Allan Little, *The Death of Yugoslavia* (London: Penguin, 1995), p. 176.

21. Off, *The Lion, the Fox, and the Eagle,* p. 298.

22. Clark, *Waging Modern War,* p. 35.

23. Meyer and Jepperson, " 'Actors' of Modern Society."

24. Ignatieff, *Virtual War,* p. 126.

25. Mike Corder, "Serb Mayor Pleads Innocent to Vukovar Massacre Charges," Associated Press, 4 July 1997.

26. Leonard Doyle, "War Crimes Suspect Held," *The Observer,* 29 June 1997, 4.

27. Reuters, "U.N. Aids War Crimes Tribunal in Croatia Arrest," *International Herald Tribune,* 28–29 June 1997, A1.

28. Steven Lee Myers, "Serb Is Held in the Killing of 261 Croats," *New York Times,* 28 June 1997, A5.

29. William Jefferson Clinton, "Statement by the President on Apprehension of Indicted War Criminal Slavko Dolmanovic," The White House, Office of the Press Secretary, 28 June 1997.

30. Off, *The Lion, the Fox, and the Eagle,* p. 301.

31. Gary Bass, *Stay the Hand of Vengeance: The Politics of War Crimes Tribunals* (Princeton: Princeton University Press, 2000).

32. Ibid., p. 208.

33. Richard McAdams, "The Origin, Development, and Regulation of Norms," *Michigan Law Review* 96 (1997): 338–86; William Goode, *The Celebration of Heroes: Prestige as a Social Control System* (Berkeley: University of California Press, 1978).

34. On loosely coupled criminal justice in the American context, see John Hagan, Duane Alwin, and John Hewitt, "Ceremonial Justice: Crime and Punishment in a Loosely Coupled System," *Social Forces* 58 (1979): 506–27.

35. McAdams, "Origin, Development, and Regulation of Norms," p. 369.

36. Ibid., p. 371.

37. Clark, *Waging Modern War,* p. 82.

38. McAdams, "Origin, Development and Regulation of Norms," p. 372.

39. Metta Spencer and Norman Dyson, "Prosecuting War Criminals," *Peace Magazine* (16) 2000: 16–23.

40. Charles Trueheart, "France Splits with Court over Bosnia: Generals Won't Testify in War Crimes Cases," *Washington Post,* 16 December 1997, A22.

41. Andre Viollaz, "U.S.-French Ties Face New Crimp After Report of Karadzic Meeting," *Agence France Presse,* 23 April 1998, 1.

42. Evelyn Thomas, "France Indicted for Failure to Bring War Criminals to Book," *The European,* 8 June 1988, 16.

43. Halpern, "Madame Justice Louise Arbour," p. 58.

44. See David Snow, Burke Rochford, Steve Worden, and Robert Benford,

"Frame Alignment Processes, Micromobilization, and Movement Participation," *American Sociological Review* 51 (1986): 464–81; William Sewell, "A Theory of Structure: Duality, Agency, and Transformation," *American Journal of Sociology* 98 (1992): 19.

45. Louise Arbour, "Crimes against Humanity," *University of Toronto Bulletin,* 11 January 1999, 16.

46. Marlise Simons, "Proud But Concerned, Tribunal Prosecutor Leaves," *New York Times,* 15 September 1999, A3.

47. Makin, "Arbour Moves from Stormy to Calm Waters," p. A3.

48. Charles Trueheart, "A New Kind of Justice," *Atlantic Monthly,* April 2000, 80–90.

49. Clark, *Waging Modern War,* p. 161.

50. Marshall Sahlins, "Culture and Agency in History," paper presented in Department of Sociology Colloquim, Northwestern University, Evanston, Illinois, 10 May 2001, p. 24.

51. Ibid. "It follows," Sahlins reasons, "that the agency of individual subjects is not independent of cultural order but authorized by it." This was the authorization process that helped create Arbour's agency. It is in this way that "persons can be empowered to represent collectivities, to instantiate or personify them, sometimes even to create them."

52. Kirk Makin, "Louise Arbour's Supreme decision: The celebrity judge would be a superstar candidate for the top court, but is the time right for her?" *Toronto Globe and Mail,* 16 March 1999, A1.

53. Mustafa Emirbayer and Ann Mische, "What Is Agency?" *American Journal of Sociology* 103 (1998): 964. They note that "the structural contexts of action are themselves temporal as well as relational fields—multiple, overlapping ways of ordering time toward which social actors can assume different simultaneous agentic orientations."

54. Ed Vulliamy and Patrick Wintour, "Hawks Smell a Tyrant's Blood; NATO's New Confidence Suggests That the Neck of Slobodan Milosevic, the Butcher of Belgrade, May Itself Now Be on the Block," *The Observer,* 30 May 1999, 15.

55. See *CNN Live Event: Milosevic,* Time 8:02, 27 July 1999.

56. Bass, *Stay the Hand of Vengeance,* p. 312.

57. Weekly Listing of Federal Cabinet Orders in Council, vol. 20, no. 21, 15 June 1999.

58. Sahlins, "Culture and Agency in History." This a change in dynamics that suggests both historical effect and some "reversal in the order of things."

59. Ibid., p. 24. Sahlins emphasizes that "we have to overcome received ideas of diametric opposition between culture and human agency in order to understand how they interact dialectically in history." Sewell, "Theory of Structure," p. 27. Sewell speaks similarly of "the dialectical interactions through which humans shape their history."

60. Neil Fligstein,"Social Skill and the Theory of Fields," *Sociological Theory* 19 (2001): 105–25. Fligstein recently has suggested that such tactics are necessary aspects of the social skill that can enable agency to be transformed into action.

61. Julia Adams, "Principals and Agents, Colonialists and Company Men: The Decay of Colonial Control in the Dutch East Indies," *American Sociological Review* 61 (1996): 12–28. Adams demonstrates that principal-agent relationships are mediated by network structures and the multivocal positions that agents may enjoy.

62. Clark, *Waging Modern War,* p. 325.

63. Bill Hemmer and Christiane Amanpour, "Justice Arbour Discusses the Indictment of Milosevic for War Crimes," CNN Morning News, 27 May 1999, Federal Department Clearing House Transcript #99052710V09.

CHAPTER FIVE

1. These external connections are a further crucial source of structural linkages and tightened couplings discussed in chapter 4. Neil Fligstein's sociological theory of fields emphasizes that "people who act as leaders in groups must stabilize their relations to their own group members to get them to act collectively and must frame their more general strategic moves toward other organizations in their field or domain." He calls the capacity to meet this dual challenge social skill, and this is exactly the challenge to which Ruez directed his skill in his work on the Srebrenica case. See Neil Fligstein, "Social Skill and the Theory of Fields," *Sociological Theory* 19 (2001): 105–25.

2. The legal and political scholar Ann-Marie Slaughter writes about the growing role of transgovernmental relationships in addressing international problems, observing that "transgovernmental networks . . . increasingly provide an important anchor for international organizations and non-state actors alike." See Ann-Marie Slaughter, "The Real New World Order," *Foreign Affairs,* September–October 1997, 196.

3. Ibid., pp. 336–37.

4. Michael Dobbs and R. Jeffrey Smith, "New Proof Offered of Serb Atrocities," *The Washington Post,* 29 October 1995, 1.

5. Gary Bass, *Stay the Hand of Vengeance* (Princeton: Princeton University Press, 2000), p. 244.

6. See Goldstone's description of the letter in Richard Goldstone, *For Humanity: Reflections of a War Crimes Investigator* (New Haven: Yale University Press, 2000), pp. 91–92.

7. David Rohde, *Endgame: The Betrayal and Fall of Srebrenica, Europe's Worst Massacre since World War II* (New York: Farrar, Straus and Giroux, 1997), pp. 264–65.

8. As the investigation grew during the following years, Frease would increasingly assume a "bridging role" that women often play in organizations, for example, bringing together individuals who otherwise would not make the link themselves. See Belinda Robnett, "African-American Women in the Civil Rights Movement, 1954–1965: Gender, Leadership, and Micromobilization," *American Journal of Sociology* 101 (1996): 1661.

9. This second-order factor model was estimated with LISREL, using the AMOS program. The simple alpha reliability score for this scale is .69.

10. See Richard Travisaro, "Alternation and Conversion as Qualitatively Different Transformations," in *Social Psychology through Symbolic Interaction,* ed. Gregory Stone and Harvey Farberman (New York: Wiley, 1981), p. 243.

11. Doug McAdam, "The Biographical Consequences of Activism," *American Sociological Review* 54 (1989): 744–60.

12. See Doug McAdam, *Freedom Summer* (New York: Oxford University Press, 1988); John Hagan, *Northern Passage: American Vietnam War Resisters in Canada* (Cambridge: Harvard University Press, 2001).

13. See John Hagan and Patricia Parker ,"White Collar Crime and Punishment: The Class Structure and Legal Sanctioning of Securities Violations," *American Sociological Review* 50 (1985): 302–16; John Hagan, Duane Alwin, and John Hewitt, "Ceremonial Justice: Crime and Punishment in a Loosely Coupled System," *Social Forces* 58 (1979): 506–27.

14. "The First Sentence," *Tribunal Update* 5, 25–29 November 1996, available from the Institute for War and Peace Reporting at www.iwpr.net/.

15. "The Appeals Chamber Judgment in the Erdemovic Case," *Tribunal Update* 47, 6–10 October 1997, available from the Institute for War and Peace Reporting at www.iwpr.net/.

16. "Erdemovic Sentence Halved," *Tribunal Update* 66, 2–7 March 1998, available from the Institute for War and Peace Reporting at www.iwpr.net/.

17. Bass, *Stay the Hand of Vengeance,* p. 254–55.

18. Elizabeth Neuffer, "Bosnia Massacre Photo Cited U2 Pictures Reveal More Than 100 Bodies, Military Says," *Boston Globe,* 21 March 1996, 1.

19. Richard Holbrooke, *To End a War* (New York: Modern Library, 1999), p. 261.

20. Report of the International Tribunal for the Prosecution of Persons Responsible for Serious Violations of International Humanitarian Law Committed in the Territory of the Former Yugoslavia since 1991, 16 August 1996.

21. Elizabeth Neuffer, *Key to My Neighbor's House: Seeking Justice in Bosnia and Rwanda* (New York: Picador, 2001), p. 243.

22. David Rohde, "Warehouse of Death," *The New York Times Magazine,* 11 March 2001, 46.

23. Neuffer, *Key to My Neighbor's House,* p. 246.

24. ICTY Report to the U.N. General Assembly, dated 8/10/98.

25. See Robnett, "African-American Women," 1661–93.

26. Charles Trueheart, "A New Kind of Justice," *Atlantic Monthly,* April 2000, 90.

27. Steven Komarow, "Two U.S. Soldiers in Tense Standoff after Serb Leader's Arrest," *USA Today,* 9 December 1998, 2A.

28. "One Man Down," *Newsweek,* 14 December 1998, 85.

29. Krstic Transcripts (IT-98-33), p. 442, found at www.un.org/icty/.

30. Ibid., p. 462.

31. Ibid., p. 474.

32. Ibid., p. 489.

33. Ibid., p. 490.

34. Ibid., p. 498.

35. Ibid., pp. 507, 509.

36. Ibid.

37. "Krstic Stands Alone," *Tribunal Update* 168, 13–18 March 2000, available from the Institute for War and Peace Reporting at www.iwpr.net/.

38. Krstic Transcripts, p. 813.

39. Ibid., p. 818.

40. "Srebrenica Trial: Dutch Soldiers Recount Fall of Enclave," *Tribunal Update* 170, 27 March–1 April, 2000, available from the Institute for War and Peace Reporting at www.iwpr.net/.

41. Krstic Transcripts, pp. 1806, 1818.

42. Ibid., pp. 1826, 1827, 1829.

43. Ibid., pp. 1842–43.

44. Ibid., p. 1850.

45. Ibid.

46. Ibid., pp. 1856–57.

47. "Dutch Feared Srebrenica Massacre," *Tribunal Update* 171, 3–9 April 2000, available from the Institute for War and Peace Reporting at www.iwpr.net/.

48. Ibid.

49. Krstic Transcripts, pp. 3124–25.

50. Ibid., pp. 3127–28.

51. Ibid., p. 3139.

52. Ibid., p. 3140.

53. Ibid., p. 3182.

54. Ibid., pp. 3486–87.

55. Ibid., p. 3488.

56. Ibid., p. 3754.

57. "General Krstic Trial," *Tribunal Update* 181, 19–23 June 2000, available from the Institute for War and Peace Reporting at www.iwpr.net/.

58. Krstic Transcripts, pp. 4170, 4211, 4216.

59. Ibid., pp. 4460–61. The slashes are part of the transcript.

60. Ibid., p. 4910.

61. Ibid., p. 4722.

62. Ibid., pp. 4725, 4735.

63. Ibid., pp. 4796, 4810.

64. Ibid., p. 4832.

65. Ibid., pp. 4831, 4837, 4850, 4854.

66. "Krstic Trial—Prosecution Employs Records of Death Transports—Tribunal Investigators Confiscate over 30,000 Documents from RSA Headquarters." *Tribunal Update* 185, 17–22 July 2000, available from the Institute for War and Peace Reporting at www.iwpr.net/.

67. Krstic Transcripts, p. 5244.

68. "British Officer Testifies in Krstic Case," *Tribunal Update* 186, 24–29 July 2000, available from the Institute for War and Peace Reporting at www.iwpr.net/.

69. Krstic Transcripts, p. 5769.

70. Ibid., p. 5769.

71. "British Officer Testifies in Krstic Case."

72. "Krstic Points Finger at Mladic and His 'Knin Clan,'" *Tribunal Update* 187, 31 July–4 August 2000, available from the Institute for War and Peace Reporting at www.iwpr.net/.

73. Krstic Transcripts, pp. 5961, 6350, 6351.

74. Ibid., pp. 6772–73.

75. Marlise Simons, "Trial Reopens Pain of 1995 Bosnian Massacre," *New York Times,* 7 November 2000, A3.

76. Krstic Transcripts, pp. 6794–95.

77. Ibid., p. 6801.

78. Ibid, pp. 6806–07. This transcription is slightly different from a report of the exchange provided in "Srebrenica Trial—A Chilling Radio Interception Puts Krstic on the Spot." *Tribunal Update* 197, 30 October–4 November 2000, available from the Institute for War and Peace Reporting at www.iwpr.net/.

79. Krstic Transcripts, p. 6812.

80. Ibid., p. 6809–10.

81. "Srebrenica Genocide Trial—Judges Subject Krstic to Two-Day Grilling," *Tribunal Update* 200, 20–25 November 2000, available from the Institute for War and Peace Reporting at www.iwpr.net/.

82. Marlise Simons, "An American with Opinions Steps Down Vocally at War Crimes Court," *New York Times,* 24 January 2002, p. A12.

83. Krstic Transcripts, p. 7398.

84. Ibid., p. 7401.

85. Mirko Klarin and Vjera Bogati, "General Krstic Trial," *Tribunal Update* 202, 4–9 December 2000, available from the Institute for War and Peace Reporting at www.iwpr.net/.

86. Mirko Klarin and Vjera Bogati, "Krstic Trial," *Tribunal Update* 203, 11–16 December 2000, available from the Institute for War and Peace Reporting at www.iwpr.net/.

87. Mirko Klarin and Vjera Bogati, "Srebrenica Trial," *Tribunal Update* 214, 19–24 March 2001, available from the Institute for War and Peace Reporting at www.iwpr.net/.

88. Krstic Transcripts, pp. 8824, 8733.

89. Ibid., p. 8750.

90. Ibid., p. 8771.

91. Ibid., p. 8828.

92. Ibid., p. 8939, cited in judgment, p. 37.

93. Ibid., pp. 8939–44.

94. Marlise Simons, "Verdict Is Due Today in Major Trial on War Crimes in Bosnia," *New York Times*, 2 August 2001, A7.

95. Marlise Simons, "Tribunal in Hague Finds a Bosnian Serb Guilty of Genocide," *New York Times*, 3 August 2001, A1, A8.

96. Simons, "Verdict Is Due Today," A7 (emphasis in original).

97. Simons, "Tribunal in Hague," A8.

98. Ibid.

99. "Radislav Krstic becomes the first person to be convicted of genocide at the ICTY and is sentenced to 46 years imprisonment," Press Release (The Hague), 2 August 2001, p. 11, available at www.un.org/icty.

CHAPTER SIX

1. Negative cases are those that present a challenge to a major hypothesis in an explanation. These cases are useful to explore because they provoke probing investigation of the necessity and validity of the core concepts in an explanation, a process that encourages moving back and forth between ideas and evidence in research and that is sometimes called "double fitting" and "retroduction." See Jack Katz, *Poor People's Lawyers in Transition* (New Brunswick, N.J.: Rutgers University Press, 1982); Charles Ragin, *Constructing Social Research* (Thousand Oaks, Calif.: Pine Forge, 1994).

2. "Another Bosnian Serb Surrenders," *Tribunal Update* 66, 2–7 March 1998, available from the Institute for War and Peace Reporting at www.iwpr.net/.

3. Slavenka Drakulic, "Viewpoint: Foca's Everyday Rapists," *Tribunal Update* 226, 18–23 June 2001, available from the Institute for War and Peace Reporting at www.iwpr.net/.

4. Kunarac, Kovac, and Vukovic Transcripts (IT-96-23-Pt), p. 4652, found at www.un.org/icty/.

5. Lauren Comiteau, "The War-Crime Fighter: A Power for the Powerless," *Time International*, 19 March 2001, p. 59.

6. Kunarac Transcripts, pp. 294–95.

7. Ibid., p. 295.

8. Ibid., pp. 332, 303.

9. Ibid., p. 304.

10. Ibid., p. 329.

11. Ibid., pp. 333, 335.

12. "The Death of Indictee Dragan Gagovic," *Tribunal Update* 107, 20 December 1998–10 January 1999, available from the Institute for War and Peace Reporting at www.iwpr.net/.

13. "Foca Suspect Commits Suicide," *Tribunal Update* 194, 9-14 October 2000, available from the Institute for War and Peace Reporting at www.iwpr.net/.

14. "Foca Trial: Rape Victims Speak Out," *Tribunal Update* 170, 27 March-1 April 2000, available from the Institute for War and Peace Reporting at www. iwpr.net/.

15. Ibid.

16. Ibid., Kunarac Transcripts, pp. 1244, 1246, 1247.

17. Ibid., p. 1253.

18. Ibid., pp. 1270, 1274.

19. Ibid., p. 1276.

20. Drakulic, "Foca's Everyday Rapists."

21. Kunarac Transcripts, pp. 1851, 1856.

22. "Foca Trial." *Tribunal Update* 171, 3-9 April 2000, available from the Institute for War and Peace Reporting at www.iwpr.net/.

23. Kunarac Transcripts, p. 2187.

24. Ibid., pp. 2206, 2207, 2208.

25. "Foca Trial," *Tribunal Update* 174, 1-6 May 2000, available from the Institute for War and Peace Reporting at www.iwpr.net/.

26. "Foca Trial," *Tribunal Update* 176, 15-24 May 2000, available from the Institute for War and Peace Reporting at www.iwpr.net/.

27. "Foca Trial," *Tribunal Update* 177, 22-27 May 2000, available from the Institute for War and Peace Reporting at www.iwpr.net/.

28. Kunarac Transcripts, pp. 4153-54.

29. Ibid., pp. 4155-56.

30. Ibid., p. 4176.

31. Ibid., p. 4179, italics added.

32. Ibid., p. 4180, italics added.

33. Mirko Klarin and Vjera Bogati, "Keraterm Case—Trial to Begin on March 19," *Tribunal Update* 208, 5-10 February 2001, available from the Institute for War and Peace Reporting at www.iwpr.net/.

34. "Foca Cases—Krnojelac Trial Set to Begin," *Tribunal Update* 192, 25-30 September 2000, available from the Institute for War and Peace Reporting at www.iwpr.net/.

35. Robert Kaplan, *Balkan Ghosts: A Journey through History* (New York: St. Martin's, 1993).

36. Kunarac Transcripts, pp. 4327, 4330.

37. "Foca Trial—Kunarac Claims He Was 'Seduced,'" *Tribunal Update* 183, 3-8 July 2000, available from the Institute for War and Peace Reporting at www.iwpr.net/.

38. Kunarac Transcripts, pp. 4541-42.

39. Ibid., p. 4542.

40. Ibid., p. 4546.

41. Ibid., pp. 4604-5.

42. Ibid., pp. 4629, 4716, 4718-19, 4720.

43. "Foca Trial—Kunarac Claims He Was 'Seduced.'"

44. "Foca Trial—Kunarac Cross-Examined over His 'Investigation' into Rapes," *Tribunal Update* 184, 10-15 July 2000, available from the Institute for War and Peace Reporting at www.iwpr.net/.

45. Kunarac Transcripts, pp. 4907-9.

46. Ibid., pp. 4917-18.

47. Ibid., pp. 4918–19.

48. Ibid., pp. 4920–21.

49. "Foca Trial—Defence Argues Lack of Medical Evidence Undermines Validity of Rape Charges," *Tribunal Update* 190, 11–16 September 2000, available from the Institute for War and Peace Reporting at www.iwpr.net/.

50. "Foca Rape Case—Prosecution Witnesses Recalled to Rebut 'Girlfriend' Claims," *Tribunal Update* 196, 23–30 October 2000, available from the Institute for War and Peace Reporting at www.iwpr.net/.

51. Kunarac Transcripts, p. 6243.

52. Ibid., p. 6292.

53. Ibid., p. 6294.

54. Ibid., p. 6323.

55. Ibid., p. 6331.

56. "Foca Rape Trial Ends—Prosecutors Say Defendants Should Be Sentenced to Lengthy Prison Terms," *Tribunal Update* 200, 20–25 November 2000, available from the Institute for War and Peace Reporting at www.iwpr.net/.

57. Marlise Simons, "Bosnian War Trial Focuses on Sex Crimes," *New York Times,* 18 February 2001, A4.

58. Jerome Socolovsky, "3 Bosnians Guilty of Wartime Rapes," *Chicago Tribune,* 23 February 2001, 1.

59. Judgement of Trial Chamber II: In the Kunarac, Kovac and Vukovic Case, Press Release No. 566, The Hague, 22 February 2001.

60. Mirko Klarin and Vjera Bogati, "Foca Rape Case," *Tribunal Update* 210, 19–24 February 2001, available from the Institute for War and Peace Reporting at www.iwpr.net/.

61. Marlise Simons, "3 Serbs Convicted in Wartime Rapes," *New York Times,* 23 February 2001, p. A1.

62. Klarin and Bogati, "Foca Rape Case."

63. Kelly Askin, "Analysis: Foca's Monumental Jurisprudence," *Tribunal Update* 226, 18–23 June 2001, available from the Institute for War and Peace Reporting at www.iwpr.net/.

64. Drakulic, "Foca's Everyday Rapists."

CHAPTER SEVEN

1. Statement of the Honorable Pierre-Richard Prosper, Ambassador-at-Large for War Crimes Issues, United States Department of State, "The U.N. Criminal Tribunals for Yugoslavia and Rwanda: International Justice or Show of Justice?" Before the Committee on International Relations, United States House of Representatives, 28 February 2002.

2. Barbara Crossette, "War Crimes Tribunal Becomes Reality, Without U.S. Role," *New York Times,* 12 April 2002, A3.

3. Jess Bravin, "Bush Presses for Closing of Tribunals—U.S. Wants Timetable to Shut Down Courts of U.N., Citing Abuses," *Wall Street Journal,* 28 February 2002, A20.

4. Andrew Buncombe, "Balkans: U.S. Ambassador Attacks Expense and Professionalism of the War Crimes Tribunals," *Independent,* 1 March 2002, 2.

5. Barbara Crossette, "Experts Dispute Bush Aide's Criticism of War Crimes Panels," *New York Times,* 2 March 2002, A6.

6. Press Release, "International Criminal Court: Statement by ICTY President Judge Claude Jorda," 12 April 2002.

7. Neil Lewis, "U.S. Rejects All Support for New Court on Atrocities," *New York Times,* May 7, 2002, A11.

8. Adam Clymer, "House Panel Approves Measures to Oppose New Global Court," *New York Times,* 11 May 2002, A3.

9. A9.

10. Mirko Klarin, "Analysis: Is the Tribunal Running out of Time?" *Tribunal Update* 257, 4–9 March 2002, available from the Institute for War and Peace Reporting at www.iwpr.net/.

11. Ibid.

12. Kevin Cullen, "Milosevic Underlings Are Called Key in Trial," *Boston Globe,* 3 July 2001, A1.

13. Kissinger states his argument against the growing use of international criminal law in his essay "The Pitfalls of Universal Jurisdiction," *Foreign Affairs,* July–August 2001, 86–96.

14. See, e.g., Wesley Clark, *Waging Modern War* (New York: Public Affairs, 2001); David Halberstam, *War in a Time of Peace* (New York: Scribner, 2001); Samantha Power, *"A Problem from Hell": America and the Age of Genocide* (New York: Basic, 2002).

15. See Thomas Schwartz, *America's Germany: John J. McCloy and the Federal Republic of Germany* (Cambridge: Harvard University Press, 1991), and more generally Yves Dezalay and Bryant Garth, *The Internationalization of Palace Wars: Lawyers, Economists, and the Contest to Transform Latin American States* (Chicago: University of Chicago Press, 2002).

16. Ian Black, "Milosevic Extradited: $1bn Aid Rewards Serbia," *Guardian,* 30 June 2001, 4.

17. Ibid.

18. "The Indictment," *Daily Telegraph* (London), 30 June 2001, 21.

19. Barbara Crossette, "Long Range Justice Raises Fears for Sovereignty," *New York Times,* 1 July 2001, 8.

20. John Meyer, "The World Polity and the Authority of the Nation-State," in *Institutional Structure: Constituting State, Society, and the Individual,* ed. George Thomas, John Meyer, Franco Ramirez, and John Boli (Newbury Park: Sage, 1987), p. 65.

21. See John Ikenberry, *After Victory: Institutions, Strategic Restraint, and the Rebuilding of Order after Major Wars* (Princeton: Princeton University Press, 2001).

22. Geoffrey Robertson, "The Court Is on Trial Too," *Guardian,* 30 June 2001.

23. "Trials, Tribulations and Tribunals," *Economist,* 28 June 1997, 50.

24. Carol Williams, "Prosecutor Is Fired up for Trial of Milosevic," *Los Angeles Times,* 3 July 2001, A1.

25. Dezalay and Garth, *Internationalization of Palace Wars,* p. 128. The authors make a similar point in the Latin American context, observing that "far from being linear, as in the typical Weberian scenario of movement from charisma to routine, the transformations of this field of practice have resulted from a competition in which strategies can change in relation to the social resources that individuals and groups are able to mobilize at a particular time and in a particular place."

26. Romesh Ratnesar, "The End of the Line," *Time,* 9 July 2001, 18.

27. Mirko Klarin and Vjera Bogati, "Milosevic Arrest Deadline Nears," *Tribunal Update* 213, 12–17 March 2001, available from the Institute for War and Peace Reporting at www.iwpr.net/.

28. Mirko Klarin, "Analysis: Belgrade's Tribunal Volte-Face," *Tribunal Update* 226, 18–23 June 2001, available from the Institute for War and Peace Reporting at www.iwpr.net/.

29. Ratnesar, "End of the Line," 18.

30. Klarin, "Belgrade's Tribunal Volte-Face."

31. Carlotta Gall, "Serbs Feared Army Would Aid Milosevic," *New York Times,* 1 July 2001.

32. Gary Bass, *Stay the Hand of Vengeance: The Politics of War Crimes Tribunals,* rev. ed. (Princeton: Princeton University Press, 2002), p. 324.

33. Ibid., p. 410, n. 46.

34. Paul Watson, "20 Killed, 10 Wounded as NATO Targets Prison," *Los Angeles Times,* 22 May 1999, 19.

35. "Allies Kill Hundred in Air Raid on 'Staging Post' Prison," *Birmingham Post,* 25 May 1999, 11.

36. Jacky Rowland, "Grilled by the Butcher," *Guardian,* 29 August 2002, 2.

37. Mirko Klarin, "Analysis: Kosovo Victims Gagged," *Tribunal Update* 263, 22–27 April 2002, available from the Institute for War and Peace Reporting at www.iwpr.net/.

38. Williams, "Prosecutor Is Fired Up."

39. Mirko Klarin, "Analysis: Milosevic's Other Indictments," *Tribunal Update* 219, 30 April–5 May 2001, available from the Institute for War and Peace Reporting at www.iwpr.net/.

40. Ibid.

41. Mirko Klarin, "Analysis: Milosevic Charge-Sheet Almost Complete," *Tribunal Update* 237, 24–29 September 2001, available from the Institute for War and Peace Reporting at www.iwpr.net/.

42. Mirko Klarin, "Analysis: The Mother of All Indictments," *Tribunal Update* 245, 19–24 November 2001, available from the Institute for War and Peace Reporting at www.iwpr.net/.

43. Marlise Simons, "Archives Force Review of Croat's Atrocity Case," *New York Times,* 21 November 2001, A12.

44. Marlise Simons, "The Briton in Charge: Sober, Polite, and Tough," *New York Times,* 4 July 2001, A6.

45. Martin Fletcher and Frances Gibb, "No-Nonsense Judge Sets the Tone," *The Times* (London), 4 July 2001, 4.

46. Joshua Rozenberg, "Milosevic Case May Be Hard to Prove," *Daily Telegraph,* 4 July 2001, 4.

47. Ian Fisher, "Power Drove Milosevic to Crime, Prosecutors Say as Trial Opens," *New York Times,* 13 February 2002, 1, 12.

48. Ian Fisher and Marlise Simons, "U.N. Details Vicious Acts Charged against Milosevic," *New York Times,* 14 February 2002, A6.

49. "Milosevic's Right Hand Man Surrenders to War Crimes Court," Reuters, 2 May 2002.

50. Marlise Simons, "Ex-President of Serbia Surrenders to Tribunal," *New York Times,* 21 January 2003, A8.

51. Milosevic Transcripts, p. 2206. Found at www.un.org/icty/.

52. Ibid., p. 2216.

53. Ibid., pp. 2252.

54. Ibid., p. 2268.

55. Ibid., p. 2285.

56. Ibid., p. 2395.

57. Ibid., p. 2497.

58. See "American Appears at Milosevic Trial," 11 June 2002; "NATO Military Head Accuses Milosevic," 13 June 2002.

59. Richard Norton-Taylor, "Complex and Historic Case Could Take Years to Finish," *Guardian,* 30 June 2001, 5.

60. Tim Franks, "Milosevic Proves a Slippery Customer," BBC, 20 September 2002, www.bbc.co.uk/.

61. Katarina Kratovac, "Yugoslavia Yields Documents Sought for Milosevic Trial: UN Tribunal Jurist Gets Action in Visit," *Chicago Tribune,* 20 July 2002, 3.

62. Marlise Simons, "Witness Links Milosevic to a Plan to Cover up Crimes in Kosovo," *New York Times,* 24 July 2002, A5.

63. "Milosevic Trial Recesses without 'Smoking Gun,'" *Washington Post,* 27 July 2002, A18; "Milosevic Finds a Friendly Face in the Witness Stand at His Trial," *New York Times,* 27 July 2002, A2.

64. Mirko Klarin, "Analysis: Milosevic Prosecution Breakthrough," *Tribunal Update* 279, 2-7 September 2002, available from the Institute for War and Peace Reporting at www.iwpr.net/.

65. Marlise Simons, "A Yugoslav Soldier's Story Poses Challenge to Milosevic," *New York Times,* 9 September 2002, A5

66. Mirko Klarin, "Milosevic Feels the Heat," *Tribunal Update* 275, 15-20 July 2002, available from the Institute for War and Peace Reporting at www.iwpr.net/.

67. Mirko Klarin, "Analysis: Penetrating Milosevic's Inner Circle," *Tribunal Update* 274, 8-13 July 2002, available from the Institute for War and Peace Reporting at www.iwpr.net/.

68. Mirko Klarin, "Comment: Milsoevic Suffers 'Exhaustion,'" *Tribunal Update* 287, 28 October-1 November 2002, available from the Institute for War and Peace Reporting at www.iwpr.net/.

69. Marlise Simons, "The Hand That Feeds Milosevic's Defense," *New York Times,* 10 November 2002, 6.

70. Chris Stephen, "Regional Report: Yugoslavia 'Threatening' Tribunal Witnesses," *Tribunal Update* 287, 28 October-1 November 2002, available from the Institute for War and Peace Reporting at www.iwpr.net/.

71. "Listening in to Milosevic: Court to Consider Admissibility of Wiretaps," Coalition for International Justice, Day 124, 22 November 2002, available at www.cij.org/.

72. Mirko Klarin, "Comment: Milosevic's Greater Serbia Project," *Tribunal Update* 290, 18-22 November 2002, available from the Institute for War and Peace Reporting at www.iwpr.net/.

73. "The Case Is Almost Proved: Insider Says Milosevic Was Responsible," Coalition for International Justice, Day 126, 27 November 2002, available at www.cij.org/.

74. Ibid.

75. Zeljko Cvijanovic, "Serbia: Vasiljevic Implicates Milosevic," 17 February 2003, available from the Institute for War and Peace Reporting at www.iwpr.net/.

76. Milanka Saponja-Hadzic, "Mladic Extradition Deadline Extended," *Tribunal Update* 310, 21-25 April 2003, available from the Institute for War and Peace Reporting at www.iwpr.net/.

77. Daniel Simpson, "Sniper Attack Leaves Leader of Serbia Dead," *New York Times,* 13 March 2003, p. 1.

78. Steven Erlanger, "Did Serbia's Leader Do the West's Bidding Too Well?" *New York Times,* 16 March 2003, p. 4.

79. Chris Stephen and Emir Suljagic, "Milosevic Linked Directly to War Crimes," *Tribunal Update* 310, 21-25 April 2003, available from the Institute for War and Peace Reporting at www.iwpr.net/.

80. Marlise Simons, "Mystery Witness Faces Milosevic at Hague Trial," *New York Times*, 19 April 2003, p. A6.

81. Crossette, "War Crimes Tribunal Becomes a Reality."

82. Serge Schmemann, "U.S. May Veto Bosnia Force in a Dispute over New Court," *New York Times*, 29 June 2002, A6.

83. Marlise Simons, "International Court Opposed by U.S. Opens for Business," *International Herald Tribune*, 1 July 2002, 1.

84. "Leaders: Not (Quite) Strangled at Birth: The International Criminal Court" and "United States Right to the Brink: The International Criminal Court," *The Economist*, 6 July 2002, 14, 47.

85. Chris Patten, "America Shouldn't Fear the International Court," *International Herald Tribune*, 10 July 2002.

86. Warren Hoge, "U.S. Veto on Bosnia Vexes Britain," *International Herald Tribune*, 2 July 2002, 1.

87. Serge Schmemann, "U.S. Peacekeepers Given Year's Immunity from New Court," *New York Times*, 13 July 2002, A3.

88. Evelyn Leopold, "U.S. Urged to Stop Fighting Global Criminal Court," Reuters, 9 July 2002.

89. Christopher Marguis, "U.S. Seeking Pacts in a Bid to Shield Its Peacekeepers," *New York Times*, 7 August 2002, A1.

90. Elizabeth Becker, "U.S. Ties Military Aid to Peacekeepers' Immunity," *New York Times*, 10 August 2002, A1.

91. Elizabeth Becker, "European Union Urges Aspirants to Rebuff U.S. on World Court," *New York Times*, 14 August 2002, A11.

92. Elizabeth Becker, "On World Court, U.S. Focus Shifts to Shielding Officials," *New York Times*, 7 September 2002, A4.

93. Paul Meller, "Europeans to Exempt U.S. from War Court," *New York Times*, 1 October 2002, A6.

94. Elizabeth Becker, "U.S. Presses for Total Exemption from War Crimes Court," *New York Times*, 9 October 2002, A6.

95. Claire Trean, "At the Origin of the Indictment, Louise Arbour's Audacity," *Le Monde*, 11 February 2002. Au: P. no.

96. "Unofficial Transcript: Ambassador Scheffer on War Crimes Charges," *NATO Security Issues Digest*, no. 105, 2 June 1999.

INDEX